SOLAR MADE SIMPLE

AND OTHER ALTERNATIVE ENERGY TOPICS

Published by
Starcott Media Services
6906 Royalgreen Drive
Cincinnati, Ohio 45244

Printed in the United States of America
Copyright © 1994 by James T. Dulley
All rights reserved
9, 8, 7, 6, 5, 4, 3, 2, 1
ISBN 0-9625583-7-0

We recommend care and adherence to standard construction safety procedures. Wear adequate protective clothing and safety gear (approved safety eyeglasses, work gloves, breathing filter mask) when working with power and hand tools, and with building and insulation materials. If you have questions about proper safety procedures or protective clothing to wear, contact your local health department, Occupational Safety and Health Administration, or Environmental Protection Agency. Neither the author nor the publisher takes responsibility for accidents that may occur during the building or use of any of the projects or products described in this book.

INTRODUCTION

Many of my readers have asked me to compile my solar and other alternative energy-related Utility Bills Updates and columns into a book. I have selected 41 Utility Bills Updates and related columns which I feel are the most helpful to readers interested in utilizing solar energy in their homes.

This book is divided into thirteen general topic sections with several Utility Bills Updates and columns in each. The topic section refers to the subject of the first primary question of each column and to the subject of the Utility Bills Update. The related Utility Bills Update is shown on the three pages following each column. The topic of the second shorter question is generally not related to the primary one.

Since some of the columns and Utility Bills Updates were written over a year ago, I have recently updated the names and addresses of manufacturers and model numbers of products to provide the most current and state-of-the-art product information. If some of the model numbers have changed very recently, a retail dealer or the manufacturer can provide you with the new model numbers based on the old one.

Before attempting any of the do-it-yourself projects, read the Update completely. Always wear adequate ***protective clothing and safety glasses/goggles.*** When these projects effect any mechanical systems in your house (furnace, air conditioner, water heater, etc.), contact a contractor or technician familiar with your specific models. Some models are unique and require specific clearances and adjustments when making improvements. Also, check your local building and fire codes.

The actual savings that you realize from making some of these solar improvements or by installing various products depend on the efficiency of your current systems and your local utility rates. Always do a payback analysis before investing your time and money in a project or product.

Several of the Utility Bills Updates show lists of manufacturers and model numbers of various types of products. Also, product information and specifications are sometimes provided. These lists of manufacturers and product information are for your information only and are <u>NOT AN ENDORSE-MENT</u> of these types of products or a specific manufacturer or model.

By following the advice, projects, and tips in this book, you should be able to reduce your utility bills. This not only saves your money, but it stretches our limited energy supplies and reduces the environmental hazards of energy production and consumption.

TABLE OF CONTENTS

Chapter I - _SOLAR SPACE HEATING_
1) Air-type collector
2) Solar wall heater
3) Insulated reflective window shutter
4) Solar window heater
5) Solar Trombe wall
6) Solar ceramic tile

Chapter II - _SOLAR WATER HEATING_
1) Water-type collector
2) Solar water heating kits
3) Passive breadbox water heater

Chapter III - _SOLAR COOLING_
1) Removable solar window film
2) Solar chimney
3) Attic foil and ventilation
4) Permanent winter/summer window film
5) Insulated exterior rolling shutters

Chapter IV - _SOLAR GREENHOUSES_
1) Greenhouse designs and construction
2) Mini garden window
3) Greenhouse kits

Chapter V - _PASSIVE SOLAR HOUSES_
1) Passive solar log house kits
2) Passive solar house layouts and techniques

Chapter VI - _SOLAR FOOD COOKING & PRESERVING_
1) Solar baking oven
2) Solar food dryer

Chapter VII - _SKYLIGHTS_
1) High-efficiency skylights
2) Cathedral ceilings for skylights
3) Sunlight tubes and build a lightwell

Chapter VIII - _SOLAR SWIMMING POOLS_
1) Solar pool heating systems
2) Solar swimming pool water purifiers

Chapter IX - _WIND ENERGY_
1) Wind-powered turbine and other attic vents
2) Portable & large electricity-generating windmills

Chapter X - _PHOTOVOLTAICS - ELECTRIC SOLAR CELLS_
1) Large solar cell systems
2) Solar-powered attic vent fans
3) Solar-powered outdoor lighting
4) Electric automobiles

Chapter XI - _WOOD ENERGY_
1) Efficient wood-burning furnaces and cost worksheet
2) Fireplace upgrade products and techniques
3) Firewood selector guide
4) Efficient wood-burning fireplaces
5) Pellet/corn-burning stoves

Chapter XII - _MISCELLANEOUS TOPICS_
1) Geothermal heat pumps
2) Emergency electric generators
3) Energy-efficient solar backyard deck
4) Natural plant indoor air purifiers

Chapter XIII - _REFERENCE CHARTS AND TABLES_
1) Sun position charts
2) Monthly sun availability chart
3) Geographic annual wind speed chart
4) Fuel cost comparison chart

Build inexpensive solar heater yourself

Q.: I want to build an inexpensive (less than $100) solar heater myself to cut my high heating bills. I want it to be able to heat one large room and a small one. What simple do-it-yourself design do you suggest?

A.: There is a simple design of solar heater that you should easily be able to build yourself for less than $100 in materials. On a sunny day, it produces enough hot air to keep your rooms warm.

This is a very simple air-type solar collector. Room air is heated as it circulates through the solar collector. You can mount the collector flat against your pitched roof, tilted up for greater efficiency, or against a south-facing wall.

The simplest design relies on "thermosiphoning". The less dense warm air naturally flows up and out the top outlet. This draws cool room air in the bottom inlet to be heated developing a continuous flow. You should close off the bottom inlet at night.

This design concept uses a slanted perforated metal collector sheet (painted black) inside a shallow insulated box. The sun shines on the collector plate and heats it. With it slanted inside the box, the room air is forced to pass through the openings in the hot metal sheet as it circulates from the inlet to outlet opening through the solar heater.

For even greater heat output, you can install an inexpensive electric blower. For a 4x8 foot collector, a small 100-cubic feet per minute blower should be adequate. This allows you to tilt it toward the sun for high efficiency.

For an inexpensive design, build a shallow box with 1/2-inch plywood. Make it 4 feet by 8 feet so that you can use standard size lumber. Leave the top of the box open. You will later cover the top with a glass or clear acrylic plastic sheet. Acrylic is inexpensive and easy to work with.

Using expanded metal lath is the easiest way to make the metal collector sheet. Wire three or four layers of it together, staggering each one a little to offset the openings.

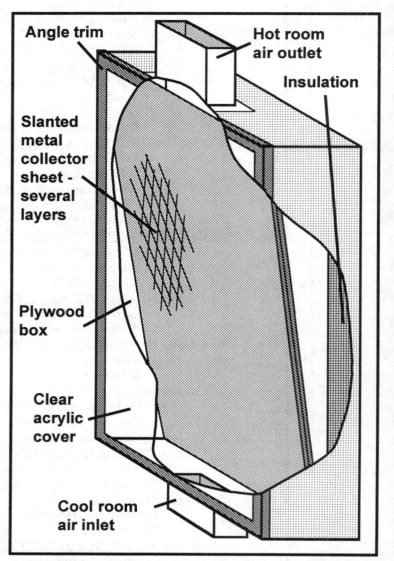

Solar heater is easy to make and very effective

In this way, the sun shines on most of metal of each layer, yet the room air can easily flow through. Punching or drilling holes in aluminum sheets and spacing them slightly apart is also effective. Saw an inlet and an outlet opening in the ends of the box nearer to the open side.

Lay standard foil-backed fiberglass batt wall insulation in the bottom of the box. Mount the metal absorber plate so it is slanted above the insulation. Attach the clear cover on the top.

Q: I have aluminum siding on my house. There is a gap between the flashing around the window and the siding. Shouldn't this gap be caulked to stop air leakage and rain?

A: The gap should not be caulked if it was installed properly. Metal siding expands as the temperature changes. The gap is needed for this expansion without buckling.

The flashing around the window frame probably was caulked and nailed in place before the siding was installed. This provides the seal.

Materials Required for Solar Heater

Expanded metal lath or	1-$\frac{1}{2}$-inch aluminum angle
Aluminum sheet with perforations	Metal wire
$\frac{1}{2}$-inch plywood	Metal washers
2X8 lumber	Rubber washers
2X4 lumber	Nails
$\frac{3}{4}$X$\frac{3}{4}$ lumber	Screws
Clear plastic or glass sheets	Stapler
Foil-faced batt insulation	Silicone caulking
Small electric blower	Hinge for cooling door
Thermostat	Foam weatherstripping
2X16 metal duct stubs	Small door latches

DO-IT-YOURSELF INSTRUCTIONS FOR MAKING AIR-TYPE SOLAR HEATER

A) Cut the 2x8 lumber for the frame. It is a good idea to use pressure-treated lumber for the structural components. Size the frame so that the outside dimensions are exactly 4 ft. by 8 ft. This is a convenient size so that you can use a standard 4 ft. by 8 ft. sheet of plywood for the back. Also, most of the other materials are also commonly available in 4 ft. and 8 ft. sizes.

B) Saw rectangular holes for the metal duct stubs (available at furnace contractor) in the 4-ft. long 2x8 end pieces. 2-inch high duct stubs are the best height to use so they fit nicely in the frame above the insulation. If you are not using a blower, get the widest duct stubs to minimize resistance to the air flow. Locate the 2-inch-high rectangular holes 1 inch from the top edge of the 2x8 lumber. Attach the duct stubs to these holes in the frame.

C) Assemble the frame using screws - not glue. With changes in temperature and moisture of the collector lumber from day to night and throughout the year, screws will resist the stresses from shrinkage and growth of the lumber.

D) Screw the plywood cover on the bottom of the 2x8 frame lumber to form the collector box. Caulk all the joints in the box with silicone caulk.

E) Cut the foil-faced fiberglass insulation to a size 4 inches larger than the size of the inside dimensions of the collector box. Carefully, cut off 2 inches of insulation around the perimeter leaving the foil facing extending out 2 inches. This will be used for stapling the insulation in place.

G) If you can't find foil-faced insulation, use unfaced insulation and cover it with a layer of attic-type reflective foil. *DO NOT USE KRAFT PAPER-FACED INSULATION.*

H) Lay the foil-faced fiberglass insulation in the bottom of the box with the foil side facing up. Staple the foil to the sides of the box to secure the insulation in place. Paint the foil surface flat black.

I) Cut a support piece from 2x4 lumber to fit the interior length dimension (a few inches less than 8 ft.) inside of the box. Screw it in place so it is flush with the open top of the collector box. This will support the clear top and the collector matrix panel.

J) Make the two collector matrix panels using expanded metal lath. You will need two panels, one on each side of the center 2x4 support piece which you already installed in the box. First measure the diagonal length from the top surface of the insulation on one end to just below the top edge of the box on the other end. Since the collector panel will be slanted upward, it will be slightly longer than the flat horizontal inside dimension of the box.

K) Carefully cut enough pieces of the lath to make the two panels of either four or five layers each. Stack the layers so that the openings are offset. This minimizes the amount of the sun's rays that pass through without striking the aluminum. Use wire to tie the layers together in many spots to form a rigid four or five layer matrix. An optional method is to use thin aluminum sheets. You can buy them at most hardware stores. Drill, saw, or punch many small holes in the aluminum sheets. Wire several of them together spacing them apart with thick washers. Stagger them so the holes are offset on each layer.

L) Cut $3/4$x$3/4$ wood collector matrix support pieces. These will be attached in a slanted position from the top of the insulation to 1 inch below the top surface of the box. You will need eight pieces total. Cut four pieces to fit between the center 2x4 support and the inside surfaces of the box. (These will be a few inches less than 2 ft., depending on the actual width of the lumber you used.)

M) Attach one piece between each side of the box and the center support directly on top of the insulation. These will support the lower edge of the collector panels. Attach the other two pieces on the other end of the box up near the top edge of the box. These will support the upper edge of the collector panels. Position these two pieces far enough down from the edge so that there is about $1/2$ inch clearance from the top edge when the collector panels are set on top of them.

N) Using the $3/4$x$3/4$ lumber, cut four collector panel side support pieces. These will be attached on an angle along the inside of the box from the lower to the upper supports. Therefore, all the edges of the collector panels will be supported by the $3/4$x$3/4$ lumber pieces. Nail or screw the collector panels to its support pieces.

O) Cut the 1-$1/2$ aluminum angle to fit around the perimeter of the top of the box. This holds the clear cover in place.

P) Make the clear cover about 1 inch smaller than the top of the box to allow for expansion and contraction. You might find it easier to make two pieces and join them over the 2x4 center support. Clear plastic is much easier and safer to work with than glass. IF YOU DO USE GLASS, CONTACT A GLASS DEALER OR EXPERT TO DETERMINE THE BEST TYPE OF GLASS FOR THIS APPLICATION. THESE ARE LARGE PIECES OF GLASS AND THEY CAN BE HAZARDOUS TO HANDLE AND DANGEROUS IF THEY BREAK. Some types of clear plastics good for solar collectors are - acrylic, polycarbonate, or fiberglass-reinforced polyester.

Q) When using a clear plastic cover, lay the clear cover over the top of the box and lay the aluminum angle over that. Drill holes through both the angle and the clear plastic. The holes should be about $1/8$-inch larger in diameter than the size of the nails or screws. This allows for expansion and contraction of both the angle and the plastic cover. Remove the cover and lay a beam of silicone caulk on the top edge of the box. Lay the clear plastic cover over the bead of caulk. Put rubber washers over the holes and lay the angle over that. Then nail or screw the angle down to the box. Don't tighten it down too much to squeeze out the caulk. A thicker bead of caulk will handle more expansion and contraction.

R) If you use a glass cover, attach the aluminum angle on the sides of the box instead of the top. By doing this, you will not have to make holes in the glass itself. Use the caulk under the top edge.

S) You should make doors or covers for the inlet and outlet opening of the ducts into your room. Once the sun goes down, the air flow will naturally reverse in the solar heater and it will actually begin to cool off your room. Hinged covers similar to the ones described below will work well. A piece of $1/2$- or 1-inch rigid foam insulation is also effective. It is very easy to cut with a knife. Cut it about $1/4$ inch smaller than the duct opening. Attach foam weatherstripping to the edge and push it into the duct openings. Screw a small drawer knob onto it so you can easily pull it out each day.

T) If you use a small blower, mount it on the lower inlet opening. This will create a positive pressure inside the solar heater and eliminate air leaks. A small squirrel cage blower is most effective and quiet, but an inexpensive small fan-type blower will also work. To be most efficient, you can install a small photovoltaic panel (electric solar cells) to operate a 12-volt d.c. blower or fan. It will produce electricity only when the sun shines, which makes it a perfect fit with solar heating. Several manufacturers of these solar-powered fans systems are:

ALTERNATIVE POWER & LIGHT CO., 701 S. Main, Westvy, WI 54667 - (608) 634-2984
EARTH OPTIONS, 6930 McKinley St., Sebastopol, CA 95472 - (707) 829-4554
SOLO POWER, 1011-A Sawmill Rd. N. W., Albuquerque, NM 87104 - (505) 242-8340

U) If you plan to use your solar heater for summer cooling, saw two square vent openings in the top (warm air outlet side) 2x8 on each side of the stringer support. Make two doors from the $1/2$-inch plywood to fit in the openings. Nail a $1/2$-inch square wood strip $3/4$ inch down from the outside. Attach $3/8$-inch thick foam weatherstripping on top of this strip. Attach the two doors over the openings with hinges. Attach latches to keep them closed. When they are closed and latched, the weatherstripping should be compressed to form a tight seal. On cool days when you are not air-conditioning, open the vents and some windows for natural ventilation.

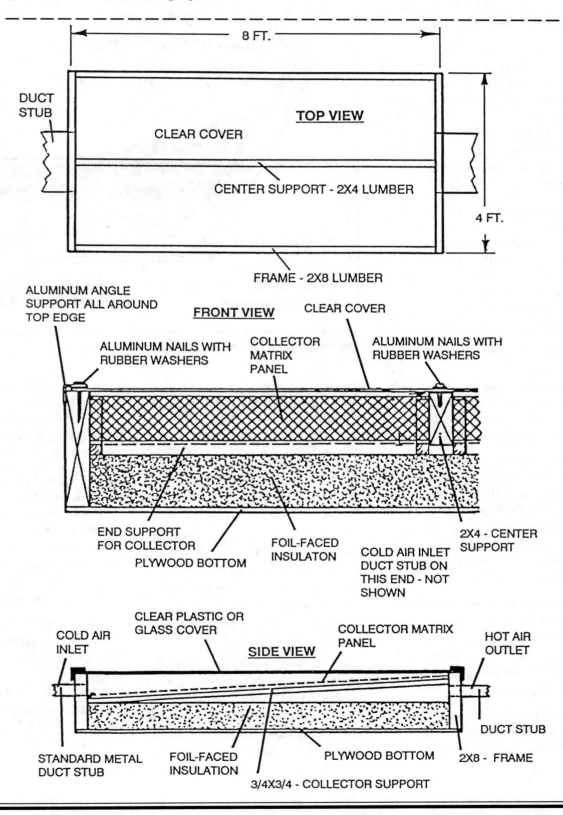

Cheap solar heater can be constructed

Q: Will you describe how to build a solar heater (not a big ugly one on my roof) that can heat one or two rooms? I'm on a limited budget, so I want to use as many low cost and scrap materials as possible.

A: A flat (only 5 inches deep) wall-mounted solar collector is the least expensive and easiest to build. Since it mounts vertically against a wall, it is not unattractive. It looks like a large window from outdoors, but can easily heat two rooms on a sunny day.

It is designed to use many scrap materials to keep the costs low. Old corrugated metal roofing, scrap printing plates, or sheet metal makes an efficient solar absorber. Secondhand window glass or inexpensive clear plastic sheet or film makes an effective cover for the solar heater.

Since standard size lumber is most reasonably priced, a 4 x 8 foot solar heater is a good size. If you have an old glass storm window or door, make it that size to avoid having to buy new clear glazing.

This solar heater design is basically a shallow plywood box with a metal solar absorber laying flat inside. Corrugated roofing, painted flat black, is good because the corrugations cause turbulence in the air flow. This increases the heat transfer to the air and boosts its efficiency.

Room air enters one opening and circulates underneath the solar-heated absorber plate. After picking up the solar heat from the absorber, the heated air blows back out into your room through an outlet register.

Use thin plywood for the solar heater back (if you mount it directly against your house) and 1 x 4's for

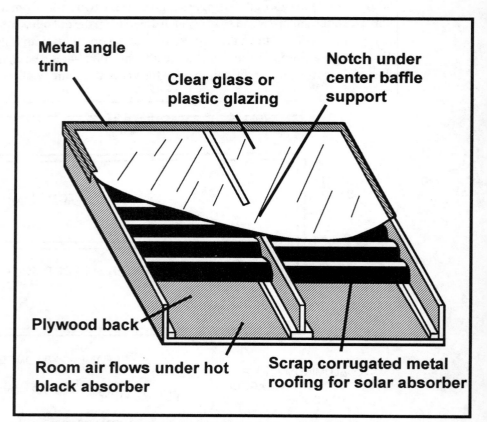

Metal angle trim

Clear glass or plastic glazing

Notch under center baffle support

Plywood back

Room air flows under hot black absorber

Scrap corrugated metal roofing for solar absorber

Inexpensive do-it-yourself solar heater

the box framing. The wall of your house provides the rigidity to the solar heater.

Split the box lengthwise with a 1 x 4 center baffle with a shallow notch cut out one-third of its length. This forms two long cavities connected by the notch under the center baffle.

Nail the corrugated roofing absorbers into the box to cover each cavity. This forces cool room air to circulate from the bottom inlet, across the hot absorber, up through the baffle notch, and back down the other side to the hot air outlet register.

Cover the entire box with the clear glazing (glass or plastic). This creates a dead air space above the hot absorber to reduce the heat loss back outdoors. Attach a small blower for increased heat output.

Q: I have a brick fireplace that I cannot use because smoke comes out into the room. The fireplace opening is 36" x 36". How can I improve the draft and stop the smoke?

A: First, you should have the chimney inspected to make sure that it is not blocked. The chimney top should be at least 2 feet above the roof peak or 3 feet above a flat roof for proper draw. If your house is airtight, you should open a window a little to provide combustion air.

The height of the top of the fireplace opening is important. If it is too high above the burning logs, the draft may be insufficient. Use a grate to raise the logs from the floor. Try adding a few bricks under the legs of the grate. If this helps, build up the entire hearth floor with fire bricks.

Construction Procedure

A) Assemble all materials before starting. Read all instructions and be sure you understand each step. A materials list is shown to the right.

B) Cut 1x4 lumber to length. Notch center baffle and attach metal ledger to notch with ¾" nails. Use aluminum ledger and aluminum nails if you use an aluminum absorber. Mixing galvanized materials with aluminum will cause electrolysis and corrosion.

C) Cut out a 2" diameter hot air vent into dead air space on upper side panel. Install screens and "temperature-vents" over the holes on the inside of the frames. This type of vent opens automatically to ventilate the dead air space when its temperature reaches 150º F. It opens to prevent overheating in summer and will remain closed during winter operation. As a substitute for "temperature-vents", you can cover the holes with small corks or wood during the winter and remove them during the summer. Locate the hot air vent on the side of the panel to prevent rain from entering the opening.

Required Materials for Solar Heater

1 each 4' x 8' x ⅜" CD exterior plywood or substitute with masonite
4 each 1" x 4" x 8' pieces of lumber
5 each 1" x 2" x 8' pieces of lumber
Wood glue
1 lbs. galvanized nails (4D to 6D)
2 each 2' x 8' sheet galvanized steel corrugated roofing or corrugated aluminum or offset printing plates or aluminum flashing. If you use a non-corrugated sheet, add baffles to cause turbulence in the air flow.
1 small bottle of vinegar, muriatic acid, or metal etcher
1 pint flat black paint (any moderate-temperature paint will work)
1 lbs. ¾" galvanized roofing nails or aluminum nails
4 tubes black silicone caulking
2 tubes of latex caulking
1 each 3" x 24" pieces of metal (to support absorber at center bar opening)
1 each 4' x 8' piece of flat icy clear fiberglass, Kalwall, or glass
3 each 8' long 90-degree angle aluminum, for holding down glazing (¾" x ¾" aluminum angle works well)
1 each 8' x ¾" flat pieces of aluminum
75 each #7 x ¾" wood screws
1 each 200 cfm squirrel cage blower
1 each thermostat (on between 90º to 155º F - off under 90º F)
1 length 2/12 UG wire (to reach from electric outlet to blower)
1 each electric plug
1 each Temp-Vent for summer ventilation
1 qt. exterior grade latex paint
Assorted lumber, duct tape and insulation for cold and hot registers
1 each 4" x 12" floor register (substitute screen for hot air opening)
8 each 3" x 3" corner braces and screws for mounting

D) Glue and nail the 1x4 frame and baffle to the plywood back. Be sure the baffle is centered properly. Caulk with latex caulking where the 1x4 meets the plywood on the inside to form a weathertight joint.

E) Cut, glue, and nail the 1x2 lip to the frame. Note: Vent openings should be in the dead air space only. Drill a series of ¼" vent holes through the center 1x4 baffle in the dead air space and install one "temp-vent".

F) Cut the absorber metal to size. Use an aluminum ledger and aluminum nails if you use an aluminum absorber. Clean any grease or oil from the metal with detergent or solvents and wash thoroughly. Etch the metal with vinegar or muriatic acid so that the paint will adhere to the metal. Again, wash the metal to remove the etching solution.

G) Fasten the absorber to 1x2 lip with ¾" galvanized roofing nails every 3". Note: Apply a thick bead of silicone caulking onto the metal ledger before laying down the absorber. This creates a formed-in-place gasket between the metal ledger and the absorber. To keep the absorber embedded in the bead of caulking, drive small nails into the 1x4 air baffle to hold the absorber down to the ledger. Be sure to put the absorber in the frame so that the corrugations in the metal are perpendicular to the air flow. This will cause the air flowing over the absorber to be turbulent and increases the heat transfer to the air.

H) Paint the absorber and the inside of the wooden frame with one coat of flat black paint and let dry thoroughly.

I) Carefully caulk (with silicone caulking) the entire edge of the absorber where it meets the wood to form an airtight seal between the wood and the metal. Also use silicone caulking on the nail heads to seal the holes.

J) Touch up any scratches with the flat black paint. Turn the frame over and paint the back of the plywood and the outside

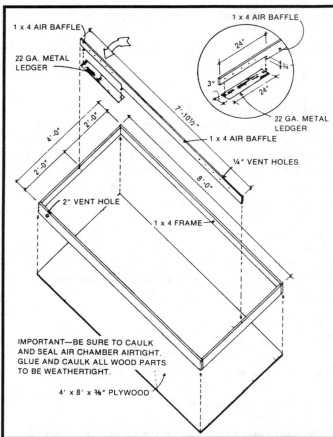

IMPORTANT—BE SURE TO CAULK AND SEAL AIR CHAMBER AIRTIGHT. GLUE AND CAULK ALL WOOD PARTS TO BE WEATHERTIGHT.

of the 1x4's with good-quality exterior house paint to seal the lumber.

K) Cut the plastic or glass glazing to size. Run a bead of caulking on the panel 1x4's and lay the glazing onto the panel. If you are using plastic with an ultraviolet coating, make sure the coating is on the outside.

L) Cut edging (wood or metal) to length and pre-drill the screw holes. Lay the edging onto the glazing and drill through the plastic glazing. If you are using glass, make the size of the glass slightly smaller so the drill will miss the edge of the glass, yet still screw into the frame. Fasten the 4 ft. edge first, the center strip next, then the sides, and finally the end. Be sure glazing does not extend beyond the outer edge of the frame to prevent ripples in the glazing.

Installation Instructions

This typical installation is for a wood framed home with siding. By using lumber, ducts can be made at the house site. For homes with stucco siding, use a masonry blade in your circular saw to cut duct openings. For a brick or concrete block house, use a hammer drill (available at most tool rental shops) or hammer and cold chisel to make the duct openings.

A) Decide where to locate the solar panel. Check inside walls for electrical outlets and obstructions. Note the floor level inside the home and its position in relation to the outside wall siding. This is to ensure that the duct comes above the inside floor height and not into the floor list area. Locate the wall framing to place the duct openings between the studs.

B) Mark openings for the ducts on the outside wall. Duct openings in the solar panel should be as close to the panel edge as possible. (For a 4" x 12" floor register, the openings should be 5 3/4" x 13 3/4".) Cut rough openings into the outside wall only. Do not cut the inside paneling or drywall at this time.

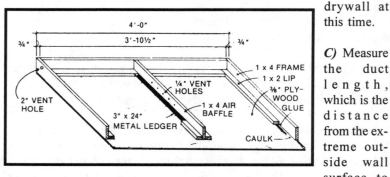

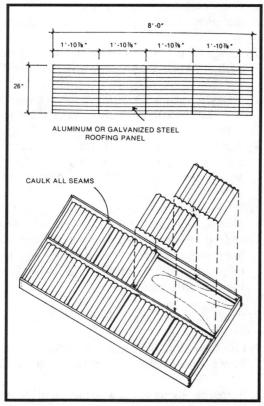

C) Measure the duct length, which is the distance from the extreme outside wall surface to the back of the interior paneling or drywall. This measurement is the length of the wall ducts. Rip a piece of 1" lumber to the duct length size. Then cut the duct lumber to size and build the ducts, gluing and nailing them together.

D) Insert the ducts into the wall openings and mark the inside dimensions on the inside wall surface through the duct. Remove the ducts and cut the wall openings. By using this method, the interior wall surface will cover the duct edge and no additional interior trim will be needed.

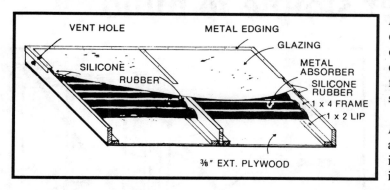

VENT HOLE   METAL EDGING
GLAZING
METAL ABSORBER
SILICONE RUBBER
SILICONE RUBBER
1 x 4 FRAME
1 x 2 LIP
⅜″ EXT. PLYWOOD

E) Run a 3 ft. length of wire (No. 2 conductor exterior grade) through the wall from the cool air opening to the hot air opening for later thermostat connection. Drill a hole into the ducts to run the wire from one duct to the other. Also drill through any studs for the wire run.

F) Latex caulk the inside edge of the ducts liberally and insert the ducts into place, running the wires into the holes drilled in the ducts. Fasten the ducts into the siding or nearby framing.

G) Caulk the rough openings around the ducts to seal openings from the weather. At this point, the wall ducts are in place and the thermostat wire is installed.

H) Next, hold the panel up against the wall and mark the duct openings on the back of the panel by reaching through the ducts from inside the house. This method will insure proper panel-to-duct alignment. Be sure to hold the panel straight so that it will look plumb and square once it is fastened to the building. Also, mark the location of the panel on the wall.

I) Lower the panel and cut the duct openings into the back of the panel. Take care not to damage the absorber by cutting or drilling too deep into the panel back. Use a circular saw, set to a shallow cut, or a short saber saw blade. Now the panel is ready to be mounted on the wall.

J) Latex caulk the outside edge of the ducts and lift the panel into place aligning the panel openings to the ducts. Fasten the panel to the wall with corner braces or angles and screws. Use two corner braces or angles at the top, sides, and bottom of the panel to fasten it securely to the wall. Latex caulk the top and sides of the panel where it meets the wall to prevent moisture from getting between the panel and the wall. Paint the wood edge of the panel with white exterior house paint or a color to match your house. At this point, the panel is mounted.

K) Inside your home, install the thermostat and blower. Drill a small hole into the absorber in the hot air opening for the self-tapping screw which holds the thermostat in place. Be sure to put the thermostat in the hot air opening so that the thermostat rests securely on the absorber to sense the absorber temperature properly. Connect the two wires to the thermostat connector screws.

L) Latex caulk all seams and joints in the hot air duct to insure an airtight seal and place the register into the duct. This completes the hot air duct installation.

M) Now latex caulk the cool air duct seams and joints. Caulk the lip of the blower opening. Fasten the blower in place over the cool air opening with the blower intake facing away from the hot air register.

N) Connect one wire from the thermostat to the blower. Connect the other blower wire and the other thermostat wire to an electrical plug. Be sure all wire connections are clean, tight, and safe. *Follow approved electrical code practices.*

    The solar heater is now installed and ready for operation. Plug the solar heater into an electrical outlet and adjust the thermostat so the blower will come on at a temperature which is reached at about 9 a.m. on a sunny morning.

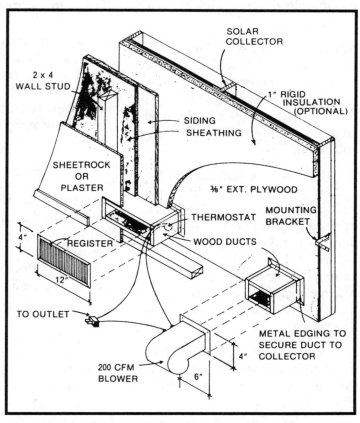

SOLAR COLLECTOR
2 x 4 WALL STUD
1″ RIGID INSULATION (OPTIONAL)
SIDING SHEATHING
SHEETROCK OR PLASTER
⅜″ EXT. PLYWOOD
MOUNTING BRACKET
THERMOSTAT
WOOD DUCTS
4″
REGISTER
12″
TO OUTLET
200 CFM BLOWER
6″
4″
METAL EDGING TO SECURE DUCT TO COLLECTOR

Mirrored shutter simple to build

Q: We leave our window shades open as much as possible to get heat from the sun, but it still doesn't shine very far into our room. Is there any simple way to get more sunshine inside?

A: The sun's rays are most intense near noon, offering the greatest potential for free solar heating. Unfortunately, it is also at its highest point in the sky then, so it often is partially blocked by a roof overhang and it doesn't shine very far into your room.

For your south-facing windows, you can easily build and install a reflective solar window shutter. It is very effective for directing additional solar heat through your windows. It also reduces the need for lights, so your electric bills are less.

If you make the shutter with an insulating material, it also stops the heat loss back outdoors when it is closed at night. Most windows, without any special covering, lose more heat than they gain over a 24-hour period. An insulating solar shutter can reduce your heating and cooling bills and greatly improve your comfort.

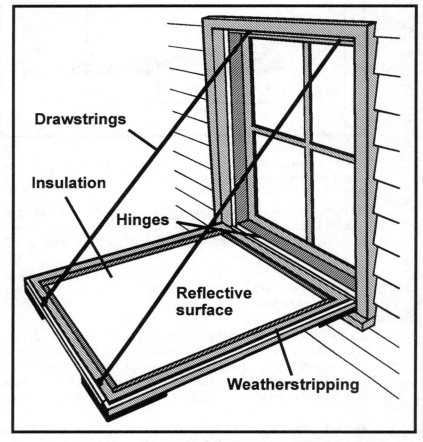

Insulating solar shutter saves energy year-round

You can easily make an inexpensive insulating solar shutter yourself. You should hinge it at the bottom of the window. Since the position of the sun changes, you can adjust the shutter for the proper open angle depending on the time of day and month of year.

First make a wooden frame of 1x2-inch pine, sized to fit snugly inside the exterior window frame opening. Redwood and cedar are more expensive, but they resist the weather better. Add gussets to the corners for strength. Attach foam weatherstripping around the edge of the frame so it seals against the window frame.

You can use any type of reflective foil-faced insulation board for the body of the shutter.

Polyisocyanurate foam has a high R-value and is durable. Extruded polystyrene is also effective. Apply foil duct tape around the edge of the foam insulation to hold it into the frame and support it with pipe strapping.

For added convenience, drill two holes through your window frame, opposite each upper corner of the shutter. Attach drawstrings to the shutter so you can adjust it, or close it completely at night, from the inside. Use tight-fitting grommets in the drawstring holes to reduce air leakage through them.

Q: We plan to duct the vent from our electric dryer indoors with just a piece of flexible ducting. What is the best way to make a filter?

A: Although it saves energy, if you already have excess indoor moisture problems, ducting the dryer indoors may worsen them. Also, check your local building codes about venting a dryer indoors.

You definitely have to add some type of filter. Stretching two layers of nylon stockings over the duct is effective. Clean out both the built-in filters and the stocking filters after each load.

You can also run the end of the duct straight down into a very shallow pan of water. As the air bubbles through, the water catches the lint. It must be shallow or it can create too much back pressure and possibly cause your dryer to overheat.

Reflective insulating shutters for your windows are easy to make and can increase the solar gain into your windows and reduce the heat loss back outside at night. When making this shutter, it is important that it fits tightly inside and against the sides of the window frame to reduce air leakage when it is closed.

Select straight lumber to start with and measure very carefully. If you want the shutter to cover the entire window, make it several inches larger than the window opening so it rests against the wall surface when it is closed. This makes it more airtight.

These shutters are most effective if you have high-quality airtight windows to start with. This is imperative for an efficient passive solar heated house. At the very minimum, you should select low-e argon gas-filled glazing. This has an R-value of about 4. Heat Mirror glass (Insol-8) has an R-value of 8. I have included a list of manufacturers of high-efficiency wood replacement windows on the bottom of page **c**.

Required Materials for Reflective Shutter

1" x 2" lumber - carefully select straight pieces
$3/4$" wood screws
1 pair of chrome plated or galvanized hinges
Pipe strapping
2" wide shiny foil or duct tape
$1/2$" plywood - exterior grade
1" thick foil-faced rigid insulation board
Waterproof glue
Staples
Heavy string
Closed-cell adhesive-backed foam weatherstripping
Spring-loaded cleats from a marine shop

DO-IT-YOURSELF INSTRUCTIONS FOR MAKING A REFLECTIVE SHUTTER

A) Saw the 1" x 2" lumber to make the frame for the shutter. Make them the proper length and height to fit snugly in the window opening.

B) Notch the ends of the pieces of lumber for lap joints when you assemble the frame. This gives strong and smooth corner joints.

C) Assemble the frame using wood screws and waterproof glue. Measure across the diagonals of the frame to make sure that it is square before you drill the holes for the screws. Then clamp the frame assembly and allow it to dry.

D) You can add stiffness to the frame by making triangular gussets for the four corners of the frame assembly. The gussets will also support the reflective foam insulation board. Make them 4" to 5" long on the sides. Drill holes and use glue and screws to secure them to the frame assembly.

E) Paint the frame assembly with good-quality wall paint to match your house. Make sure to get good coverage over all the joints since this will be exposed to the worst winter weather.

F) After the frame has dried, you can cut the reflective foam insulation to fit it. Lay the frame flat with the gussets against the table. Carefully measure the inside dimensions of the frame. You can usually cut the foam insulation with a sharp knife. Cut slowly and carefully.

G) Lay the piece of insulation into the frame against the gussets.

H) Using the foil duct tape, lay a strip of the tape overlapping the foil and the frame. This will seal the edge of the foam insulation and help to hold it in place in the frame. Use the tape on both sides of the frame and insulation joint for the greatest strength, airtightness, and reflectivity. You can use staples to better secure the tape to the frame and insulation.

I) Cut 2" lengths of the pipe strapping. These will be used to help hold the insulation into the frame. Cut enough to space them about every 2-1/2 ft. around the frame. Mount them so they extend about 1-1/4" out over the insulation.

J) Stick the adhesive-backed foam weatherstripping around the edge of the frame where it will lay against the window frame. That will produce a good seal when it is closed.

K) Have a helper hold the assembled shutter up against the window where it will be mounted. Mark the locations for the hinges to be attached to the shutter frame and the window frame. It should be hinged at the bottom.

L) If you want to operate the shutter from outdoors (this is the easiest method), attach the boat cleats to the wall above the window.

M) Attach small eyelet to the top of the shutter frame and tie the strings to them. Run the other end of the strings through the cleats above them. You can then adjust the angle that the shutter is opened for the maximum heat gain or close it tightly at night.

N) If you plan to operate the shutter from indoors, then you will have to drill two holes through the window frame opposite the eyelets on the top of the shutter frame. Make sure to drill the holes big enough to install plastic grommets for the string to slide through. That will reduce wear on the string and reduce air leakage through the holes.

O) Feed the strings through the grommets into your house. The strings should be about three times the height of the shutter. Tie the indoor ends of the strings to a 1" dowel and glue them so they won't slide around the dowel. You will roll the string up on the dowel to control the position of the shutter on the outside. Hammer a small nail partially into the center of the dowel.

P) Using the pipe strapping, make an upside-down J-hook to mount under your window sill inside your house. You may be able to purchase a strong wire hook at your hardware store. This will hold the dowel. You wind up the strings on the dowel to position the shutter and then hook the nail in the dowel under the pipe strapping J-hook to hold that position.

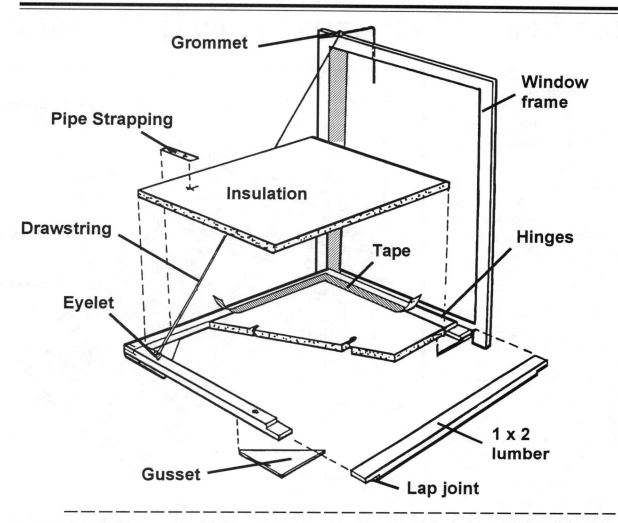

Grommet

Window frame

Pipe Strapping

Insulation

Drawstring

Tape

Hinges

Eyelet

1 x 2 lumber

Gusset

Lap joint

MANUFACTURERS OF HIGH-EFFICIENCY WOOD REPLACEMENT WINDOWS

ANDERSEN CORP., 100 Fourth Ave. N., Bayport, MN 55003 - (612) 439-5150
ARCHITECTURAL COMPONENTS, 26 N. Leverett Rd., Montague, MA 01351 - (413) 367-9441
BILT-BEST WINDOWS, 175 Tenth St., Ste. Genevieve, MO 63670 - (314) 883-3571
CARADCO CORP., PO Box 920, Rantoul, IL 61866 - (217) 893-4444
CENTURY WINDOWS, 1301 Newark Rd., Mt. Vernon, OH - (614) 397-2131
CRAFTLINE, 1125 Ford St., Maumee, OH 43537 - (800) 283-3311 (419) 893-3311
CRESTLINE, PO Box 8007, Wausau,WI 54402 - (800) 552-4111 (715) 845-1161
HURD MILLWORK, 575 S. Whelan Ave., Medford, WI 54451 - (715) 748-2011
KOLBE & KOLBE MILLWORK, 1323 S. Eleventh Ave., Wausau, WI 54401 - (715) 842-5666
LINCOLN WOOD PRODUCTS, PO Box 375, Merrill, WI 54401 - (800) 967-2461 (715) 536-2461
LOUISIANA-PACIFIC, 324 Wooster Rd. N., Barberton, OH 44203 - (800) 358-2954 (216) 745-1661
MALTA WINDOWS, PO Box 397, Malta, OH 43758 - (614) 962-3131
MARVIN WINDOWS, PO Box 100, Warroad, MN 56763 - (800) 346-5128 (218) 386-1430
PEACHTREE WINDOWS, PO Box 5700, Norcross, GA 30091 - (404) 497-2000
PELLA CORP., 102 Main St., Pella, IA 50219 - (515) 628-1000
PEERLESS, PO Box 2469, Shawnee Mission, KS 66201 - (800) 279-9999 (913) 432-2232
POZZI WOOD WINDOWS, PO Box 5249, Bend, OR 97708 - (800) 821-1016
TISCHLER UND SOHN, 51 Weaver St., Greenwich, CT 06830 - (203) 622-8486
VETTER, PO Box 8007, Wausau, WI 54402 - (800) 552-4111 (715) 845-1161
WEATHER SHIELD MANUFACTURING, PO Box 309, Medford, WI 54451 - (715) 748-2100

Solar heater inexpensive, easy to make

Q: We have a room with a south-facing window. Can I make a small inexpensive solar heater that mounts in the window? It should not show from indoors.

A: There are several basic designs of small do-it-yourself solar heaters that you can make over a weekend for less than $50 in materials. One can produce enough free solar heated air (at about 100 degrees) to keep a room comfortably warm on a sunny day.

One simple solar heater mounts in your window and angles downward outdoors. The window closes down against the air inlet and outlet. It's barely noticeable from indoors.

If you air-condition your home in the summer, you can easily remove the solar heater and just close the window as always. If you rely on natural ventilation, you can add a summer vent door in the outdoor portion of the heater. By opening this vent, the solar heater becomes a free exhaust fan by naturally drawing hot air out of your home.

Most do-it-yourself solar heater designs utilize a shallow plywood box with a clear top. An old storm door or window works well for the top. Mount the box in the bottom of your window and angle it downward.

The box is split inside by a collector panel (flat black) which creates two shallow chambers, above one another. This panel is shorter than the box leaving a gap at the bottom that connects the chambers.

The sun shines through the glass on to the black collector panel and heats the air above the panel in the upper chamber. This hot air naturally rises upward (since the box is angled upward to the window) and flows out into your room. Cool room air is then

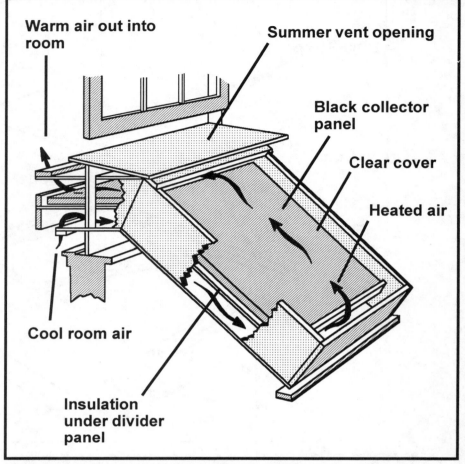

Solar room heater is cheap and easy to build

drawn into the lower chamber.

Insulating the sides and bottom of the box increase overall effectiveness. This reduces the heat loss from the room air entering the heater and from the solar heated air as it flows back into your room. Since the solar heater does not get extremely hot, you can easily attach rigid foam insulation to the sides and bottom.

There are several designs you can use for the divider panel. A plywood sheet with insulation attached underneath is effective. You can also lay fiberglass insulation over the panel and paint the vapor barrier black.

Another design uses a corrugated aluminum collector sheet di-

rectly under the clear cover. The air is circulated beneath it in insulated chambers. This reduces heat loss back outdoors through the clear top.

Q: I am remodeling my house. What is the most efficient location for the thermostat?

A: The best location for the thermostat is where is gets the truest reading of the average temperature of your house. Chest height is generally a good vertical location.

Locate it away from rooms that are heated by the sun. Also, keep it away from furnace registers and breezes from the opening of doors.

DO-IT-YOURSELF SOLAR WINDOW HEATER DESIGNS

Design #1

This solar window heater is basically a wooden box with a glass top that collects heat from the sun. As the air inside gets hot, it flows out into your room drawing in more cool room air to be heated.

Before you begin this project, make sure you wear adequate safety clothing and safety glasses. You will be handling glass, so be careful. Also, if you are going to use spray paint, use it outdoors and do not smoke while you spray it.

These are general instructions. Since everyone's application and design will be a little different, modify it for your specific home. Other than the 3" and 4" dimensions shown in the diagram, the rest of the dimensions are not extremely critical to its effectiveness.

A) You will first have to determine the proper size of the box for your window. It should be slightly narrower than your window so it fits through the window and snugly against the sides of the window frame. You will use foam weatherstripping to seal it.

B) Once you have determined the basic dimensions for the solar window heater, begin to build the plywood box. You can use 2x2's or 2x4's to make the basic frame, and then cover it with $3/8$ inch plywood. Remember that the width will be $3/4$ of an inch wider after the plywood sides are added, so make the frame small enough to fit into the window. Screws will hold up better than nails since it will get warm in the sun. Use silicone caulking to seal all the joints in the box.

C) Leave the top of the box open for the piece of glass. It is a good idea to build a two-inch wide plywood lip around the open top. This will add rigidity to the box, and provide support for the glass, without blocking much of the sun's heat.

D) For the most effective operation, you should insulate the inside of the box with rigid foam board insulation. This will reduce the heat loss from the cool room air in the lower portion and from the solar heated air in the upper portion.

E) Make the plywood divider piece to fit as shown in the diagram. Attach a layer of foam insulation board to the underside of it and paint the top flat black. Mount the divider as shown in the diagram. Seal all around it with silicone caulking. It is very important that the air is forced to flow down around the end of the divider and back up under the glass.

F) Cut an opening in the solid horizontal top piece by your window. This will be the location of the outdoor vent flap. If you cut carefully, you can use this piece for the flap door itself. Otherwise, cut another piece for the door. Attach that piece with hinges to use as the vent door. Use foam weatherstripping around the edge to seal the flap when it is closed.

G) Make another flap door to mount on the inside opening from the upper chamber into your room. Mount it with hinges and use weatherstripping again to seal it. You should close it when the sun goes down and in the summertime. You can also add a small plywood apron where the bottom section comes into your window.

H) The next step is to add the glass cover. ***Wear safety glasses***. It may be easier and cheaper to use two or three pieces of glass instead of one. Have the glass cut to fit the finished box. Unless you're an accomplished cabinetmaker, the finished box will not end up exactly the same size as you planned.

I) Place the glass on the box and hold it in place with glazier points. Don't putty the glass in place. That won't hold up to the temperature changes of the box. Instead, use duct tape stapled to the sides of the box, or caulk the glass all the way around the edges so you get a good seal.

J) Paint the wood box with house paint before you put it into your window. Seal it against the window frame with adhesive foam weatherstripping.

K) In the winter, close off the indoor top flap at night to minimize heat loss. During the summer, you can store the solar window heater in your garage or basement. Or, close the top flap inside the house and open the outdoor top flap. Open the window on the other side of your room for cross-ventilation. Select a shady window for the coolest air to be drawn in.

Illustrations for Making Design #1

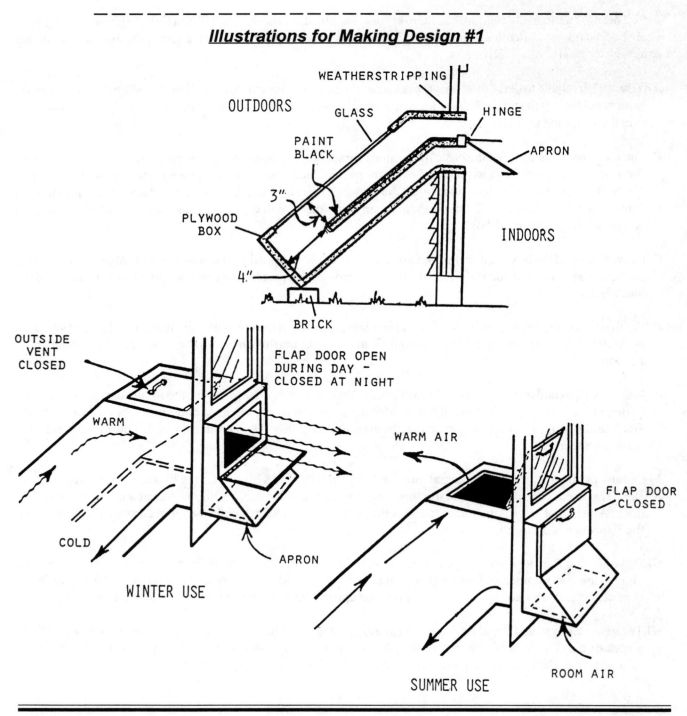

Design #2

A) Actual dimensions vary depending on the size of your window. The basic relationship of dimensions shown in the illustration below provide efficient operation. Before you begin to assemble the collector, paint both sides of all wood parts with two coats of outdoor paint. First make a box by sawing 1x4's at an angle forming a hockey stick shape by attaching the two pieces with a sheet metal strip. Add a top lip and nail on the bottom sheet plus the end piece.

B) Make another assembly like the first. When the two assemblies are piggybacked and fastened together, the two air-circulation channels will be created. This puts the heat-absorbing surface on a $1/8$" hardboard sheet that is fixed 1-$3/4$" over the hardboard bottom. This creates the lower cold-air channel. (See illustration).

C) Use a 23"-wide section of 2-$3/4$"-thick fiberglass insulation batt with kraft-paper or foil backing painted black. Secure the batt at each end with screen mold and small nails. You can also cover the insulation batt with a thin sheet of metal (aluminum is easy to cut and work with) and paint it black. Complete the assembly as shown in the illustration. Seal all the edges between the hardboard and the screen stock with duct tape on the outside.

D) You can use glass (an old storm door), clear rigid acrylic, or 5 to 10-mil acetate for the clear top. The flexible acetate is easiest to use. You can either tack or staple it down and trim off the excess around the edges.

E) When you install the collector in your window, the hot-air outlet to the room must be either horizontal or pitched upward slightly. This allows for proper air flow. Add a rain cover and seal any gaps between the collector and the window frame with insulation and duct tape.

F) To prevent reverse convection at night or on cloudy days, make two snug fitting wood doors to plug up the intake and outlet openings. If you plan to mount the collector on a roof under a window, bolt it with angle braces. You can remove it in the summer.

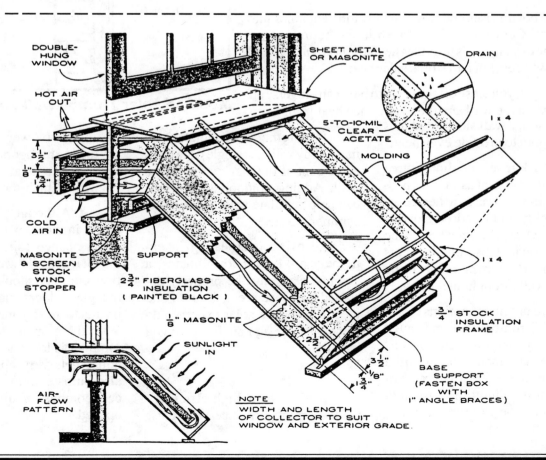

Trombe wall easy method of solar heat

Q: I would like to use some free solar heating to lower my utility bills. Would you explain how a solar Trombe wall works. Is it something that I can attach to my house myself?

A: A Trombe wall can be a very effective solar heating method for new and existing houses. With the proper design, size, and amount of air vents, you can control the amount and timing of heat output into your house.

You should be able to add a Trombe wall yourself. If your house already has masonry walls, you can add a glass covering over a small section of it. For a frame house, you can remove part of the wall and add a small masonry section. A modified design can also be built below a window.

A Trombe wall is basically a large glass window placed a few inches outside of a masonry wall. It is often called one of the "mass under glass" solar heating techniques which requires no fans or pumps.

Vent holes are cut through the wall at its bottom and top. Therefore, as the sun heats the brick, block, or stone wall section behind the large glass, the air between the wall and the glass gets hot.

This hot air rises and flows out the top vent holes into your room. Cool room air is drawn in the bottom vents. During the daytime, this provides heated air flow as the wall itself slowly gets hot and stores solar heat

At night, you close off the vents to block any reverse air flow between the wall and the glass. Then heat from the warm masonry wall slowly radiates into the room to provide even heat.

For a kitchen or dining area where you want heat as early as possible, larger vents carry in heated air more quickly. For a bedroom or living room, where you want heat in the evening, you may use smaller vents or close them to store more heat in the masonry wall throughout the day.

There are many options available for a Trombe wall and much depends on your climate. In cold climates, a selective solar coating on the wall is often necessary for maximum effectiveness. Nighttime insulated coverings for the glass are helpful.

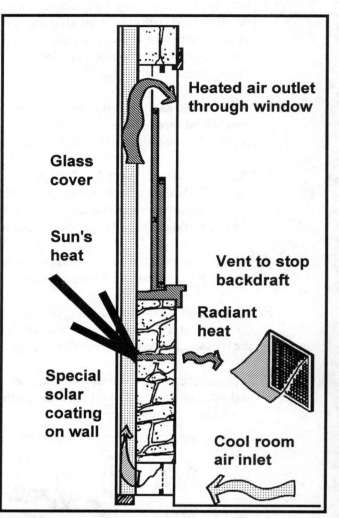

Modified solar Trombe wall under window

Glass cover

Sun's heat

Special solar coating on wall

Heated air outlet through window

Vent to stop backdraft

Radiant heat

Cool room air inlet

In more moderate climates, you may get by with just single pane glass and a coat of flat black paint on the wall. Adding outdoor upper vents can help ventilate your house in the summer too.

To avoid overheating in extremely mild southern climates, a Trombe wall must be properly-designed. In these areas, it is a good idea to contact a solar expert to do some basic design analysis for you initially.

Q: I have a high-efficiency wood-burning fireplace with glass doors and a blower. The instructions say to keep the doors closed, but I feel much more heat when they are opened. Which should I do?

A: Although you feel warm directly in front of the fire with the doors opened (direct radiant heating), it is actually wasting energy and firewood. You should definitely keep the glass doors closed if you are trying to heat your house with it. With them open, too much heated room air is lost and the rest of your house gets very chilly. Firewood also burns extremely fast from excess combustion air with the doors opened.

For the greatest daytime heating, you can add upper and lower vents through the masonry wall. This allows room air to circulate between the warm wall and the glass. The heated room air will naturally flow out the top vent and draw cool room air in the bottom. This provides some heat during the day and reduces the heat output from the warm wall at night. The vents should be closed at night (have some type of backdraft damper or cover for the vents) to block the flow of room air in reverse.

The chart on page **c** shows the basic design features for various zones of the country. A selective surface refers to a special solar material that is applied over the outdoor-facing side of the wall. This special material improves the solar absorption of the wall and reduces reradiation of the heat back outdoors through the glass.

DESIGN GUIDELINES FOR A SOLAR TROMBE WALL

It is easy to build a solar Trombe wall. The actual design and dimensions are not critical to its performance. Following the basic design features for climate zones (shown on the following pages) is most important.

The diagram on page **c** shows a modified Trombe wall built under a window. This looks "more-normal" from the outside of your house. You can use the window (a double-hung is best) for the upper vent holes.

If you plan to use a single-glazed window for the glass covering, you can probably make a simple wood frame. Use 1x2 or 2x2 lumber. Silicone caulk around the glass is the longest-lasting type. If, due to climate zone or problems with condensation, use double pane insulated glass. You should have the window made by a replacement window manufacturer. It is difficult to handle the desiccant and seal the glass well enough to avoid fogging in between the glass panes.

A rule of thumb is that the wall should be from 8 to 16 inches thick if made of concrete. You can use the chart to determine the equivalent thickness for the same heat capacities for other wall materials. For example, you will need slightly more brick and the actual amount of stone will depend on the density of the particular type of stone you use. Leave a gap of approximately 3 to 4 inches between the glass and the wall.

Thermal Mass Heat Storage Capacities			
Material	Specific Heat Btu/lb X	Density lb/ft³ =	Heat Capacity Btu/ft³/°F, no voids
Water	1.00	62.4	62.4
Concrete	0.22	140	30.8
Stone	0.21	90 to 170	18 to 36
Brick	0.21	130	27.3
Stucco	0.22	116	25.5
Drywall	0.26	50	13.0
Dry Soil	0.21	105	22.0
Wet Soil	0.44	125	55.0
Wood, hardwood	0.30	45	13.5

If you are seeking daytime heating also, you will need upper and lower vents through the wall for room air circulation. A rule of thumb is that both the top (outlet) and bottom (inlet) vents should each be equal to one half the area of the horizontal cross section of the collector. For example, if the Trombe wall is 10 feet wide and the air gap between the glass and wall is 4 inches, the collector cross section area is 3.33 square feet. Therefore, the size of the upper vents (and lower vents) should be 1.67 square feet.

The easiest way to make a backdraft damper is to make a light wood frame just slightly smaller than the size of each vent opening. First staple a piece of thin plastic film to the top edge of the frame. (See diagram). Then staple hardware wire over the frame on the same side as the plastic film. Recess this back several inches into the vent opening and caulk around it. This will allow room for a piece of insulation to cover the vent openings at night.

SPECIAL DESIGN FEATURES FOR TROMBE WALLS IN VARIOUS CLIMATES

ZONE 1:

The severe climate in this zone calls for special design features. The most effective Trombe walls are those with a selective absorber surface, night insulation, and single glazing. This combination yields good daytime performance and nighttime heat retention. If the Trombe wall is freestanding, single glazing can cause condensation problems. Using double insulated glazing can reduce the condensation problem. A Trombe wall with a selective coating and insulation is fairly expensive, but the additional cost is generally offset by improved performance.

If the initial cost of this type of wall is too great for your budget, the next best option is a Trombe wall with a combination of triple glazing and night insulation. In this zone, all other types of design will generally result in a net energy loss throughout the entire year.

ZONE 2:

The only Trombe walls that perform well in this zone are those that use a selective surface or night insulation. A combination of both is best. Single glazing will work well and can reduce the total cost of the project.

Another option for this zone is a Trombe wall with a selective surface, double insulated glazing, and no night insulation. Also, a wall with night insulation, triple glazing, and no selective surface is workable. Trombe walls without either a selective surface or night insulation will be net energy losers throughout the entire year.

ZONE 3:

A Trombe wall is a good fit with this zone's relatively mild climate. Although a Trombe wall with a selective surface and night insulation is most effective, the increased cost may not be justified. Generally, a wall with triple glazing and night insulation is best. Another option is double glazing and a selective surface. It is only slightly less effective than the first option. Since summertime heat gain can be a problem with a Trombe wall in this zone, it should have summer shading and be vented. A large roof overhang or deciduous trees are good shading devices.

ZONE 4:

You have many options for the design of a Trombe wall in this zone. The only wall that will be a net energy loser is just a plain wall (no selective surface or night insulation) and single glazing. Any combination of one or more of the other wall design options will be effective. You will definitely need summertime shading and ventilation in this zone to avoid overheating.

ZONE 5:

In this zone, the thermal performance is not important. Any design from a plain wall to a more high-tech one with the selective surfaces and night insulation will be effective. Since this climate is so mild, the payback from using selective surfaces and night insulation is not generally worth the added expense.

Summertime overheating is probably your greatest problem. In Zone 5A, the humidity is relatively low, so a simple roof overhang can provide effective shading. In Zone 5B, the high level of humidity can diffuse and scatter the sunlight. Therefore, a simple roof overhang may not block enough of the heat. Exterior shading devices that actually cover the glass are the best option. In both zones, venting of the Trombe wall will reduce the heat buildup.

ZONE 6:

In this zone, any design works well. Summertime overheating can be a significant problem. You should contact a local solar designer to give you some advice about the feasibility and payback of installing a Trombe wall.

TROMBE WALL CLIMATE ZONES

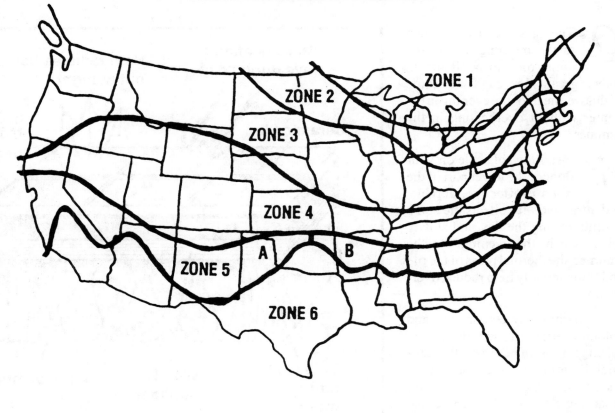

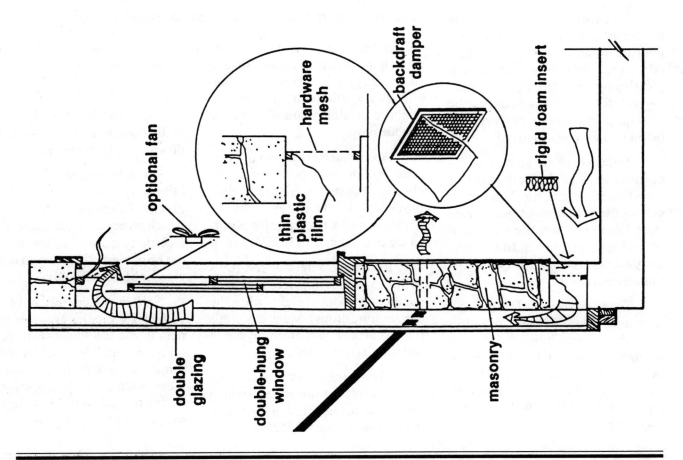

Solar tile stores a.m. heat for p.m. usage

Q. The sun shines in my kitchen in the morning and in the dining room in the afternoon. It feels great. How can I save some of this free heat for the evening in the winter without overheating in the summer?

A. Installing solar tile on your floor or the lower part of the walls is effective, durable, and attractive. It collects the sun's warmth during the day and slowly releases it in the evening. In the summer, the thermal mass of the tile and floor actually help reduce overheating.

Traditionally, certain types and colors of ceramic tile have been used for this purpose. These have the natural ability to efficiently conduct, store, and reradiate the solar heat at night. Installing ceramic tile properly for passive solar is a simple do-it-yourself project.

For existing homes, you can lay it directly over your standard floor. Pouring a thin layer of cement first raises your floor only a little, but it greatly improves efficiency. For the highest efficiency, you should put the solar tile over a heavier masonry floor (ideal for new construction).

Today there are some new attractive earth-friendly tile alternatives to traditional ceramic tile. These products use recycled or cement-based materials to produce tile with good passive solar qualities and durability. They are also available in a variety of finishes and colors.

The wide variety of shapes and sizes available in ceramic tile offer many design possibilities. For south facing rooms especially, one alternative is to install tile on the walls as well as the floor. This increases the passive solar area as well as being very attractive.

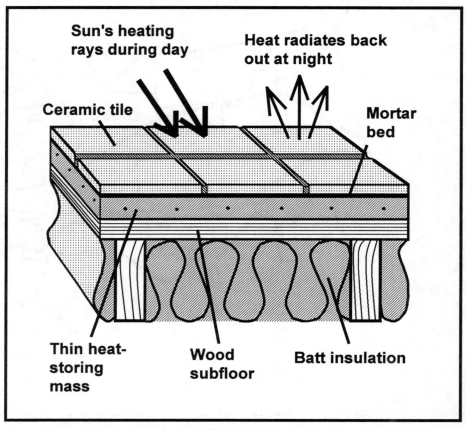

New floor and wall tile is ideal for passive solar

When you go out to select the tile, it is important to consider several solar energy properties of the specific tile and color: solar absorptance, emittance, and thermal diffusivity and conductivity.

Absorptance refers to the percentage of the sun's heat the material absorbs. I installed a special dark brown tile in the entryway of my home. It has a higher solar absorbance than other tiles would.

Emittance refers to the tile's ability to release its stored heat back out into the room at night (when the temperature drops). Many materials readily absorb and store heat, but they don't emit it well.

Thermal diffusivity and conductivity both relate to the speed at which solar heat passes through the tile to the subfloor material. It also affects how fast the tile gives off the heat at night to warm your feet.

Q: I watch a lot of TV at night. Will it use less electricity if I turn down the brightness knob?

A: A large color TV uses a lot of electricity. You can feel the heat given off from the back of your TV which gives you an idea of how much electricity it uses. Just turning down the brightness a little won't cut your electric bills noticeably.

Often you can still have an excellent TV picture at lower brightness if you use lower wattage light bulbs in your TV room. Better yet, turn off some of the lights. Adding all these wattage savings together over an entire year of TV watching can save quite a bit of electricity.

The natural thermal properties of ceramic tile are ideal for passive solar heating. Ceramic tile readily absorbs the sun's heat and transmits it through to the thermal mass below. At night, it reradiates the stored solar heat back out into your home. Although ceramic tile is somewhat effective for passive solar heating when it is laid directly over a wood floor, it is most effective over a concrete, brick, or stone floor.

If you have ever been in a sun room with inadequate thermal mass in the floors and walls during the winter, it overheats very quickly in the sun. With the proper amount of thermal mass, the room heats up slowly and does not get too hot. In the summer, the thermal mass (shaded with a roof overhang or window shades) tends to moderate temperature changes throughout the day inside your home. This delays the indoor temperature rise and makes you more comfortable. You can often set your air conditioner thermostat several degrees higher and save electricity.

Several ceramic tile floor and wall installation methods are shown on pages **b** and **c**. Each diagram lists the thermal capacity of the complete floor and wall structure. A higher thermal capacity indicates that more solar heat can be stored for each degree increase in its temperature. This improves efficiency and the length of time in the evening that heat reradiates out into your home.

Depending on the amount of glass area, the orientation to the sun, and your climate, there is an optimum total thermal capacity value. Although most homes generally have to little thermal capacity, you can actually have too much thermal capacity in the walls and floor. When this occurs, the floor or walls do not get warm enough throughout the day to properly reradiate the heat back out at night. As a result, you will not feel as comfortably warm as you should. The solar thermal properties of different colors and types of ceramic tile varies. The properties of several common tiles are shown on page **c**. When you select tiles for your home, compare their thermal specifications discussed in the newspaper column.

MANUFACTURERS OF SOLAR CERAMIC TILES

AMERICAN OLEAN TILE, 1000 Cannon Ave., Lansdale, PA 19446 - (215) 855-1111

AMERICAN MARAZZI TILE, 359 Clay Rd., Sunnyvale, TX 75182 - (214) 226-0110

CONGOLEUM CORP., 3705 Quakerbridge Rd., Mercerville, NJ 08619 - (800) 934-3567

EPRO INC., 156 E. Broadway, Westerville, OH 43081 - (614) 882-6990

FLORIDA TILE, P.O. Box 447, Lakeland, FL 33802 - (800) 352-8453 (813) 687-7171

INNOVATIVE CERAMICS, 800 Community Cir., Roswell, GA 30075 - (404) 640-0819

INTERCERAMIC, 1624 W. Crosby Rd. #120, Carrollton, TX 75006 - (800) 365-6733

LAUFEN INTERNATIONAL, 4942 E. 66th St. N, Tulsa, OK 74117 - (800) 331-3651

LONE STAR CERAMICS CO., P.O. Box 75381, Dallas, TX 75234 - (800) 256-5248

KPT INC., P.O. Box 468, Bloomfield, IN 47424 - (800) 444-5784 (812) 384-3563

METROPOLITAN CERAMICS, P.O. Box 9240, Canton, OH 44711 - (216) 484-4876

MONARCH TILE, P.O. Box 999, Florence, AL 35631 - (800) 289-8453 (205) 764-6181

QUARRY TILE, Spokane Industrial Park #12, Spokane, WA 99216 - (800) 423-2608

RO-TILE INC., 1615 S. Stockton, Lodi, CA 95240 - (800) 688-1380 (209) 334-3136

STONEWARE TILE CO., 1650 Progress Dr., Richmond, IN 47374 - (317) 935-4760

SUMMITVILLE TILES, P.O. Box 73, Summitville, OH 43962 - (216) 223-1511

TILECERA, 300 Arcata Blvd, Clarksville, TN 37040 - (800) 782-8453 (615) 645-5100

TYPICAL CERAMIC TILE SOLAR PROPERTIES (shown for American Olean tiles)

AO CRYSTALLINE® TILE

Absorptance*

362 Cr. Charcoal 0.8

345 Cr. Cobalt... 0.7

Specific Heat .... 0.18 BTU/lb, F
Specific Heat .... 0.53 BTU/sq. ft, F
Emittance 0.81
Diffusivity .... 0.00102 in²/sec.
Thermal Conductivity .... 6.0 BTU/hr, ft², in, F
Thermal Expansion .... 4.3 × 10⁻⁶ in/in, F

AO CERAMIC MOSAIC TILE

Absorptance*

A42 Cinnabar,
A49 Sepia, ... 0.7

Specific Heat .... 0.19 BTU/lb, F
Specific Heat .... 0.40 BTU/lb, sq. ft, F
Emittance 0.82
Diffusivity .... 0.00135 in²/sec.
Thermal Conductivity .... 10.1 BTU/hr, ft², in, F
Thermal Expansion .... 3.3 × 10⁻⁶ in/in, F

AO QUARRY TILE

Absorptance*

Q07 Umber 0.8
Q02 Ember Flash 0.8
Q01 Canyon Red 0.7
Q04 Sand Flash 0.7
Q06 Fawn Gray 0.7
Q16 Gray Flash 0.7
Q03 Sahara 0.7

Specific Heat .... 0.18 BTU/lb, F
Specific Heat .... 1.08 BTU/sq. ft, F
Emittance 0.82
Diffusivity .... 0.00128 in²/sec.
Thermal Conductivity .... 9.5 BTU/hr, ft², in, F
Thermal Expansion .... 3.4 × 10⁻⁶ in/in, F

AO QUARRY NATURALS® TILE

Absorptance*

N07 Timber Brown 0.8
N02 Fire Flash 0.8
N22 Burnt Sequoia 0.8
N01 Lava Red 0.7
N16 Stone Flash 0.7
N06 Stone Gray 0.7
N04 Prairie Flash 0.7
N24 Burnt Adobe 0.7

Specific Heat .... 0.18 BTU/lb, F
Specific Heat .... 0.96 BTU/sq. ft, F
Emittance 0.82
Diffusivity .... 0.00128 in².sec.
Thermal Conductivity .... 9.5 BTU/hr, ft², in, F
Thermal Expansion .... 3.2 × 10⁻⁶ in/in, F

CERAMIC TILE INSTALLATION METHODS ON WALLS

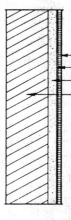

CEMENT MORTAR ON 8″ HOLLOW CONCRETE BLOCK

CERAMIC TILE-⁵⁄₁₆″
BOND COAT-¹⁄₁₆″
MORTAR BED-¾″
8″ × 8″ × 16″ HOLLOW CONCRETE BLOCK, DENSE

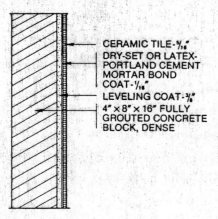

DRY-SET MORTAR ON 4″ GROUTED CONCRETE BLOCK

CERAMIC TILE-⁵⁄₁₆″
DRY-SET OR LATEX-PORTLAND CEMENT MORTAR BOND COAT-¹⁄₁₆″
LEVELING COAT-⅜″
4″ × 8″ × 16″ FULLY GROUTED CONCRETE BLOCK, DENSE

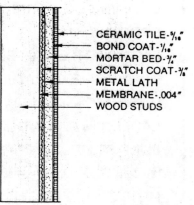

CEMENT MORTAR ON WOODS STUDS

CERAMIC TILE-⁵⁄₁₆″
BOND COAT-¹⁄₁₆″
MORTAR BED-¾″
SCRATCH COAT-⅜″
METAL LATH
MEMBRANE-.004″
WOOD STUDS

THERMAL CAPACITY:

10.8 BTU's per sq. ft. of wall surface per degree F temperature rise when American Olean glazed wall tile are used.

Thermal diffusivity for the AO ceramic tile is 0.00102 in² per second. Average diffusivity for this wall is 0.00211.

THERMAL CAPACITY:

9.4 BTU's per sq. ft. of wall surface per degree F temperature rise when American Olean glazed wall tile are used.

Thermal diffusivity for the AO ceramic tile is 0.00102 in² per second. Average diffusivity for this wall is 0.00124.

THERMAL CAPACITY:

2.9 BTU's per sq. ft. of wall surface per degree F temperature rise when American Olean glazed wall tile are used.

Thermal diffusivity for the AO ceramic tile is 0.00102 in² per second. Average diffusivity for this wall is 0.00122.

CERAMIC TILE INSTALLATION METHODS ON FLOORS

EPOXY GROUT AND MORTAR ON CEMENT MORTAR, 4″ CONCRETE SLAB.

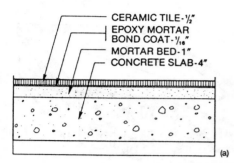

- CERAMIC TILE-½″
- EPOXY MORTAR BOND COAT-⅟₁₆″
- MORTAR BED-1″
- CONCRETE SLAB-4″

(a)

THERMAL CAPACITY:

12.5 BTU's per sq. ft. of floor surface per degree F temperature rise when American Olean quarry tile, Quarry Naturals tile or Primitive tile are used.

Thermal diffusivity for the AO ceramic tile is 0.00128 in² per second. Average diffusivity for this floor is 0.00110.

CEMENT MORTAR ON WOOD SUB FLOOR

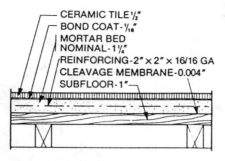

- CERAMIC TILE-½″
- BOND COAT-⅟₁₆″
- MORTAR BED NOMINAL-1¼″
- REINFORCING-2″×2″×16/16 GA
- CLEAVAGE MEMBRANE-0.004″
- SUBFLOOR-1″

THERMAL CAPACITY:

4.2 BTU's per sq. ft. of floor surface per degree F temperature rise when American Olean quarry tile, Quarry Naturals tile or Primitive tile are used.

Thermal diffusivity for the AO ceramic tile is 0.00128 in² per second. Average diffusivity for this floor is 0.00128.

DRY-SET MORTAR ON CEMENT BOARD AND WOOD FLOOR

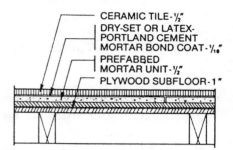

- CERAMIC TILE-½″
- DRY-SET OR LATEX-PORTLAND CEMENT MORTAR BOND COAT-⅟₁₆″
- PREFABBED MORTAR UNIT-½″
- PLYWOOD SUBFLOOR-1″

THERMAL CAPACITY:

2.4 BTU's per sq. ft. of floor surface per degree F temperature rise when American Olean quarry tile, Quarry Naturals tile or Primitive tile are used.

Thermal diffusivity for the AO ceramic tile is 0.00128 in² per second. Average diffusivity for this floor is 0.00117.

CEMENT MORTAR BONDED

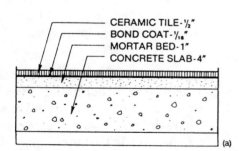

- CERAMIC TILE-½″
- BOND COAT-⅟₁₆″
- MORTAR BED-1″
- CONCRETE SLAB-4″

(a)

THERMAL CAPACITY:

12.5 BTU's per sq. ft. of floor surface/degree F temperature rise when AO quarry tile, Quarry Naturals tile, or Primitive tile are used.

Thermal diffusivity for the AO ceramic tile is 0.00128 in² per second. Avg. diffusivity for this floor is 0.00110.

DRY-SET MORTAR BONDED

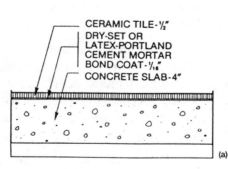

- CERAMIC TILE-½″
- DRY-SET OR LATEX-PORTLAND CEMENT MORTAR BOND COAT-⅟₁₆″
- CONCRETE SLAB-4″

(a)

THERMAL CAPACITY:

10.5 BTU's per sq. ft. of floor surface/degree F temperature rise when AO quarry tile, Quarry Naturals or Primitive tile are used.

Thermal diffusivity for the AO ceramic tile is 0.00128 in² per second. Avg. diffusivity for this floor is 0.00109.

EPOXY GROUT AND MORTAR BONDED

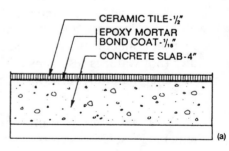

- CERAMIC TILE-½″
- EPOXY MORTAR BOND COAT-⅟₁₆″
- CONCRETE SLAB-4″

(a)

THERMAL CAPACITY:

10.5 BTU's per sq. ft. of floor surface/degree F temperature rise when AO quarry tile, Quarry Naturals or Primitive tile are used.

Thermal diffusivity for the AO ceramic tile is 0.00128 in² per second. Avg. diffusivity for this floor is 0.00108.

Home solar system is easy to construct

Q: I want to make an inexpensive solar system to help heat my home. I heard that a water-type of collector is better than an air-type. Is that true and can I easily make a solar collector myself?

A: A solar collector that circulates water instead of air is generally more effective. Water can hold more solar heat energy than air and it offers a greater range of uses. It is possible to cut your utility bills by up to several hundred dollars per year with a do-it-yourself system.

In the summer, when you aren't heating your home, you may be able to use your solar collectors to heat your domestic water or your swimming pool. This year-round utilization yields the greatest total savings.

If you can do any simple plumbing, like replacing a kitchen faucet, you should be able to build your own solar collector inexpensively. All of the materials you need should be available at most hardware stores.

With some designs, you won't even need a pump to circulate the water. By locating a storage tank above the collector, the solar-heated water (hot water is less dense than cold water) naturally flows up to the tank.

You need not mount your "homemade" solar collectors on your roof. A south-facing location on the ground near your house is fine. This provides easy access for keeping the glass top clean.

A typical do-it-yourself solar collector is basically a shallow insulated box with a clear cover over it. Water, which flows through pipes inside the box, is heated by the sun.

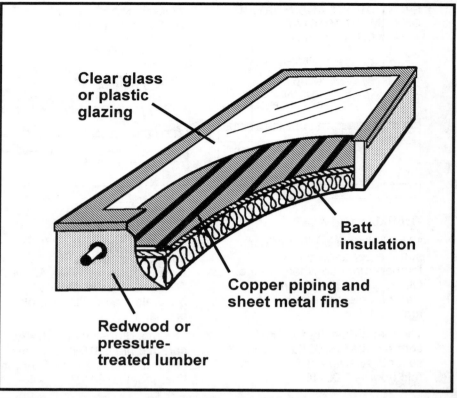

Clear glass or plastic glazing

Batt insulation

Copper piping and sheet metal fins

Redwood or pressure-treated lumber

Do-it-yourself water-type collector is effective

Make the frame for the collector box with 2x6 lumber. Redwood works, but pressure-treated lumber is best. Cover the bottom of the frame with plywood to form the shallow box.

You can use standard wall-type of fiberglass insulation in the bottom of the box. It blocks heat loss out the back of the collector. The clear cover on top reduces heat loss to the cold outdoor air above.

For the simplest design, you can use copper piping which you paint black. The pipes run vertically in the collector with the inlet at the bottom. As the water heats in the copper collector pipes, it flows up and out the top of the collector.

For more effective operation, solder flat copper fins to the copper collector pipes. These fins increase the area exposed to the sun, so the collector's heat output is greater.

Q: Our toilet always seems to be hissing and gurgling. I am sure that it is wasting a lot of water. How can I fix it myself?

A: A leaky toilet can increase your water bills because it runs continuously. The noise is often caused by water leaking past a deteriorated stopper bulb in the tank. It may also be a bad float bulb or shut-off valve which lets the water level rise too high.

You can usually buy replacements parts to fix either problem. Simple installation instruction are shown on the packaging or check your library for "fix it" books. They all cover toilet repair.

DO-IT-YOURSELF WATER-TYPE SOLAR COLLECTOR

This type of solar collector utilizes a header/riser panel design. Copper pipes and absorber plates are energy efficient and copper is fairly easy to work with. The glazing cover can be made of many materials - glass (tempered and annealed or low-iron tempered and annealed), acrylic, polycarbonate, fiberglass reinforced polyester, or polyvinyl fluoride. Check with local plastic material suppliers for the non-glass glazing materials.

A) A good collector size is 96" by 48" outside dimensions. Lumber and other materials for this size are easy to find.

B) Make the frame for the solar collector using 2x6 lumber. Standard lumber will work, but pressure-treated lumber is best. When using pressure-treated lumber, follow the suppliers guidelines for handling and safety precautions. You might want to consider treating the lumber after assembly. Therefore, the treating chemicals won't reduce the adhesion power of any glues that you use. Using dowels at the corner joints will increase the strength.

C) Nail and glue the plywood base on to the bottom of the frame. Drill several small weep holes in the back of the frame to let any moisture escape. Paint the inside and outside of the frame.

D) Cut a wood center support to fit across the frame. This supports the glazing in the center of the frame. Do not nail it into place yet.

E) You need 8 copper riser pipes and two header pipes. Make the header pipes using $3/4$" copper pipe and the risers using $1/2$" copper pipe. The header pipes should be cut to lengths of about 4-$1/8$" long to fit between the $3/4$"x$3/4$"x$1/2$" tees. The riser pipes should be about 90 inches long. This will allow for expansion as the pipes heat in the sun. If they are too long, the header pipe will be too close to the inside of the frame. Trial assemble all the pipes together in the collector frame to make sure they fit properly.

F) Make the 8 absorber plates using .020" copper sheet metal. They should be about 88" long and 5-$1/4$" wide after they are formed with the groove for the riser pipe. Trim one of the center absorber plates narrower to leave clearance for the center wood support for the glazing. An easy way to form the groove is to make a simple 8-foot long wood jig. See the diagram. Press a $1/2$" steel pipe down to form the groove in the copper.

G) Clean the copper risers and the grooves in the absorber plates with steel wool. Place the riser pipes in the plates. Using a propane torch, sweat solder into the joint attaching the risers to the plates. Make sure you get a continuous bead of solder connecting the two pieces. This is essential for good heat transfer from the absorber plates to the water in the risers.

H) Solder the tees and header pipe pieces to the riser/absorber plate assemblies. Cap off one end of both header pipes (same end of each). The other ends are the inlet and outlet that extend out the holes in the sides of the frame.

I) When the entire piping system is soldered and assembled, pressure test it with water and resolder any leaky spots.

J) Paint the copper assembly with high-temperature flat black paint to increase the solar heat gain. A flat black barbecue or automotive engine paint should work.

K) Use 3-$1/2$" foil-faced fiberglass or rock wool insulation batts in the bottom of the frame. Install the insulation with the foil facing upward. Staple the edges of the foil facing to the sides of the frame. This keeps it from settling when the collector is mounted up on an angle to face the sun. Seal the joints of the foil facing with duct tape.

L) Drill holes in the side of the frame for the inlet and outlet header pipes. Gently, slip the inlet and outlet pipes through the holes in the sides of the frame and lower the absorber assembly into the frame on top of the insulation. Using pipe strapping, secure the header pipes to the sides of the frame. Seal the gap between the inlet and outlet pipes and the frame.

M) Nail the wood support for the glazing across the center of the collector. You may have to notch it to clear the header pipes. Lay a bead of caulk along the top edge of the frame and the center support. Place the glazing on top of the frame. Lay another bead of caulk on top of the glazing and place aluminum angle over that. If you used plastic glazing you can drill through that and nail it on from the top. If you use glass, nail on the angle piece from the side.

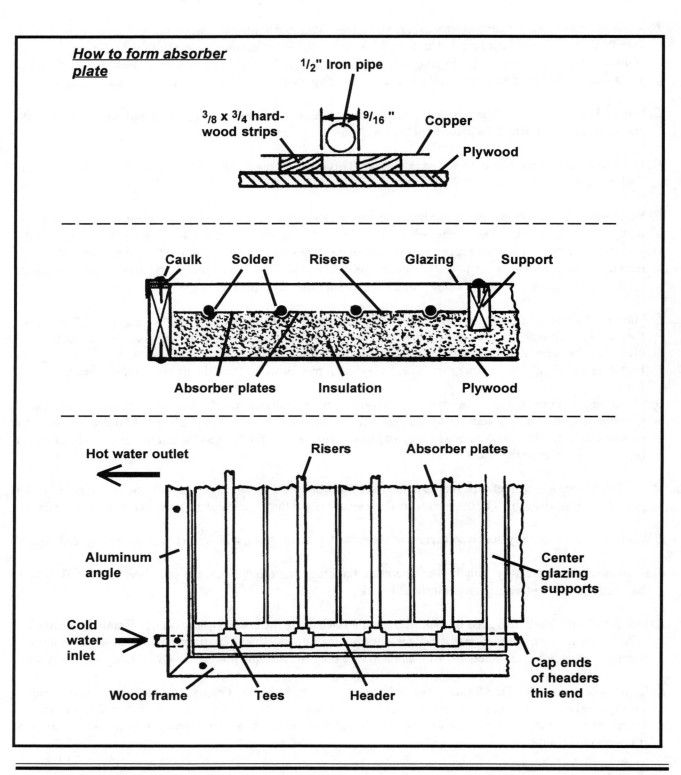

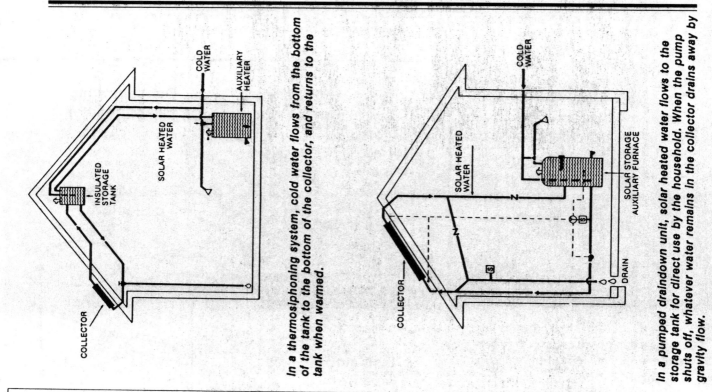

In a thermosiphoning system, cold water flows from the bottom of the tank to the bottom of the collector, and returns to the tank when warmed.

In a pumped draindown unit, solar heated water flows to the storage tank for direct use by the household. When the pump shuts off, whatever water remains in the collector drains away by gravity flow.

In an indirect (or closed-loop) system, an antifreeze solution is pumped through a heat exchanger, where it gives up its heat to the house water supply.

Though there are dozens of solar collector manufacturers, each of whom has their own uniquely designed system, all the systems fall within four main categories: draindown, drainback, indirect and phase change.

Draindown

In a draindown system, water is pumped from the hot water storage tank up to the collectors and back again. It derives its name from the electrically powered draindown valve which is the key to its freeze protection system. When the sun is out, the valve is open and the pump circulates water through the pressurized solar loop. When there is not enough solar gain and the outdoor temperature drops near 32°F (in clear, dry climates like Arizona and New Mexico, night sky radiation can draw enough heat from collectors to cause freezing at an ambient temperature of 40°F), a sensor signals the central controller to close the valve. This causes the pressure in the loop to drop, and all the water in the collectors and the exposed plumbing empties out through a special opening into a house drain. When the temperature rises above 32°F, the draindown valve will open and the pump will once again begin circulating the water.

Drainback

When the temperature falls near the freezing point the drainback system, like the draindown system just described, empties its collectors of water to avoid freeze damage. The difference between the two is that the water from the collectors in the drainback system empties back into a holding tank and is saved. Another difference is that the loop between the holding tank and the collectors is not pressurized. Therefore, when the thermostat signals the pump to turn off, the water drains by force of gravity. No electric valves are used which might fail.

Thermosiphon Water Heaters

Thermosiphon systems consist of a solar collector panel to absorb solar heat and a separate storage tank, either built-in at the top of the collector or placed inside the house, to hold solar-heated water. The solar collector is faced true south at an angle equal to the latitude. It must be mounted at least a foot below the storage tank to permit thermosiphoning - upward movement of water by natural convection. When the water in the collector is heated, it becomes less dense and rises to the top of the storage tank. At the same time, cool water from the bottom of the tank flows into the bottom of the collector.

Although thermosiphon systems can be quite efficient and supply 40 to 60 percent of your hot water, two problems keep them from being used more often. First, because the storage tank must be installed above the collector, it is often placed on an upper floor or high in the attic above the roof rafter. In some cases, the roof or flooring may have to be reinforced because water tanks are quite heavy. Of course, the collectors can be placed on the ground if an adequate site is available.

Second, thermosiphon collectors in their simplest form contain no safeguard against freezing. This is important because water remains in the collector whenever convection stops (during sunless periods). If this water freezes it can expand with enough force to burst the piping or the tank. Freezing can be prevented by using movable insulation, an antifreeze/water solution or by installing a valve allowing the water to be drained at night. But operating a thermosiphon water heater is cheaper and easier in areas where freezing does not occur. If used elsewhere, the simplest solution is to drain them before the first frost.

Active Systems

Unlike passive systems, active domestic hot water systems use electrically driven pumps and valves to control the circulation of the heat absorbing liquid. This allows a greater degree of flexibility than their passive counterparts since the hot water storage tank does not have to be above or near the collectors. Also, active systems are designed to operate all year round without any danger of freezing.

New designs for roof solar heaters

Q: I want to install a simple solar system myself to heat our hot water. Are there any new types of small solar systems that won't look ugly on my roof and are easy to install?

A: There are new designs of solar systems that are simple to install and are not "ugly". Installing one yourself can cut your annual water heating costs by as much as $200 and can easily payback its cost several times over its lifetime.

One of the most unique and simplest designs uses the coffee percolator concept. This eliminates the need for an electric pump to circulate the solar heated water. It uses your existing water heater.

Specially-designed tubes in the flat collector on your roof cause a water/alcohol solution to boil. As the bubbles rise, they carry the solar heated solution with them. This is how a coffee percolator works.

This heated water/alcohol solution flows through a sealed heat exchanger base that you set your water heater on top of. Since the heat exchanger gets hot, the water from your water heater naturally circulates through it (hot water is less dense) without any pumps.

This solar system is very simple to install yourself. The water/alcohol solution also provides for winter freeze protection for year-round use.

Another unique solar system also needs no pumps. This system uses a small concentrating collector. The reflective collector focuses the sun's heat on a small pipe in its center. For super high efficiency, it has an automatic sun sensor to slowly rotate the collector to follow the sun's

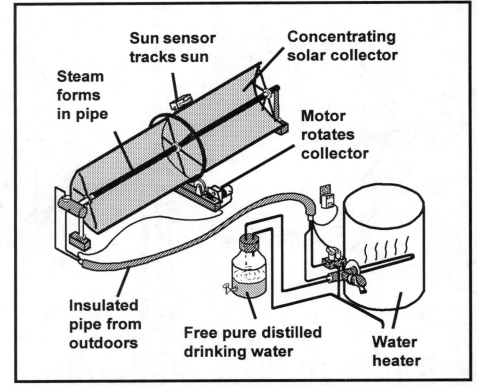

Solar water system tracks sun for efficiency

path all day.

The water gets hot enough to form steam inside the pipe. This creates a slight pressure that forces the steam through an insulated tube to a heat exchanger in your water heater.

There it gives off its heat to the water heater and the steam condenses to pure distilled water. You can store this pure water for drinking and cooking. Combining the hot water savings and the savings from not buying bottled water, the return on the investment is good.

If you are really concerned about the appearance of the solar collectors on your roof, there is a new type of shallow solar collector that is designed to look like a skylight on your roof. It lays flush against your roof surface and is less than 2-1/2 inches deep. It has durable plastic tubes inside it to handle year-round tem-

perature extremes and it is very efficient.

Q: I always hear the size of electric motors described in horsepower, like my half horsepower air conditioner blower. How much energy is one horsepower and how does that relate to my other electric appliances?

A: One horsepower of energy is equivalent to 746 watts of electricity or 2,545 Btu of heat per hour. The amount of electricity your furnace blower draws is not constant. As the load on the motor increases, so does the electricity usage.

For comparison, a typical hand-held hair blower dryer uses the equivalent of 1.5 horsepower. Your stereo system may use about one-quarter horsepower.

Domestic hot water solar systems usually are the most economically feasible solar system because they are effective year-round. A target for having solar energy provide 60% to 80% of your hot water needs is often used. In the summer, it will probably provide nearly 100% of your needs because of the longer days, warmer air temperature, and cooler showers taken. The water usage chart on this page will help you to determine your hot water needs and the size of solar system you will need.

A list of manufacturers of hot water solar systems is shown on page **b**. Most of these are the typical flat plate solar collector systems that are mounted on your roof. The solar-heated water is piped to a heat exchanging coil inside a water heater tank. A small electric pump circulates the water when the solar collectors get hot. There is usually a temperature sensor in the collector to detect when the water is hot enough to switch on the circulation pump.

Information on three unique solar systems is shown on pages **b** and **c**. The first (American Solar Network) works like a standard solar system as described above. It is unique in that the collector looks like a skylight. The collector is shallow and lays flat against your roof. In addition to being attractive, it's efficient. The typical price is about $1,300.

Page **c** shows a unique system (by BSAR) that produces pure distilled drinking water as it heats your water. It uses a concentrating collector that focuses the sun's heat on to a water-filled tube. This creates steam. This also increases pressure that forces the steam through a heat exchanger in your water heater. Therefore, a circulating electric motor is not used. When the heat from the steam is given off to the water in your water heater, the steam condenses to produce <u>free</u> pure distilled drinking water.

Another unique feature of this system is that it has a sun-tracker sensor to follow the sun throughout the day. This slowly tilts the collector so that it is always facing most directly toward the sun. A typical price for this system is about $3,000.

Page **c** shows a unique solar system that moves the solar heated water/alcohol (does not freeze in winter) through the system without a circulating pump. A special design of tubing inside the collector on your roof causes tiny steam bubbles to form. As they rise in the tubes, they force the heated water up with them. This is exactly how a coffee percolator works to raise the hot water.

A special heat exchanger is designed to be the base for an existing electric water heater. Cold water from the bottom drain in the tank flows out into the heat exchanger base. You unscrew and remove the lower electric heating element. You screw a fitting in that hole and it carries the heated water from the heat exchanger back into the tank. This is natural flow with no pump. The typical price for this system is about $2,200.

Worksheet to determine daily hot water needs			
Fixture/Use	_# of times/week_	_Gallons/use_	_Gallons/week_
Bath (standard)		x 15 =	
Bath (large/jacuzzi)		x 25 =	
Shower (regular head)		x 15 =	
Shower (low-flow head)		x 8 =	
Laundry (hot wash/warm rinse)		x 25 =	
Laundry (hot wash/cold rinse)		x 20 =	
Laundry (warm wash/cold rinse)		x 15 =	
Dishwasher		x 15 =	
Hand-wash dishes (full sink)		x 4 =	
Hand-wash dishes (just a few)		x 2 =	
Hand and face wash		x 1 =	
Others _____		x ____ =	
		Total =	
		Total/7 = Gallons per day	

MANUFACTURERS OF RESIDENTIAL SOLAR WATER HEATING SYSTEMS

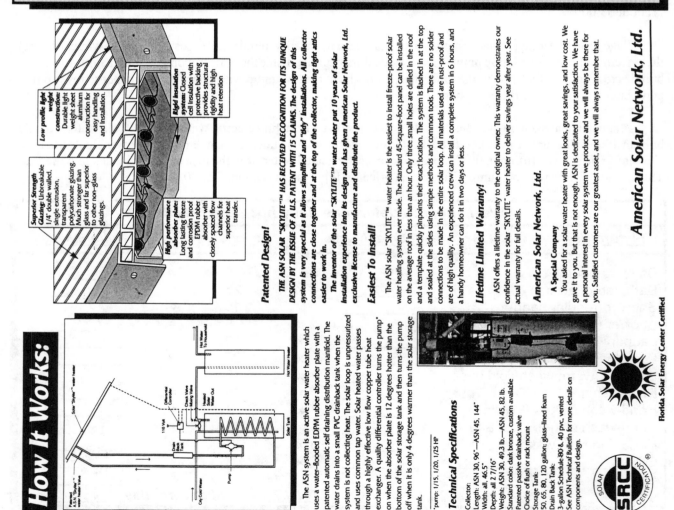

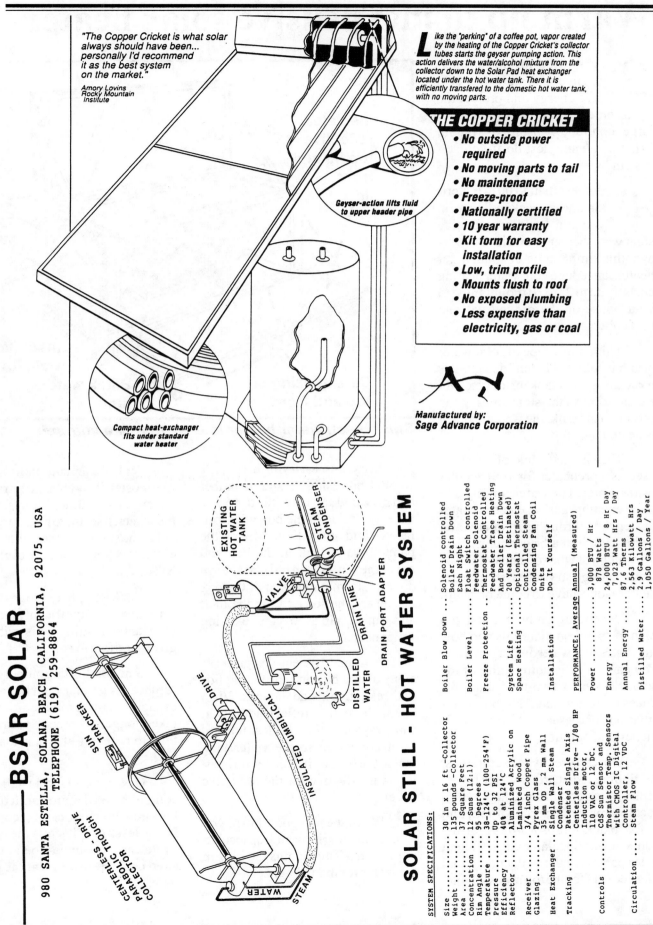

"The Copper Cricket is what solar always should have been... personally I'd recommend it as the best system on the market."

Amory Lovins
Rocky Mountain
Institute

Like the "perking" of a coffee pot, vapor created by the heating of the Copper Cricket's collector tubes starts the geyser pumping action. This action delivers the water/alcohol mixture from the collector down to the Solar Pad heat exchanger located under the hot water tank. There it is efficiently transfered to the domestic hot water tank, with no moving parts.

THE COPPER CRICKET

- **No outside power required**
- **No moving parts to fail**
- **No maintenance**
- **Freeze-proof**
- **Nationally certified**
- **10 year warranty**
- **Kit form for easy installation**
- **Low, trim profile**
- **Mounts flush to roof**
- **No exposed plumbing**
- **Less expensive than electricity, gas or coal**

Geyser-action lifts fluid to upper header pipe

Compact heat-exchanger fits under standard water heater

Manufactured by:
Sage Advance Corporation

BSAR SOLAR

980 SANTA ESTELLA, SOLANA BEACH, CALIFORNIA, 92075, USA
TELEPHONE (619) 259-8864

SOLAR STILL - HOT WATER SYSTEM

SYSTEM SPECIFICATIONS:

Size	30 in x 16 ft -Collector
Weight	135 pounds -Collector
Area	37 Square Feet
Concentration	12 Suns (12:1)
Rim Angle	95 Degrees
Temperature	38-124°C (100-254°F)
Pressure	Up to 32 PSI
Efficiency	40% at 124°C
Reflector	Aluminized Acrylic on Laminated Wood
Receiver	3/4 inch Copper Pipe
Glazing	Pyrex Glass
Heat Exchanger	35 mm OD , 2 mm Wall Single Wall Steam Condenser
Tracking	Patented Single Axis Centerless Drive- 1/80 HP Induction motor, 110 VAC or 12 DC.
Controls	CdS Sun Sensor and Thermistor Temp. Sensors with CMOS IC Digital Controller, 12 VDC
Circulation	Steam Flow

Boiler Blow Down	Solenoid controlled Boiler Drain Down
Boiler Level	Float Switch controlled Feedwater Solenoid
Freeze Protection	Thermostat Controlled Feedwater Trace Heating And Boiler Drain Down
System Life	20 Years (Estimated)
Space Heating	Optional Thermostat Controlled Steam Condensing Fan Coil Units
Installation	Do It Yourself

PERFORMANCE: Average Annual (Measured)

Power	3,000 BTU / Hr 878 Watts
Energy	24,000 BTU / 8 Hr Day 7,023 Watt Hrs / Day
Annual Energy	87.6 Therms 2,563 Kilowatt Hrs
Distilled Water	2.9 Gallons / Day 1,050 Gallons / Year

EXISTING HOT WATER TANK

STEAM CONDENSER

VALVE

DRAIN LINE

DRAIN PORT ADAPTER

DISTILLED WATER

INSULATED UMBILICAL

DRIVE

SUN TRACKER

CENTERLESS-DRIVE

PARABOLIC COLLECTOR

CENTERLESS-DRIVE

STEAM

WATER

Warm up to inexpensive solar heater

Q: I would like to build an inexpensive solar water heater to save energy and protect the environment. I can't afford to buy a large contractor-installed system. What is the simplest do-it-yourself system?

A: For less than $100 in materials and a weekend's work, you can build an effective solar water heater yourself. On average, this simple type of solar water heater can reduce your water heating costs by up to 25%. It mounts next to your house on the ground with no roof collectors.

This simple type of solar water heater is called a "batch" design. It is basically a water tank inside box with a clear top. As the sun shines in the box on to the tank, the water inside it is heated.

This heated tank of water is used as a preheater for your regular water heater. The water coming into your existing gas or electric water heater runs through the solar water heater first. On a bright sunny day, the water from the solar heater can be warm enough so your existing water heater won't have to come on at all.

Depending on how much you plan to spend on materials and how much solar hot water output you want, you can vary the complexity of the solar design. A two-tank unit produces more hot water. Nighttime insulation increases the overall efficiency and output.

You can greatly reduce the cost by finding a discarded water heater tank in good condition. Check with a local plumber. Strip it down and paint it flat black to absorb more of the sun's heat. Special extra-efficient solar paints for the tank and special clear covers for the top are available.

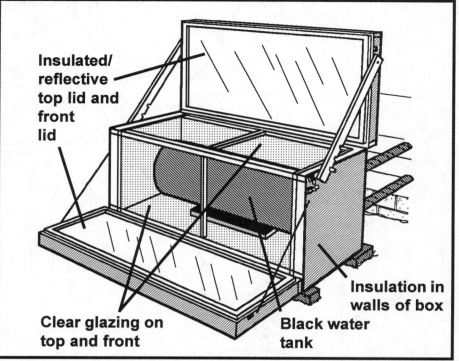

Insulated/ reflective top lid and front lid

Clear glazing on top and front

Black water tank

Insulation in walls of box

Solar batch water heater is easy to make yourself

In its simplest form, just make a wooden box using cheap 2x4 lumber and plywood and leave the top open. Line the inside of the box with foil-faced rigid insulation. Mount the painted water tank in the box and cover the top with an old glass storm door or storm window. Tilt the box up toward the sun and run the inlet and output pipes to your existing water heater.

A more efficient design, uses an insulated box and insulating lids with reflective inside surfaces. When open, these lids reflect additional sun's rays through the clear top and front covers on to the water tank inside the box. Foil-faced rigid insulation is effective for the reflective covers.

When the sun goes down, you should close the front and top insulating covers. This retains the heat in the water for many hours.

Q: I use an automatic setback thermostat for both my central heating and air-conditioning systems. In the winter, it seems to heat up quickly, but in the summer, it seems to take an extremely long time to cool after setback. Why?

A: Setting back your thermostat can save a significant amount on your annual utility bills without a great sacrifice in comfort.

Since the heating output of most furnaces is greater than the cooling capacity of most air conditioners, it takes longer to recool your house than to reheat it after a setback period.

One option is to install a new computerized thermostat. It remembers how long it took to recool your house last time. It starts the cooling cycle early enough to be at the desired cool temperature at the proper time.

This type of solar water heater is most often used as a preheater for your standard electric or gas water heater. It is not designed to be the only heat source for hot water. Used as a preheater, it can reduce your water heating costs and can easily pay back its material costs.

- -

Required Materials for Batch Solar Water Heater

Lumber - 2x4, 2x3, 1x4, 1x3, 1x2
Plywood - $1/4$" sheet
Water tank - stripped discarded water heater tank - check with plumbers
Insulation - Thermax foil-faced $1/2$" sheet and 2" sheet, tubular foam for pipes
Glazing - clear acrylic, special solar glazing, or glass
$1/2$" wood dowel
Aluminum angle
Caulking - silicon
Weatherstripping - adhesive-backed foam
Plumbing Supplies - copper pipe, solder, teflon tape, fittings
Paint - flat black or special solar paint, marine epoxy or exterior house paint
Glue - wood glue, foamboard/panel adhesive
Tape - aluminum foil duct tape
Fasteners - nails, screws, strapping, butt hinges

DO-IT-YOURSELF INSTRUCTIONS FOR MAKING A BATCH SOLAR WATER HEATER

When completed, this solar water heater will be approximately 31" high, 28" wide, and 61" long. If you happen to have an old storm window or door, you can make the solar heater any size. The size shown here makes efficient use of most standard size building materials and water tanks Diagram #1.

A) Cut four 21" long 2x4 uprights and four 53-$3/4$" long 2x4 crosspieces. Cut four 21" long 2x3 upright supports. Measure in 16-$1/2$" from each end of the crosspieces and mark a line. Glue and nail these pieces together per Diagram #2 to form the back and bottom of the box.

B) Cut four 24-$1/2$" long and four 24" long 2x4 pieces. Glue and nail pieces together per Diagram #2.

C) Make the frames for the insulating and reflective front and top lids. For the top lid, cut two 25-$1/8$" long and two 61-$1/2$" long 2x4 pieces and two 25-$1/8$ long 2x3 pieces. Glue and nail together per Diagram #2. For the front lid cut two 21" long and two 61-$1/4$" long 2x4 pieces and two 21" long 2x3 pieces. Glue and nail together per Diagram #2.

D) Make two glazing frames to cover the top and the front of the box from the 1x4 lumber. Rip it to four 3/4" square strips. For the top glazing frame, cut three 18" long and two 53-$3/4$" long. To assemble the glazing frame, nail through the longer strips into the shorter ones at both ends. A support is centered between the two end pieces. Mark its position and nail it in place. From the remaining $3/4$" strips, cut three 21" long pieces and two 53-$3/4$" long pieces. Assemble these for the front glazing frame.

E) Cut and install the insulation in the box frame. It is very important that the insulation fits tightly in the box with no gaps. Measure each side and carefully cut the pieces. It is easy to do a final trim with a utility knife. For the front lid, cut a piece of the $1/2$" Thermax insulation. It should measure roughly 21"x58-$1/4$". Spread adhesive on the supports and place the Thermax in the lid against the support with the reflective foil surface facing up. Tape it to the frame with strips of the foil duct tape.

F) Cut pieces of 2" Thermax insulation to fit between the supports in the top lid. Two pieces should be roughly 15"x21" and one piece should be 25-1/2"x21". Spread adhesive on the supports and the 1/2" Thermax already installed. Place pieces of 2" Thermax in the lid. Allow adhesive to dry. Cover the top of the lid with plywood. The foil surface should be showing on the other side. Install insulation in the top lid and finish it the same as the front lid.

G) Insulate the box framing in the same fashion. The reflective side of the 1/2" insulation should face inside the box. This directs as much heat as possible on to the water tank. Seal the insulation to the lumber with the foil duct tape. With the insulation in the bottom, back, and side sections of the box frame, glue and nail the framing together to form the box. Caulk all the wood to wood joints on the inside with silicon caulking. Cut plywood pieces to cover and finish the outside of the box. Paint the exterior of the box with an epoxy marine-type paint or exterior house paint.

H) Using 2x4 lumber, make two cradle pieces to support the water tank. Cut a long shallow "V" to form the cradle. Nail these through the 1/2" Thermax into the supports in the bottom frame section. This will position the tank about 2" above the bottom of the box.

I) Paint the water tank with flat black paint. For greater efficiency, use a special selective solar paint. The tank should be positioned with the hot water outlet fitting directly above the cold water inlet. Since the hottest water will rise to the top, this positioning will minimize mixing of the hot and cold water. Screw a short nipple into the tank fittings and solder on 90-degree elbows. Measure the position of the elbows and drill inlet and outlet holes in the back of the box. Tilt the pipes slightly downward to your house so they will drain out when you want to drain it. Secure the tank in the cradles with metal strapping.

J) Rip the 1x4 lumber to 3/4" strips to form ledgers to support the clear glazing. Nail these ledgers 3/4" below the top and front surface of the box frame - Diagram #3. Set the glazing frames in the box against the ledgers. The outside edge of the glazing frames should be flush with the surfaces of the box. For greater efficiency, you can staple clear teflon film to the bottom of the glazing frames first. This produces a double-clear cover when completed. Nail the front edges of the glazing frames together to complete the box. Caulk all the joints.

K) For the clear top and front of the box, you can use clear acrylic, polycarbonate, fiberglass reinforced polyester (FRP), low-iron glass (best for solar), or standard glass. Cut the glazing pieces to cover the entire top and front surface of the box (you'll have to have glass professionally cut). Lay a thin bead of caulking on the frame and place the clear glazing covers in position. Finish the edges over the glazing with an aluminum angle. Place another thin bead of caulk under the aluminum angle. Drill through the aluminum and the acrylic glazing into the wood. When using glass, screw the angle on from the sides since it is difficult to drill through glass. Secure it in place with screws every six inches. If you ever have to remove it for maintenance, you can slip a thin knife under the angle and then the glazing to cut it loose.

L) Lay the front reflective lid on the ground in front of the box. Attach the butt hinges at the bottom so it will close snugly against the front cover. Lay the top reflective lid on top of the box. Attach it with the butt hinges. Drill 1/2" holes in the tops of the ends of the box and insert a 1/2" dowel. It should extend out about 2". Make two lid supports from 1x3 lumber. Cut notches in them and drill a hole 17/32 holes in one end. Install a short piece of the 1/2" dowel in each side of the top lid. Slip the lid supports over the dowels. Adjust the position of the top lid with the notches in the lid supports. Place the adhesive-backed weatherstripping around the edge of the lid so it seals against the box when it is closed.

M) Position the solar water heater as close to the south side of your house as possible. Leave adequate space to get behind it in case any work has to be done. Contact your local weather service to find the exact true solar south direction in your area. It is not the same as the south on your compass.

N) Run the inlet and outlet pipes into your water heater. Pipe it into your water heater system as shown in the plumbing diagram. Wrap the tubular foam pipe insulation over the outdoor sections of the pipes.

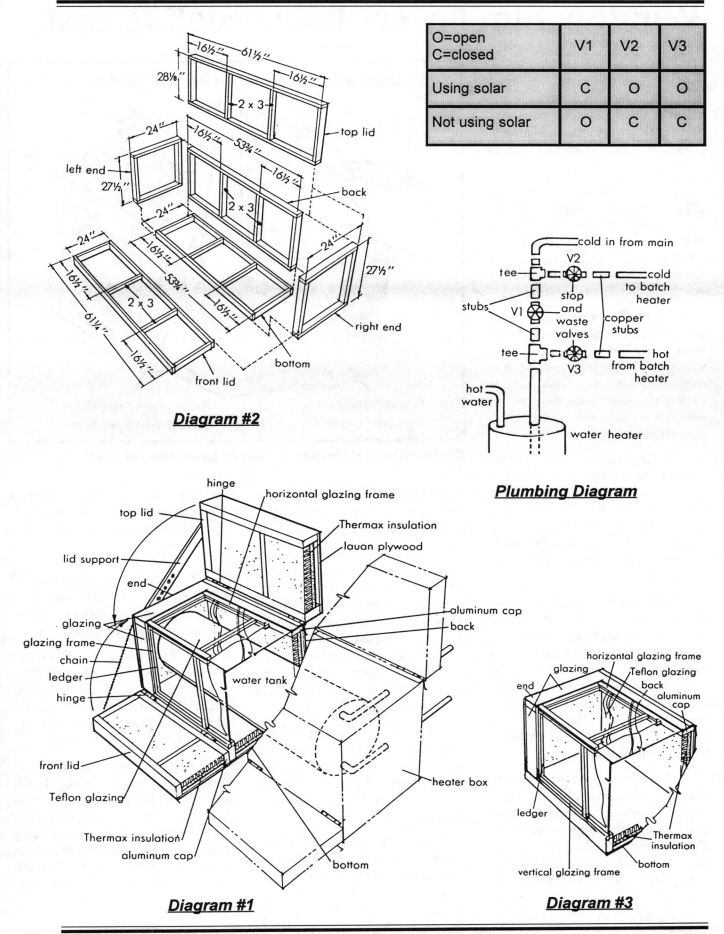

O=open C=closed	V1	V2	V3
Using solar	C	O	O
Not using solar	O	C	C

Diagram #2

Plumbing Diagram

Diagram #1

Diagram #3

Window film lowers home cooling cost

Q. The hot sun shining in our windows literally bakes us and fades our furniture and carpets. What can I do to our windows to block the sun in the summer, but still let it shine in for solar heat in the winter?

A: Blocking the intense summer sun through your windows reduces your air-conditioning costs and increases your comfort. It also greatly reduces the fading and deterioration of your furniture, curtains, and carpeting.

There are several inexpensive do-it-yourself methods to block the summer sun from shining in your windows. These sun control methods are designed so you can remove them each winter if you want to capture some free solar heat through your windows.

A very effective summer-only sun control method is installing a new type of self-cling reusable tinted (grey or bronze) window film yourself. You can reinstall it each spring in just a couple of minutes. Peel it off again each fall and roll it up until you install it again next spring.

Unlike standard year-round sun-control window film which uses a permanent adhesive, the durable reusable film sticks to the window glass by static electricity. The natural properties of the thin tinted vinyl film create the tiny natural static charge to hold it firmly to the glass. To remove it in the fall, you just lift up a corner, and pull it off the glass.

This tinted vinyl blocks more than 50% of the sun's heat, yet still provides a sharp, undistorted view through your windows. The sun's ultraviolet rays, which fade and destroy your furniture through your windows, are reduced by more than 80%.

Ordinary window cleaner on film and window

Newspapers or drop cloth

Self-cling reusable tinted window film

Self-cling window film is simple to install yourself

With the film applied, the window glass is also more shatter-resistant from impacts and high winds.

You can purchase self-cling window film in small rolls. Using a scissors, cut a piece of film slightly larger than your window. Wet the window and the film (either side since there is no adhesive) with a common spray window cleaner. Place it on the window and squeegee it flat to the glass. When it dries, cut off the excess with a sharp utility knife.

You can also install special fiberglass sun-control window screening in your existing window screen frames. This very durable screening blocks 70% of the sun's heat and fading rays.

Although this screening is a closer weave than standard screening, you can still easily see through it

and it won't block breezes through an open window. You should be able to install the screening yourself.

Q: I have been told that roof felt under the shingles is needed as a vapor barrier for unvented attics. Does roof felt save much energy?

A: First of all, roof felt is not used as a vapor barrier and all attics should be vented. The thin layer of material directly under the shingles has no significant effect on the energy efficiency of your house.

There are several benefits from using roof felt when roofing. The felt provides a quick protective covering for the roof deck and the interior of the house while the roofing is being applied. It also provides extra leak protection against strong wind-driven rain or when a shingle is blown off.

Sun-control window film and window screening are very effective methods to reduce the heat entering your house in the summer. If you choose to use natural ventilation through windows most of the time in the summer and your screens cover the entire window area, the sun-control window screening is your best choice. For double-hung windows, with screening only on the top or bottom half, use a combination of screening and window film to be most effective.

The self-cling window film is effective because you can remove it in the winter for the greatest solar gain. It is also very easy to install yourself. Self-cling film is not quite as distortion-free as permanent window film because of the removable nature of the material. There is also a type of self-cling opaque window film with many tiny perforations. You can easily see through the film, yet it blocks much of the sun. All of these products block the sun's heat and fading rays through your windows. The sun control specifications are shown below.

MANUFACTURERS OF REUSABLE SELF-CLING WINDOW FILM

MIDWEST MARKETING, P.O. Box 2063, East Peoria, IL 61611 - (309) 688-8858
Perforated opaque window film

SOLAR STAT, 511 N.E. 190th St., Miami, FL 33179 - (800) 783-0454
Non-reflective tinted window film

MANUFACTURERS OF SUN-CONTROL WINDOW SCREENING

PHIFER WIRE PRODUCTS, P.O. Box 1700, Tuscaloosa, AL 35403 - (205) 345-2120

VIMCO, 9301 Old Staples Mill Rd., Richmond, VA 23228 - (804) 266-9638

SUN-BLOCKING SPECIFICATIONS FOR SELF-CLING WINDOW FILM

	Grey	Bronze
TOTAL SOLAR ENERGY REJECTION	55.2%	55.3%
TOTAL SOLAR ENERGY TRANSMISSION	44.8%	44.6%
TOTAL ULTRAVIOLET REJECTION	82.3%	87.5%
TOTAL ULTRAVIOLET TRANSMISSION	17.7%	12.4%
VISIBLE LIGHT TRANSMITTANCE	37.2%	38.0%
SHADING COEFFICIENT	0.58	0.58
R-FACTOR	1.75	1.75
U-FACTOR	0.57	0.57

INSTRUCTIONS FOR INSTALLING SELF-CLING WINDOW FILM

A) Avoid working in direct sunlight or wind. For best results, apply when the temperature is between 45 and 90 degrees. Clean window thoroughly with a glass cleaner. Make sure all corners and edges are as clean as possible. Wipe window dry with a lint free cloth.

B) Measure window. Unroll self-cling film on a flat surface and cut one inch larger on sides to insure proper sizing.

C) Spray the window thoroughly with a glass cleaner before applying film. Never reinstall on a dry surface. For easier handling, spray the surface of the film before applying. This will prevent the film from clinging to itself as you handle it. Starting at the top, apply the film to the inside of the window. If you have double pane thermal windows, apply the film to the outdoor surface of the window.

Installation Tools Needed

- Squeegee
- Tape Measure
- Straight Edge Ruler
- Single Edge Razor Blade
- Utility Knife
- Glass Cleaner
- Lint-free Cloth

D) Position the film by using your hands to work out wrinkles until it overlaps the frame on all sides. On larger windows and doors, some assistance will be helpful.

E) Spray the surface of the film generously. Beginning at the center of the window, firmly squeegee out bubbles and water toward the sides, working in a side to side and up and down direction.

F) After you squeegee out the excess liquid and bubbles, use a straight edge ruler to press the film to the inside edge of the window frame. Trim the excess film with a sharp razor blade or knife.

G) After trimming the excess around the entire window, firmly squeegee the edges toward the frame. At this point, you may wish to repeat step *E*. Any remaining small bubbles or excess liquid should evaporate in a few days. During the first ten hours after installation, the film should not be disturbed.

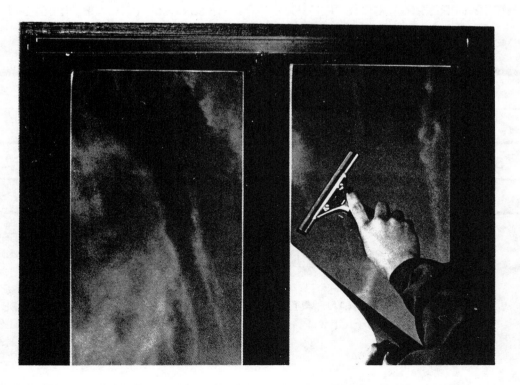

DOT MATRIX UV-X removeable, reusable window tinting is a permanent or temporary relief to heat, glare, fading, and privacy control in automobiles, homes, and offices. UV-X is available prepacked for Do-it-yourself use or bulk 100 foot rolls for the professional. This high tech patent pending product adheres to smooth, clean, dry glass, Plexiglass, Lexan, or film by a permanent static charge. Once sucessfully applied, DOT MATRIX UV-X will stay attached in all types of weather, temperature, interior or exterior, until you pull it off. Removal is fast and easy; just lift a corner and pull. The material can be rolled up, stored, and reinstalled over and over. Most installations are quick and easy.

INSTALLATION INSTRUCTIONS

1. Thoroughly clean glass to be covered. Scrape wet glass with razor blade if needed, especially in corners. Squeegee or towel completely dry.

2. Pre-cut material at least 1'' - 2'' larger than glass. Place shiney side towards glass. Start in the center and press the material to the glass moving your hands toward the edges. Material should lay flat against the glass. If air bubbles are present, peel back a corner, holding material off the glass, repress as you gradually allow material to touch the glass. Small air bubbles can be pressed down without peeling back a corner. If small specks or dots appear and will not smooth out, it is probably dirt. Peel back and remove.

On large windows (patio doors, plate glass, etc.) start smoothing film from the top downward. After the top 10''-12'' has smoothly been applied, the remaining area can be pulled from the glass. Spray the glass with water or window cleaner, then squeegee out air and water. After step 4, remove excess water from the holes in the material by wiping with cloth or paper towels. NOTE: DOT MATRIX UV-X does not stick to wet glass. As the water drys, the film will begin to adhere. Repeat step # 4 later if needed.

3. Place a flat 1/16''-1/8'' straight edge (installation tool , ruler, etc.) next to window frame. Place a single edge razor blade next to the straight edge on the opposite side of the window frame and cut. This will allow the excess material to be cut a proper 1/8'' from the frame. Scrap can be used for windshield visor strips or movable sun spots.

4. To create a uniform dot matrix look from the outside, smooth down material with installation tool, kitchen spatula, or credit card.

5. If film has been stored and is being reused, wash first with a soap and water solution, rinse, let dry, then reapply. Wrinkles will come out with a little heat and pressure from an installation tool.

6. AUTO INSTALLATION. Many curved rear windows will have to go on in several vertical pieces. Overlap 1'', cut through both pieces and peel off the excess. DOT MATRIX UV-X should be below the bottom rubber on roll down windows to prevent material from coming loose. On front side frameless windows, move the razor blade along the glass edge as a guide. Windshields should not be done lower than 6'' from the top.

TEMPERATURE - This material reacts to both extreme temperatures of heat and cold during installation. After a successful installation, material is not affected by temperature. The best temperature range is between 65º-90º, and out of direct sun. Too much heat may cause air pockets to appear later. This could happen once. Peel back and reapply. Cold and moisture will affect the static cling.

TECHNICAL SPECIFICATIONS
SOLAR OPTICAL PROPERTIES

	Black	Almond
TOTAL SOLAR ENERGY		
Transmitted	25%	
Reflected	12%	
Absorbed	63%	
VISIBLE LIGHT TRANSMITTED	33%	
ULTRA-VIOLET LIGHT TRANSMITTED	18%	
SHADING COEFFICIENT	.49	
EMMITTANCE	.78	
U-VALUE	1-10	
TOTAL ENERGY REJECTED	51%	

Independent testing of DOT MATRIX UV-X applied to 1/4'' clear plate glass is in accordance with ASHRAE STANDARD 74 - 73

WARRANTY - 5 year interior application
2 year exterior application

PRICING AND SIZES
DO-IT-YOURSELF PRE-PAK KITS - BLACK ONLY

SIZE		COST $1.40 SQ. FT
5'' x 72''	SUN STRIP	$ 3.50 EACH
14'' x 20''	SUN SPOT	$ 2.75
20'' x 40''	SUN ROOF	$ 7.75
20'' x 5'	REAR GLASS	$11.70
20'' x 10'	SIDE GLASS	$23.35
30'' x 5'	HATCH BACK	$17.50

PROFESSIONAL BULK ROLLS - BLACK OR ALMOND

SIZE	COST $1.20 SQ. FT.
20'' x 100'	$200 ROLL
24'' x 100'	$240
30'' x 100'	$300
36'' x 100'	$360
48'' x 100'	$480
54'' x 100'	$540
60'' x 100'	$600

DIY INSTALLATION KIT INCLUDES:
SQUEEGEE / EDGE TOOL, TRIM KNIFE. $3.20

ORDERS SHIPPED SAME DAY.
MINIMUM ORDER $25
UPS-COD (WITHOUT PRIOR CREDIT APPROVAL)

MIDWEST MARKETING

ALSO AVAILABLE, TRANSPARENT MYLAR **SUN-SHADES, MADICO** WINDOW FILM, **AUTO ROOF** POP UP SUNROOFS, CUSTOM VINYL STICK ON LETTERS

Using solar energy to cool, heat house

Q. I would like to use free solar energy to help cool my house in the summer without sacrificing solar gain in the winter. Are there any do-it-yourself solar-cooling projects?

A. You can use free solar energy to help cool your home in the summer. Building a solar ventilation chimney is an effective and simple project. With the proper use of solar heat mass storage, you can have cooling well into the evening hours too.

First, you should make some simple do-it-yourself improvements. Extend the roof overhang on the south and west sides of your house. This blocks the summer sun which is high in the sky. The winter sun, which is lower in the sky, still shines under the large overhang on to your walls and in your windows for solar heating.

It is not a difficult task to increase the overhang. Remove the soffit sheathing and extend the roof rafters or joist. Cover this with roof sheathing and match the old shingle color. Cover the soffit area again and add inlet air vents to the attic.

A do-it-yourself solar chimney is basically a natural whole-house exhaust vent from the ceiling in your home up through the roof. As the portion of the solar chimney extending up past the roof gets warm from the sun, the hot air inside it naturally flows upward and out.

This pulls cool air indoors. Air inlet can be located in a crawl space or through windows or vents near the floor. Install screens on both openings.

A solar chimney has clear glazing (acrylic plastic, glass, etc.) on the south and west sides. A two-foot-square size is ideal because there is less material waste when using inexpensive standard 4 foot by 8 foot lumber and other materials. Seven feet high is a typical size.

Install clear glazing on only the top half of the south side. Otherwise, since the sun is so high at noon, it will shine down into your room below and actually heat it. Glaze the entire west side of the solar chimney.

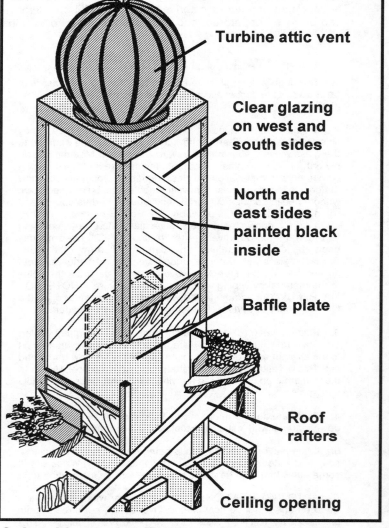

- Turbine attic vent
- Clear glazing on west and south sides
- North and east sides painted black inside
- Baffle plate
- Roof rafters
- Ceiling opening

Solar chimney is effective and easy to build

Install foil-faced rigid insulation board on the inside of the plywood north and east sides of the solar chimney. Paint the foil flat black so it becomes an effective solar heat collector when the sun shines in the glazed west or south sides. You can also install an 18-inch turbine attic vent on top of the chimney to improve the draw in windy weather.

Q: I have a problem with rusty water coming out of my hot water faucets. My electric water heater is only a couple of years old. What is the source of the rust and how can I get it out?

A: Since your water heater is fairly new and it is glass-lined, it probably is not the source of the rust. The most likely source is one or more of the hot water supply pipes between the water heater and faucets.

Try flushing the pipes to remove the rust. First turn off the power to your water heater. Open all the hot water faucets and allow the water to run for 15 minutes. If this doesn't help, contact your plumber for a more thorough analysis.

Building a solar chimney can be a very effective method to ventilate your house. It also adds natural lighting like a skylight without the direct sun's heat getting in. Not only does it operate for free, but it does not contribute to air pollution and global warming as electric fans do.

A schematic diagram showing how a solar chimney draws cool air into your house is shown on page **c**. Be sure to keep your windows tightly closed so that the cooler air is drawn in crawl spaces or basement windows or vents. If you are allergic to molds and mildew and live in a humid climate, the air from a crawl space or basement may aggravate your allergy. In this case, open windows on the ground level floor of your home.

Installing an optional turbine vent on top of the chimney helps to increase the vertical draft when it is breezy outdoors during the day. An 18-inch turbine vent is a good size to use on top of a 2 ft. by 2 ft. solar chimney. In the winter, you can close the insulated hinged plywood 2 ft. by 2 ft. door in the ceiling. Also close it when you run your air conditioner.

I have included a schematic construction diagram of a sample solar chimney. You can make the solar chimney any size you want. The bigger it is, the more ventilation it will create. If you make it too big, it may detract from the exterior appearance of your house. A height of seven feet above your roof is a good initial target height. A steeper pitched roof, as in the northern climates, can accommodate a taller solar chimney.

Check the location of trees around your roof to find a location for the solar chimney that is not shaded. Keep in mind that neighbors' trees will grow and you probably will not be able to prune them. Consider the orientation of your roof to the south and west. If possible, locate it near an outside wall where the roof slopes downward. This makes the lightwell channel shorter between the roof and the ceiling. Also the solar chimney will be less obvious sticking up from your roof. To be effective, it must be in the sun from late morning to early evening.

You should be able to find most of the materials at a home center or building supply outlet. There are several options for the clear glazing on the south and west sides of the solar chimney. Clear acrylic plastic (Plexiglas) sheet is easy to work with. Fiberglass reinforced polyester is another durable option. Clear polycarbonate (Lexan) is unbreakable (used for bulletproof windows), but it is more expensive.

Always wear appropriate safety equipment and eye protection. I would avoid using ordinary window glass because it can break during installation or from the impact from a bird, hail, or baseball. Most local plastic supply outlets (look in your Yellow Pages) carry these types of plastic sheeting.

Required Materials for Building a Solar Chimney

Clear acrylic, polycarbonate sheet glazing	Silicon caulking
2x4 lumber	Adhesive-backed foam weatherstripping
2x2 lumber	Nails
$1/2$x$1/2$- inch wood strip	Wood and sheet metal screws
$1/2$-inch plywood	Paint - exterior house and flat black
Roofing flashing	18-inch turbine vent
Aluminum angle trim	Hinges
Aluminum sheet metal for top	Foil-faced rigid foam insulation board

DO-IT-YOURSELF INSTRUCTIONS FOR BUILDING A SOLAR CHIMNEY

A) To keep the costs down and simplify the availability of the materials, build the solar chimney with standard size building materials. Make it a size that divides evenly into 4 x 8 sheets (both glazing and plywood) to minimize waste.

B) Go up into your attic and find the exact location where you plan to cut through the ceiling. Cut the 2-foot square hole in the ceiling. Frame the hole with double 2 x 4's. Make sure to keep the blocking plumb because you will cover it with plywood to connect the hole in the ceiling to the hole in the roof. This will create the lightwell channel for the breeze and provide natural lighting to your room or hall.

C) Using a plumb line, find the locations for the four corners of the hole in the roof directly above the hole in the ceiling. Drill small holes through these four spots in the roof. These will mark the desired location of the opening in the roof.

D) Go up on your roof and carefully remove the shingles surrounding the four locator holes. Saw through the roof sheathing at the holes to make the square roof opening. Frame the opening with 2x4's making sure to keep them plumb for when you nail on the vertical 2x4's to form the lightwell channel between the ceiling and the roof.

E) Cut and nail vertical 2x4's to the inside of the openings to form the lightwell channel from the roof to the ceiling. These should then be recessed so the inside surface is flush with the very edge of the hole in the ceiling. You will nail the uprights for the chimney portion to these 2x4's in the lightwell. You will then later cover the inside of these 2x4's with plywood so they will enclose and finish the lightwell.

F) For three of the corners, between east and south, east and north, and north and west, you will nail other vertical chimney 2x4 uprights to the ones below. Attach these in a suitable manner for adequate support. These 2x4's will form the corners of the solar chimney above the roof. Use a 2x2 on the south and west corner so that less of the glazed area is blocked. Nail horizontal 2x4's between the uprights at the top to support the uprights and provide a mounting surface for the top over and turbine vent.

G) If you have a very short lightwell, the sun at high noon may shine down into your room through the lightwell. If you find that this happens in your area, secure a horizontal 2x4 across the east to west side at the top of the lightwell. Cut and nail a plywood baffle to the 2x4 and to the plywood on the sides. This baffle will block any sun from shining directly down into your room below.

H) Cut foil-faced rigid foam insulation board to cover all the inside unglazed surfaces in the chimney. Paint the foil surface flat black and glue and nail it to the plywood surfaces with the black foil facing inward. This black surface will become the solar absorber to capture the sun's heat.

I) Use some type of clear plastic sheets for the south and west sides. The various types of materials are listed in the materials list. Glaze only the upper half of the south side to avoid direct sunlight from shining in your room around noontime.

J) Lay a bead of silicon caulking on the 2x4 and 2x2 uprights and place the sheets against the uprights. Cut four lengths of the aluminum angle trim and drill holes in it every one foot. Place a bead of caulking under each leg and screw these in place through the glazing sheets along the exterior corners to finish them.

K) You can either have a 2-foot square sheet metal top made to cover the chimney and mount the turbine vent or you can make a plywood top. If you make a plywood top, use the aluminum angle to finish the edges. Use silicon caulking under the top.

L) Paint all the unglazed exterior surfaces with house paint to match your house or roof. Attach flashing around the chimney and replace the shingles. Finish the inside of the lightwell with plywood or drywall.

M) Make a plywood door to fit the opening in your ceiling. Attach a $1/2 \times 1/2$ strip around the inside of the opening about $3/4$ of an inch above the opening. Stick adhesive-backed foam weatherstripping against the strip. Attach the door with hinges and attach a latch to hold it closed when you are air-conditioning or in the winter. Glue several inches of foam insulation board on top of it to block heat flow when it's closed.

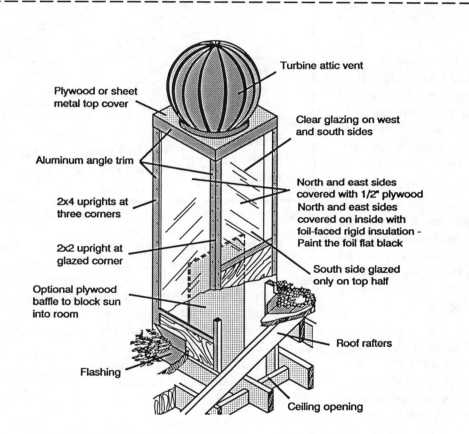

Changes in attic can foil the sun's rays

Q: My house has plenty of attic insulation, but the heat still blasts down from the ceiling all day. What is an inexpensive and simple do-it-yourself method to block the sun's heat and lower my cooling bills?

A: The afternoon sun can heat your roof and attic to over 150°. Much of this intense heat radiates down right through your attic insulation to your ceilings. Adding more insulation will not help much.

The easiest and most effective do-it-yourself method is to install radiant barrier foil under your roof rafters and add more ventilation in your attic. You can buy the reinforced foil for as little as 9 cents per sq. ft. and attic ridge vent for $2 to $3 per lineal foot.

In just a few hours, I installed foil in my own attic and it lowered the temperature in my second floor bedrooms by 10 degrees. The rooms cool off faster in the evening so I can sleep comfortably with just my ceiling paddle fan on low speed.

Reinforced aluminum foil is used as the radiant heat barrier material. The primary heat reduction property of aluminum is that little heat is radiated from the shiny underside to the insulation and ceiling below.

Stapling the foil on the underside of the roof rafters is the easiest method. The heat is trapped between the foil and the roof. This heats the air and it naturally flows up and out the vents, drawing in cooler air.

Don't lay the foil, even if it is perforated, over the attic insulation on the floor. This can trap moisture in the insulation during the coldest winter weather.

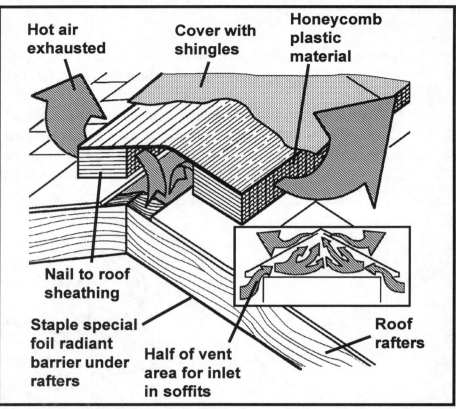

Foil radiant barrier and roof vents block heat

Double-sided aluminum foil (shiny on both sides) is often used, although the less expensive single-sided foil is almost as effective. If you install single-sided foil (reinforcing kraft paper on one side), face the shiny side downward, away from the roof. Overall, this blocks the heat radiation to your ceiling better than facing it upward.

For maximum comfort, install additional attic ventilation. Continuous ridge vents are the most effective method and the easiest to install.

These vents are only a couple of inches high. When they are covered with shingles, you cannot notice them from the ground. As a minimum, you should have about 0.5 to 1.0 sq. ft. each of ridge vent outlet area and soffit vent inlet area for each 300 sq. ft. of attic floor area.

Q: I leave my home several times each day to go shopping, pick up the children, etc. Should I turn the air conditioner off each time I leave or does it just use more electricity to cool it down again?

A: It is a common misconception that more electricity is used to cool your house down again. Unless you leave for just 10 minutes or less, you will save electricity overall by turning your air off or setting the thermostat higher.

Heat, which your air conditioner must remove, is constantly leaking into your house. The cooler your house is, the faster the heat leaks in. If you let your house warm up while you are gone, heat flows in more slowly. Overall, then, your air conditioner has fewer Btu of heat to remove.

Attic foil can have a great impact of the amount of heat that radiates down from a hot roof in the summer. In the winter, it has negligible impact on your heating bills.

The chart on the right shows how much foil you will have to buy. A higher pitched roof requires more foil for a given attic floor area. Foil is often available in rolls that are four feet wide. This is a convenient size to work with in your attic. You can do the installation yourself, but it is much quicker if you have a helper to position the foil as you staple it up under the rafters. The neatness of the job is not critical to the heat rejecting properties of the foil.

Area of Foil Needed For Various Size Houses

House Size in feet	Slope of Roof - Rise Over Run of 12						
(a,b)	2	3	4	5	6	7	8
(20,30)	609	619	633	650	672	695	722
(20,40)	811	824	843	866	894	926	961
(20,50)	1014	1031	1054	1083	1118	1157	1202
(30,30)	913	928	949	975	1007	1042	1082
(30,40)	1217	1237	1265	1300	1342	1389	1442
(30,50)	1521	1546	1581	1625	1677	1736	1803
(30,60)	1826	1856	1898	1950	2013	2084	2164
(40,30)	1217	1237	1265	1300	1342	1389	1442
(40,40)	1623	1650	1687	1734	1790	1852	1924
(40,50)	2028	2061	2108	2166	2236	2316	2404
(40,60)	2434	2474	2530	2600	2684	2778	2885

The price on the foil ranges from about 12 cents per square foot for single-sided kraft paper-backed foil to about 25 cents per square foot for reinforced double-sided foil. If you install single-sided foil, face the foil down toward the floor to be most effective.

Another option to using foil, is painting the underside of your roof with a low-emissivity silver paint. Information on this special paint is shown on page **c**. Applying this paint most often requires a professional painter.

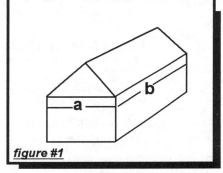

figure #1

MANUFACTURERS OF DO-IT-YOURSELF REFLECTIVE ATTIC FOILS

AAE SYSTEMS, 7962 C Mission Center, San Diego, CA 92108 - (619) 296-0970

ADVANCED FOIL SYS., 4471 E. Santa Ana St, Ontario, CA 91761 - (714) 988-8365

DENNY SALES CORP., 3500 Gateway, Pompano Beach, FL 33069 - (800) 327-6616

INNOVATIVE ENERGY, 1119 W. 145th Ave., Crown Point, IN 46307 - (800) 776-3645

INNOVATIVE INSULATION, 2710 SE Loop 820, Ft. Worth, TX 76140 - (800) 825-0123

KEY SOLUTIONS, 7529 E. Woodshire Cove, Scottsdale, AZ 85258 - (800) 776-9765

LAMOTITE, 2909 E. 79th St., Cleveland, OH 44104 - (800) 841-1234 (216) 883-8484

RABAR PRODUCTS, 3243 Blair St., Cocoa, FL 32926 - (407) 636-4104

RICH'S ENTERPRISES, 2734 El Dorado Pl., Snellville, GA 30278 - (404) 979-9671

RISI, P.O. Box 2846, Wichita, KS 67201 - (800) 798-3645 (316) 265-6712

SIMPLEX PRODUCTS DIV., P.O. Box 10, Adrian, MI 49221 - (517) 263-8881

SOLAR SHIELD, 1054 Branch, Alpharetta, GA 30201 - (800) 654-3645 (404) 343-8091

THERMONICS INT'L, 4513 Old Shell Rd., Mobile, AL 36608 - (800) 334-3431

VAN LEER, 9505 Bamboo Rd., Houston, TX 77041 - (800) 825-3766 (713) 462-6111

BEFORE YOU BEGIN

Be sure you have the following tools and materials:
A. Proper amount of INSUL-FOIL™ RB
B. Tape measure, drop light, shears, utility knife and stapler (mechanical, electrical or air - squeeze or hammer type)
C. Two movable support surfaces such as 2' x 3' x ½" plywood or 1" x 12" x 3' piece of wood (lengthen for 24" O.C. trusses)

SAFETY PRACTICES

Be sure you observe the following safety rules:
A. **DO NOT** lay RB on top of exposed electrical wiring or boxes.
B. Make sure trusses or rafters are sound before placing your weight on them.
C. Be sure you have adequate ventilation and lighting. A dust mask is suggested.
D. Protective headgear (bump cap) and safety glasses are suggested.
E. WARNING: *DO NOT attempt to stand or lay on existing insulation. Failure to follow these instructions can and may result in serious injury and damage.*

FIG. 1 - BOTTOM OF TRUSS APPLICATION

Measure, roll out and cut material in lengths best handled by two people.
1. Whether you start at the bottom (nearest soffit vent) or at peak (nearest ridge) leave spacing as shown in Fig. 3.
2. Slit or trim RB at uprights or obstructions as necessary. It is not necessary to have a tight fit.
3. Staple RB to truss face approximately 6" on center the entire width of the product. Suggested staple size is a corrosive resistant type with a 9/16" crown and a 5/16" leg.

FIG. 2 - BETWEEN TRUSS ALTERNATE

Lay pre-scored piece of RB flat and bend each edge as shown in Fig. 2-1A and place between trusses. Position material and space as shown in Fig. 3. Flush left side bottom edge of RB with bottom edge of truss and staple entire length. Repeat stapling on right side bottom edge.

FIG. 3 - VENTILATION

Because ventilation can greatly enhance your RB performance, it is important to consider the following:
A. Where no existing ridge or gable vents exist you should install one system or the other. Consult mfrs. instructions for proper location and installation.
B. Where no soffit vents exist, be sure ridge, pan or gable end vents are of adequate size to properly ventilate area.

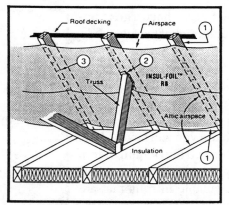

FIGURE 1   BOTTOM OF TRUSS APPLICATION

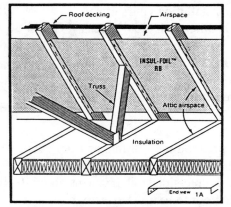

FIGURE 2   BETWEEN TRUSS ALTERNATE

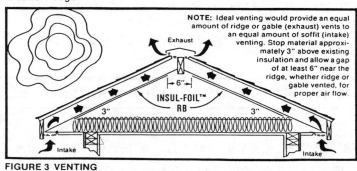

NOTE: Ideal venting would provide an equal amount of ridge or gable (exhaust) vents to an equal amount of soffit (intake) venting. Stop material approximately 3" above existing insulation and allow a gap of at least 6" near the ridge, whether ridge or gable vented, for proper air flow.

FIGURE 3 VENTING

RECOMMENDED NET FREE VENT AREA FOR ATTIC - (sq. in.)

		20	22	24	26	28	30	32	34	36	38	40
	20	192	211	230	269	288	307	326	348	365	384	403
	24	230	253	276	300	323	346	369	392	415	438	481
	28	269	296	323	349	376	403	430	484	511	538	564
	32	307	338	369	399	430	461	492	522	553	584	614
	36	346	380	415	449	484	518	553	588	622	657	691
	40	384	422	461	499	538	576	614	653	691	730	768
	44	422	465	507	549	591	634	676	718	760	803	845
	48	461	507	553	599	645	691	737	783	829	876	922
	52	499	549	599	649	699	749	799	848	898	948	998
	56	538	591	645	699	753	807	860	914	967	1021	1075
	60	576	634	691	749	807	864	922	979	1037	1094	1152

ATTIC WIDTH in feet (column headers); *ATTIC LENGTH in feet* (row headers)

LO/MIT-I ™

RADIANT BARRIER COATING

For Energy Conservation and Light Reflection

LO/MIT-I is a silver colored, non-thickness dependent, low emissivity coating. Its superb ability to reflect both heat (infrared radiation) and light make it an excellent, low cost substitute for metallic foils or metallized plastic films. High temperature tolerance, excellent adhesion and the ability to produce uniformly low emissivities on a wide variety of substrates make LO/MIT-I unique in the field of high technology coatings.

OPTICAL CHARACTERISTICS

Laboratory application of LO/MIT-I on glass substrates has lowered emissivity from .86 to .22 and increased spectral reflectivity from 7.3% to 85%. LO/MIT-I can be applied to a wide variety of substrates and normally will create a surface emissivity of .21–.26, and a spectral reflectivity of 81%-85%, depending on the substrate used. The chart on the rear of this bulletin shows optical properties on specific materials.

CONSTITUENTS

Aromatic hydrocarbons, aliphatic ketones, proprietary pigments and binders.

SOLVENT

Solsolv 301 or xylene.

VISCOSITY

29 seconds #1 Zahn's cup.

HARDNESS

Extremely strong 3H hardness after 24 hour room temperature cure. Hardness increases with age.

DEGRADATION & OUTGASSING

Unaffected by UV or elevated temperatures. Thermally tolerant to 1000° F (538°C). No outgassing when correctly cured.

COVERAGE

400-800 square feet/gallon, depending on surface and application method.

CLEAN UP

Clean application equipment with Solsolv 301 or Xylene. Use Isopropyl Alcohol for operator clean up and removal from clothing.

MIXING

Coating supplied ready for use. No thinning is required or suggested. Shake well before using. If possible, agitate during application.

SURFACE PREPARATION

Normally, adhesion is the only factor that will be affected by surface preparation. Optical properties will remain constant except on surfaces that are very porous such as brick and cement. To improve optical properties on porous substrates, appropriate fillers and primers may be used to increase surface smoothness. This will also increase coverage. On metallic substrates, such as cold rolled or galvanized steel, that may be subject to possible corrosion or oxidation, appropriate primers should be used before applying LO/MIT-I. Where a surface is already primed or painted, apply a test patch of LO/MIT-I to ascertain that the prepared surface is compatible with the solvents used in LO/MIT-I. Plastics may require surface treatment to increase adhesion and should be tested for compatibility with LO/MIT-I. Most building materials, such as wood, plasterboard, paper faced insulation batts, fibrous ceiling tiles and painted metal roof decking require no surface preparation except that they be clean and dust free. Masonry surfaces should be allowed to cure for one month prior to the application of LO/MIT-I.

Any surface preparation questions not answered in this section should be referred to our Technical Services Department.

APPLICATION

Air Atomization: Use DeVilbiss pressure gun #JGA-502-704-FX; gun pressure of 30 psi (2.11 kg/cm²); tank pressure of 4-6 psi (.14-.42 kg/cm²). Remote paint supply pots should be equipped with an air driven agitator to keep coating thoroughly mixed during application.-OR-DeVilbiss suction gun #JGA-502-43-FF, gun pressure of 25 psi (1.76 kg/cm²). Needle adjustment = ½ open. Hold spray gun 8-14″ from work. Spraying at the lower pressure (25-30 psi) indicated will lessen overspray and effect better coverage. Use 2 horsepower or larger compressor.

Airless and Electrostatic: Test airless and electrostatic equipment for compatability with LO/MIT-I before using. Remote paint supply pots should be equipped with an air driven agitator to keep coating thoroughly mixed during application.

Portable Compression Sprayer: The SOLEC Model LS-1 portable compression sprayer is a low cost, self-contained coating application device for the field application of LO/MIT-I to roof decks, cinder block walls, attics, or new construction where power is unavailable. Ask for Bulletin LS-1.

Brush and Roller: LO/MIT-I may also be applied using a solvent resistant paintbrush or roller. However, coverage may be substantially reduced.

Note: Good ventilation is necessary for operator safety and drying and curing of the applied coating.

DRYING AND CURE

Coating will skin dry within one minute after application. Drying to touch will generally occur within 15 minutes to one hour depending on ambient temperature and humidity. Curing can be accelerated by application of heat up to 500°F (260°C) for 4 to 30 minutes. Experimentation will determine the best curing procedures for your particular environment.

STORAGE

Keep at room temperature in tightly sealed container. Keep out of direct sunlight to avoid pressure increase in container. Full containers will remain usable for 1 year from date of manufacture.

CAUTION

Contains flammable solvents. Do not expose to elevated heat or open flames. Use with adequate ventilation and avoid excessive breathing of vapor or spray mist. Avoid contact with eyes. OSHA regulations, Sections 1915.24—Painting, 1915.25—Flammable Liquids and 1915.82—Respiratory Protection give additional helpful safety suggestions.

FIRST AID

Remove from skin using isopropyl alcohol and warm soapy water. In case of contact with eyes, flush with clean water for at least 15 minutes and get medical attention. If swallowed, get immediate medical attention. If headache, dizziness or nausea result from excessive inhalation of vapors, remove to fresh air and administer oxygen if necessary.

SOLAR ENERGY CORPORATION, BOX 3065, PRINCETON, NJ 08543-3065, U.S.A.

(609) 883-7700

Window film aids furniture

Q: I want to stop the fading of my curtains and furniture near windows, yet still have a clear view outdoors. Does clear year-round insulating window film also stop fading. Can I install the window film myself?

A: New clear insulating summer/winter window films save energy, your furniture and curtains. Once this type of film is installed on your windows, unless someone told you, you could not tell film was applied. The highest-quality professionally-installed films have up to ten-year warranties.

I installed do-it-yourself summer/winter film on a west window in my own home. It is above the garage roof. I could definitely notice the reduction in midday glare and heat, and the view is still clear. Film always looks darker or more reflective before you install it on the glass.

All window films block 95% to 99% of the sun's fading ultraviolet (UV) rays. Most films also block more than half of the sun's heat and glare, which also contribute to fading. Not only does UV fade furniture, it actually weakens the material's fibers (patio furniture is an example).

Summer/winter film is made of many layers of films and scratch resistant coatings. Its year-round savings come from a low-emissivity (low-e) coating between the inner layers. This is the same coating used on expensive super-efficient replacement windows. Multi-layer film is tough and safe. It can keep the glass from shattering should a child hit it.

This window film blocks the summer sun's heat just like standard window film. You can get darker-tinted films for more summer heat rejection. In the winter, since indoors is warmer than outdoors, the low-e

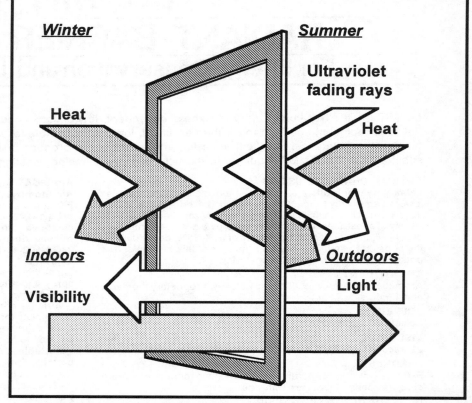

Insulating window film saves year-round

coating works in reverse and blocks the radiant heat loss outdoors.

Tests conducted on summer/winter window film show that it can reduce winter heat loss from your windows by up to 30%. In the winter, you can feel the comfort difference when standing near a window with film. Glare is also reduced significantly and houseplants quickly adjust to the new lighting. Many plants prefer the reduced UV radiation.

Do-it-yourself window film can be purchased at home centers, but you cannot tell if it is low-e insulating film just by looking at it. Check the specifications because most salespersons will not even know what low-e means.

It is easy to install window film yourself, especially on small to average-size windows. Having it professionally installed costs more, but you get a long warranty and you are sure it is done properly.

Q: I removed the metal housing from around my central air conditioner compressor outdoors to clean out the debris. Can I just leave some of the small access panels off since I plan to clean it each year?

A: It is important to replace all the metal panels, no matter how small and screw them tightly together. The condenser fan creates a vacuum inside the outdoor unit drawing air through the heat transfer coils. If you leave the panels off, air will be drawn in the openings instead of through the coils. This reduces efficiency.

It is also important to replace them for safety. Air conditioners are 220 volts and have moving parts which can harm an inquisitive child.

Insulating summer/winter window film is sold in home centers for do-it-yourselfers. The suggested retail price is about $1.50/sq.ft. in a kit. Depending on the retail outlet, it may sell for more or less than this. Although low-e window film may look reflective and darkly-tinted, once your entire window is covered with it, it is not very noticeable. Most window films, even the darker tinted ones, look more natural when they are installed.

Figure #1 compares the fading-blocking characteristics of two types of film with clear glass with no film. Nearly all of the ultraviolet light is blocked by window film (see specs. on page **b**). Varying degrees of light (glare) and summer heat are blocked depending on the specific films.

The most effective insulating summer/winter films have a low-emissivity (low-e) coating on one of the interior layers of the film (page **c**). This blocks reflected heat in the summer (reflected from roofs, driveways, patios - anything outside your window). In the winter, the coating blocks the heat loss back outdoors through your windows.

Although it is not difficult to install window film yourself, most window films are professionally-installed. Manufacturers provide a warranty for the highest-quality films when they are professionally-installed.

Professionally-installed window film often has up to a 10-year warranty . Cost ranges from $3/sq.ft. and up depending on the film and the installer's profit margins. Get quotes from several installers in your area.

If you have double-pane thermal windows now, you should avoid the darkly-tinted films. These films block much of the sun's heat from coming in by absorbing the heat, not reflecting it away. This causes the glass to heat up and can result in a seal failure over time and fogging of the glass.

The nearly clear summer/winter film should be okay for all windows, but you should <u>check</u> with your window manufacturer or contractor to be sure. It may void the glass warranty.

When comparing films, a "**30%**" film (usually somewhere in its product #) means it allows 30% of the sun's heat to get through the window. "**SR**" at the end indicates a scratch-resistant coating is on the window film.

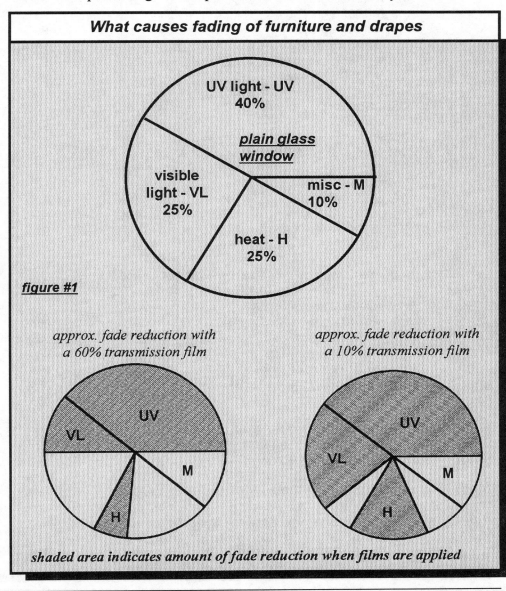

What causes fading of furniture and drapes

UV light - UV
40%

plain glass window

visible light - VL
25%

misc - M
10%

heat - H
25%

figure #1

approx. fade reduction with a 60% transmission film

UV
VL
M
H

approx. fade reduction with a 10% transmission film

UV
VL
M
H

shaded area indicates amount of fade reduction when films are applied

MANUFACTURERS OF WINDOW FILMS FOR HOME USE

Product # - color	Solar heat reduction	Heat loss reduction	UV light reduction	Glare reduction
COURTAULDS PERFORMANCE FILMS, P.O. Box 5068, Martinsville, VA 24115				
"Vista" and "Llumar" brands - (800) 345-6088				
"Gila Sunshine" brand - (800) 528-4481				
"VISTA" brand - professionally installed only				
V30 - gray	59%	1%	99%	66%
V45 - gray	46%	1%	99%	48%
V58 - gray	35%	1%	99%	60%
"LLUMAR" brand - professionally installed only				
E-1220SR	79%	30%	99%	81%
DL15 - bronze	61%	8%	99%	84%
DL15G - gray	58%	10%	99%	83%
DL30GR - green	54%	4%	99%	66%
N-1020 - gray	63%	4%	99%	73%
N-1035 - gray	52%	4%	99%	60%
N-1050 - gray	44%	3%	99%	45%
N-1065 - gray	31%	1%	99%	28%
N-1020B - bronze	77%	14%	99%	77%
N-1035B - bronze	62%	11%	99%	58%
N-1050B - bronze	51%	8%	99%	57%
"GILA SUNSHINE" brand - do-it-yourself from retail outlets				
Low-e	55%	30%	99%	81%
3M, 3M Center Bldg 225-4S-08, St. Paul, MN 55144				
(800) 328-1684 ext. 228				
Professionally installed only				
LE35AMARL - amber	70%	30%	99%	65%
LE20SIAR - silver	73%	23%	97%	81%
LE30CUARL - copper	64%	26%	98%	64%
LE50AMARL - amber	55%	29%	97%	44%
MADICO INC., 64 Industrial Pky, Woburn, MA 01888				
(800) 225-1926 (617) 935-7850				
Professionally installed only				
SB-340 - bronze	66%	17%	96%	65%
TSG-335 - gray	53%	12%	98%	55%
NG-50 - gray	51%	5%	96%	48%
NB-50 - bronze	51%	5%	96%	48%
NG-35 - gray	61%	10%	96%	59%
NB-35 - bronze	61%	10%	96%	59%
METALLIZED PRODUCTS, 2544 Terminal Dr. S., St. Petersburg, FL 33712				
(800) 777-1770 (813) 327-7132				
Professionally installed only				
SW150 SILVER 15	84%	29%	96%	84%
SW150 SILVER 30	65%	20%	96%	60%
Sold do-it-yourself or professionally installed				
SW150 GRAY 30	60%	15%	96%	58%
SW150 BRONZE 30	61%	15%	96%	57%

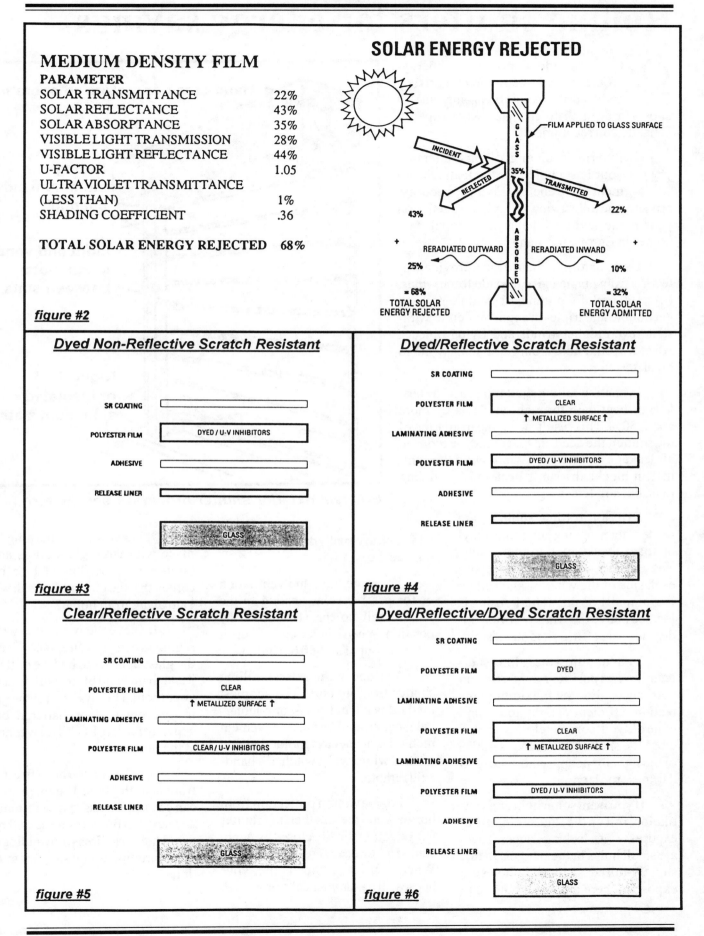

MEDIUM DENSITY FILM

PARAMETER	
SOLAR TRANSMITTANCE	22%
SOLAR REFLECTANCE	43%
SOLAR ABSORPTANCE	35%
VISIBLE LIGHT TRANSMISSION	28%
VISIBLE LIGHT REFLECTANCE	44%
U-FACTOR	1.05
ULTRA VIOLET TRANSMITTANCE (LESS THAN)	1%
SHADING COEFFICIENT	.36
TOTAL SOLAR ENERGY REJECTED	**68%**

SOLAR ENERGY REJECTED

FILM APPLIED TO GLASS SURFACE

INCIDENT

REFLECTED 43%

TRANSMITTED 22%

GLASS 35% ABSORBED

RERADIATED OUTWARD 25%

RERADIATED INWARD 10%

= 68% TOTAL SOLAR ENERGY REJECTED

= 32% TOTAL SOLAR ENERGY ADMITTED

figure #2

Dyed Non-Reflective Scratch Resistant

- SR COATING
- POLYESTER FILM — DYED / U-V INHIBITORS
- ADHESIVE
- RELEASE LINER
- GLASS

figure #3

Dyed/Reflective Scratch Resistant

- SR COATING
- POLYESTER FILM — CLEAR — ↑ METALLIZED SURFACE ↑
- LAMINATING ADHESIVE
- POLYESTER FILM — DYED / U-V INHIBITORS
- ADHESIVE
- RELEASE LINER
- GLASS

figure #4

Clear/Reflective Scratch Resistant

- SR COATING
- POLYESTER FILM — CLEAR — ↑ METALLIZED SURFACE ↑
- LAMINATING ADHESIVE
- POLYESTER FILM — CLEAR / U-V INHIBITORS
- ADHESIVE
- RELEASE LINER
- GLASS

figure #5

Dyed/Reflective/Dyed Scratch Resistant

- SR COATING
- POLYESTER FILM — DYED
- LAMINATING ADHESIVE
- POLYESTER FILM — CLEAR — ↑ METALLIZED SURFACE ↑
- LAMINATING ADHESIVE
- POLYESTER FILM — DYED / U-V INHIBITORS
- ADHESIVE
- RELEASE LINER
- GLASS

figure #6

Rolling shutters for energy savings

Q: I want to add some type of energy-efficient window covering for privacy and security against break-ins, but still allows for an unobstructed view when I open it. What do you recommend?

A: Exterior insulating rolling shutters are your best choice for the features you mention - energy savings, security, privacy, and a clear view. They are attractive on your home and they have been popular on homes in Europe for many years.

Exterior rolling shutters also provide protection from hurricane or tornado force winds, over 100 mph for a standard shutter. You can get double and triple-strength models to withstand even higher winds and flying objects. Also, it would take a burglar a long while to break through one.

Insulating rolling shutters reduce the heat loss or heat gain through windows by more about 50%. This results from the insulation of the shutter, the dead air space, and the reduced air leakage around your window. In the summer, it blocks the sun's heat and UV fading rays, but still lets in light.

Exterior rolling shutters are made of interlocking horizontal vinyl or foam insulated aluminum slats. These slide in aluminum channels on each side of the window and roll up into a small housing. This housing is located above the window, often under the roof soffit, so it is out of sight.

You can adjust the rolling shutter in several positions depending on your needs. For the maximum protection, efficiency, light and sound control, you completely lower and close the shutter. It can block 100% of the light for people who need total darkness to sleep.

If you want some light and ventilation, roll up the shutter slightly to expose the interlocking flanges. There are small holes in the flanges. In this slightly-raised position, the holes are exposed. There are enough holes to

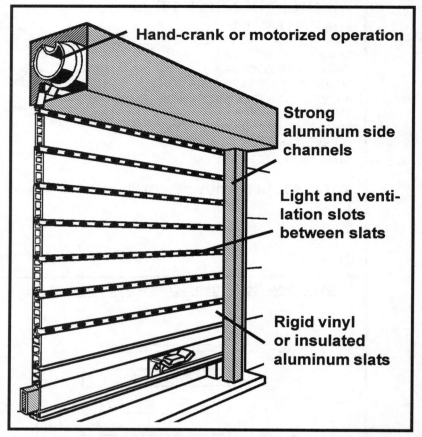

Hand-crank or motorized operation

Strong aluminum side channels

Light and ventilation slots between slats

Rigid vinyl or insulated aluminum slats

Efficient exterior shutter provides security too

allow you to visually distinguish forms outside the window.

For more light and ventilation or for passive solar heating in the winter, roll up the shutter to any position. When it is completely up, it is totally out of sight from indoors.

You operate an exterior rolling shutter from indoors. The simplest method is a hand crank or counter-balanced strap. The most convenient method is an electric motor that you control with a wall switch or a hand-held remote.

For maximum protection from burglars and the weather, the shutter can be automatically closed by wind, sun, rain, or heat sensors or timers. When you leave your home, your house will be automatically protected.

Q: I have a wood-burning fireplace with large glass doors and a built-in blower. Should I be concerned that the glass may break when I am away from home?

A: Never leave home with a raging fire in your fireplace. Even if the glass appears to be free of flaws, it can shatter and blow sparks out into your room. I know because the glass in my fireplace door shattered for no apparent reason. Luckily, I was home at the time.

Do not build too hot a fire in the front near th glass. The intense heat can cause the glass to lose its temper and develop fine stress cracks. Try to avoid hot flash fires from adding too much crumpled newspapers at one time.

Exterior rolling shutters have been popular in Europe for many years because they provide energy savings, privacy, and security. The energy savings comes from the insulation value of the shutter slats and the dead air space created between the shutter and window.

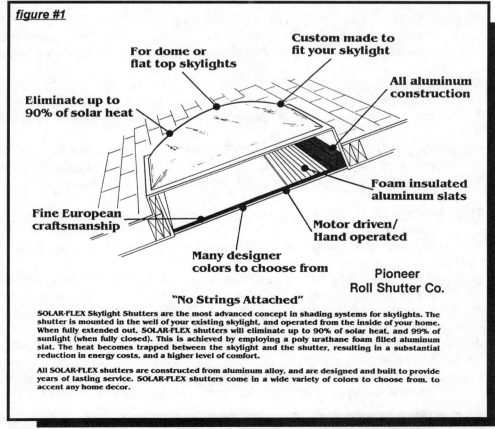

ventilation through slots

figure #2

The unique feature of all exterior rolling shutters is the small slots or holes in the flanges between the slats (figure #2). These slots allow for ventilation and light without actually raising the shade. You just start to raise the shutter until the slats begin to separate and the slots are exposed. In the fully lowered position, with the slot covered, these shutters virtually block all the light.

Although these rolling shutters are most often used on vertical windows, they are also ideal for mounting under a skylight. Figure #1 shows how one can be mounted. The one shown is made by Pioneer Roll Shutter Co. This particular model can be operated with a crank, 12-volt motor, or 120-volt motor. A 12-volt motor, makes it easier to run an electric wire to the motor.

Page **b** lists information about the various manufacturers' shutters. The foam-filled aluminum slats are flatter, so they roll up tighter into a smaller storage box above your window. The PVC slats are strong and come in various cross-sections. For large windows, a heavy cross-section slat design is needed. This also requires a larger storage box. The manufacturers or local dealers can recommend the best slat design for your specific home and weather conditions - tornadoes, hurricanes, extreme temperatures, sun exposure, etc.

Page **b** shows detailed information about exterior rolling shutters. Foam insulation filled aluminum and hollow (air-filled) are the most common slat materials. Several manufacturers also offer Lexan. This is a very tough plastic (used as bulletproof glass) and it is often tinted in shutters. It is more often used for commercial installations.

Most rolling shutters work in a similar fashion. The unique special features of some are the types of automatic controls. In areas where there are sudden storms, automatic wind sensors can close the shutters before a storm strikes. In hot areas, sun sensors are useful. A hand-held remote, like for a TV, is a convenience. Seven-day programmable timers allow for a different schedule each day.

A typical installed cost for a 3.5 ft. by 5 ft. PVC shutter with a hand crank is $650 and an aluminum shutter is $715. Motorized controls and special wind and sun sensors can cost an additional $300 depending on your specific home.

figure #1

For dome or flat top skylights

Custom made to fit your skylight

Eliminate up to 90% of solar heat

All aluminum construction

Fine European craftsmanship

Foam insulated aluminum slats

Motor driven/ Hand operated

Many designer colors to choose from

Pioneer Roll Shutter Co.

"No Strings Attached"

SOLAR-FLEX Skylight Shutters are the most advanced concept in shading systems for skylights. The shutter is mounted in the well of your existing skylight, and operated from the inside of your home. When fully extended out, SOLAR-FLEX shutters will eliminate up to 90% of solar heat, and 99% of sunlight (when fully closed). This is achieved by employing a poly urathane foam filled aluminum slat. The heat becomes trapped between the skylight and the shutter, resulting in a substantial reduction in energy costs, and a higher level of comfort.

All SOLAR-FLEX shutters are constructed from aluminum alloy, and are designed and built to provide years of lasting service. SOLAR-FLEX shutters come in a wide variety of colors to choose from, to accent any home decor.

MANUFACTURERS OF ROLLING SHUTTERS

AC ROLLING SHUTTER, 2310 Superior Ave., Cleveland, OH 44114 - (216) 621-4577
    material - aluminum or PVC   *insulation* - air
    operation - manual crank or electric motor   *colors* - aluminum - 5 / PVC - 3

ALUTECH UNITED, INC., PO Box 40547, Raleigh, NC 27604 - (919) 954-8012
    material - aluminum   *insulation* - foam
    operation - manual crank/strap or electric motor   *colors* - unlimited
    unique features - remote control, timers, temperature and wind sensors

AMERICAN ROLL SHUTTER, 31843 W. 8 Mile, Livonia, MI 48152 - (800) 331-1205 (313) 478-9311
    material - aluminum, extruded aluminum or PVC   *insulation* - foam for Al, air for PVC
    operation - manual crank or electric motor   *colors* - aluminum - 12 / PVC - 4

PIONEER ROLL SHUTTER CO., PO Box 21240, Reno, NV 89515 - (702) 355-8686
    material - aluminum   *insulation* - foam
    operation - manual crank or electric motor   *colors* - 7 standard
    unique features - remote, wireless, wind/sun sensor, light sensor, temperature sensor

ROLLAC SHUTTER OF TEXAS, INC., 10800 Blackhawk, Houston, TX 77089 - (713) 485-1911
    material - aluminum, PVC or Lexan   *insulation* - foam for Al, air for PVC
    operation - manual crank/strap or electric motor   *colors* - aluminum - 10 / PVC - 5
    unique features - seven day programmable digital timer

ROLL-A-SHIELD, 3964 N. Oracle Rd., Tucson, AZ 85705 - (800) 457-8723 (602) 293-0666
    material - aluminum with a baked enamel finish   *insulation* - foam
    operation - manual crank/ pull strap or electric motor *colors* - 5 standard / 10 special order
    unique features - remote control, wind/sun sensor, quick release system/manual override

ROLL-A-WAY, 10597 Oak St. NE, St. Petersburg, FL 33716 - (800) 683-9505 (813) 576-1143
    material - aluminum, PVC, or Lexan   *insulation* - foam for Al, air for PVC
    operation - manual crank/pull strap or electric motor   *colors* - aluminum - 3 / PVC - 4

SHUTTERHAUS-NUSASH, 2501 N. Anvil St., St. Petersburg, FL 33710 - (800) 330-7210 (381) 6522
    material - PVC   *insulation* - air
    operation - manual crank or electric motor   *colors* - 7 standard

SOLAROLL SHADE & SHUTTER, 915 S. Dixie Hwy E., Pompano Bch., FL 33060 - (305) 782-7211
    material - aluminum or PVC   *insulation* - foam for Al, air for PVC
    operation - manual crank or electric motor   *colors* - 6 standard

THERMO ROLLING SHUTTER, 5100 Jackson Rd., Ann Arbor, MI 48103 - (313) 995-0577
    material - PVC   *insulation* - air
    operation - manual crank/pull strap or electric motor *colors* - 3 standard

TOP ROLL SHUTTERS, PO Box 2585, Salmon Arm British Columbia, VIE 4R5 - (800) 665-5550
    material - aluminum or PVC   *insulation* - foam for Al, air for PVC
    operation - manual crank/strap or electric motor   *colors* - 8 standard

WHEATBELT INC., PO Box 201, Hillsboro, KS 67063 - (800) 264-5171 (316) 947-2323
    material - aluminum   *insulation* - air
    operation - manual crank/strap or electric motor   *colors* - 3 standard
    unique features - remote radio control, seven day programmable timer

Roll·a·way INSULATING SECURITY SHUTTERS

PP / PRODUCT PRESENTATION

Engineering Capabilities—

Roll-A-Way Insulating Security Shutters have proven to be effective protection and insulating barriers for windows, sliding glass doors, screened enclosures, balconies and various other openings. The shutter and its components can be easily retrofitted for existing structures or integrated and completely hidden within a wall or soffit in new construction.

Security & Energy Conservation—

When fully closed, Roll-A-Way shutters deter break-ins and form an insulating dead-air barrier between the shutter and the opening that dramatically improves the "R" factor of the opening (see page 7).

Weather Protection—

Tested to withstand windloads of up to 140 miles per hour, Roll-A-Way shutters also protect the opening from heavy storm winds, driving rain, hail, snow and dangerous flying debris.

Noise Control—

There is no other product that can provide security, privacy, insulation and sun/solar control in one application as does the exterior rolling shutter. The Roll-A-Way Insulating Security Shutter provides substantial security, noise and energy control characteristics to a structure, and enhances the aesthetic and monetary value of the structure.

Patented Slat Design—

Roll-A-Way's patented, step-down slat design (standard J and reverse J configurations) provides maximum strength and wind deflection along with an attractive appearance. When the interlocking slats are extended, the vent holes open to allow air infiltration and sun control. As the shutter closes, the slats come to rest one on top of the other, thereby concealing the vent holes and turning the shutter into an insulating, security barrier.

Major Components:

1. BOX: ESP finished roll formed aluminum. The box is available in three (3) configurations, (4, 5 and 6 sided). Customized box designs using various building materials may be utilized.

2. SIDEFRAME: Urethane finished cast aluminum for rigidity and strength. The sideframe is also available in three (3) configurations.
3. OPERATORS: Four (4) different operators are available:
   a. Pull Strap Coiler
   b. 3/1 Crank with Strap-Coiler
   c. Gear & Crankhandle
   d. Electric Motor—by SIMU
4. MANUAL OVERRIDE: Optional safety device installed with electric motor that permits the shutter system to be manually cranked in the event of a power failure.
5. SWITCH: Rocker Switch and Key Switch are available for indoor and/or outdoor applications as well as master switch controls with optional Sun/Wind sensors.
6. TRACK: ESP finished aluminum extrusion available in four (4) configurations for single or multi-span applications.

7. PURLIN ASSEMBLY: ESP finished aluminum extrusion available in five (5) configurations to provide fixed or removable storm bars.
8. SLAT: Roll-A-Way slats are manufactured in 10 configurations in a wide range of materials and colors to meet the most demanding shutter applications. See page 8 for technical details.
9. SLAT HANGERS: Stainless Steel spring design for improvement of energy conservation, lock-down position and reduced noise infiltration.
10. REELS: Octagonal galvanized steel reel in two (2) sizes and round 6063-T6 aluminum reel in four (4) sizes are utilized to minimize slat deflection.
11. SLAT REINFORCEMENT: Aluminum extrusion used to strengthen 2" PVC extruded slats when required for windloading.

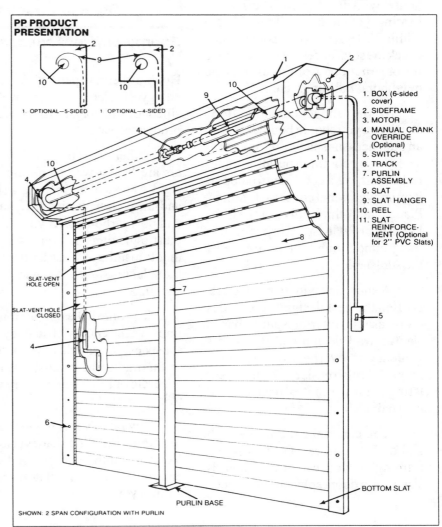

PP PRODUCT PRESENTATION

1. OPTIONAL—5-SIDED
1. OPTIONAL—4-SIDED

1. BOX (6-sided cover)
2. SIDEFRAME
3. MOTOR
4. MANUAL CRANK OVERRIDE (Optional)
5. SWITCH
6. TRACK
7. PURLIN ASSEMBLY
8. SLAT
9. SLAT HANGER
10. REEL
11. SLAT REINFORCEMENT (Optional for 2" PVC Slats)

SLAT-VENT HOLE OPEN

SLAT-VENT HOLE CLOSED

BOTTOM SLAT

PURLIN BASE

SHOWN: 2 SPAN CONFIGURATION WITH PURLIN

Sunspace saves energy, aids resale

Q: I want to build a sunspace (greenhouse) myself from scratch. I want to attach it to my house for living space and to add some heat. What design features should I consider to build an energy-efficient one?

A: Building a properly-designed sunspace can provide some heat for your house. In addition to saving energy, providing living space, and growing plants, a sunspace increases the resale value of your house.

The south side of your house is the best location for a sunspace, especially if you plan to help heat your house with it. For most effective heating, your house wall should face within 30 degrees of true south. Also, check the solar access of the sunspace for obstructions from trees, fences, neighbors' buildings, etc..

If the above considerations check out, you should be able to build an attached-sunspace very inexpensively using common building materials. First, it's a good idea to support it on conventional concrete footings. Place 1-inch-thick polystyrene insulation board at least 24 inches deep in the ground around the perimeter of the sunspace.

A sunspace with vertical walls is often the best design. It provides more usable interior space than a slanted-wall design and it has less tendency to overheat in mid-afternoon. It is also easier to install insulating shades to control heat loss and heat gain.

You can make the frame with 2x4 or 2x6 lumber. Try to size the framing so you can use standard-sized patio door replacement panels.

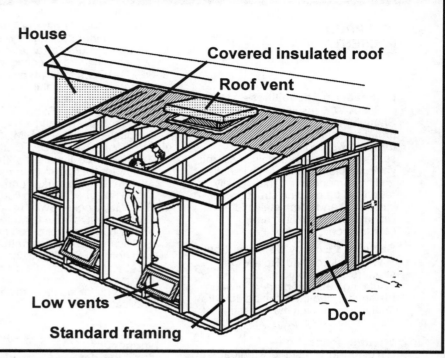

Energy-efficient sunspace is easy to build

Double thermal pane glass is most energy-efficient. Seal them well with silicone caulk for an airtight and leak-proof sunspace.

Other types of glazing materials are heavy-weight plastic films, rigid translucent fiberglass sheets, and fairly-clear plastics such as acrylic and polycarbonate. If you choose a plastic glazing material, select one that transmits at least 85 percent of the solar rays and is ultraviolet light-stabilized.

To control the temperature and improve the energy efficiency of the sunspace, you should have some type of thermal storage mass. A heavy concrete or brick floor is very effective.

Operable vents in the roof and movable insulating shades also help. You can purchase thermostatically-controlled fans to circulate the heated air into your house.

Q: The walls of a house we just bought are insulated with urea-form-aldehyde foam and I want to replace it with fiberglass. Is there any way to remove it without totally destroying the siding?

A: The primary concern about having urea-formaldehyde (U-F) insulation is that it may give off formaldehyde fumes. If the insulation was blown in years ago, there are probably very little fumes still being given off.

If you want to remove the insulation, it should not be difficult. Over time the insulation probably has shrunk a little. Take off several bands of the siding and the sheathing under it.

Since the insulation should be loose from shrinkage, you can easily break it apart and pull out the pieces. Wear a mask and safety glasses when you break it apart.

Footings

A footing in the ground is intended to make sure that the weight of the greenhouse-along with any superimposed weight load, such as snow or wind-is evenly distributed. A typical solar greenhouse weighs very little. However, wind could be troublesome when it is an upward force that could conceivably shake your greenhouse loose if you leave the door open. Anchoring in a good solid footing will prevent both the problems of weight distribution and the vagaries of the wind. Moreover, a good footing below the frost line will prevent winter frost from heaving the structure.

You can use a wooden footing if you desire, as long as it is anchored securely in the ground. Why not use concrete? Build your greenhouse to last-and leave something for archeologists to ponder 500 years from now. Here is one footing option: The figure below depicts a conventional footing that conforms to the Uniform Building Code. The footing and stem wall insulation should extend at least 24 inches below the ground on the outside of the masonry. This assures that the heat transmitted through the glazing is soaked up in the floor and not lost to the ground outside.

Framing

Methods of framing a solar greenhouse vary, depending on the type of glazing you plan to use, the weather in your area, and the way in which the greenhouse will communicate with your house. The type of glazing you choose will determine the frame spacing you will need to construct; refer to the section on glazing for the choices available.

A greenhouse that has a vertical south face will be cooler in the summer. A vertical wall will collect 25 percent less solar energy from October through April than a wall built at a 60° angle, but the same wall will conduct only half as much heat energy in the summer months. A vertical wall also allows for more interior space, and is easier to insulate against nighttime heat loss.

You will have to make some compromises in deciding upon the right design for your location and purposes. You may want maximum winter performance, which means an angled south wall. In this case the summer heat can be reduced only by an additional investment in some kind of shading device, swamp cooler, or powered exhaust fan.

Good ventilation is extremely important for proper temperature control. A vent should promote the natural flow of air from a low entry to a high exit across the greenhouse. The vent placement should be such that the prevailing summer breeze pushes right through the vents. When you design the vents, try to recall the direction the summer wind comes from most of the time in your location. The low vent should face the prevailing wind.

A word about finishing: paint all components that will be in contact with water or soil with copper naphthenate; paint all framing a light color before the glazing is applied. Use latex base paint.

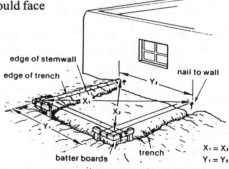

Make sure your walls and footings are really square.

Glazing

No glazing material is best. Every product has advantages and disadvantages. The type you choose is determined by appearance, cost, and how you intend to use your greenhouse. An optically clear product like glass will let direct rays through, while a plastic like fiberglass will scatter the rays into what is known as a diffuse pattern. This diffuse lighting is preferable for plant growth.

Glass is optically clear, can withstand high temperatures, and can be heat-treated to withstand impact. If you choose to use glass, one convenient technique is to design your framing for double glazed patio door replacement panels. They come in 28-inch x 76-inch, 34-inch x 76-inch, 46-inch x 76-inch, 34-inch x 92-inch, 46-inch x 92-inch, and other sizes. Check your glass supplier for prices and availability. Be sure to pinch off the vent in the panel before installation since this stabilizes the air pressure. Use a generous amount of silicone sealant around all sides of the window.

There is an optically clear, 7-mil laminated plastic available which is very tough and has been successfully tested for long-term weatherability. It comes in a 4-foot-wide roll. All other plastics, like fiberglass, are translucent - they let the light in but you can't see through them. If you prefer plastic, be sure the product you choose transmits at least 85 percent of the solar spectrum and is ultraviolet stabilized. Your dealer can help you with this.

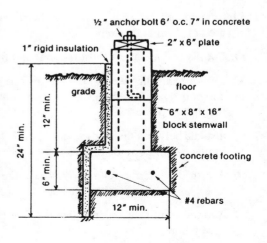

A very convenient but expensive material is a cellular vinyl or polycarbonate which comes in a very strong, lightweight, and double-glazed 4-foot-wide sheet. You can nail it with self sealing nails after you thoroughly seal the cells with silicone. Use nothing but silicone, and be sure that penetration is at least one-half-inch on all cells. The most important aspect of the glazing process is to be sure to seal every joint. Your greenhouse must be airtight. Use good quality sealant- at least a polymer and preferably silicone.

Heat Storage

Without a lot of dense materials (such as adobe, cement block, water containers, etc.), the air temperature inside your greenhouse could vary considerably from day to night. The addition of mass will tend to stabilize greenhouse temperatures. When you have completed your greenhouse, install as many dark-colored (black, brown, or green) 55-gallon drums as your space will comfortably allow. Fill them with water, add one-fourth cup of sodium dichromate as a corrosion inhibitor in each drum, cover them, and use them as supports for the benches you will construct on which you will place planting boxes for vegetables, flowers, and so on. The growing beds, insulated floor, massive north wall, and water-filled drums should provide the heat storage you need. To make sure the heat stored in the greenhouse is transferred into your house, install a thermostatically-controlled window fan to blow warm air into the house during the winter.

Building a Typical Solar Greenhouse: Step-by-Step Instructions

A) Lay out the footing and stem wall using batter boards and strings. The strings define the edge of the footing trench and the stem wall. Dig a trench that is 12 inches wide and 18 inches deep.

B) Place $1/2$ inch rebar 3 inches from the bottom. Block it in place with flat stones or stakes with the rebar wired onto the stakes. Pour concrete into the trench at least 6 inches deep. Use a level and trowel to form a smooth level top surface.

C) When the footing is firm, lay the stem wall, using mortar mix for the joints: stagger the vertical joints.

D) Every 4 feet, fill the core with concrete or mortar mix. Fill the other cores with vermiculite insulation or tamped dirt if most of the stem is below grade. Leave 4 inches of each core unfilled and then pour in concrete or mortar. Don't forget to install the anchor bolts for the sill plate.

E) Place a minimum of 1-inch thick polystyrene bead board 24 inches into the ground on the outside of the stem wall and footing. This assures that the heat transmitted through the glazing is soaked up in the floor and not lost to the ground outside. The foundation and stem wall should now be complete.

F) Place the front sill plate in position by indenting each anchor bolt location and drilling holes to slide the plate in place. Using the sill plate as the first member, lay out the south face on level spot and nail the sill, studs, and headers with 16-penny nails, as shown below.

G) Place the front face in position with strips of insulation, weather-stripping, or caulk between the sill and stem wall to cut off any possible air leaks. Brace to the desired upright angle.

H) Cut the side sills, permanently seal, and put into position.

I) Affix a 2x6 ledger on the house. You can nail through the existing siding into the house studs; use lead anchors and lag screws; or whatever means are appropriate for your house.

J) Place roof joist hangers on the ledger in their proper locations.

K) Cut and nail 2x6 roof joists to fit the angle of the roof, the joist hanger, and the front face. If the house and south face are not parallel, custom-fit each joist.

L) Cut the end members to fit the roof and front face contour, door, and vents. The framing is now complete.

M) Let's assume that the roof is made of corrugated steel. The safest method for avoiding roof air leaks is to caulk all seams and pop-rivet the sections into a continuous strip. You can also use an abundance of lead-headed roofing nails to put the roof in place.

N) Insulate between the joists with roll fiberglass insulation (6-inch fiberglass has a heat resistance rating of R-19), stapled in place with no folds or tucks.

O) Finish the interior ceiling with masonite, paneling, or green waterproof sheetrock. Seal and nail rigid corrugated fiberglass to roof portions that are not opaque. (A polyethylene vapor barrier could be installed if desired.)

P) Add the front fascia plate when the roof is completely built. Paint the entire frame with a light-colored exterior latex base paint.

Q) Glazing is next. Nail Tedlar-coated rigid fiberglass on the inside and outside of the studs. Be sure to generously apply caulking to the studs before attaching each sheet. Finish the inside and outside seams with trim amde of pre-painted batten strips. Don't skimp on the nails for these operations.

R) Construct the vents and doors to fit the openings you provided. The main key is the provision of strong corners. Test the hinges by simulating the movement of the device before notching or attaching hinges. Weather-strip all moving joints.

S) Place dark-colored 55-gallon drums inside the greenhouse (as discussed in Heat Storage). If you can comfortably fit more than five heat storage drums inside the greenhouse, add as many as you desire.

T) Acquire a fan and 110-volt thermostat that can be set at 90°F. Wire the thermostat into the lead and plug into a socket. The fan will blow hot air into your house when the greenhouse reaches 90°F during the winter. You should also get a minimax thermometer which will tell you the temperature swings within your greenhouse. Adjust the house blower so the greenhouse temperature does not rise above 95°F and harm your plants. Each installation requires individual experimentation to achieve optimum results.

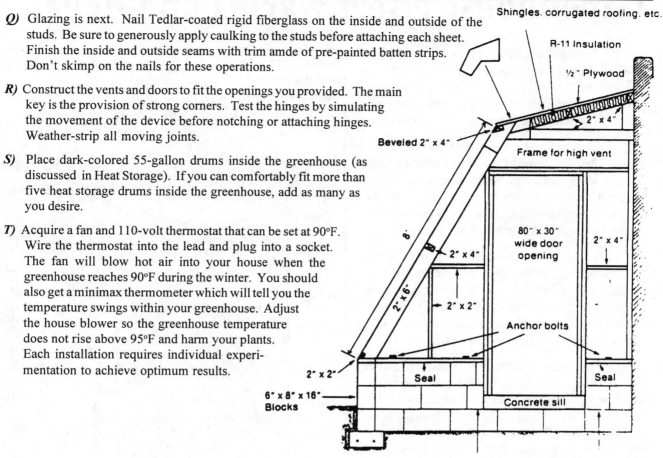

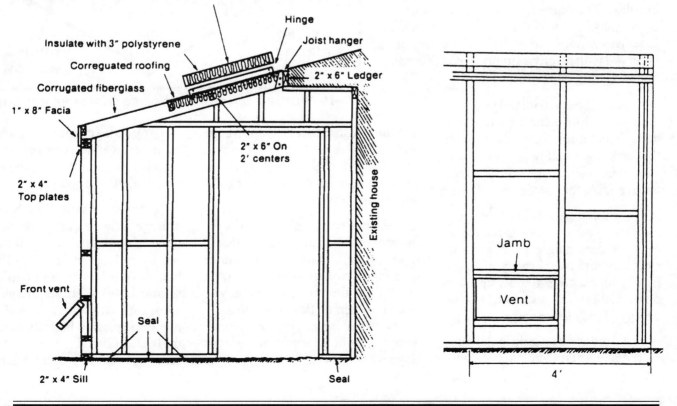

Greenhouse effect warms up kitchen

Q.: I would like to make or buy a kitchen window mini-greenhouse to start and grow small plants. How can I make or install one that can also help heat my kitchen in the winter and cool it in the summer?

A: A window mini-greenhouse can be an attractive addition to any kitchen window. Adding one to your window can create a natural and more spacious feel to the room, without a major expense. You can purchase a complete kit or build one yourself.

In addition to growing flowers and plants, a window mini-greenhouse saves energy year-round. In the winter, it reduces heat loss by adding additional insulation value to your window. The glass area can also capture some of the sun's heat to help heat your kitchen.

In the summer, a mini-greenhouse can act as a natural ventilation exhaust fan. As the air inside it gets hot and rises out a top vent or side windows, hot humid stale air is drawn out of your kitchen. With operable windows in the sides, as in many purchased kits, it can also catch and direct cool evening breezes into your house.

One new window mini-greenhouse kit uses super-efficient low-E, argon-gas-filled insulating glass. The frame is made of insulating composite plastic material and it has tight-sealing casement windows in each side. The front glass is curved with no cross supports, so the outdoor view is totally unobstructed.

A kit is easy to install yourself. You just remove the existing sash and mount the mini-greenhouse over the existing window opening and frame. Jamb extension kits and trim are available for a professional look.

You can also build an inexpensive do-it-yourself mini-greenhouse. Since it uses single pane glass or clear acrylic plastic sheets, you should leave your existing window sashes in place. Otherwise, instead of saving energy, it may lose energy.

To reduce heat gain in the summer, make a slanted clear roof with

Slats provide shade from summer sun

Adjustable vent in top

Acrylic glazing

Hinged window

Do-it-yourself mini-greenhouse fits over window

1x4 lumber slats mounted up on edge and spaced about four to six inches apart. The slats allow diffused light to enter from above, but block the sun's direct rays.

Using acrylic plastic sheet for the roof makes it easy to cut and drill holes. Mount a roof ventilation door on hinges so that it swings down away from the roof slats when you open it. Opening this door naturally vents heated air out of your house. Simple acrylic windows in the sides improve house ventilation.

Q: I cut a couple of 3-inch holes in the drywall to pour in additional wall insulation. What is the easiest way to fix these holes?

A: One way to fix a hole is to enlarge it (large enough to get your hand through) and square it up. Using drywall screws, attach 1x3 backer boards (top and bottom behind the square hole) with about one inch showing. Cut a square drywall patch piece and place it in the hole against the backer boards. Use more drywall screws to secure it to the boards.

MANUFACTURERS OF MINI-GREENHOUSE GARDEN WINDOWS

BOTANICAL GARDEN, 8300 Grand Ave., Minneapolis, MN 55420 - (800) 876-4884 (612) 884-4329

DELSAN INDUSTRIES, 1644 Lotsie Blvd., St. Louis, MO 63132 - (314) 423-5900

FOUR SEASONS, 5005 Veterans Mem. Hwy., Holbrook, NY 11741 - (800) 368-7732 (516) 563-4000

GALLATIN ALUMINUM PROD., P.O. Box 1987, Gallatin, TN 37066 - (800) 333-0111 (615) 452-4550

GREAT LAKES, P.O. Box 1896, Toledo, OH 43603 - (800) 666-0000 (419) 666-5555

FENTECH, 431 Tower Ave., Superior, WI 54880 - (715) 392-9500

FLORIAN GREENHOUSES, 64 Airport Rd., W. Milford, NJ 07480 - (800) 356-7426 (201) 728-7800
   Large garden windows "Bump-Out", 5 ft. by 5 ft. by 2 ft. deep

THERMO INDUSTRIES, 4884 Duff Dr., Cincinnati, OH 45246 - (513) 874-0501

VEGETABLE FACTORY, 71 Vanderbilt Ave., New York, NY 10169 - (800) 221-2550 (212) 867-0113
   Do-it-yourself blueprints and materials

VINYL MAX, 891 Redna Ter., Cincinnati, OH 45215 - (800) 837-9103 (513) 772-2247

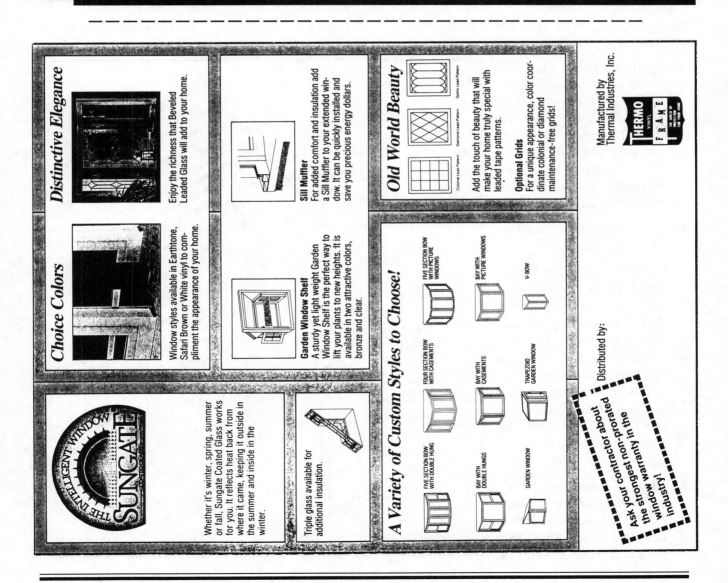

DO-IT-YOURSELF INSTRUCTIONS FOR MAKING A GARDEN WINDOW

A) Plan the dimensions of this unit carefully before beginning construction. Allow enough space in the vertical measurements to accommodate the back-to-front slope of the slatted roof. Plan the width of the boxlike base so that your plants will be easy for you to tend.

B) Build the base first. Start by rabbeting the plant box 1x8's (*A,B*) to accommodate the plywood bottom to be attached later. Then glue and nail the 1x8's together, using butt joints.

C) Cut the bottom of the plant box (*C*) from 3/4-inch exterior plywood. Size it to fit flush with the bottom of the 1x8's. Drill 1/2-inch drain holes in the plywood. Treat it and the inside of the 1x8's with wood preservative to prevent rot. Let dry. Nail the bottom piece to the 1x8's.

D) Cut two 1x4 verticals for the front of the greenhouse (*D*) and two longer ones for the back (*E*). Miter the tops of the verticals to the appropriate angle. Notch the longer verticals (*E*) to accept the 1x4 roof slat that will butt against and attach to the sidewalls of your house.

E) Fasten the verticals to the plant box as shown in the sketch. Use glue and screws.

F) Construct 1x6 "rafters" (*F*) as shown in the sketch. You'll need to angle-cut each end of the rafters and notch the back end to accommodate the roof slat closest to the house. Then cut the notches for the roof slats. Cut both boards at the same time to ensure matching notches. Fasten the rafters to the uprights with glue and screws.

G) Cut 1x4 slats (*G*) to fit into the notches in the rafters. Cut small notches in the bottoms of the slats for drainage. Nail the slats to the rafters.

H) Build a frame for the front "window" of the unit from mitered 1x2's (*H,I*) and a 1x4 top piece (*J*). Notch the ends of the 1x2's as shown so that the 1x4 top piece will fit around the 1x6 rafters. Using glue and nails, fasten the frame members together.

I) Paint or stain the unit inside and out. Let dry.

J) Have pieces of 1/8-inch clear acrylic sheet cut to fit the top, sides, and front of the unit. Drill holes in the acrylic (drill slowly to avoid cracks) and screw the top and side sheets to the inside of the greenhouse as shown. Attach the remaining piece of acrylic to the window frame, then screw the entire frame to the rest of the unit.

K) Fasten the greenhouse securely to the wall studs of the house, using lag screws driven through the rear 1x8 box member and the rear 1x4 roof slat.

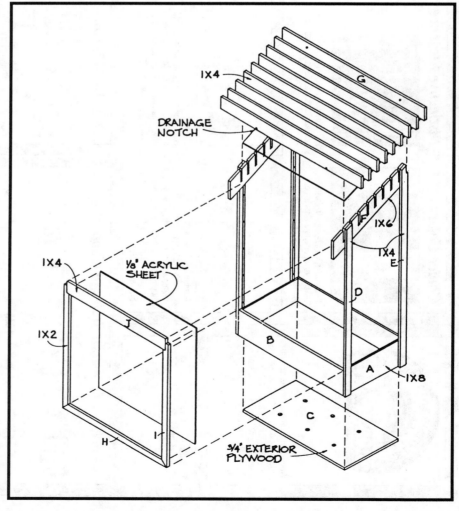

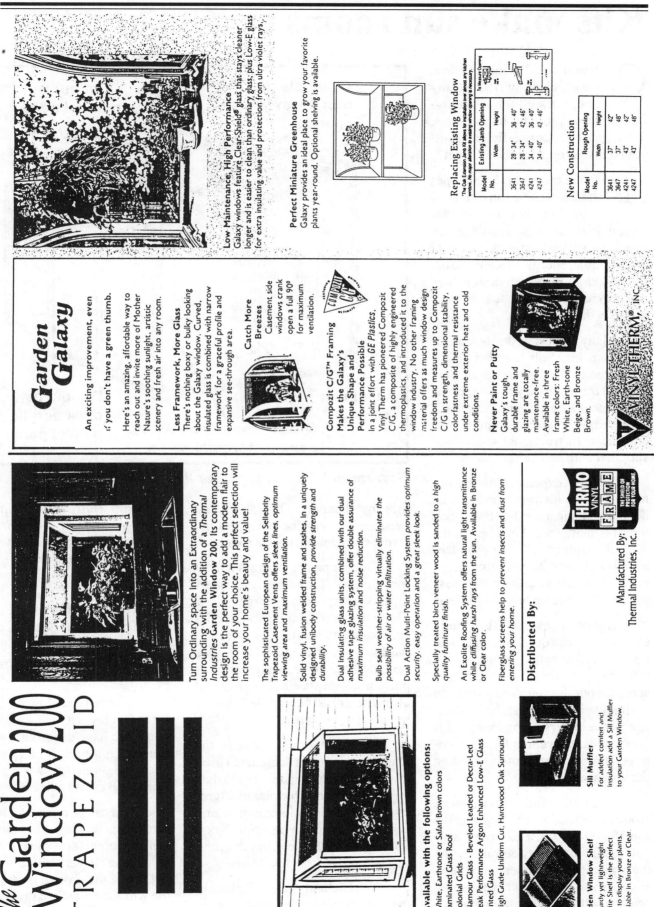

Garden Galaxy

An exciting improvement, even if you don't have a green thumb.

Here's an amazing, affordable way to reach out and invite more of Mother Nature's soothing sunlight, artistic scenery and fresh air into any room.

Less Framework, More Glass
There's nothing boxy or bulky looking about the Galaxy window. Curved, insulated glass is combined with narrow framework for a graceful profile and expansive see-through area.

Catch More Breezes
Casement side windows crank open a full 90° for maximum ventilation.

Compozit C/G™ Framing Makes the Galaxy's Unique Shape and Performance Possible
In a joint effort with *GE Plastics*, Vinyl Therm has pioneered Compozit C/G, a composite of highly engineered thermoplastics, and introduced it to the window industry. No other framing material offers as much window design freedom and measures up to Compozit C/G in strength, dimensional stability, colorfastness and thermal resistance under extreme exterior heat and cold conditions.

Never Paint or Putty
Galaxy's tough, durable frame and glazing are totally maintenance-free. Available in three frame colors: Fresh White, Earth-tone Beige, and Bronze Brown.

Low Maintenance, High Performance
Galaxy windows feature Clear-Shield® glass that stays cleaner longer and is easier to clean than ordinary glass; plus Low-E glass for extra insulating value and protection from ultra violet rays.

Perfect Miniature Greenhouse
Galaxy provides an ideal place to grow your favorite plants year-round. Optional shelving is available.

Replacing Existing Window

The Oak Extension Jamb Kit allows for installation over almost any kitchen window. No major alteration to existing window opening is necessary.

To Measure Opening

Model No.	Existing Jamb Opening	
	Width	Height
3641	28 - 34"	36 - 40"
3647	28 - 34"	42 - 46"
4241	34 - 40"	36 - 40"
4247	34 - 40"	42 - 46"

New Construction

Model No.	Rough Opening	
	Width	Height
3641	37"	42"
3647	37"	48"
4241	43"	42"
4247	43"	48"

VINYL THERM®, INC.

The Garden Window 200 TRAPEZOID

Turn Ordinary space into an Extraordinary surrounding with the addition of a *Thermal Industries* Garden Window 200. Its contemporary design is the perfect way to add a modern flair to the room of your choice. This perfect selection will increase your home's beauty and value!

The sophisticated European design of the Sellebrity Trapezoid Casement Vents offers *sleek lines, optimum viewing area and maximum ventilation.*

Solid vinyl, fusion welded frame and sashes, in a uniquely designed unibody construction, *provide strength and durability.*

Dual insulating glass units, combined with our dual adhesive tape glazing system, offer double assurance of *maximum insulation and noise reduction.*

Bulb seal weather-stripping virtually eliminates the *possibility of air or water infiltration.*

Dual Action Multi-Point Locking System *provides optimum security, easy operation and a great sleek look.*

Specially treated birch veneer wood is sanded to a *high quality furniture finish.*

An Exolite Roofing System offers natural light transmittance while *diffusing harsh rays from the sun.* Available in Bronze or Clear color.

Fiberglass screens help to *prevent insects and dust from entering your home.*

Available with the following options:
- White, Earthtone or Safari Brown colors
- Laminated Glass Roof
- Colonial Grids
- Glamour Glass - Beveled Leaded or Decra-Led
- Peak Performance Argon Enhanced Low-E Glass
- Tinted Glass
- High Grade Uniform Cut, Hardwood Oak Surround

Garden Window Shelf
A sturdy yet lightweight Exolite Shelf is the perfect way to display your plants. Available in Bronze or Clear.

Sill Muffler
For added comfort and insulation add a Sill Muffler to your Garden Window.

Distributed By:

THERMO VINYL FRAME — THE SHIELD OF PROTECTION FOR YOUR HOME.

Manufactured By:
Thermal Industries, Inc.

Kits make sun rooms easy to build

Q. I want to add an inexpensive, yet efficient, sun room to my house myself for casual living area and growing houseplants. What type of energy efficient do-it-yourself sun room kit should I get?

A. There are several new types of inexpensive sun room kits available. By using modern materials and accessories, these sun rooms are very attractive and can add comfortable, energy efficient casual living area. With proper design, they can provide some solar heat for your house in the winter too.

Many of the new do-it-yourself sun room kits bolt together like a huge erector set. They are predrilled with all the necessary screws, bolts, seals, etc. Once the ground area is prepared, you can build one in several days. Instructional videos are supplied with most kits.

The least expensive kits use aluminum extrusion frames and special double-pane clear acrylic plastic glazing. It is shatterproof and resists the sun's damaging rays. This produces a very lightweight, yet strong, sun room. You can actually build these sun rooms right over an existing deck.

One new convertible (to a porch) sun room kit has quick-change clear double wall acrylic glazing panels that expose screens creating a screened porch. You simply snap out the lightweight panels and store them against the lower glazing panels. This provides natural ventilation with continuous roof ridge vents to exhaust the warm summer air.

You will definitely need some type of summertime shading over the roof. Several kits use external channels mounted to the roof framing. At the beginning of summer, you simply slide in special dense-weave shading screens with light aluminum frames,

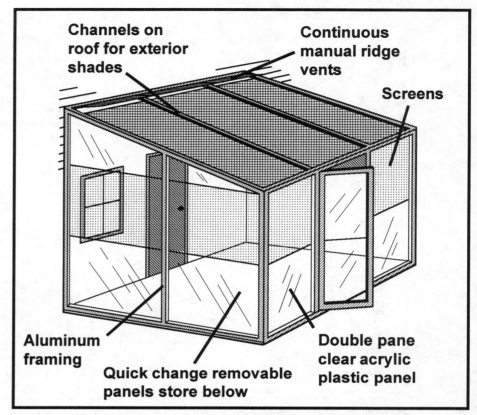

Sun room kit bolts together like erector set

into the channels. This is efficient because it blocks the sun's heat before it even enters the sun room.

Double pane glazing is a must for efficiency. The most efficient glazing is double pane low-e argon glass. These are used in the good quality sun rooms and require more substantial framing for the weight. Double pane clear acrylic or supertough clear polycarbonate plastic are lighter and also efficient. Bronze-tinted glazing helps in hot climates.

A vinyl thermal break in the aluminum frame is sometimes used to reduce heat loss and sweating during cold weather. One manufacturer uses an exterior aluminum frame combined with an interior wood frame. This is efficient, durable, and very attractive from the inside.

To efficiently gain solar heat in the winter, you need heat storage mass in the sun room. A simple heavy brick or concrete floor or wall is effective. This reradiates heat in the evening keeping it warm.

Q: I have done some rewiring in my older house so that I can efficiently zone heat it with electric space heaters. How can I tell if I wired the ground properly to each receptacle?

A: You'll need heavier wiring for the high-current heaters. It is important to have the ground and neutral wired properly. Most plugs have one wide prong and wiring it backwards can create a hazard.

You can purchase an inexpensive receptacle tester at many home center stores. You plug it into the receptacle. It has a series of lights to tell you if the ground is good and if the wires are attached properly.

Do-it-yourself sun room kits are also often referred to as sunspaces or greenhouses. I have listed the highest-quality and easiest to build kits on page **b** along with other information that you will find helpful on selecting the proper one for your needs. The estimated prices shown are for their sun room kits nearest the 9 x 12 foot size.

Most of the kits listed are designed for casual living space. The glazing is crystal clear plastic or glass and there are windows and vents to control the temperature. You can buy less expensive greenhouses with translucent glazing and less finish for growing plants only. This is usually some type of durable plastic glazing.

These sun room kits are easy to build yourself. The lighter-weight models using aluminum frames and plastic glazing do not even require a foundation. They can be built right over a standard wood deck. Check your local building code requirements for additions to your house. Sometimes, any attached addition must be supported by an approved foundation.

You can build any width sun room just by adding more bays side-by-side. Most manufacturers have standard bays, often 3 to 4 feet wide. The assembly of each bay is identical and they offer instructional videos. This makes building one simple because once you learn how to build one of the bays, the others assemble the same way.

One of the less expensive models (made by Vegetable Factory) is convertible into a porch (see detailed information on page **c**). The top half of the glazing panels can be easily taken out and stored against the lower panels. This creates a porch atmosphere in the summer if you want natural ventilation. With a continuous roof ridge vent, there is more than adequate air flow. All of the other sun room kits have optional slider or awning windows which can be opened. Information on one more-expensive model by another manufacturer is shown below.

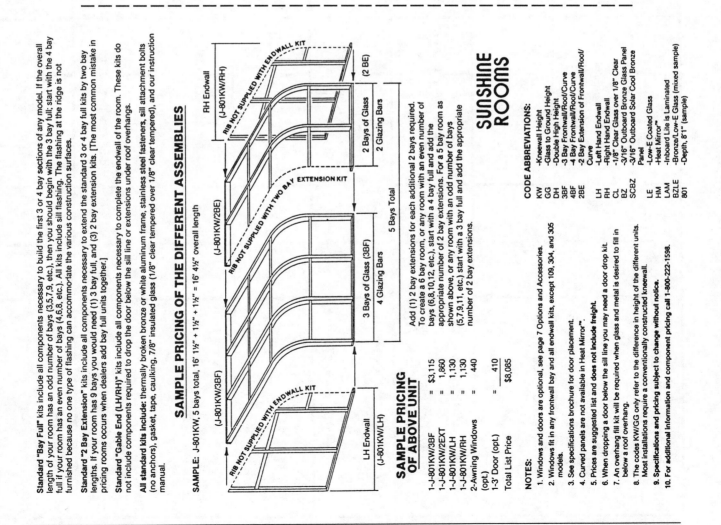

Standard "Bay Full" kits include all components necessary to build the first 3 or 4 bay sections of any model. If the overall length of your room has an odd number of bays (3,5,7,9, etc.), then you should begin with the 3 bay full; start with the 4 bay full if your room has an even number of bays (4,6,8, etc.). All kits include sill flashing. The flashing at the ridge is not furnished because no one type of flashing can accommodate the various construction surfaces.

Standard "2 Bay Extension" kits include all components necessary to extend the standard 3 or 4 bay full kits by two bay lengths. If your room has 9 bays you would need (1) 3 bay full, and (3) 2 bay extension kits. [The most common mistake in pricing rooms occurs when dealers add bay full units together.]

Standard "Gable End (LH/RH)" kits include all components necessary to complete the endwall of the room. These kits do not include components required to drop the door below the sill line or extensions under roof overhangs.

All standard kits include: thermally broken bronze or white aluminum frame, stainless steel fasteners, sill attachment bolts (no anchors), gasket, tape, caulking, 7/8" insulated glass (1/8" clear tempered over 1/8" clear tempered), and our instruction manual.

SAMPLE PRICING OF THE DIFFERENT ASSEMBLIES

SAMPLE: J-801KW, 5 bays total, 16' 1½" + 1½" + 1½" = 16' 4½" overall length

SAMPLE PRICING OF ABOVE UNIT

1-J-801KW/3BF	=	$3,115
1-J-801KW/2EXT	=	1,860
1-J-801KW/LH	=	1,130
1-J-801KW/RH	=	1,130
2-Awning Windows (opt.)	=	440
1-3' Door (opt.)	=	410
Total List Price		$8,085

Add (1) 2 bay extensions for each additional 2 bays required. To create a 6 bay room, or any room with an even number of bays (6,8,10,12, etc.), start with a 4 bay full and add the appropriate number of 2 bay extensions. For a 5 bay room as shown above, or any room with an odd number of bays (5,7,9,11, etc.) start with a 3 bay full and add the appropriate number of 2 bay extensions.

SUNSHINE ROOMS

CODE ABBREVIATIONS:

KW	-Kneewall Height
GG	-Glass to Ground Height
DH	-Double High Height
3BF	-3 Bay Frontwall/Roof/Curve
4BF	-4 Bay Frontwall/Roof/Curve
2BE	-2 Bay Extension of Frontwall/Roof/Curve
LH	-Left Hand Endwall
RH	-Right Hand Endwall
CL	-1/8" Clear Glass over 1/8" Clear
BZ	-3/16" Outboard Bronze Glass Panel
SCBZ	-3/16" Outboard Solar Cool Bronze Panel
LE	-Low-E Coated Glass
HM	-Heat Mirror™
LAM	-Inboard Lite is Laminated
BZLE	-Bronze/Low-E Glass (mixed sample)
801	-Depth, 8'1" (sample)

NOTES:

1. Windows and doors are optional, see page 7 Options and Accessories.
2. Windows fit in any frontwall bay and all endwall kits, except 109, 304, and 305 models.
3. See specifications brochure for door placement.
4. Curved panels are not available in Heat Mirror™.
5. Prices are suggested list and does not include freight.
6. When dropping a door below the sill line you may need a door drop kit.
7. An overhang fill kit will be required when glass and metal is desired to fill in below a roof overhang.
8. The codes KW/GG only refer to the difference in height of the different units. Most installations require a conventionally constructed kneewall.
9. Specifications and pricing subject to change without notice.
10. For additional information and component pricing call 1-800-222-1598.

Sun Room Manufacturers	Frame Type		Glazing Options			Shading Systems		Ventilation		Thermal Break?	Price 9x12'
	Curved	Straight	Glass	Acrylic	Other	Interior	Exterior	Fan	Windows		
BRADY & SUN 97 Webster St. Worcester, MA 01603 (508) 755-9580 (800) 888-7177	☼	☼	☼ Low "E" argon filled, light tint adds solar protection				☼ Fiberglass mesh material mounted in aluminum frames		☼ Awning type, also sliding doors	All wood w/aluminum exterior	$7,500
DUO-GARD INDUSTRIES 6232 Executive Dr. Westland, MI 48185 (313) 595-7181 (800) 872-4404	☼	☼			☼ PCSS-polycarbonate structured sheet	Insulated ceiling available			☼ Vertical sliding, also hinged door	No	8' x 10.5' $3,500
FLORIAN GREENHOUSES 64 Airport Rd. West Milford, NJ 07480 (201) 728-7800 (800) 356-7426	☼	☼	☼ Low "E" Argon filled or any other glass, plastic avail.		☼	☼ Manual or motorized in variety of materials	☼		☼ Awning type, also sliding and hinged doors	Yes Also wood w/aluminum exterior	$8,000-$12,000
LINDAL CEDAR SUNROOMS P.O. Box 24426 Seattle, WA 98124 (206) 725-0900 (800) 426-0536	☼	☼	Tempered thermal is standard, many others available					☼	☼ Vent Axia exhaust fans w/thermostat, awning windows	Cedar	$5,500-$12,000
OMEGA SUNSPACES 4401 Ellison N.E. Albuquerque, NM 87109 (505) 344-0333 (800) 753-3034	☼	☼	☼ GE Lexan® roof and curve 5' removable glass windows		☼	☼ Roman pleat shades with metal mylar center layer			☼ Horizontal sliding w/security ventilation latch	No	$6,000
SUNGLO SOLAR GREENHOUSES 4441 26th Ave. W. Seattle, WA 98199 (206) 284-8900 (800) 647-0606	☼	☼		☼ Double wall "Thermal Truss"		☼ Bronze fiberglass shading material avail. in 60" width		☼ Exhaust fan, fresh air shutter available		No	$2,600
SUNSHINE ROOMS P.O. Box 4627 Wichita, KS 67204 (316) 838-0033 (800) 222-1598	☼	☼	☼ Insulated glass standard, other varieties available			☼ 3 types exterior, 5 types interior	☼	☼	☼ Vent axia exhaust fan, windows & doors available	Yes	$7,500
VEGETABLE FACTORY 71 Vanderbilt Ave. New York, NY 10169	☼	☼		☼ GE Lexan® roof, double pane acrylic sides				☼ Polyester mesh fabric w/vinyl coating		☼ Self-storing windows w/screens	No	$3,000-$5,000

VEGETABLE FACTORY®, INC.
Sales Offices:
655 Washington Boulevard, Stamford, CT 06901-3793
OUT-OF-STATE CALL TOLL FREE (800) 221-2550
CONNECTICUT CALL (203) 324-0010
FAX (203) 324-0520

Convertible Sun-Porch™

PRICE LIST
January 15, 1992

F.O.B. Factory, Louisville, KY
TERMS: 25% Deposit with order, Balance C.O.D.,
unless other arrangements are made.

NOTE: All prices noted are subject to change without prior notice.

SUN-PORCH™ STANDARD FEATURES & OPTIONS
WITH EXAMPLE BELOW OF 9' x 12' L (NOMINAL SIZE) STRUCTURE

STRUCTURE: Heavy-guage hollow aluminum extrusions for arches, eaves, purlins, base channels, brackets, with a factory-baked enamel finish. Stainless-steel screws, bolts, EPDM rubber gasketry. Front wall gutter with down spouts at each end included for rain-free protection. Roof and wall glazing panels are of shatter-resistant, insulated double-wall materials, with special weathering surfaces, engineered for snow and wind load factors, and ultraviolet (UV) treated against yellowing and haze.

FRAME COLOR OPTIONS: Elegant White or Architectural Bronze. Indicate choice on Order Form.

GLAZING COLOR OPTIONS: ROOF-GE Lexan® Thermoclear® insulated double-wall, light-diffusing sheeting. Choice of Bronze-Tint, Opal-White, Clear. Indicate choice on Order Form. WALLS/DOOR - Plexiglas®DR® insulated double-wall aluminum framed panels. Choice of Bronze-Tint, Glass-Clear. Indicate choice on Order Form.

QWIK™ SYSTEM: All vertical panel areas in front and end walls are fitted with our patented QWIK™ System (Quick Window Insert Kit). This allows for rapid window/screen changeovers. The top 3' x 3' panel areas, screen covered on the outside, are quickly deployed into the lower self-storing area. The exterior screens are spring steel loaded for easy removal from inside.

VENTS: All Sun-Porch™ models come with continuous full-length screened ridge vents, operable by pole from the inside in 3' sections. A practical extra, exclusively ours, at no extra charge.

SUNSHADE TRACKS: All Sun-Porch™ models come equipped with exterior vertical roof battens that have built-in tracks ready to accept aluminum framed fiberglass sunshades. Another very practical Sun-Porch™ exclusive feature.

DOORS: All Sun-Porch™ models include a storm/screen combination door which may be placed in any QR38/QX38 section, hinged right or left at your option, and swings outward.
a) EXTRA-DOOR (Replaces QR38/QX38 panel area) - $215. Order "SUBDKC/QR38C".
b) NO DOOR (Replaces QR38/QX38 panel area) - Deduct $100. Order "SUBQR38C/DKC".
c) DROPPED-DOOR - Door is at ground level when structure is mounted on knee wall. Specify QR38/QX38 area desired, plus height of wall, except outer corners, and add $150.
d) PET DOOR - Staywell magnetic door with lock, mounted in QX38 panel. Order as follows: #PD7 (Small)-$115., #PD11 (Medium)-$135., #PD12 (Large)-$155.

FOOTING/FOUNDATION: Dimensions noted are outer dimensions of structure. Unit may be readily mounted on decks, patios, or landscape ties. IMPORTANT - Add 3" in width and length to outer dimensions for mounting surface. This also allows for wood verticals and headers that are attached to wall of house before surface is mounted. It also allows for any optional foundation such as blocks or pressure-treated landscape ties.

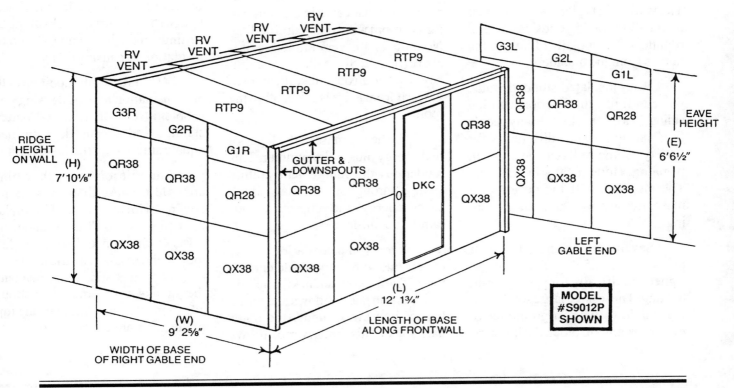

Log homes both attractive and efficient

Q: I have seen some very attractive large (over 2,500 sq. ft.) build-it-yourself log home kits. They are super-efficient and designed for free passive solar heating too. How can they make log homes efficient?

A: You are referring to insulated "half-log" kit homes. These are super-efficient and range in size from 1,000 sq. ft. cabins to 7,000 sq. ft. mansions. Your monthly utility bills will be just a fraction of those for a similar size conventional house.

These homes are ideal for the inexperienced do-it-yourself builder/helper. You can dramatically reduce the overall building costs by doing some of the construction work yourself with friends. With the heavy log exterior and insulated studded wall interior, these kit homes are extremely durable.

The half log design uses an insulated 2x6 studded wall behind the exterior half logs. This provides a wall insulation value of up to R-32. The walls of a typical house are less than R-20. The log ends can be full round so they look just like full log homes from the outside.

With insulated studded walls, you can finish the interior with log siding for a true log look. Many people finish several rooms differently for variety. Some walls can be drywall, paneling, stone, heavy beams, etc. The insulated half log design also makes it easy to run wiring and plumbing.

Several of the standard kit floor plans (up to 3,500 sq. ft.) are designed specifically for passive solar heating. These have large south-facing windows with large attractive roof overhangs to block the hot sum-

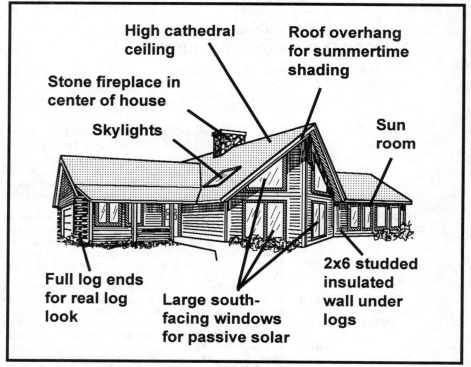

High cathedral ceiling · **Roof overhang for summertime shading** · **Stone fireplace in center of house** · **Skylights** · **Sun room** · **Full log ends for real log look** · **Large south-facing windows for passive solar** · **2x6 studded insulated wall under logs**

New easy-to-build passive solar log home kit

mer sun. A relatively open floor plan with high ceilings and lofts provides a spacious feeling and natural heat circulation.

A large masonry or stone fireplace is often located in the center of a great room with a cathedral ceiling. Not only is this very attractive, it is also efficient. Since the stone chimney is not on an outside wall, more of the heat from a fire is given off to the room.

The heavy mass of the logs is a real energy plus in the summer. This moderates the indoor temperature swings throughout the day which saves energy and improves your family's comfort.

When you select a log home, choose one with energy-efficient features. The most efficient kits include low-e argon gas windows and an air barrier housewrap under the outer half logs. This housewrap allows moisture to escape, but blocks air leaks through the walls.

Q: Ever since we put several inches of insulation in our attic, I notice straight dirty streaks along the ceilings in the bedrooms. Could the insulation be causing this?

A: Indirectly, the addition of the attic insulation may be causing your problem. It is often called pattern staining and is caused by an inadequate amount of attic insulation.

The attic joists over the ceiling are cold because their tops are not covered with insulation. This makes the ceiling areas directly under the joists colder. Since there is slightly more condensation on the colder areas, more dust sticks there causing the streaks over time. You should add more attic insulation so the tops of the joists are covered too.

Log home kits are relatively easy to build yourself, they are by no means low quality. Stock floor plans of up to 4,000 sq. ft. are available; however, most of the larger log houses are built to custom floor plans. In the chart below, I have listed several of the manufacturers of high-quality log homes. The ones that also make the insulated half-log wall designs are indicated with an (*). On the following pages, I have included floor plan layouts and exterior diagrams of several passive solar and other energy efficient log home kits. I have shown floor plans of only two manufacturers. Since many of the standard styles of all the manufacturers are similar, these will provide you with an idea the range of styles of log homes available.

If you are interested in building a high-efficiency log home, the insulated half-log wall design is best. Many of these houses are designed to utilize passive solar or other alternative energy sources for heating. The floor plans on page **c** are all ideal for solar heating.

An insulated half-log wall design consists of half logs on the outside of an insulated studded wall. It looks just like a solid full log house from the outside. Some even have full-round log ends for a true log look. You can finish the inside of the studded walls with log siding or half logs for a true log look indoors too. You may also want to finish some of the rooms with conventional drywall.

There are many advantages of an insulated wall half log design. Although wood logs are a natural insulator, solid logs do not compare to a 2x6 insulated studded wall for energy efficiency. A half log wall is much lighter weight than a full log house, so there is less chance of settling. The electrical wiring and plumbing are much easier to install in a studded wall. It can be very tricky for a do-it-yourselfer to wire a full log home. These homes have total wall insulation levels of R-30 or more.

If you are interested in passive solar heating for your log home, it should have large south-facing windows, a large roof overhang for summer shading, and an open floor plan for easy distribution of the solar heat. One of the floor plans shown locates the fireplace in the center of the house. This is very efficient because the heat from the warm chimney stays inside the house. A chimney located on an outside wall wastes a lot of its heat.

When selecting your insulated half-log home, carefully study the specifications of the materials in the kits. On page **b**, I have listed the materials from one very high-efficiency kit. A good indication of high efficiency is the air barrier housewrap and the efficient (low-e, argon gas-filled) windows which are standard features.

MANUFACTURERS OF LOG HOME KITS**

APPALACHIAN LOG HOMES, 11312 Station W., Knoxville, TN 37922 - (615) 966-6440
GARLAND LOG HOMES, PO Box 12, Victor, MT 59875 - (800) 642-3837 (406) 642-3095
***GASTINEAU LOG HOMES**, Rt. 2, Box 248, New Bloomfield, MO 65063 - (800) 654-9253 (314) 896-5122
***GREATWOOD LOG HOMES**, PO Box 707, Elkhart Lake, WI 53020 - (800) 558-5812 (414) 876-3378
KUHNS BROS. LOG HOMES, Rd. 2, Box 406A, Lewisburg, PA 17837 - (717) 568-1422
LINCOLN LOG HOMES, Riverside Dr., Chestertown, NY 12817 - (800) 833-2461 (518) 494-4777
LOG STRUCTURES, PO. Box 470009, Lake Monroe, FL 32747 - (407) 321-5647
MAJESTIC LOG HOMES, PO Box 772, Ft. Collins, CO 80522 - (800) 279-5647 (303) 224-4857
MONTANA IDAHO LOG HOMES, 995 S. US Hwy., Victor, MT 59875 - (406) 961-3092
NEW ENGLAND LOG HOMES, PO. Box 5427, Hamden, CT 06518 - (800) 243-3551 (203) 562-0541
REAL LOG HOMES, PO Box 202, Hartland, VT 05048 - (800) 732-5564 (802) 436-2121
SATTERWHITE LOG HOMES, Rt. 2, Box 256A, Longview, TX 75605 - (800) 777-7288 (903) 663-1729
***TRAVERSE BAY LOG HOMES**, 6446 M-72, E. Traverse City, MI 49684 - (616) 947-1881
***WILDERNESS LOG HOMES**, Route 2, Plymouth, WI 53073 - (414) 893-8416
***WISCONSIN LOG HOMES**, 2390 Tampamperin, Green Bay, WI 54307 - (800) 678-9107 (414) 434-3010

(*) indicates insulated half log wall kits available
(**) each of these manufacturers sells its homes nationally through
a dealer/builder network or directly to the homeowner.

A. SUB-FLOOR PACKAGE (BASEMENT CAP)

- 2" x 10" Floor joist or as plan specified (Conventional floor system)
- 3/4" T&G underlayment grade plywood
- Wood bridging as per plan
- Wood main beams as per plan
- 2" x 10" box joist or as plan specified
- Box insulation – Kraft backed (R-19)
- Sill seal
- Treated sill plates
- Conventional stair stringers and treads
- Joist hangers where applicable
- Sub-floor adhesive

B. EXTERIOR WALLS

- Hand dressed "Whole Log Look" Thermal-Log™ with Tru-Fit™ precut full log corners or Hewn Beam™ with 10" x 10" square corners or Vert-A-Log™ with 10" x 10" square vertical corners or Colonial Beam™ with 8" x 8" square vertical corners
- 2" x 6" Precut studs – full 8 foot ceiling 1st floor
- 4" x 5" Window and door trim (Tru-Fit™ and Vert-A-Log™)
- 4" x 4" Window and door trim (Colonial Beam™ and Hewn Beam™)
- Sole/top plates
- 1/2" CDX corner bracing
- 1/2" Insulated sheathing
- Tyvek™ housewrap
- Fiberglass batt insulation (R-19)
- 4 Mil vapor barrier
- 2" x 12" Window and door headers
- Sill seal (if built on slab)
- High performance, LOW-E argon filled insulated, aluminum clad double hung wood windows including storm and screen combination, wood window grilles, and extension jambs
- Prehung insulated steel, 9 lite crossbuck exterior doors with adjustable oak thresholds, and extension jambs
- Keylock knobs (for exterior doors)
- Acrylic-rubber sealant caulk
- Specially formulated exterior log oil, choice of colors
- High performance, LOW-E patio doors included as per plan

C. INTERIOR WALL PARTITIONS

- 2" x 4" Precut studs
- 2" x 6" Precut studs for plumbing wall as per plan
- 2" x 4" Sole and double top plates
- Interior door headers as per plan

D. SECOND FLOOR

- 2" x 10" Floor joist or as plan specified (Conventional floor system)
- 3/4" T&G underlayment grade plywood
- Joist hangers where applicable
- Wood bridging as per plan
- Conventional stair stringers, treads and risers
- Box insulation – Kraft backed (R-19)
- Square railings as per plan
- Hand crafted 1st floor ceiling 6" x 6" pine beams 4' o.c.
- High performance, LOW-E argon filled insulated, aluminum clad double hung wood windows including storm and screen combination, wood window grilles and extension jambs
- Sub-floor adhesive

E. STANDARD ROOF

- All conventional roof framing
- Pre-manufactured energy trusses as per plan where applicable
- 12" Kraft backed insulation (R-38)
- 5/8" CDX roof plywood
- 15# Roof felt
- Choice of asphalt or fiberglass shingles
- 2" x 8" Rake overhang 24" o.c. – 2' overhang on gable ends
- Brown "T" edging
- 1" x 10" Cedar fascia trim
- 2" x 8" Subfascia nailer
- Continuous ridge and soffit vents
- Knotty pine soffits (1" x 8" tongue and groove)
- Aluminum valley as per plan
- Asphalt cement as per plan
- Aluminum flashing as per plan
- C-5, C-9 Hurricane clips for both sides of rafters
- Energy vents
- Plywood spacing clips

F. CATHEDRAL CEILING

- 2" x 12" Ridge board
- 2" x 14" Ceiling rafters (2" x 12" and 2" x 2")
- 12" Kraft backed insulation (R-38)
- 15# Roof felt
- 5/8" CDX roof plywood
- Choice of asphalt or fiberglass shingles
- Brown "T" edging
- 2" x 8" Subfascia nailer
- 1" x 10" Cedar fascia trim
- Hand dressed log rafters
- Hand dressed log collar ties
- Continuous ridge and soffit vents
- Knotty pine soffit
- C-5, C-9 Hurricane clips for both sides of rafters
- Continuous "Energy" vents (full length of rafters)
- Proper vents where trusses apply as per plan
- Plywood spacing clips

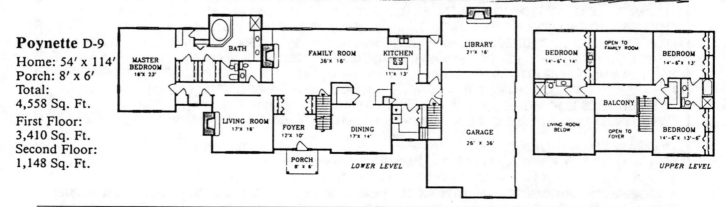

Poynette D-9

Home: 54' x 114'
Porch: 8' x 6'
Total:
4,558 Sq. Ft.

First Floor:
3,410 Sq. Ft.

Second Floor:
1,148 Sq. Ft.

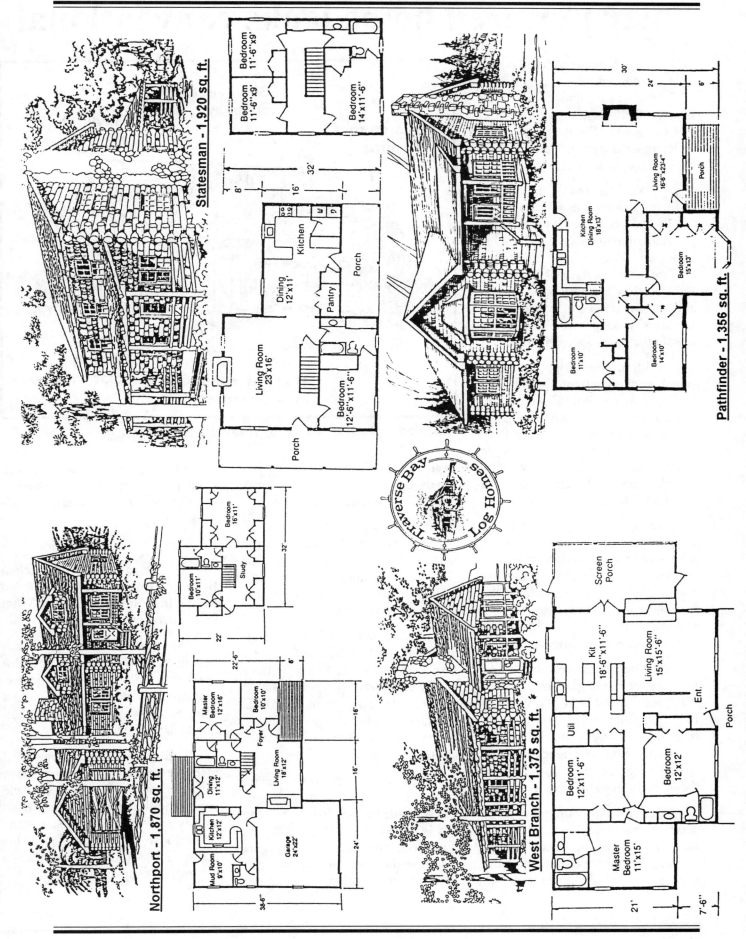

Statesman - 1,920 sq. ft.

Bedroom 11'-6"x9'
Bedroom 11'-6"x9'
Bedroom 14'x11'-6"

32'
8'
16'

Kitchen
Dining 12'x11'
Pantry
Porch
Living Room 23x16'
Bedroom 12'-6" x11'-6"
Porch

Pathfinder - 1,356 sq. ft.

30'
24'
6'

Living Room 16'-6"x23'-4"
Porch
Kitchen Dining Room 18'x13'
Bedroom 15'x13'
Bedroom 11'x10'
Bedroom 14'x10'

Traverse Bay Log Homes

Northport - 1,870 sq. ft.

Bedroom 16'x11'
Bedroom 10'x11'
Study

32'
22'
22'-6"
6'

Master Bedroom 12'x16'
Bedroom 10'x10'
Foyer
Dining 11'x12'
Living Room 18'x12'
Kitchen 12'x12'
Mud Room 9'x10'
Garage 24'x22'

16'
16'
24'
38'-6"

West Branch - 1,375 sq. ft.

Screen Porch
Kit 18'-6"x11'-6"
Util
Living Room 15'x15'-6"
Bedroom 12'x11'-6"
Bedroom 12'x12'
Master Bedroom 11'x15'
Ent.
Porch

21'
7'-6"

Solar powered home looks conventional

Q: Is it possible to build a conventional-looking house that is heated and cooled with nearly 100% passive solar energy (no furnace)? What are the most efficient solar design features to incorporate in it?

A: You can build a house that uses only free solar energy to heat and cool it year-round. Other than having many south-facing windows and a sunspace, 100% passive solar houses can look "normal". Indoors, they are very open, bright, and spacious. Several house manufacturers make passive solar house kits for the do-it-yourself builder.

With proper design, a passive solar house can stay comfortably cool in the summer without air-conditioning. The heavy thermal mass absorbs excess heat in the daytime to keep your house cool. Building a simple passive solar whole-house ventilation chimney creates a natural breeze throughout the house.

The keys to designing a passive solar house are high-insulation, much south-facing glass, and thermal mass inside the floors and walls. This mass stores solar heat during the day in the winter to keep your house warm. Having the proper ratio of glass area and thermal mass is important.

The basic passive solar design features are direct gain, solar walls, sunspaces, and solar roofs. You will need a combination of these features to attain near 100% solar. Consider installing a high-efficiency wood or gas burning fireplace, both for aesthetics and unusually-severe weather.

Direct solar gain with large south-facing windows is most common. The sun shines in on a thick concrete floor (covered with ceramic tile) or wall which stores the solar

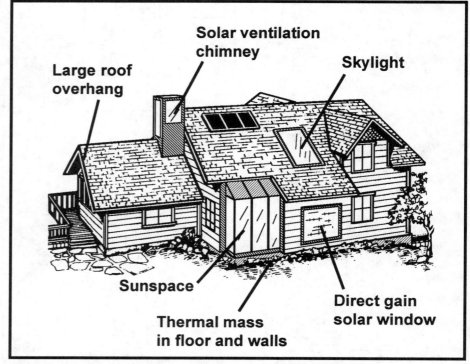

Methods of passive solar heating and cooling

heat. This provides even heating during the day and comfortable warmth that slowly radiates up at night.

A solar wall is a heavy masonry wall that is built just inside a large south-facing window. As the sun shines on the wall, it stores the heat during the day. At night, the heat is given off into the room.

A sunspace is effectively a giant solar collector. Some of the solar heat is stored in the sunspace floor and walls. The remainder of the heated air circulates throughout the house. A solar roof utilizes large windows in the roof and your entire attic becomes a solar collector.

For summer comfort, design your house with large roof overhangs. These shade the windows when the sun is higher in the summer sky. A do-it-yourself solar chimney gets warm in the sun. The hot air in it naturally rises which draws cooler

air in through the windows. If you want to air-condition, the thermal mass lets you run it at nighttime off-peak rates.

Q: The cabinets in my kitchen fit snugly around my refrigerator and there is little room for air flow. What can I do to get more air to it?

A: It is important to get adequate air flow to your refrigerator condenser coils. Inadequate air flow reduces efficiency and creates a "hot spot" behind your refrigerator making it harder to stay cool.

Add a false back, leaving 3 inches behind it, to the cabinets above the refrigerator. Saw holes in the cabinet bottom behind the false back so it is open to the floor. Saw some holes above the cabinet door. This creates a passage for the warm air to naturally rise up and out.

Although it is possible to build a nearly 100% passive heated house in most climates, it requires much glazing (glass) area on the south side. The chart at the top of page b shows an estimate of the amount of glass area needed compared to the size of the house in square feet of floor area. You may find it more economically feasible to design for 70% to 80% passive solar heating and install a small furnace or space heaters. Four primary passive solar methods are direct gain windows, solar walls, sunspaces (greenhouses), and solar roofs. The floor plan layouts of the passive solar houses on the following pages use one or several of these methods in each. These will give you some idea of possible functional solar layouts.

Heat Capacity in Btu/ft³/°f	
Water	62.4
Concrete	30.8
Stone	18-36
Brick	27.3

Direct gain windows are just large south-facing windows. A solar wall is a heavy masonry wall built directly inside a south-facing window. The wall absorbs the heat. A solar roof has much glass area and the attic becomes the solar collector and heat storage area. These houses also have large roof overhangs to block the summer sun. You need thermal heat storage mass in a passive solar house to store the heat during the day and release it at night. Some typical materials are water in drums, concrete, stone, or brick. Heat capacity is measured in Btu/ft³/°F. This indicates how much heat each cubic foot of the material can store for each degree warmer it gets. The chart on this page shows the thermal capacities for these materials.

If your floor plan is a very open design, you should size the amount of thermal mass to absorb about one half of the solar heat. If you use direct gain through windows in a more-closed or partitioned room, you will need more thermal mass, enough to absorb three-quarters of the solar heat. At this point in your design, definitely have a solar designer/engineer estimate the solar heat gain and the needed thermal mass. The above rules of thumb are useful only for the preliminary planning. Your house must be well insulated and airtight. The heat gain during the day must last throughout the night. With an airtight solar house, you should consider installing a heat recovery ventilation system. These systems circulate fresh outdoor air through your home. The heat from the stale exhaust air is captured before it goes outdoors.

Listed below are manufacturers of home kits. By kits, it is meant that they are designed so you can do much of the construction work yourself. A true passive solar house generally costs a little more to build because it is highly insulated and uses airtight construction techniques.

These manufacturers have designs that are very effective for passive solar heating or they can modify designs to meet your solar goals. Several types of construction methods are listed - steel frame, panelized, geodesic dome, modular, circular panelized, log, and cedar. For nearly 100% passive solar, you will have to modify their standard designs. Depending on your climate, their basic "passive solar" homes are designed for solar to contribute about 50% of the heating load. Panelized (stress-skin) construction methods are well suited for passive solar because window locations are easily modified and the self-supporting walls offer an open floor plan.

MANUFACTURERS OF KIT HOMES

AMOS WINTER HOMES, RR. 5, Box 168B, Brattleboro, VT 05301
  panelized   (802) 254-3435
DELTEC HOMES, P.O. Box 6279, Asheville, NC 28816
  circular panelized   (800) 642-2508 (704) 253-0483
ENERCEPT INC., 3100 Ninth Ave. SE, Watertown, SD 57201
  panelized   (605) 882-2222
HELICON DESIGN CORP., Rt. 66 N., Cavetown, MD 21720
  circular panelized   (301) 824-2254
LINDAL CEDAR HOMES, P.O. Box 24426, Seattle, WA 98124
  cedar home   (206) 725-0900
NORTH AMER. HOUSING, P.O. Box 145, Point of Rocks, MD 21777
  modular   (301) 694-9100
TIMBERLINE GEODESICS, 2015 Blake St., Berkeley, CA 94704
  geodesic dome   (800) 366-3466 (510) 849-4481
TRI-STEEL, 5400 S. Stemmons, Denton, TX 76205
  steel-framed   (800) 874-7833 (817) 497-7070
WILDERNESS LOG HOMES, Rt. 2, Plymouth, WI 53073
  log home   (800) 237-8564 (414) 893-8416
YANKEE BARN HOMES, HCR 63, box 2, Grantham, NH 03753
  panelized   (800) 258-9786 (603) 863-4545

Glazing Requirements for a Thermally-efficient House

City	Amount of Solar Glazing In Proportion to Floor Area	Solar Contribution to Heating Needs												
		Annual Total	Monthly Percentage											
			J	F	M	A	M	J	J	A	S	O	N	D
Asheville, NC	25%	99%	99	100	100	100	100	100	•	•	100	100	100	99
Boise, ID	25%	95%	89	100	100	100	100	100	•	100	100	100	100	92
Boston, MA	25%	93%	88	95	97	100	100	100	•	100	100	100	100	90
Burlington, VT	100%	92%	87	94	97	98	100	100	100	100	100	100	98	83
Chicago, IL	25%	93%	90	96	98	100	100	100	•	•	100	100	100	89
Denver, CO	25%	99%	98	99	99	100	100	•	•	100	100	100	100	99
Des Moines, IA	25%	91%	85	95	96	100	100	100	•	•	100	100	100	87
Detroit, MI	50%	94%	89	97	98	100	100	100	•	100	100	100	100	89
Dodge City, KA	25%	99%	98	100	100	100	100	100	•	•	100	100	100	98
Duluth, MN	100%	90%	83	94	96	96	97	100	100	100	100	100	95	79
Fargo, ND	100%	91%	83	96	97	99	100	100	100	100	100	100	97	83
Green Bay, WI	50%	91%	84	94	96	99	100	100	100	100	100	100	98	83
Harrisburg, PA	25%	94%	91	97	99	100	100	•	•	•	100	100	100	91
Indianapolis, IN	25%	91%	86	95	98	100	100	100	•	100	100	100	100	86
International Falls, MN	100%	86%	76	93	96	97	99	100	100	100	100	100	91	73
Louisville, KY	25%	97%	94	99	100	100	100	100	•	•	100	100	100	95
Madison, WI	33%	90%	84	94	95	100	100	100	100	100	100	100	98	81
Minneapolis/St. Paul, MN	50%	90%	83	94	96	100	100	100	100	100	100	100	98	81
New York, NY	25%	94%	91	96	98	100	100	•	•	•	100	100	100	92
Omaha, NE	25%	91%	83	95	96	100	100	100	•	100	100	100	99	87
Portland, OR	25%	96%	93	100	100	100	100	100	100	100	100	100	100	95
Rapid City, SD	25%	92%	85	95	95	100	100	100	100	100	100	100	99	88
Reno, NV	25%	99%	98	100	100	100	100	100	100	100	100	100	100	98
Richmond, VA	25%	99%	99	100	100	100	100	•	•	•	100	100	100	99
St. Louis, MO	25%	97%	95	99	100	100	100	•	•	•	100	100	100	96
Salt Lake City, UT	25%	96%	93	100	100	100	100	100	•	100	100	100	100	94
Seattle, WA	25%	94%	89	100	100	100	100	100	100	100	100	100	100	90
Spokane, WA	33%	90%	81	99	100	100	100	100	100	100	100	100	100	80
Springfield, MO	25%	98%	97	100	100	100	100	100	•	100	100	100	100	98
Syracuse, NY	50%	90%	86	93	96	100	100	100	100	100	100	100	100	83
Youngstown, OH	50%	92%	87	94	96	100	100	100	100	100	100	100	100	86

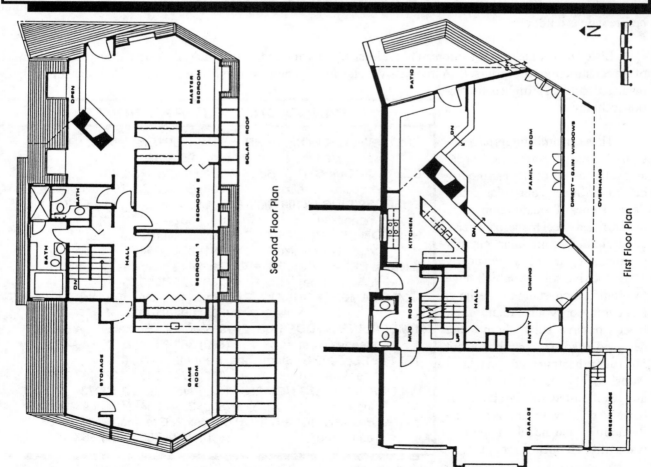

Second Floor Plan

First Floor Plan

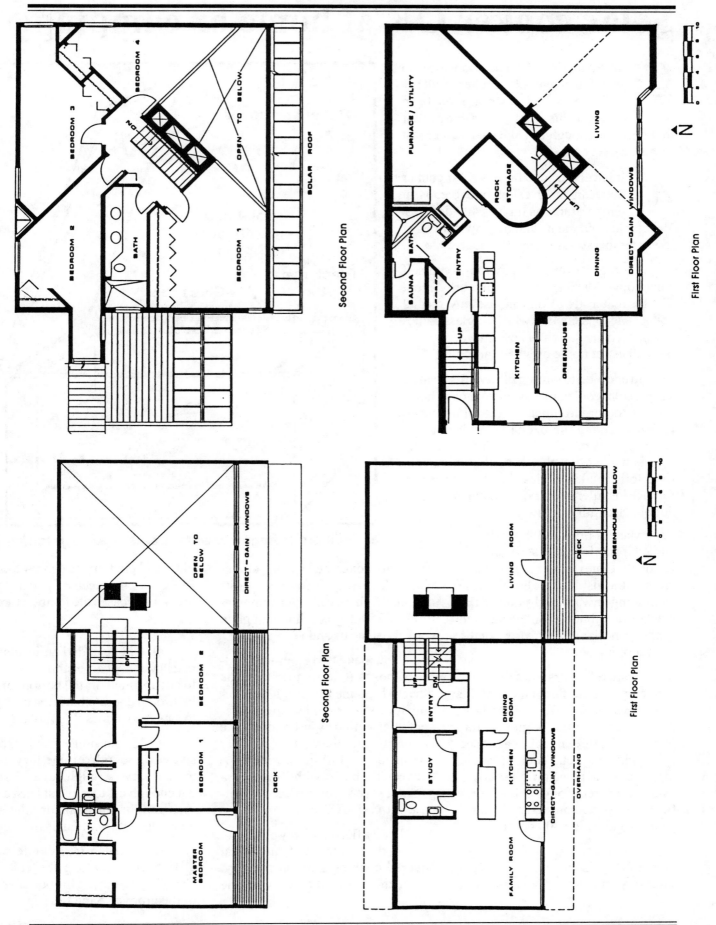

Second Floor Plan

First Floor Plan

Second Floor Plan

First Floor Plan

Solar cooker OK at home or camping

Q.: My kitchen gets hot and I want to make an inexpensive solar cooker to cut my utility bills and cut pollution from power plants. Can I make one myself that gets hot enough to bake cakes and roast meats

A.: It is very easy to build a solar cooker that can bake cakes and breads at temperatures as high as 400 degrees. Vegetables and meats can be slow cooked at lower temperatures under 300 degrees.

There are several effective do-it-yourself solar cooker designs, one costing only about $10 for materials. You can also buy special collapsible solar cookers with fiberglass frames and hi-tech insulation. These are very convenient to use at home or when camping.

In addition to cutting utility bills, using a simple solar cooker instead of your oven helps protect the environment - no pollution, no global warming, no ozone layer damage. A simple, yet very effective, do-it-yourself design is made with plywood, aluminum foil, rigid foil-faced fiberglass insulation (from a furnace installer), cardboard or masonite, and double-strength window glass.

Make a plywood box with an angled front (faces the sun) which is left open. Glue rigid fiberglass insulation to the inside of the box with the foil facing inward and paint it flat black. Mount hooks on the sides to support a horizontal wire tray for the food cooking pot.

Make reflectors from foil-covered cardboard to direct more of the sun's rays into the front of the box. The proper mounting angles are important to capture enough heat. Place a dark glass or metal cooking pot in the cooker and place the glass cover over the slanted front. With the reflectors adjusted properly, the temperature can reach 400 degrees.

The least expensive design (about $10) of solar cooker (called a solar box cooker) is made from old

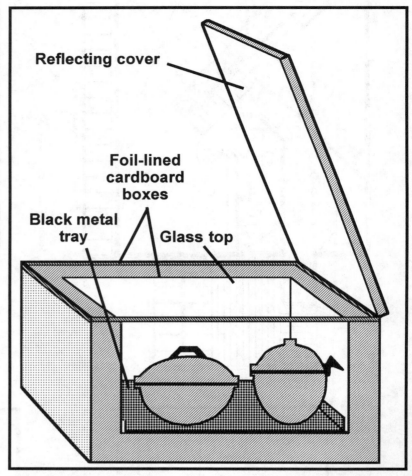

Simple solar heater roasts meats and vegetables

cardboard boxes, newspaper, aluminum foil, and old window glass. In its simplest form, it can reach temperatures of 250 degrees, hot enough to cook most meats and vegetables.

You make two open-top cardboard boxes (one smaller than the other). Line the boxes with aluminum foil. Lay crumpled up newspaper for insulation in the bottom of the larger box and then set the smaller box inside it. Fill in the side gaps between the boxes with more newspaper or several more pieces of foil-covered cardboard.

Paint a flat metal tray black and lay it in the bottom. Put dark metal covered cooking pots on the tray. Cover the top of the box with the

glass and put it in the sun. Adding a foil-covered reflector tilted up from the top increases the temperature.

Q: I have added an insulating pad under my carpet and now I have to cut one inch off the bottom of my bathroom door. What is the best way to saw it so it doesn't splinter?

A: If your house has inexpensive wood doors like mine, they splinter and leave a rough edge. Plan to cut enough off to leave at least a 1/2-inch gap for adequate air inlet area when the bath vent fan is running.

Using a sharp utility knife, score a deep groove along the cut line. Carefully saw along the bottom edge of the groove. Sand the edge.

INSTRUCTIONS FOR MAKING CARDBOARD SOLAR COOKER

Glue foil thoroughly to toppers and reflector flap to withstand wear and tear. Use a 50-50 mixture of glue (water-based white glue or carpenter's glue) and water. On the other pieces, foil can be wrapped, taped, or spot-glued. Put shiny side out, and overlap foil edges slightly.

PART A - INNER BOX - Foiled both sides. Size is important. If the box is too small, it won't collect enough solar energy to get hot enough to cook reasonable quantities of foods. Start with a box that is 19"x23"x8-$^1/_2$" or proportionally bigger. Cover any holes with cardboard patches, then cover both sides with foil. To make a box from flat cardboard, see the diagrams below. It is easier to glue aluminum foil onto both sides after making creases for the folds, but before actually folding the box. Fold the box and use full-strength glue or tape to make the box.

PART B - OUTER BOX - Foiled inside only. 24"x28"x10" or larger. It needs to be bigger than the inside box so that there is about 2-$^1/_2$" space between all four sides of the two boxes and 1" between bottoms. The outer box can be made of material other than cardboard, like plywood.

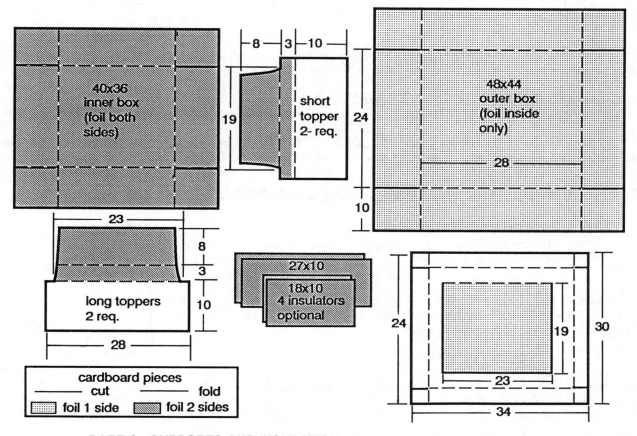

PART C - SUPPORTS AND INSULATION - Glue or tape small stacks of 2" cardboard squares to make 8 supports in the bottom of the outer box. Fill the rest of the bottom with small balls of newspaper or other insulation material. Place the inner box so that there is 2-$^1/_2$" space between the two boxes on all sides. There are many ways to insulate the boxes. Crumpling newspaper is one way. A little crumpled newspaper with four foiled insulators is better. The bottom of each insulator piece is against the outside box, and the top is against the inner box, with crumpled newspaper in the spaces. Other clean dry materials may be used such as wool, straw, or rice hulls. For a hotter box, add foiled layers in the insulation. While cooking, a well-insulated cooker should not feel hot on the outside except the glass.

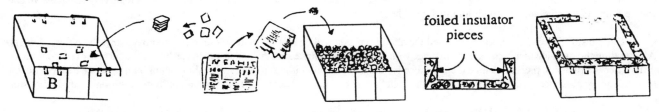

PART D - SEALING THE SPACE BETWEEN THE BOXES- When the insulation is installed, seal the top spaces between the boxes with 4 cardboard toppers. The two short and two long ones are foiled on both sides just to the outside fold. The 4 toppers fold to cover the inside of the inner box and the outer side of the outer box. Glue the toppers in place.

PART E - LID WITH REFLECTOR FLAP - This can be made in several ways, but you must provide a snug-fitting seal. After a basic lid is made, cut three side of an opening that will frame the glass window. Fold back the flap created from the 3 cuts and cover its inside surface with foil to make a reflector. Put silicone caulk or papier mache around the edge if the glass on one side. Then press the glass into the inside of the lid so that there is a seal all the way around.

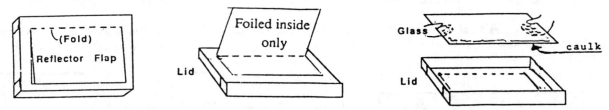

PART F - PROP STICK - These diagrams show one way to prop up the reflector flap. Its free end is set in one of the holes in a stick glued to the lid. Hold the flap in position against the stick with a string looped from the flap to a hole in the lid.

PART G - BLACK LINER TRAY - On the bottom of the inner box, place a thin metal tray painted black. It catches spills and also draws heat to the cooking pots. A cardboard piece covered with aluminum foil and painted black will work.

PART H - DARK COOKING POTS WITH LIDS - It is important to use dark pots with dark, tight-fitting lids. Metal, black enamelware, ceramic, or brown glassware works well.

PLYWOOD HIGH-TEMPERATURE SOLAR COOKER INSTRUCTIONS

OVEN BOX
Start by making the plywood body. Use $3/4$" plywood. Cutting the side, top, and bottom pieces at a rectangular angle will help save wood and make construction easier.

SIDES - #A & #B
Cut the rectangular sides carefully so the top, bottom and back pieces will fit correctly. Draw a line to divide the two side pieces as shown on page **c**. Steady the board and saw along the pencil line. Sand the edges of the two matching pieces.

TOP AND BOTTOM - #C & #D
Glue and nail the sides to the larger uncut rectangle. Glue only the edges that will meet the two side pieces. Line the two side pieces up with the edges at the back of the oven. Nail the sides in place with 2" finishing nails. The uncut piece will stick out after both sides are secure. Draw guide lines on the piece sticking out and carefully cut from line to line. This piece should now fit between the sides to form the top of your solar oven.

BACK - #E
The back of the oven is now ready to go into position. Put glue on all four sides and nail the back to the frame. It is important that all the edges are even and square so the glass cover will lay flat on the oven.

INSULATION
Without the insulation the oven temperature would only reach about 250°. By adding about an inch of fiberglass insulation, the oven will reach an appropriate cooking temperature. Fiberglass insulation with an aluminum foil backing is relatively inexpensive and can be found at heating and air-conditioning supply houses.

Cut the side pieces first, keeping in mind the aluminum side will be on the inside of the oven and not against the plywood walls. After cutting the two side pieces, tack them in place with roofing nails. Make sure the nail is not driven below the surface of the aluminum foil. After the two side pieces are intact, cut a piece for the back and nail it into place. Since shiny aluminum makes a better reflector than an energy absorber, paint the insulation with black "nontoxic" paint. Before you put food in, let it dry thoroughly in the hot sun.

GLASS DOOR
The glass door should be 18-$3/4$" square. This is so the glass will overlap the frame of the oven. Next drill a $3/16$" hole about 2" from the edge and centered. This hole is for a wooden drawer knob. Take the wooden drawer knob and drill a hole in the front center.

Insert a short nail, removing the head first. Let the nail protrude about $3/4$". File and round off the sharp edge. (This is a helpful sun tracking device, no shadow means the oven is pointing directly at the sun.) After filing the top of the nail attach the knob to the glass, using a fiber washer to avoid cracking. Three $1/8$"x $3/8$"x 36" strips of balsa wood are needed to attach the glass cover on the front of the oven. Glue the wood strips to the oven face. Use pins to keep them in place.

The solar cooker is now ready for use. Reflector panels can also be attached to collect more solar heat and make the temperature in your solar oven higher.

REFLECTORS

The best and most inexpensive materials to use are cardboard and aluminum foil. Cut eight 18" squares of corrugated cardboard. Glue two pieces together (making 4 panels) to increase the strength of the reflector. You can use white glue or contact cement. Place a large book on them to make sure they remain flat as they dry. You can also use $1/2$" rigid foam insulation board instead of cardboard.

Cover the panels with heavyweight aluminum foil. Heavier foil is easier to keep flat and smooth producing an effective reflective surface. Glue the foil to the panels with the shiny side outward.

Make aluminum angle brackets to attach the reflectors around the glass cover. The following reflector angles are usually effective. The two side reflectors should be angled out at 145° from the side . The bottom reflector should be parallel with the bottom of the box. The top reflector should be angled at 115° from the top. For more heat, you can make foil-covered corner pieces to mount between the main four reflectors. These also add rigidity to the reflector assembly.

TILT SPACERS

Using the $3/4$" plywood, make two triangular supports with 2" steps cut in them. You will use these to place under the back of the box to adjust the tilt of the glass surface. You will want it to face up higher at midday so it faces the sun more directly. In morning or afternoon, place the spacers under the back of the box to face the glass more directly toward the lower sun.

COOKING RACK

Since the spacers will change the angle of the box, you should make a cooking rack that stays horizontal. Otherwise, when you tilt up the back of the box, the food may spill out of the cooking utensil.

One good method is to use a wire rack from a barbecue grill. Braze a wire hook at each end of the rack to form a triangle at each end. Drill a $1/2$" hole into the inside of each side of the box. Glue short pieces of $1/2$" dowels in these two holes. The wire hooks at each end of the rack will hang over the dowels. Then, as you tilt the box, the rack will always swing to a level position.

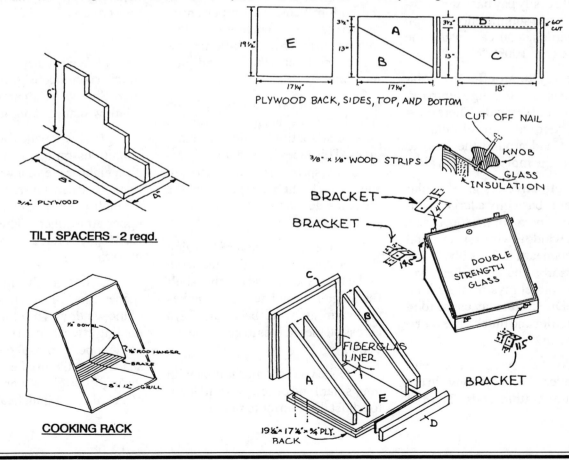

PLYWOOD BACK, SIDES, TOP, AND BOTTOM

TILT SPACERS - 2 reqd.

COOKING RACK

Solar food dryer easy to construct

Q: When fruits and vegetables are on sale, I want to buy large quantities and preserve them by natural drying with no chemical preservatives or cooking. How can I make a simple inexpensive solar food dryer myself?

A: You should be able to build a simple solar food dryer over a weekend for less than $50. Not only will you save money on your groceries, but you won't heat up your kitchen with cooking and canning.

Drying food is a perfect fit with solar and it is the most natural and nutritious method to preserve foods. Dried food takes up little space and lasts a very long time. Using heat from the sun is free and it does not create pollution or contamination of the environment or your food.

The savings from buying larger quantities of fruits and vegetables on sale should easily pay back the material costs in one summer alone. If you have a garden, you can insure the dried foods are 100% "clean".

The key to an effective solar food dryer is maintaining a temperature of about 110° inside. There must also be adequate air circulation through it and around the food to carry away the moisture-laden air.

One effective design of a solar food dryer is basically a large open-top plywood box. For the top, use an old storm window with a sheet metal collector beneath it. This black collector absorbs the sun's heat, yet blocks the direct rays from striking the food. Direct sun may cause food to lose its color and much of its nutritional content.

Build the plywood box with screen-covered vent openings in the top and the bottom ends. The hot

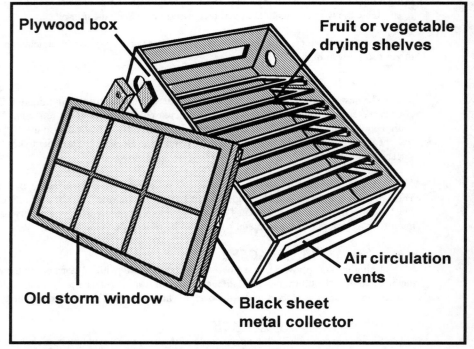

Plywood box — **Fruit or vegetable drying shelves** — **Air circulation vents** — **Old storm window** — **Black sheet metal collector**

Simple solar dryer preserves food naturally

moist air naturally exhausts out the top vent, thus drawing cool dry air in the bottom vent. It is important to properly size the vent holes, or there may be too much or too little air flow to keep the dryer at the proper drying temperature.

Attach legs to the box to tilt it up from horizontal at an angle equal to your area's latitude minus five degrees. This faces it most directly toward the spring, summer, and fall sun. Attach shelf supports on the interior sides so they are level when the box is tilted up.

Make screen covered drying shelves slightly shorter than the depth of the box. Stagger every other shelf flush against the back. This makes the warm air wind back and forth across all the shelves to get to the top outlet.

Once you become familiar with your solar food dryer, you will learn to adjust the interior temperature by

tilting it slightly higher or lower and adjusting optional small movable side vent covers.

Q: We usually run our air conditioner continuously during the summer. Should we open or close our window shades at night?

A: This depends on the weather conditions on a given night. On a clear night, leave your window shades open. Heat can then radiate outdoors through your windows to the cold upper atmosphere. This is most effective if you have double pane thermal windows.

On hot cloudy nights, close the shades to increase the insulation value of the window. The clouds block the cooling effect of heat radiation to the cold upper atmosphere. With the shades open, more heat transfers in through the glass than the cooling effect of the radiant heat loss.

The easiest fruits to dry are apples, apricots, cherries, dates, nectarines, peaches, pears, and plums. The easiest vegetables are beans, carrots, corn, and peas. You can make fruit strips by mixing the fruits in a blender and then spreading the mixture on wax paper. Place it on the drying trays. You can also make pasta and dry breakfast cereals in the solar dryer.

A solar food dryer is basically a plywood box that gets hot in the sun. The heat does two things - 1) it warms the air to speed the drying of your foods, and 2) the warm air creates a natural air flow over the foods to be dried. Since warm air is less dense than cool air, the solar heated and moist air flows out the top vent while cooler dry air is pulled in the bottom. There is a metal solar collector sheet under the storm window glass top. This sheet absorbs the solar heat, yet blocks the sun's rays from striking the food directly. The screen-covered drying shelves hold the pieces of foods. The ideal interior dryer temperature is 110°. It will take about two sunny days to dry most foods. Vegetables must be drier than fruits because of their lower acid content.

Required Materials for Solar Dryer
$3/_4$" or 1" CDX plwood sheet (4x8)
1" x 2" fir or spruce lumber
1" x 3" pine lumber
2" long bolts, washers, and nuts
1 $1/_4$" and 1 $1/_2$" wood screws
Old storm window
Nylon or stainless steel screening
Waterproof glue
Old aluminum printing plates or sheet metal
Silver or white paint in spray can
Non-toxic flat black paint in spray can
Plastic waste basket
Sandpaper or steel wool

In the following do-it-yourself design, the drying shelves are staggered - alternate ones are toward the front or back. This causes the air to wind around all the shelves somewhat as it rises from the lower inlet vent to upper outlet vent.

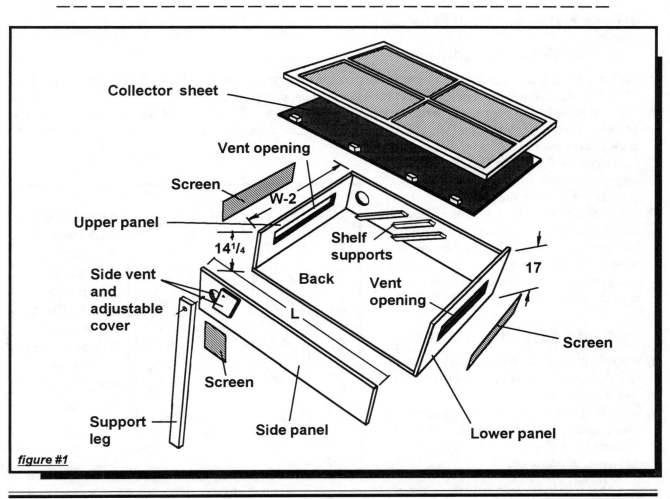

figure #1

DO-IT-YOURSELF INSTRUCTIONS FOR SOLAR FOOD DRYER

1. Construct the box

A) Measure the outside dimensions of your storm window. This will be used for the top of your dryer. If you do not have a storm window and must make the clear top, make it to a size that will divide easily into 4 x 8 sheets of lumber and glazing.

B) Cut the back of your box from the $^3/_4$" plywood. Make the back the same length as the length of your window, but decrease the width by 2".

C) Also from the plywood, cut the side panels of the box. The left and right side panels should be cut the same length as the length of the window and 15" wide. The upper panel should be cut to the same width as the back piece and 14$^1/_4$" high. The lower panel should be cut to the width of the back and 17" high. Cutting the bottom side higher than the top side creates a ledge for the storm window to rest on when the box is tilted toward the sun.

2. Locate the shelf supports

A) Choose and label the "inside" and "outside" of each side piece. Starting with the inside of the left side panel, measure 4" from the top and make a mark at the right edge. From this mark measure in 4" intervals down the rest of the side, marking each at the right edge. Use these marks to draw angle lines (see *figure #2* for the proper angle) down from the right to the left. Repeat this procedure with the right side piece, marking the left edge and drawing the angle lines down from the left to the right. When facing together, the lines on both side pieces should match up exactly.

B) To make the supports for the shelf trays, cut as many 1"x1"x15" slats of wood as you have angle lines. Attach these with glue and screws, staggering their placement. That is, the first support on each side should be positioned 1" from the back edge, the second support 1" from the front edge, the third support 1" from the back edge, etc. This provides for more efficient air circulation.

3. Make the vents

A) At the top of each side panel in the 4" area located before the first support strip, locate the center and cut a hole 3" to 4" in diameter. Take care to avoid cutting the shelf support pieces.

B) The vent holes in the upper and lower panels should be no more than 20% of the surface area of each panel. For instance, if your lower panel is 24" wide and 18" high, cut a rectangular vent approximately 4" high and 18" wide in the center of the board.

C) Cut pieces of nylon screening material about 1" larger than the four vent openings and staple them to the inside of the plywood.

D) Using plastic from an old flat waste basket, cut round or square flaps, big enough to cover the side vent holes. Screw them to the side panels with one screw above the vent holes, so that you can rotate them to adjust the open area of the vent holes.

4. Assemble the box

A) With a helper, pre-assemble the box, as shown in the diagram, to make sure all the pieces fit together properly.

B) Since the box will be exposed to the weather, you should use both waterproof glue and screws to assemble it. Countersink the screw holes for a finished appearance.

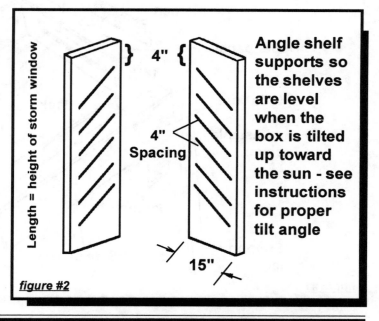

figure #2

C) Starting with the upper panel, attach it with glue and screws to the back piece. Attach each side panel in the same way. The support pieces should be angled down and out. Finally, attach the lower panel to the back and side panels.

D) Spray the outside of the box with a flat black paint. Spray paint the inside of the box with shiny aluminum paint.

E) Let it get hot in the sun for several days before you use it. This makes sure that the solvents have baked out of the paint.

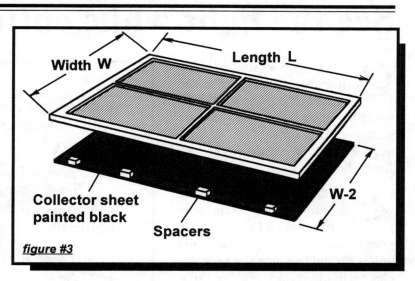

Width W

Length L

W-2

Collector sheet painted black

Spacers

figure #3

4. *Assemble the box*

A) With a helper, pre-assemble the box, as shown in the diagram, to make sure all the pieces fit together properly.

B) Since the box will be exposed to the weather, you should use both waterproof glue and screws to assemble it. Countersink the screw holes for a finished appearance.

C) Starting with the upper panel, attach it with glue and screws to the back piece. Attach each side panel in the same way. The support pieces should be angled down and out. Finally, attach the lower panel to the back and side panels.

D) Spray the outside of the box with a flat black paint. Spray paint the inside of the box with shiny aluminum paint.

E) Let it get hot in the sun for several days before you use it. This makes sure that the solvents have baked out of the paint.

6. *Make the top and collector sheet*

A) Size the collector sheet (*figure #3*) about 2" smaller than the storm window you are using. Use an old aluminum printing plate from a print shop or any other piece of thin aluminum sheet. Clean the plate with steel wool and wipe it with solvents.

B) Spray paint the aluminum plate and the frame of the storm window with flat black paint. This improves the solar heat absorption.

C) Cut eight spacers from the 1" x 2" lumber, each 3" long. Mount these, four on each side, between the aluminum plate and the inside of the storm window, centering the plate over the window frame. When the top is set on the box, the spacers should fit just inside the sides, so that the aluminum plate slips down inside the box. This will position the storm window top on the box.

7. *Position the dryer*

A) You will have to experiment with the tilt angle and the opening of the vents to get the desired temperature and air flow for proper food drying. During the summer, you will get the greatest amount of solar heat by tilting it up at your area's latitude angle minus ten degrees. Since the summer is the hottest season, you will generally tilt it higher or lower to avoid overheating, even with the vents open.

B) During fall and spring, tilting it at the latitude angle absorbs the greatest amount of solar heat. With the cooler weather, you may have to close the side vents or even block the upper and lower vents a little to maintain the proper temperature.

C) It is a good idea to install a bulb-type outdoor thermometer in the dryer. As the sun moves throughout the day, you may want to check the thermometer and change the tilt angle several times.

See the light while cutting energy costs

Q: My neighbor installed a skylight in her family room and it really made the room look much larger and brighter. There are so many different skylight designs available, which would be the best for my home?

A: Installing a skylight can make a dramatic improvement in any room and can increase your home's resale value. Not only will a skylight reduce the need for electric lights, but a new super-high-efficiency one can ventilate and cool your room in the summer and capture free solar heat in the winter.

It is important to select a skylight with the proper design features for durability and energy efficiency. Don't just choose one that is on sale. Select the proper size for your room. An undersized skylight does not provide enough light and an oversized one looks bad and causes glare.

A venting skylight (one that opens) installed in your ceiling will naturally vent the hottest air from your room. This is particularly effective when you don't air-condition in the fall and spring because the evening and morning air is cool. Many skylights are designed so that when they are only partially opened, rain is still blocked from coming in.

You can get either a manual crank or electric motor-operated venting skylight. The electric models operate from a wall switch. You can even get a water-sensing switch to close it automatically when it rains. Since skylights close on compression weatherstripping, they are airtight.

The most efficient type of glazing is low-emissivity (low-e) argon gas-filled insulated glass. The low-e coating reduces heat loss in the winter and heat gain in the summer. It

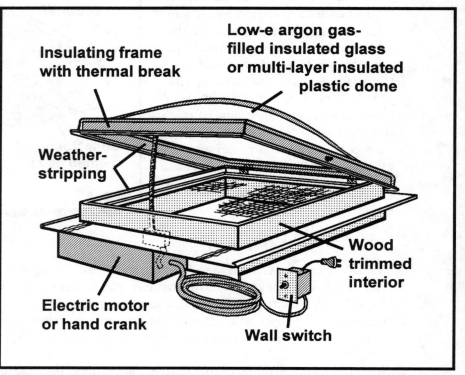

Skylight brightens room and ventilates naturally

Labels: Insulating frame with thermal break · Low-e argon gas-filled insulated glass or multi-layer insulated plastic dome · Weather-stripping · Wood trimmed interior · Electric motor or hand crank · Wall switch

also blocks the sun's fading rays. Argon-gas between the panes saves more energy and blocks noise.

Although glass provides the most clear and distortion-free view, domed multi-layer insulated plastic glazing (often acrylic or polycarbonate) is efficient. The view is slightly distorted, but the amount of light coming in is unaffected and the skylights are virtually unbreakable.

You have several options of materials for the skylight frame and curb. The most common materials are vinyl, aluminum, fiberglass, and clad wood. Fiberglass is one of the strongest materials and shows little thermal expansion and contraction. If you select aluminum, make sure it has a thermal break to avoid energy loss and wintertime condensation.

You can install one of several types of easy-to-open insulated shades for your skylight to save dur-

ing both summer and winter. In my home, I also mount a lightweight magnetically-attached clear plastic storm window under my low-e argon gas-filled skylight in the winter.

Q: I have an old refrigerator that makes a high-pitched sound like a turkey. It still runs fine, so I don't want to replace it. Is this wasting electricity and how can I fix it?

A: From your description of the sound, the sound is probably coming from one of the fan motors that is wearing out. It probably won't waste much electricity until it finally stops or burns out.

There are usually two fans - one condenser and one evaporator. Listen to each motor running to determine which is the noisy one. You should replace it immediately to avoid any serious problems.

The most energy efficient skylight glazing is the Heat Mirror 66 glass. This has two low-e films between two panes of glass and has an insulating R-value of R-7. Double pane low-e/argon gas filled glass has an R-value of about R-4. Regular double pane low-e glass and triple pane clear plastic are R-3. Regular double pane glass (no low-e) and double pane plastic are R-2.

In cold climates, higher R-value glazings are best to save energy and minimize window condensation. Consider installing a skylight with a thermally-broken aluminum, fiberglass, FRP (fiberglass reinforced polyester), or vinyl frame to minimize condensation in the winter.

Recommended Size of Skylight - sq. ft.	
Room size	**Skylight size**
80	3.5
100	4.6
140	6.3
160	7.0
225	9.5
340	14.5

In hot climates, you should consider tinted glazings to reduce the heat buildup. The low-e coating, in addition to saving energy year-round, also blocks much of the sun's fading rays. The plastic glazing is also effective at blocking the fading rays.

In my own home, I installed a double pane low-e argon gas filled skylight with a thermally-broken aluminum frame. In the winter, I attach a magnetic clear acrylic storm window in the skylight opening about one inch below the skylight. This reduces heat loss in the winter and further blocks the sun's fading rays.

Thermo-Vu Sun lite®

FEATURES	INSULATED GLASS WITH RIBBED ALUMINUM FRAME	INSULATED ACRYLIC DOUBLE-DOME WITH RIBBED ALUMINUM FRAME	INSULATED ACRYLIC DOUBLE-DOME "Classic Series"
Glazing	Full 1" AdvantagE™ High Performance Low-E™ Insulated Safety Glass. Clear or Bronze Tint.	Two Insulated DuPont Lucite® "L" Layers. Inner & Outer. Clear or Bronze Tint. Special Colors Available.	Two Insulated DuPont Lucite® "L" Layers. Inner & Outer. Clear or Bronze Tint. Special Colors Available.
Complete Unit (Includes Hatch-Top, Full Curb & Copper Flashing)	Vented (opening) or Fixed (non-opening)	Vented (opening) or Fixed (non-opening)	Vented (opening) or Fixed (non-opening)
Pitched Roof (Standard) Min. 3/12 Pitch Flat Roof (Optional) Curb Mounted (Hatch-Top Only)	Yes (6" curb) Yes (9" curb) Available	Yes (6" curb) Yes (9" curb) Available	Yes (6" curb) Yes (9" curb) Available
Weatherstripping	Co-extruded vinyl bulb and fin seals.	Co-extruded vinyl bulb and fin seals.	Vented: Heavy-duty EPDM closed cell insulating gasket. Fixed: Heavy-duty vinyl foam insulating gasket.
Glazing Seal Thermal-Break Condensation Gutter	Butyl, Top & Bottom One-piece welded vinyl construction. Yes	Butyl Top & Bottom One-piece welded vinyl construction. Yes	Same as Above Gasket Not Applicable
Frame	6063 T-5 Extruded Aluminum with Ribbed Surface. Welded corners. Electrostatically coated bronze paint finish. Assembly screws are concealed under the frame.	6063 T-5 Extruded Aluminum with Ribbed Surface. Welded corners. Electrostatically coated bronze paint finish. Assembly screws are concealed under the frame.	Vented: 6063 T-5 Extruded Aluminum, mill finish. Fixed: Not Applicable.
Copper Flashing Pittsburgh Lock & Corrugated	Premium 16 oz., cold rolled with hand-soldered seams.	Same	Same
Curb	5/8" thick moisture-resistant MDO wood. Other fine furniture woods available.	Same	Same
Hinge	Rain Diverter Hinge	Rain Diverter Hinge	Stainless Steel
Operator (Vented Models Only)	Modular, high gear reduction, low torque, hardened steel drive worm gear, sprocket & concealed chain. Motor optional.	Same	Same
Telescoping Extension Pole (Optional)	Lightweight aluminum, adjusts from 6' to 12'.	Same	Same
Pleated Shade	Available	Available	Available
Insect Screen (Vented Models Only)	Included	Included	Included
Sun Screen (Optional)	Yes	Yes	Yes
Interior Acrylic Storm Panel (Optional)	Yes	Yes	Yes
Mulled Units	Available	Available	Available
Motorization	Available	Available	Available

MANUFACTURERS OF HIGH-EFFICIENCY SKYLIGHTS

AMERICAN SKYLITES, INC., 7451 Dogwood Park, Fort Worth, TX 76118
Aluminum frame   (800) 772-7401   (817) 589-7199

APC CORP., 50 Utter Ave., Hawthorne, NJ 07506
Aluminum frame   (201) 423-2900

BRISTOLITE SKYLIGHTS, 401 E. Goetz Ave., Santa Ana, CA 92707
Fiberglass frame   (800) 854-8618   (714) 540-8950

FOX LITE, INC., 8300 Dayton Rd., Fairborn, OH 45324
Aluminum frame   (800) 233-3699   (513) 864-1966

INSULA-DOME SKYLIGHTS, 83 Horseblock Rd., Yaphank, NY 11980
Aluminum frame   (516) 924-7890

KENERGY SKYLIGHTS, 3647 All American Blvd., Orlando, FL 32810
FRP frame   (800) 347-9334   (407) 293-3880

LANE-AIRE MFG. CORP., P.O. Box 4485, Carson, CA 90749
Aluminum frame   (213) 636-2324

LESLIE-LOCKE, INC., 4501 Cir. 75 Pkwy., Atlanta, GA 30339
Aluminum frame   (800) 755-9392   (404) 953-6366

NATURAL SKYLIGHTS, 925 Orchard Lake Rd., Pontiac, MI 48341
Aluminum or vinyl frame   (800) 222-1502

ODL INC., 215 E. Roosevelt Ave., Zeeland, MI 49464
Aluminum or vinyl frame   (800) 288-1800   (616) 772-9111

O'KEEFE'S INC., 75 Williams Ave., San Francisco, CA 94124
Aluminum frame   (800) 227-3305   (415) 822-4222

PLASTECO, INC., P.O. Box 24158, Houston, TX 77229
Aluminum frame   (800) 231-6117   (713) 453-8696

SKYMASTER SKYLIGHTS, 413 Virginia Dr., Orlando, FL 32803
Aluminum frame   (800) 327-1911   (407) 898-2881

SUN-TEK INDUSTRIES, 10303 General Dr., Orlando, FL 32824
Aluminum frame   (800) 334-5854   (407) 859-2117

THERMO-VU SUNLITE INDUSTRIES, INC., 51 Rodeo Dr., Edgewood, NY 11717
Aluminum frame   (800) 883-5483   (516) 243-1000

VELUX-AMERICA INC., P.O. Box 5001, Greenwood, SC 29648
Aluminum-clad wood frame   (803) 223-3149

VENTARAMA SKYLIGHT CORP., 303 Sunnyside Blvd., Plainview, NY 11803
Aluminum frame   (800) 237-8096   (516) 349-8855

WASCO, P.O. Box 351, Sanford, ME 04073
Vinyl frame   (800) 388-0293   (207) 324-8060

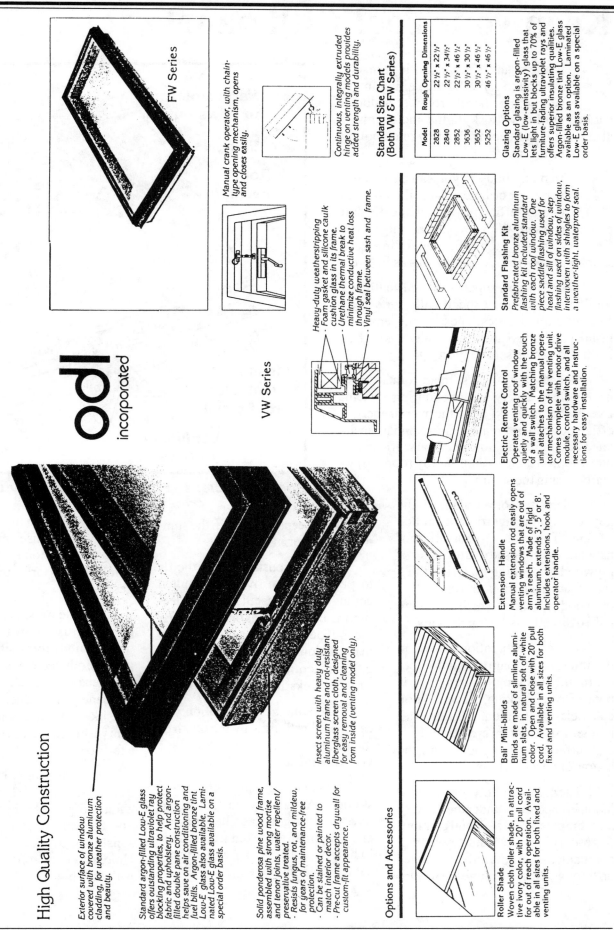

odl incorporated

FW Series

Manual crank operator, with chain-type opening mechanism, opens and closes easily.

Continuous, integrally extruded hinge on venting models provides added strength and durability.

Standard Size Chart
(Both VW & FW Series)

Model	Rough Opening Dimensions
2828	22½″ x 22½″
2840	22½″ x 34½″
2852	22½″ x 46½″
3636	30½″ x 30½″
3652	30½″ x 46½″
5252	46½″ x 46½″

Glazing Options

Standard glazing is argon-filled Low-E (low-emissivity) glass that lets light in but blocks up to 70% of furniture-fading ultraviolet rays and offers superior insulating qualities. Argon-filled bronze tint Low-E glass available as an option. Laminated Low-E glass available on a special order basis.

VW Series

Heavy-duty weatherstripping
Foam gasket and silicone caulk cushion glass in its frame.
Urethane thermal break to minimize conductive heat loss through frame.
Vinyl seal between sash and frame.

Standard Flashing Kit

Prefabricated bronze aluminum flashing kit included standard with each roof window. One piece saddle flashing used for head and sill of window, step flashing used on sides of window, interwoven with shingles to form a weather-tight, waterproof seal.

Electric Remote Control

Operates venting roof window quietly and quickly with the touch of a wall switch. Matching bronze unit attaches to the manual operator mechanism of the venting unit. Comes complete with motor drive module, control switch, and all necessary hardware and instructions for easy installation.

Extension Handle

Manual extension rod easily opens venting windows that are out of arm's reach. Made of rigid aluminum, extends 3', 5' or 8'. Includes extensions, hook and operator handle.

High Quality Construction

Exterior surface of window covered with bronze aluminum cladding, for weather protection and beauty.

Standard argon-filled Low-E glass offers outstanding ultraviolet ray blocking properties, to help protect fabric and upholstery. And argon-filled double pane construction helps save on air conditioning and fuel bills. Argon-filled bronze tint Low-E glass also available. Laminated Low-E glass available on a special order basis.

Solid ponderosa pine wood frame, assembled with strong mortise and tenon joints, water repellent/preservative treated.
- Resists fungus, rot, and mildew, for years of maintenance-free protection.
- Can be stained or painted to match interior decor.
- Pre-cut frame accepts drywall for custom-fit appearance.

Insect screen with heavy duty aluminum frame and rot-resistant fiberglass screen cloth, designed for easy removal and cleaning from inside (venting model only).

Options and Accessories

Bali' Mini-blinds

Blinds are made of slimline aluminum slats, in natural soft off-white color. Open and close with 20' pull cord. Available in all sizes for both fixed and venting units.

Roller Shade

Woven cloth roller shade, in attractive ivory color, with 20' pull cord for out of reach operation. Available in all sizes for both fixed and venting units.

Keep your cool with panel roof

Q: Is there any simple (do-it-yourself) method to remodel the ceiling in my bedroom or family room to a sloped vaulted ceiling with skylights and beams? I also want it to keep my heating and cooling bills low.

A: In many houses, you can easily convert your ordinary flat ceiling into an energy-efficient vaulted or cathedral ceiling yourself. With new super-energy-efficient skylights and the high open ceiling, your room will seem twice as spacious as before.

There are new super-insulated ventilated roof panels designed specifically for sloped ceilings without attics. These strong, easy-to-install panels have insulation values as high as R-40 and can be self-supporting.

Constructed with shiplap joints, these panels form a very airtight roofing system. Even with a large skylight, the overall energy-efficiency can be greater than a standard insulated flat ceiling/attic design. You will also feel more comfortable in your family room, especially during the summer.

Adequate roof ventilation is the key to building an efficient vaulted ceiling. These do-it-yourself roof panels are composed of a top layer of plywood or decking material, thick rigid foam insulation, and drywall or plywood on the bottom. Shingles are nailed directly to the top decking.

There are ventilation grooves in the thick rigid foam insulation beneath the decking. When this is bonded to the decking, the ventilation channels are formed. The drywall bonded to the bottom creates the ceiling surface in your room with the beams exposed below.

The grooves allow for air circulation immediately under the decking and shingles. With a special continuous roof ridge vent (made by several companies), air naturally circulates up through the roof above the insula-

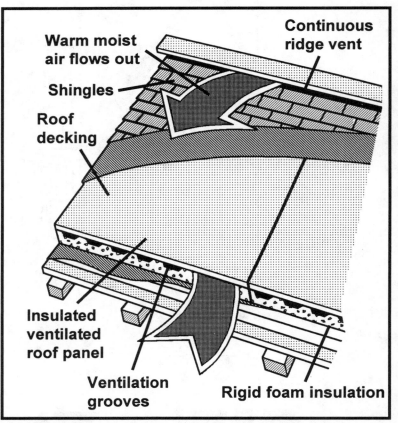

Energy-efficient vaulted ceiling is easy to build

tion. This keeps it cooler in the summer and dryer in the winter.

Another construction method is to put insulation over the vaulted ceiling drywall. Install special reflective insulation shields one inch under the roof decking. These hold blown-in insulation in place and create an air gap for ventilation. The reflective surface blocks the summer sun's heat.

The amount of insulation you can install is limited by the depth of the rafters. Install continuous ridge vents for adequate ventilation.

Select a super-high-efficiency skylight. At the very least, it should have low-e argon-gas filled glazing and a thermally-broken frame. This is the type of skylight I installed in my cathedral ceiling.

Q: What is a bio-gas generator and could we use one to produce energy for our home? I heard of their being used on farms to make natural gas.

A: The most common bio-gas generator uses cow manure to produce combustible methane gas. The gas is produced when organic material decays in a closed tank. The methane gas produced can be used just like natural gas in your home. The waste sludge can also be used as a fertilizer.

Unfortunately, it generally requires a fairly large bio-gas unit (capacity to process the manure from 30-40 cows a day) to provide a reasonable payback on the investment. Unless you work on a farm, it usually isn't feasible.

It is important to have a high attic insulation value with adequate ventilation above it. Without ventilation, the insulation can become damp in the winter and lose it effectiveness. It also will get extremely hot in the summer sun. The easiest method to build a vaulted ceiling is with ventilated insulated stress-skin panels. Manufacturers of these panels are listed on page **b** and product information is shown on page **c**. The cost of an R-25 ventilated panel is roughly $2.50 per sq. ft.. They are available in 4x8 ft. sizes with larger sizes in increments of 2 ft. (4x10 or 4x12).

Stress-skin panels are delivered complete to your home with sheathing on the top for shingles and drywall on the bottom interior side. You can attach these directly over exposed ceiling beams and your roof is basically complete. You can also use other non-ventilated types of stress-skin (means self-supporting) and standard foam core panels for the roof. You will have to add spacers to the top of the panels and lay sheathing over these. These create the ventilation air gap above the insulation. Manufacturers of the foam core panels are listed below. The cost of these is somewhat less than the pre-ventilated designs.

You should install a continuous ridge roof vent to exhaust the air from the ventilation channels in the roof panels. You will also need inlet soffit vents under the roof overhang. The cost of the ridge vents is roughly $2.50 per foot length and they are available in 4 to 10 ft. lengths. Many are made of plastic or aluminum. You just lay the shingles over the top of the installed ridge vent and it is barely perceptible from the ground.

If you plan to build a conventional vaulted roof with rafters, it is easiest to use reflective insulation shields to maintain the ventilation air gap above the insulation. (See page **b** for the manufacturer). With these shields in place, you can blow in insulation for a very energy-efficient roof. The foil covered paper panel also blocks the sun's radiant heat in the summer from getting through to your room.

When you select a skylight, choose a high-efficiency and high-quality unit. I have a low-e, argon-gas filled skylight in the cathedral ceiling in my own house. I also attached an acrylic storm window (with magnetic seals) under my skylight. It saves energy, blocks the noise of rain, and helps to block even more of the sun's fading rays. If you don't air-condition in the fall and spring, a venting type of skylight is particularly effective in a cathedral or vaulted ceiling. The hottest air rises up and is naturally vented out of the skylight.

MANUFACTURERS OF FOAM CORE AND STRESS SKIN PANELS

AFM CORP., P.O. Box 246, Excelsior, MN 55331 - (800) 255-0176 (612) 474-0809
ADVANCE ENERGY TECH., P.O. Box 387, Clifton Park, NY 12065 - (518) 371-2140
ADVANCED FOAM PLASTICS, 5250 N. Sherman St., Denver, CO 80216 - (303) 297-3844
ATLAS INDUSTRIES, 6 Willow Rd., Ayer, MA 01432 - (508) 772-0000
BRANCH RIVER FOAM PLASTICS, *see page b*
CORNELL CORP., *see page b*
ENERCEPT INC., 3100 9th Ave. S.E., Watertown, SD 57201 - (605) 882-2222
FISCHER INDUSTRIES., 1843 Northwestern Pky., Louisville, KY 40203 - (502) 778-5577
FUTUREBILT, A-104 Plaza del Sol, Wimberley, TX 78676 - (512) 847-5721
HARMONY EXCHANGE, Rte. 2, Box 843, Boone, NC 28607 - (800) 968-9663 (704) 264-2314
HOMASOTE CO., P.O. Box 7240, W. Trenton, NJ 08628 - (609) 883-3300
J-DECK BULDING SYS., 2587 Harrison Rd., Columbus, OH 43204 - (614) 274-7755
MARNE INDUSTRIES, P.O. Box 88465, Grand Rapids, MI 49588 - (616) 698-2001
NASCOR INC., 2820 Center Ave., NE, Calgary, Alberta T2A 7P5 - (403) 248-9890
POND HILL HOMES, 4334 Lindell Blvd., St. Louis, MO 63108 - (314) 534-4170
RADVA CORP., P.O. Box 2900, FSS, Radford, VA 24143 - (703) 639-2458
WINTER PANEL CORP., R.R. 5, Box 168B, Brattleboro, VT 05301 - (802) 254-3435

MANUFACTURERS OF ROOF PANELS

VENTED ROOF PANELS
BRANCH RIVER FOAM PLASTICS, 15 Thurber Smithfield, RI 02917 - (800) 336-3626 (401) 232-0270

CORNELL CORPORATION, Box 338, Cornell, WI 54732 - (715) 239-6411

REFLECTIVE INSULATION SHIELDS
INSUL-TRAY, INC., P.O. Box 3111, Redmond, WA 98073-3111 - (206) 427-5930

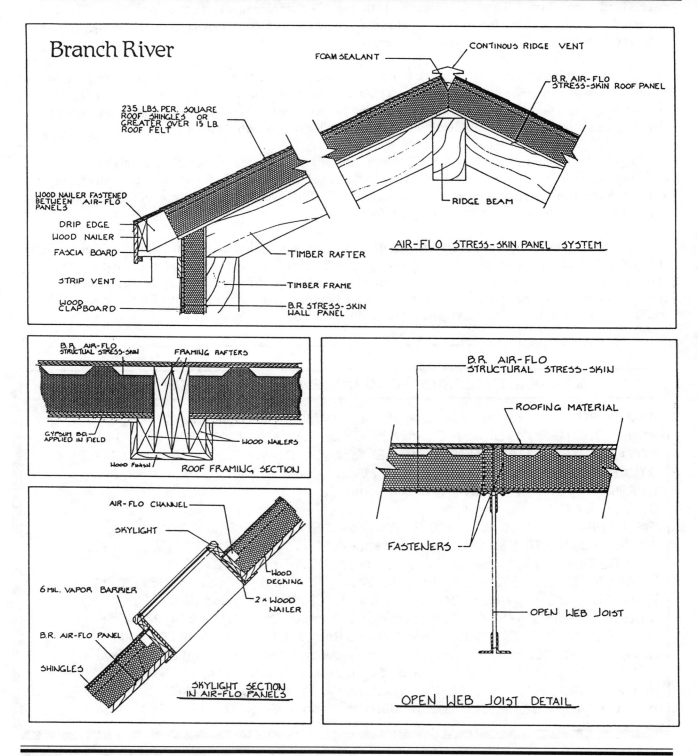

Vent-Top ThermaCal
Ventilated Roof Insulation

Product Description

*Vent-Top ThermaCal is a ventilated nail base roof insulation composed of two layers of waferboard with an air space between them combined with a urethane or isocyanurate foam and a felt skin.

*Patent Applied For

Uses

Vent-Top was designed for ventilating and cooling the sheathing below the shingles. Vent-Top is used with eave and ridge vents over exposed roof decking on cathedral type ceilings. It combines the high R-value of urethane or isocyanurate foam with a ventilated top surface that many users prefer.

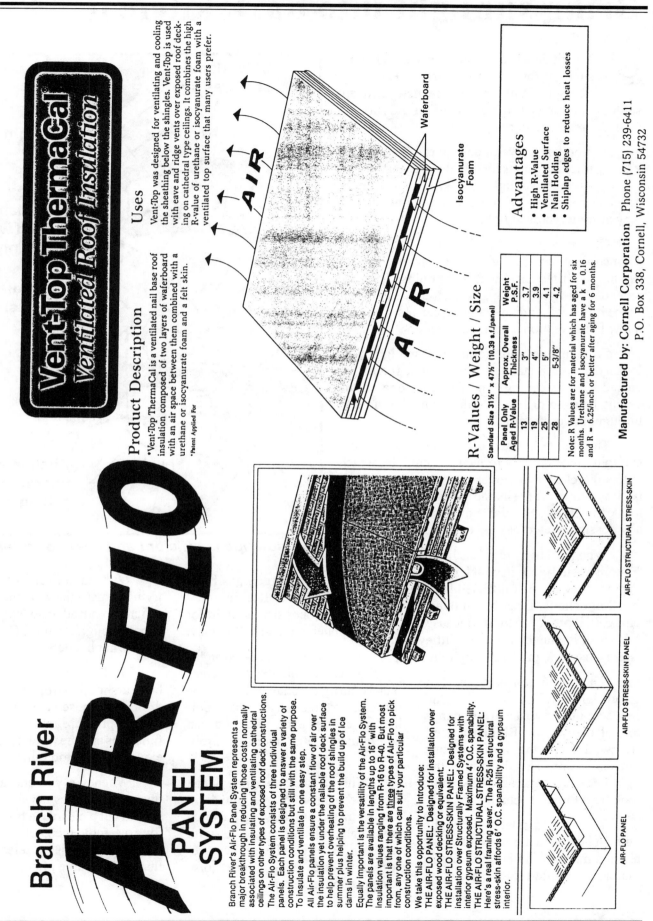

AIR

AIR

AIR

Waferboard

Isocyanurate Foam

Advantages

• High R-Value
• Ventilated Surface
• Nail Holding
• Shiplap edges to reduce heat losses

R-Values / Weight / Size

Standard Size 31½" x 47¾" (10.39 s.f./panel)

Panel Only Aged R-Value	Approx. Overall Thickness	Weight P.S.F.
13	3"	3.7
19	4"	3.9
25	5"	4.1
28	5-3/8"	4.2

Note: R Values are for material which has aged for six months. Urethane and isocyanurate have a k = 0.16 and R = 6.25/inch or better after aging for 6 months.

Manufactured by: Cornell Corporation Phone (715) 239-6411
P.O. Box 338, Cornell, Wisconsin 54732

Branch River
AIR-FLO
PANEL SYSTEM

Branch River's Air-Flo Panel System represents a major breakthrough in reducing those costs normally associated with insulating and ventilating cathedral ceilings on other types of exposed roof deck constructions. The Air-Flo System consists of three individual panels. Each panel is designed to answer a variety of construction conditions but still with the same purpose. To insulate and ventilate in one easy step.

All Air-Flo panels ensure a constant flow of air over the insulation yet under the nailable roof deck surface to help prevent overheating of the roof shingles in summer plus helping to prevent the build up of ice dams in winter.

Equally important is the versatility of the Air-Flo System. The panels are available in lengths up to 16' with insulation values ranging from R-16 to R-40. But most important is that there are three types of Air-Flo to pick from, any one of which can suit your particular construction conditions.

We take this opportunity to introduce:
THE AIR-FLO PANEL: Designed for installation over exposed wood decking or equivalent.
THE AIR-FLO STRESS-SKIN PANEL: Designed for installation over Structurally Framed Systems with interior gypsum exposed. Maximum 4' O.C. spanability.
THE AIR-FLO STRUCTURAL STRESS-SKIN PANEL: Here's a real framing saver. The R-25 in structural stress-skin affords 6' O.C. spanability and a gypsum interior.

AIR-FLO PANEL

AIR-FLO STRESS-SKIN PANEL

AIR-FLO STRUCTURAL STRESS-SKIN

Bring sunlight into dark kitchen

Q. My kitchen is dark and needs more natural sunlight, but I can't afford an expensive skylight. Will one of the new efficient sunlight tubes help brighten my room and should I consider recessed lighting?

A. You have several energy efficient and attractive options for brightening your kitchen - natural sunlight tube kits, a small high-efficiency skylight with a tapered lightwell, or a new airtight recessed light.

On a sunny day, a do-it-yourself 10-inch- or 13-inch-diameter sunlight tube can provide the lighting of fifteen 100-watt light bulbs. The tube extends from your ceiling to just above the roof. Since it is small in diameter, you can install one in a few hours without cutting any rafters.

From inside your room, the sunlight tube looks just like a standard round light fixture attached to your ceiling. The frosted globe on the ceiling helps to diffuse and distribute the sunlight throughout your room.

The inside surface of the small aluminum sunlight tube is highly reflective. Sunlight, which enters the clear tube cover on your roof, reflects back and forth off the inside tube surface with little loss of intensity. Special roof flashing eliminates any possible water leaks.

When the light rays reach the bottom frosted globe in your kitchen ceiling, they are just diffused light in all directions. Even on an overcast day, it produces light. Because it is small in diameter, there is little energy loss as with a larger skylight.

Another option is to install a small high-efficiency skylight. This reduces both the cost and the energy loss of a larger one. Build a tapered lightwell from the roof to your kitchen ceiling. This distributes the light better and makes the skylight look larger than it actually is.

You should select a skylight with an insulated thermally-broken aluminum, vinyl, or fiberglass frame material. Triple-pane plastic or double-pane low-e argon gas filled glass is most efficient. It is important to select the proper size skylight for balanced appearance and efficiency.

There are new recessed lighting fixtures available that are completely airtight. Standard can-type recessed fixtures can lose many dollars of energy each year and can contribute to attic moisture problems.

With this new design, you can lay attic insulation over the light fixture instead of leaving a 3-inch uninsulated clearance gap as with standard fixtures. These new recessed fixtures also reduce noise transmission into your home.

Q: I have heard of someone trying to make the water heater more efficient caused it to explode and shoot through the roof. Can you explain what happened?

A: There are reports of water heaters shooting from a basement up through a house. This may happen when a pressure release valve malfunctions and the water tank literally explodes from too much pressure.

Whenever you add an insulation jacket to a water heater, make sure to cut a clearance hole to allow for free movement of the moving parts in the pressure release valve. Inspect the valve often.

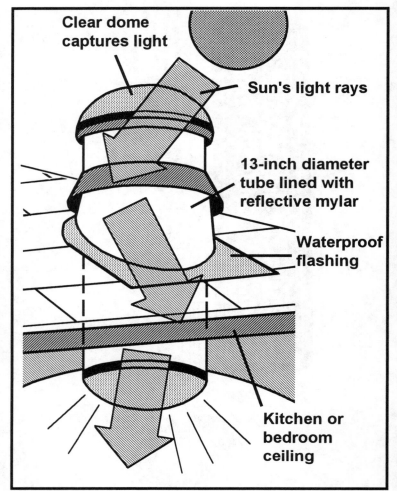

Clear dome captures light

Sun's light rays

13-inch diameter tube lined with reflective mylar

Waterproof flashing

Kitchen or bedroom ceiling

New sunpipe is efficient and easy to install

Natural light reduces electric bills and heat buildup inside your home in the summer. The SunPipe and SolaTube are probably the most efficient methods. Since they are small in diameter (SunPipe - 13 in. and SolaTube - 10 in.), there is little energy loss through the hole in the ceiling. Information on these kits is shown on page **b.**

The basic SunPipe kits retails for $395 and the SolaTube kit for under $260. Both the 10-inch and 13-inch units fit between them without cutting. You can extend them fairly high above the roof to capture more direct light.

A small high-efficiency skylight is also efficient. The smaller, the less the energy loss through the uninsulated ceiling and roof openings. By building a tapered lightwell between the roof and the ceiling, the sunlight from the skylight can be better distributed. Figure #1 below shows recommended skylight sizes for various-sized rooms. "No Lightwell" refers to installation in a cathedral ceiling. Instructions for building a lightwell are shown on page **c.**

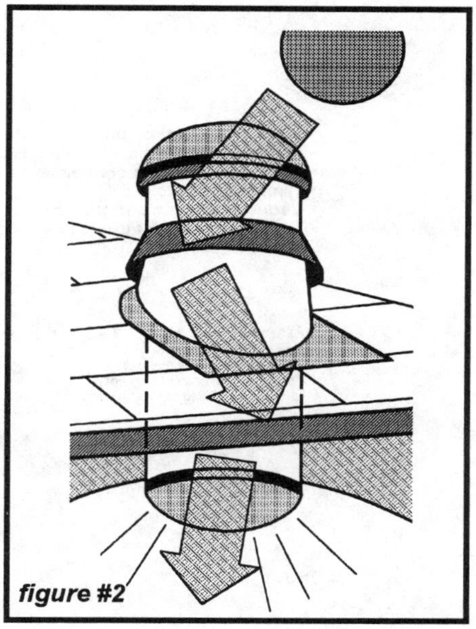

figure #2

Select a skylight with high-efficiency glazing like low-e argon gas-filled glass or triple pane acrylic plastic. In cold climates, an aluminum frame with a thermal break reduces condensation and energy loss year-round. If you do not air condition in the summer, select an operable venting skylight.

If you plan to install recessed lighting, select an energy efficient, airtight design. With most recessed lighting, you must keep attic insulation at least three inches away from the can that extends into the attic. This results in an uninsulated hole and they are very leaky, creating drafts inside your home. The energy loss from a single standard recessed light can be significant.

There are also new types of airtight recessed lights. With the double wall aluminum housing, you can safely cover it with insulation in your attic. One model is made by Juno Lighting, P.O. Box 5065, Des Plaines, IL 60017 - (708) 827-9880 (see page **b**). Check with your local electrical supply outlet for other similar brands.

Recommended Skylight Sizes

Room size	No Lightwell	Straight Lightwell	Tapered Lightwell
feet	square feet	square feet	square feet
8x8	3.2	3.8	3.5
8x10	4.0	4.8	4.4
8x12	4.8	5.8	4.4
8x14	5.6	6.7	6.2
10x10	5.0	6.0	5.5
10x12	6.0	7.2	6.6
10x14	7.0	8.4	7.7
10x16	8.0	9.6	8.8
12x12	7.2	8.6	7.9
12x14	8.4	10.0	9.2
12x16	9.6	11.5	10.6
14x14	9.8	11.8	10.8
14x16	11.2	13.4	12.3
16x16	12.8	15.4	14.0

figure #1

MANUFACTURERS OF SUNLIGHT TUBES

SUNPIPE CO., P.O. Box 2223, Northbrook, IL 60065 - (708) 272-6977

SOLATUBE, 5825 Avenida Encinas #101, Carlsbad, CA 92008 - (619) 929-6060

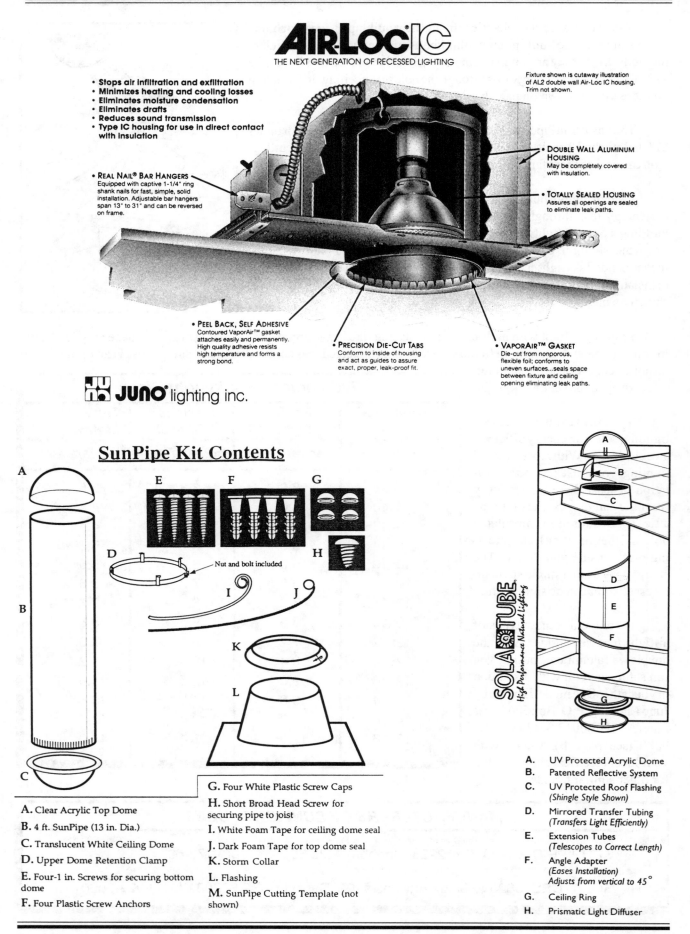

Air-Loc IC
THE NEXT GENERATION OF RECESSED LIGHTING

- Stops air infiltration and exfiltration
- Minimizes heating and cooling losses
- Eliminates moisture condensation
- Eliminates drafts
- Reduces sound transmission
- Type IC housing for use in direct contact with insulation

Fixture shown is cutaway illustration of AL2 double wall Air-Loc IC housing. Trim not shown.

• **REAL NAIL® BAR HANGERS**
Equipped with captive 1-1/4" ring shank nails for fast, simple, solid installation. Adjustable bar hangers span 13" to 31" and can be reversed on frame.

• **DOUBLE WALL ALUMINUM HOUSING**
May be completely covered with insulation.

• **TOTALLY SEALED HOUSING**
Assures all openings are sealed to eliminate leak paths.

• **PEEL BACK, SELF ADHESIVE**
Contoured VaporAir™ gasket attaches easily and permanently. High quality adhesive resists high temperature and forms a strong bond.

• **PRECISION DIE-CUT TABS**
Conform to inside of housing and act as guides to assure exact, proper, leak-proof fit.

• **VAPORAIR™ GASKET**
Die-cut from nonporous, flexible foil; conforms to uneven surfaces...seals space between fixture and ceiling opening eliminating leak paths.

JUNO lighting inc.

SunPipe Kit Contents

Nut and bolt included

SOLATUBE High Performance Natural Lighting

A. Clear Acrylic Top Dome
B. 4 ft. SunPipe (13 in. Dia.)
C. Translucent White Ceiling Dome
D. Upper Dome Retention Clamp
E. Four-1 in. Screws for securing bottom dome
F. Four Plastic Screw Anchors

G. Four White Plastic Screw Caps
H. Short Broad Head Screw for securing pipe to joist
I. White Foam Tape for ceiling dome seal
J. Dark Foam Tape for top dome seal
K. Storm Collar
L. Flashing
M. SunPipe Cutting Template (not shown)

A. UV Protected Acrylic Dome
B. Patented Reflective System
C. UV Protected Roof Flashing *(Shingle Style Shown)*
D. Mirrored Transfer Tubing *(Transfers Light Efficiently)*
E. Extension Tubes *(Telescopes to Correct Length)*
F. Angle Adapter *(Eases Installation)* *Adjusts from vertical to 45°*
G. Ceiling Ring
H. Prismatic Light Diffuser

INSTRUCTIONS FOR MAKING A SKYLIGHT LIGHTWELL

A) Determine the size of the skylight that you need for your room. Select a width that will fit between the roof rafters and attic floor joists. Most skylights are made to fit joists and rafters on 16-inch and 24-inch centers. They will be roughly 1-1/2 inches narrower to allow for the thickness of the 2x lumber.

B) Carefully remove the shingles around the area for the skylight. You will have to replace some of these after the skylight is installed. Saw the hole for the skylight in the roof sheathing. Saw it large enough to allow room for the headers. You may have to saw through a rafter if you selected a wide skylight. Follow the manufacturer's installation instructions very carefully to avoid. Also follow recommended **SAFETY GUIDELINES** when working on a roof.

C) Get up into your attic and remove the insulation from the location on the floor where you plan to make the lightwell opening. Locate the position of the ceiling opening for the lightwell. Saw the opening in the floor. You may have to saw through some of the floor joists if you selected a wide skylight.

D) Using the same size lumber as used for the rafters and joists, build headers across the openings. (See drawing below). If you had to saw through the rafters and joists, you may want to use a double thickness of headers. Install cripple studs to frame the lightwell opening and to support the cut rafters. Double these in the corners to provide extra support for the roof and more rigidity to the lightwell itself.

E) Rigid foam board insulation is the best to use. It forms a natural vapor barrier and has much more insulation value per inch thickness. It is also easy to nail up in the vertical position on the sides of the lightwell frame. If you plan to use this type of insulation, 2x4 lightwell framing lumber is best.

F) If you plan to use fiberglass batt insulation, you should probably use 2x6 or 2x8 lumber to allow adequate space for the thicker insulation. Either use faced-insulation or staple polyethylene vapor barrier to the inside of the lightwell opening. Nail the drywall over it when you finish the lightwell opening. With faced-insulation, the vapor barrier facing should be toward the interior. After you finish the inside of the lightwell, paint it white to reflect as much light as possible.

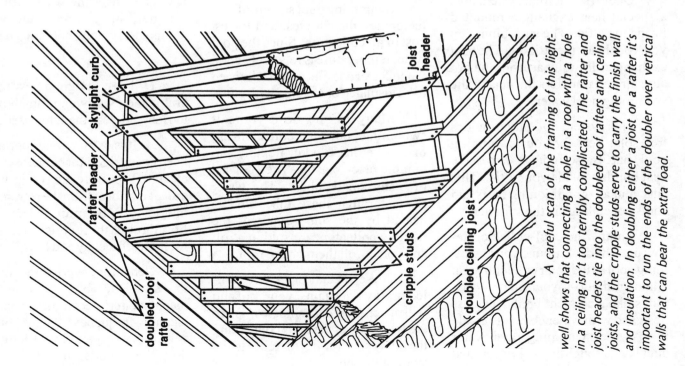

A careful scan of the framing of this lightwell shows that connecting a hole in a roof with a hole in a ceiling isn't too terribly complicated. The rafter and joist headers tie into the doubled roof rafters and ceiling joists, and the cripple studs serve to carry the finish wall and insulation. In doubling either a joist or a rafter it's important to run the ends of the doubler over vertical walls that can bear the extra load.

Solar heat can keep you in the swim

Q.: I want to get several more months use of my swimming pool each year. I would like to use a solar heating system, but I don't want big collectors on the roof. What solar energy options do I have?

A: Heating swimming pool water is probably the most efficient and effective use of solar energy. Installing an inexpensive solar system can easily extend your swimming season by several months. Most of these systems are designed for the do-it-yourselfer to reduce costs. Your existing filter pump circulates the water through the solar system.

There are new designs of swimming pool solar systems that don't require big collectors on your roof. Some don't use any roof collectors at all. Others use special flat collectors that can barely be seen from the ground.

One efficient solar system uses a special heat exchanger mounted inside the attic. The sun shining on your roof heats the attic air. The heat exchanger draws heat from the hot attic air and transfers the heat to the swimming pool water.

This system not only provides free solar heat for your swimming pool, but it also reduces excessive heat buildup inside your attic. This cuts your air-conditioning costs and cools hot ceilings in the summer.

Another no-roof-collector design uses the deck around your swimming pool as the solar collector area. Although the do-it-yourself pool deck looks like a conventional deck, it is designed with water channels inside it. As the swimming pool water circulates through the deck, it is heated

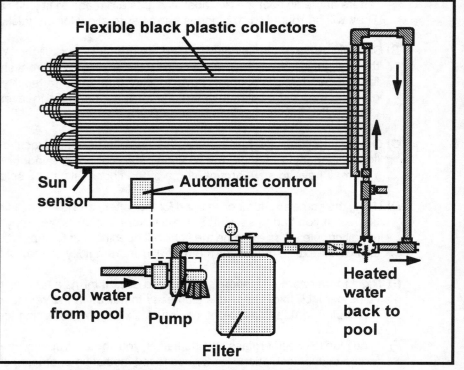

Do-it-yourself pool solar system is effective

by the sun. The pool water also keeps the deck area cooler on hot sunny days.

Swimming pool solar roof collectors are the simplest and lowest cost of all collectors. Since the pool water temperature is relatively cool, the collector does not necessarily need to be insulated or covered with glass.

Many of the do-it-yourself swimming pool solar collectors are made of either rigid or flexible and durable black plastic. They consist of many small tubes. The water flows through these tubes and is heated by the sun. Some of the flexible collectors are sold in a roll and you unroll them on the roof.

These special black pool collectors lay flat against your roof and will match most dark shingles. There are two pipes at the ends connecting the many small collector tubes to the swimming pool.

You can install an automatic sensor that lets water flow through the collector only when the sun is hot enough to heat the water. In midsummer, you can operate the system at night to actually cool the water.

Q: I just bought a new refrigerator and I was wondering how often I should clean the condenser coils?

A: It is extremely important to keep the refrigerator condenser coils clean. These are the coils which transfer the heat from the refrigerator interior to the room air. Adequate air flow through these coils is necessary for high efficiency and long life.

Generally, every three months is enough, but follow the manufacturer's recommendations for cleaning frequency. If your house is very dusty or you have a long-hair dog that sheds, more frequent cleanings are advisable.

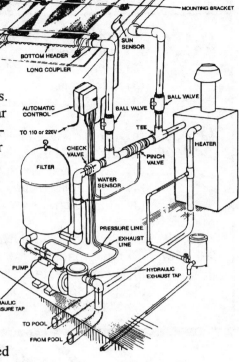

Solar systems for heating swimming pool water are one of the most effective and efficient uses of solar energy. Since the pool water temperature is about the same or cooler than the air temperature, there is very little heat loss to the air. This makes simple and inexpensive collector design and materials very efficient.

Information on several solar systems is shown on the following pages. I have listed the manufacturers of the best priced and most efficient solar systems below. The "inside-the-attic-mounted" solar system heat exchanger is made by Solar Attic (see page **b**). The deck used as solar collector is made by Fanta-Sea. Page **c** shows this deck and typical rigid on-the-roof collector information. The illustration to the right shows a typical Fafco solar installation.

Foolowing the manufacturers' names and addresses below are listed the types of collector - rigid or flexible - they offer and the trade names of their systems. Flexible collectors are easy to mount to a roof, since they generally lay against the roof. They can even be formed to a tile roof. Page **b** shows the typical required materials and solar system size for a flexible collector (Bio-Energy Systems). This is for a moderate climate. The complete material cost for a do-it-yourself installation is about $5 per square foot of collector area. A typical professionally-installed price is $7.50 per square foot.

MANUFACTURERS OF SWIMMING POOL SOLAR SYSTEMS

BIO-ENERGY SYSTEMS, Box 191, Ellenville, NY 12428 - (800) 882-3628   (914) 647-6700
    "SolaRoll" - Flexible on roof

FAFCO INC., 2690 Middlefield Rd., Redwood City, CA 94063 - (415) 363-2690
    "Fafco" - Rigid on roof

FANTA-SEA POOLS, 10151 Main St., Clarence, NY 14031 - (800) 845-5500   (716) 759-6951
    "Solar Pool" - Solar pool deck

HARTER INDUSTRIES, P.O. Box 502, Holmdel, NJ 07733 - (908) 566-7055
    "Hi-Temp" - Flexible on roof

HELIOCOL, 13620 49th St., N., Clearwater, FL 34622 - (813) 572-6655
    "Heliocol" - Rigid on roof

SEALED AIR, 3433 Arden Rd., Hayward, CA 94545 - (800) 451-6620 (510) 887-8090
    "HCP and FP-series" - Rigid on roof

SOLAR ATTIC, 15548 95th Cir. N.E., Elk River, MN 55330 - (612) 441-3440
    "Solar without Panels" - Attic-mounted

SOLAR INDUSTRIES, 1985 Rutgers Univ. Blvd., Lakewood, NJ 08701 - (800) 227-7657
    "Aqua-Therm" - Flexible on roof

SIZE AND SOLAR SYSTEM COMPONENTS THAT YOU WILL NEED

Typical Pool Sizes - gallons		Typical Spa Sizes - gallons	
16' x 32' **(19,200)**	(3) 4' x 30' x 2" SolaRoll = 360 sq. ft. (1) case mastic (1) 3-way diverter valve (1) quick splice repair (1) 2" PVC check valve	**400**	(1) 4' x 30' x 2" SolaRoll (6) tubes mastic (1) 3-way diverter valve (1) quick splice repair (1) 2" PVC check valve
18' x 36' **(24,300)**	(4) 4' x 30' x 2" SolaRoll = 480 sq. ft. (2) case mastic (1) 3-way diverter valve (1) quick splice repair (1) 2" PVC check valve	**500**	(1) 4' x 35' x 2" SolaRoll (6) tubes mastic (1) 3-way diverter valve (1) quick splice repair (1) 2" PVC check valve
20' x 40' **(30,000)**	(4) 4' x 35' x 2" SolaRoll = 560 sq. ft. (2) case mastic (1) 3-way diverter valve (1) quick splice repair (1) 2" PVC check valve	**600**	(1) 4' x 30' x 2" SolaRoll (1) case mastic (1) 3-way diverter valve (1) quick splice repair (1) 2" PVC check valve

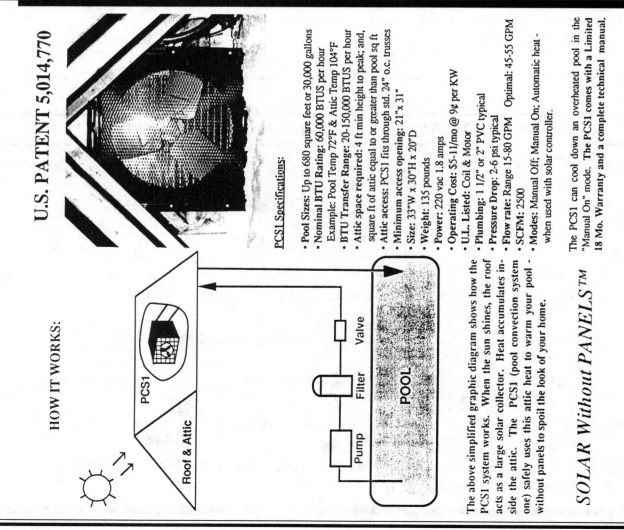

U.S. PATENT 5,014,770

HOW IT WORKS:

Sun → Roof & Attic → PCS1

Pump — Filter — Valve — POOL

PCS1 Specifications:

- Pool Sizes: Up to 680 square feet or 30,000 gallons
- Nominal BTU Rating: 60,000 BTUS per hour
  - Example: Pool Temp 72°F & Attic Temp 104°F
- BTU Transfer Range: 20-150,000 BTUS per hour
- Attic space required: 4 ft min height to peak; and, square ft of attic equal to or greater than pool sq ft
- Attic access: PCS1 fits through std. 24" o.c. trusses
- Minimum access opening: 21"x 31"
- Size: 33"W x 30"H x 20"D
- Weight: 135 pounds
- Power: 220 vac 1.8 amps
- Operating Cost: $5-11/mo @ 9¢ per KW
- U.L. Listed: Coil & Motor
- Plumbing: 1 1/2" or 2" PVC typical
- Pressure Drop: 2-6 psi typical
- Flow rate: Range 15-80 GPM   Optimal: 45-55 GPM
- SCFM: 2500
- Modes: Manual Off; Manual On; Automatic heat - when used with solar controller.

The above simplified graphic diagram shows how the PCS1 system works. When the sun shines, the roof acts as a large solar collector. Heat accumulates inside the attic. The PCS1 (pool convection system one) safely uses this attic heat to warm your pool - without panels to spoil the look of your home.

The PCS1 can cool down an overheated pool in the "Manual On" mode. The PCS1 comes with a Limited 18 Mo. Warranty and a complete technical manual.

SOLAR *Without PANELS*™

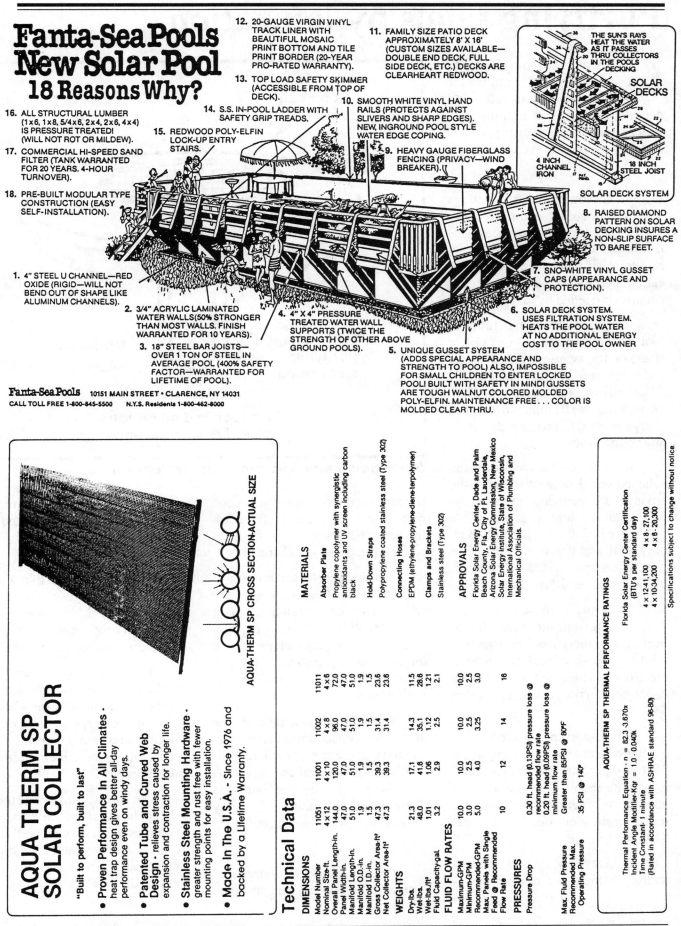

Purifying pools by ionization

Q: Are there any low-electricity usage devices to reduce the amount of chemicals that I need to purify my swimming pool water? The chemicals are expensive and they irritate my eyes.

A: The lowest-electricity-usage types of swimming pool purification devices use the ionization principle to kill algae, bacteria, etc.. Using an ionization purifier can reduce the amount of standard chemicals needed by up to 90%.

One new type of small (about 1 foot in diameter) ionization purifier floats on the swimming pool water and is powered by free solar energy. Solar cells are built into its top. They provide the small amount of electric charge needed to produce the silver and copper ions.

It takes several weeks for the solar-powered ionizer to build up the silver and copper ion levels to the point of adequate purification. Once the water is at the proper ion level, only small additional amounts of ion generation are needed. It then requires just several days use per week.

The purifying ions are not quickly lost from the water due to heat and evaporation like standard pool chemicals. Replacement ion electrodes, which last several years depending on pool usage, cost about $40.

House-current electric-powered ionization devices cost only about $5 to $10 per year for the electricity to operate them. The water is exposed to only very low voltage. The replacement electrodes cost about $100 per set.

In this type of system, the ionization chamber and electrical con-

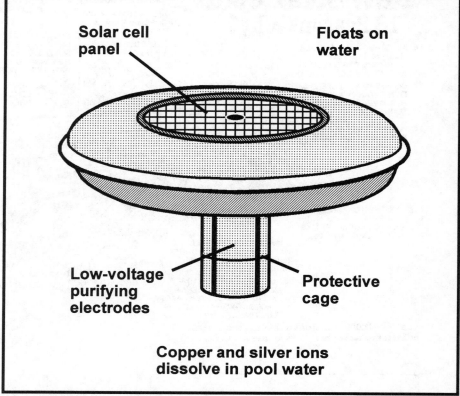

Solar-powered swimming pool water purifier

trols are located outside of your pool, often near the filter pump. The existing water filtration pump circulates water through the ion chamber.

You use a water test kit to measure the level of copper ions in the water. The concentration of silver ions is much lower than for the copper. There is an adjustment dial on the electronic controls that allow you to maintain the desired ion concentration level.

Even though you maintain the proper ion concentration level, you still have to use some standard purification and pH-level chemicals. A periodic "shock treatment" is needed if the water gets cloudy after very heavy usage, a rain storm, etc.

Q: I have made my house more airtight to save energy and my aller-

gies seem to bother me more now. What exactly are dust mites and what can I do to control them?

A: Dust mites are very small animals, about the size of a grain of sand, that live in your bed, carpets, and furniture. Many thousands of these survive by eating tiny flakes of dead skin that drop off our bodies.

They stay pretty well anchored, but their tiny feces pellets and worn out shells become airborne when you walk on the carpet, shake out the bedding, and vacuum clean. These get on your mucous membranes and cause allergies.

The best way to control them is to keep the relative humidity lower. The mites don't survive well below 50% relative humidity. A high-quality air cleaner can also help to remove some of the airborne particles.

Ionization types of swimming pool and spa purifiers are effective. You will still need to use some chemicals with these systems, but the amount is greatly reduced. This generally involves a shock treatment several times a swimming seasons. You will also still have to use some chemicals to control the pH of the water.

Two of the companies listed below make solar-powered ionization purifiers. Floatron makes the model shown in figure #1. (Basic operating instructions are shown on page **b**. It actually floats on the surface of the water. Obviously, it is most effective in areas where there is a lot of sunshine. The other two models have solar panels that mount on the ground. These panels are attached the electrode that are inserted in the water, often in the filter plumbing. Information on a solar powered system (Miller Technology) is shown on page **b** and a diagram of a typical 110-volt installation is shown on page **c**.

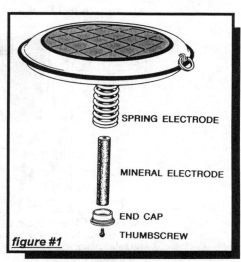

SPRING ELECTRODE

MINERAL ELECTRODE

END CAP

THUMBSCREW

figure #1

MANUFACTURERS OF IONIZATION SWIMMING POOL PURIFICATION SYSTEMS

AQUATECH POOL PURIFC'N, 2061 NW Boca Raton Blvd. #104, Boca Raton, FL 33431
large 110-volt house power   (407) 362-0836

CAREFREE CLEARWATER, 2307-A Browns Bridge Rd., #148, Gainesville, GA 30501
110-volt house power   (706) 778-9416

CARIBBEAN CLEAR, 101 Watersedge Shelter Cove, Hilton Head, SC 29928
110-volt house power   (803) 686-3424

CRYSTAL KING INC., P.O. Box 455, Middleville, MI 49333
110-volt house power   (800) 243-5464

ELECTRON PURE, 1300 Slaughter Rd., Madison, AL 35758
110-volt house power   (800) 525-7458   (205) 430-8041

ENVIRONMENTAL WATER PRODUCTS, 9353 Eton Ave., Chatsworth, CA 91311
110-volt house power   (818) 718-1795

FLOATRON, P.O. Box 51000, Phoenix, AZ 85076
solar-powered   (602) 345-2222

LIFEGUARD PURIFICATION SYS, 4806B N. Coolidge Ave., Tampa, FL 33614
solar & 110-volt house power (800) 678-7439 (813) 875-7777

MILLER TECHNOLOGY, P.O. Box 1651, Ballwin, MO 63011
solar-powered   (314) 825-2841

OXYGEN TECHNOLOGY, 8229 Melrose Dr., Lemena, KS 66214
110-volt house power   (913) 342-9436

SUPERIOR AQUA ENTERPRISES, 7350 S. Tamiami Tr., Sarasota, FL 34231
110-volt house power   (813) 923-2304

LIQUITECH INC., 241 S. Frontage Rd. #40, Burr Ridge, IL 60521
110-volt house power   (800) 635-7873

VAK PAK, 9731 Beach Blvd., Jacksonville, FL 32246
110-volt house power   (800) 877-1824 (904) 942-2267

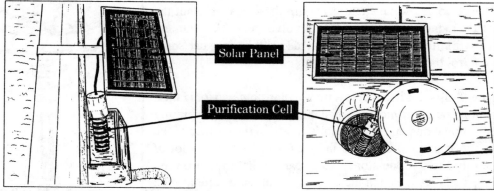

Above Ground Pools

In Ground Pools

Solar Panel

Purification Cell

The SOLARCIDE unit can be installed for an above ground pool by mounting the solar panel in an optimum location and placing the purification cell in the skimmer.

The same installation can be used for in ground pools by installing the solar panel in an optimum location and placing the purification cell in the skimmer

In-Line Option

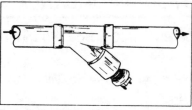

Installation of the SOLARCIDE purification cell can also be made permanent by use of the optional in-line equipment.

SPECIFICATIONS

Solar panel measurements:
(3 sizes)
  5 1/4" x 5 1/4"
14 5/8" x 8 1/8"
14 5/8" x 16 1/4"

Purification cell:
7" long x 2 1/2" dia.

Shipping Weight:
5-8 lbs. (approx)

"Solarcide" by Miller Technology

Getting Started

1) Begin with normally chlorinated water, approx. 1.0 ppm (parts per million) chlorine, and a normal pH of 7.2 - 7.4. Use your regular chlorine test kit.

2) Place your Floatron in the water in bright sunlight.

3) Keep circulation pump on when ionizing, i.e. sunlight hours.

4) Read and understand the copper test kit instructions and test water for copper content. It should read 0 ppm at this beginning point. If you have a positive reading at this point, consult the factory.

The First Few Weeks

1) Float daily.

2) Maintain normal chlorine level and pH.

3) Inspect spring electrode for accumulation of white, scaly deposits. Scaling is more rapid in hard water. Clean according to electrode cleaning instructions.

4) Test copper level every few days. Normal range is .20 - .40 ppm copper.

Upon Reaching Copper Level (.20 - .40 ppm)

1) Allow chlorine to fall to approximately .20 - .40 ppm over the next few days. This is a trace amount and is all that is normally necessary.

Note: Hard or hot water conditions or high swimmer load requires a greater amount of chlorine

2) If copper ion reading exceeds .40 ppm, remove unit from water.

Routine Care

1) Test copper level once a week, more often if water is added.

2) When copper level falls off to low range reading, replace Floatron into water until .20 - .40 ppm is reestablished.

3) Keep electrodes clean, very important.

4) Maintain approx. .20 - .40 ppm chlorine.

5) Maintain pH at 7.2 - 7.4 in normal manner.

Floatron startup instructions

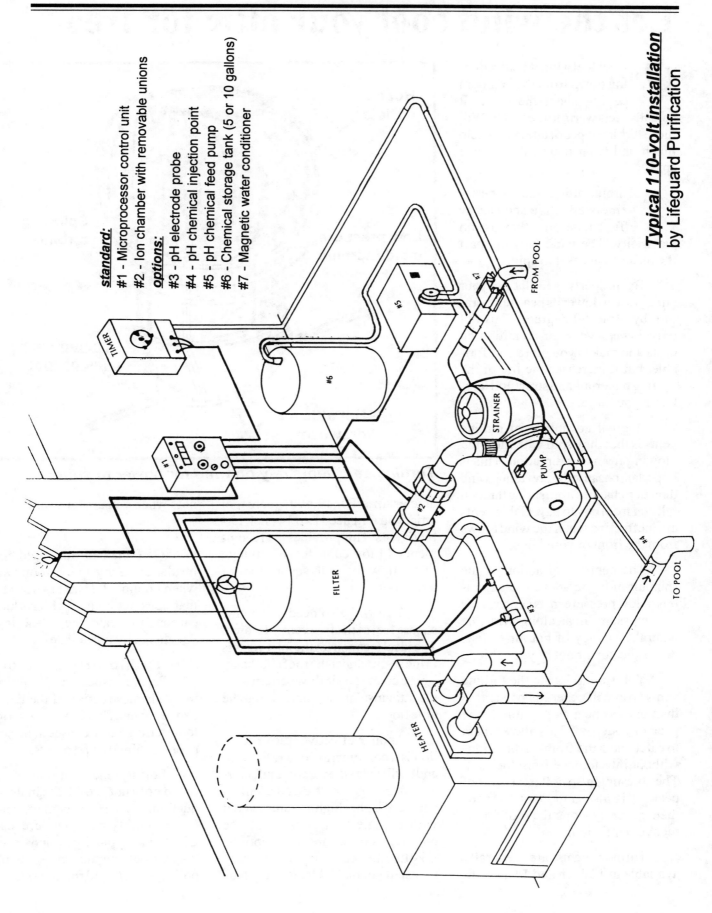

Typical 110-volt installation
by Lifeguard Purification

standard:
#1 - Microprocessor control unit
#2 - Ion chamber with removable unions

options:
#3 - pH electrode probe
#4 - pH chemical injection point
#5 - pH chemical feed pump
#6 - Chemical storage tank (5 or 10 gallons)
#7 - Magnetic water conditioner

TIMER

FILTER

HEATER

STRAINER

PUMP

FROM POOL

TO POOL

Let the wind cool your attic for free

Q: I can feel a lot of heat radiating down from the bedroom ceiling under the attic. It actually feels warm to the touch. Will those turbine types of attic vents help much and what makes the turbine spin?

A: Turbine attic vents can be extremely effective and energy efficient because they use no electricity. The wind blowing past the turbine causes it to spin.

By properly ventilating your attic, you can lower its peak temperature by 40 to 50 degrees. This not only lowers your air-conditioning costs and makes you more comfortable, but it increases the life of the roofing materials and structural lumber in your attic.

A great advantage of turbine vents is that they spin with the wind blowing from any direction. This is important because the prevailing wind direction changes from spring through fall and from day to day. Gable vents are ineffective when the wind blows from the front of your house.

The centrifugal action of the spinning turbine blades creates a nimbus of low pressure in its center. This low pressure area, along with the natural tendency of hot air to rise, draws the hot air out of your attic.

You should locate the turbine vents (you will generally need more than one) as near as possible to the peak of your roof. This allows them to catch the wind from all directions without interference from the roof. The attic air is also hottest at the roof peak. It is also important to space them properly along the roof for effective ventilation.

Turbine vents are generally available in 12-inch and 14-inch di-

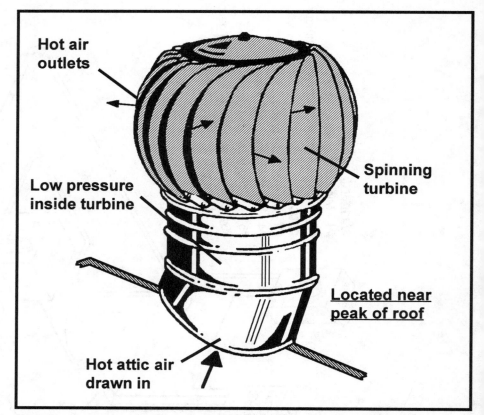

Hot air outlets

Low pressure inside turbine

Spinning turbine

Located near peak of roof

Hot attic air drawn in

Turbine attic vents rely on wind for power to spin

ameter sizes. For a 1,500 square foot attic, you will need two 14-inch turbine vents. This provides the recommended 1 to 2 cubic feet per minute of air flow for each square foot of attic floor area.

You will also need about five square feet of net free vent inlet area. The ideal location for the inlet vents is in the soffits under the roof overhang. These create an air flow pattern over the attic insulation, thus cooling the attic floor.

Another effective attic vent option is a combination of a ridge vent and soffit vents. Several manufacturers offer ridge vents that are only a couple of inches high and are covered with shingle material. From the ground, they are barely perceptible. Like turbine vents, they are very easy to install yourself. Use a safety har-

ness when you are on a roof.

Q: I plan to add rigid foam insulation to my living room walls when I remodel. I want to use a type that does not contain chlorofluorocarbons that hurt the ozone layer. Are there any type made?

A: Chlorofluorocarbons (CFC's) are suspected of contributing to the destruction of the Earth's ozone layer. This has very serious long-term health consequences for people, animals, and plants.

Polystyrene foam insulation board does not use CFC's in its production. Generally pentane and a flame modifying agent are used. CFC's are typically found in urethane, isocyanurate, and some phenolic types of rigid foam insulation.

You should be able to buy attic turbine vents at most building supply and home center outlets. You may have to contact the manufacturers of the continuous ridge vents for the names of local dealers. When installing a ridge vent, you should have about one square foot of vent area for each 300 square feet of attic floor area. Information on the ridge vents is shown on pages **b** and **c**.

MANUFACTURERS OF CONTINUOUS ATTIC RIDGE VENTS

AIR VENT INC., 4801 N. Prospect Rd., Peoria Hts., IL 61614 - (800) 247-8368 (309) 688-5020
   "Filter Vent" - $20 for 10 ft. section

BENJAMIN OBDYKE, John Fitch Ind. Park, Warminster, PA 18974 - (215) 672-7200
   "Roll Vent" - $49.95 for 20 ft. roll

COBRA VENTILATION CO., 1361 Alps Rd., Wayne, NJ 07470 - (800) 688-6654
   "Cobra Ridge Cent" - $45 for 20 ft. roll

COR-A-VENT INC., 16250 Petro Dr., Mishawaka, IN 46544 - (800) 837-8368 (219) 255-1910
   "Cor-A-Vent" - $12 for 4 ft. section

LOMANCO, PO Box 519, Jacksonville, AR 72076 - (800) 643-5596 (501) 982-6511
   "SOV-4" - $17.89 for 4 ft. section

SIZING TURBINE VENTILATION SYSTEMS

Square feet of attic floor area	Number of turbine vents required	Turbine vent size (inches)	Min square feet of inlet louver area required	Min. number * and size (inches) of eave vents
1,200	2 each	12	4.0	9 ea. 8 x 16
1,500	2 each	14	5.0	12 ea. 8 x 16
1,800	3 each	12	6.0	14 ea. 8 x 16
2,100	3 each	14	7.0	16 ea. 8 x 16
2,400	4 each	12	8.0	18 ea. 8 x 16

* Use twice the number of 4 x 16-inch eave vents

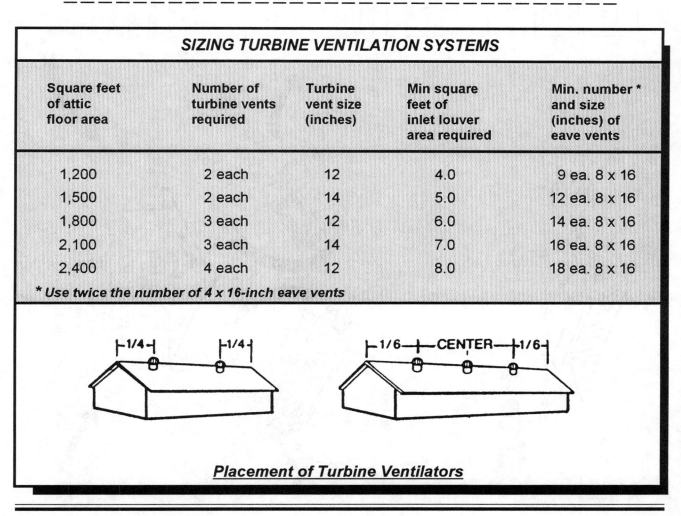

Placement of Turbine Ventilators

COR-A-VENT

IS MADE FROM EXTRUDED, HIGH DENSITY POLYETHYLENE SHEETS LAMINATED INTO A CORRUGATED STRUCTURE.

Cor-A-Vent recommends that the entire main ridge of the house be covered with the ridge vent.
Reason: The architectural beauty of a continuous ridgeline & balanced ventilation.
Continuous orientation of ridge & soffit vents is the most efficient ventilation.

	Steps to determine ventilation required	
Good Ventilation One to One Rule Use 3 lineal feet (Per 100 Sq. Ft. attic)	Cor-A-Vent required for each 100 sq. ft. of attic area	Superior Ventilation One Percent Rule Use 4 lineal feet (Per 100 Sq. Ft. attic)
1/260th Ventilation	Your answer represents the amount of Cor-A-Vent required. (Without Soffit Vents, ratio equals)	1/200th Ventilation
1/130th Ventilation	An equal amount of ventilation must also be placed in the overhangs or Soffits, to insure proper ventilation. (This ratio equals)	1/100th or One Percent
One to One Rule ONE SQ. INCH (VENT) TO ONE SQ. FOOT (ATTIC)	**NOTE:** Air flow 7½ M.P.H. using one percent rule. Equals - 1.5 Cubic foot per minute. Superior ventilation for summer and winter.	One Percent Rule. 1½ SQ. INCH (VENT) TO ONE SQ. FOOT (ATTIC)

For every square inch of exhaust vent you must balance it with one square inch of intake vent.

COR-A-VENT ROOF RIDGE VENTILATOR INSTALLATION INSTRUCTIONS

STEP 1. Cut a 3½" slot at ridge (1¾" slot each side of center line of ridge).
STEP 2. Apply roof shingles in normal fashion. (Trim top of shingles flush with slot in roof sheathing).
STEP 3. Nail one shingle ridge cap at each end of ridge, as with conventional ridge cap application.
STEP 4. Slip metal end cap over end of first and last pieces of Cor-A-Vent. Align Cor-A-Vent over center line of ridge and nail in place.
STEP 5. Apply asphalt shingle ridge caps. Go over Cor-A-Vent with shingle ridge caps using the same color for the caps as the roof shingles. Nail in conventional manner using long nails provided.
STEP 5-A. (Mission Tile) or (Cedar Shakes). (FOLLOW DETAILED INSTRUCTIONS IN CARTON)

HIP ROOF — If the ridge length is too short for proper ventilation, Cor-A-Vent may be applied in equal lengths to the upper end of the hips to provide the required ventilation. (FOLLOW DETAILED INSTRUCTIONS IN CARTON)

SOFFIT VENT — To help create this flow of air out of the top of the building, there must also be soffit vents installed under the eaves. Soffit vents may be larger in square inches of free air, but not less than the square inches of free air provided by the ridge vent.
Recommend S-400 STRIP VENT. (FOLLOW DETAILED INSTRUCTION IN CARTON)

As a natural ventilator Cor-A-Vent meets all building code requirements when installed according to the instructions.

COR-A-VENT SPECIFICATIONS

Product	Cat. No.	Net Free Vent Area Per. Lin. Ft.	Fan Capacity Per Lineal Ft.	Units Per Carton	Size		Carton Weight	Color
Ridge Vent	V-400	18 Sq. Inches Per. Lin. Ft.	240 C.F.M.	12	4 Ft. Length	1" x 2"	28 Lbs.	Black
Strip Vent	S-400	9 Sq. Inches Per. Lin. Ft.	120 C.F.M.	84	4 Ft.		36 Lbs.	Black or White
End Cap	E.C. .400	ALUMINUM		12	Eleven Inches		1¼ Lbs.	White

COR-A-VENT INC.
16250 Petro Drive
MISHAWAKA, INDIANA 46544
(219) 255-1910

YOUR LOCAL DEALER IS

COR-A-VENT INC.
16250 PETRO DRIVE • MISHAWAKA, INDIANA 46544 • (219) 255-1910

DRAWS ATTIC AIR

RELATIVE WIND

LOW AIR PRESSURE

HIGH PRESSURE

AIR

VENT

SHEATHING

TRUSS

SNOW DRIFT TEMPORARY SEALS

RIDGE

PLYWOOD

RAFTER

OR

HOW DOES COR-A-VENT WORK?
Three Natural Forces
1. Aero-Dynamic Principle (Lift of an Airplane)
2. Thermo Effect (Hot Air Rises)
3. Diffusion (Moisture Movement)

SOFFIT AIR

INTAKE

ROLL VENT — Product Description:

Roll Vent™ attic ventilation system is the only self-contained ridge vent on a roll. This space age material is a durable, two layer composite consisting of a NYLON-POLYESTER, non-woven, non-wicking fabric, heat bonded to a compression-resistant, open nylon matting of three-dimensional construction.

Composition and Materials:

1. Matting: NYLON 6 plus carbon black for UV resistance.
2. Fabric: NYLON-POLYESTER non-woven

Dimensions:

Weight: .174 lbs/lin. ft.
Thickness: .8 inches minimum
Width: 10.25 ± 10.5 inches
Length: 20' & 50' rolls

Color:

Standard: Black on Charcoal grey

Maintenance:

Roll Vent™ is completely hidden by shingles and requires no maintenance.

Net Free Area:

Total NET FREE AREA is 18 sq. inches per linear foot minimum.

Codes:

Roll Vent™ installed properly is in compliance with nationally recognized model codes, including CABO, BOCCA, SBCCI, and ICBO, and meets requirements of FHA, and U.S. Department of Housing and Urban Development.

Technical Data:

Property	Test	Values	Property	Test	Values
Fabric Air Permeability	ASTM D737	215 cu.ft. per minute @ .01 in. of water pressure differential	Resiliency	100 PSI (3 cycles)	80% recovery in 30 min.
			Deflection vs. load	100 PSF / 1000 PSF	.051 in. / .131 in.

MARKETED BY BENJAMIN OBDYKE, INCORPORATED
John Fitch Industrial Park, Warminster, PA 18974, 215/672-7200

COBRA™ RIDGE VENT SPECIFICATIONS.

Product Description COBRA™ RIDGE VENT attic ventilation system is the only single-layer, non-fabric-covered ridge vent on a coil. It is a strong, durable, modified polyester, non-woven, non-wicking, fiber-based matting of three-dimensional construction.

Composition and Materials UV stable, polyester composite.

Dimensions
Weight: 4.5 oz./lin. ft.
Thickness: 5/8 inches minimum
Width: 10.5 ± 0.125 inches
Length: 20 ft. or 50 ft. rolls

Maintenance COBRA™ RIDGE VENT properly installed is maintenance-free.

Color Black

Installation COBRA™ RIDGE VENT is easily installed without special tools. Joints can be simply cut square, butted and caulked without connectors or baffles. COBRA™ cannot dent, crack, or rust, and has no sharp edges. Cobra is flexible, easy to handle and transport, and conforms to any roof pitch.

Availability and Cost COBRA™ RIDGE VENT is available through an extensive distributor network. For quotations, contact Berger Building Products for the location of your nearest distributor or representative.

Net Free Area Minimum NET FREE AREA is 12 sq. in. per lin. ft. COBRA™ RIDGE VENT must be installed with soffit vents to meet HVI recommendations. Air flow is unrestricted by any fabric covering. COBRA™ exceeds NET FREE AREA flow indicated due to a venturi action allowing constant air siphoning.

Codes COBRA™ RIDGE VENT installed properly is in compliance with nationally recognized model codes, including CABO, BOCA, SBCCI and ICBO, and meets requirements of FHA and the U.S. Department of Housing and Urban Development. COBRA™ RIDGE VENT is licensed for sale under U.S. Patent Pending.

COBRA™ RIDGE VENT Testing Certified by Construction Research Laboratories, Miami, FL (Report #5515B, Static Pressure Structural Uplift Test, Report #5515C, Wind Driven Rain Test @ 8 in. rainfall per hr. at 100 MPH), ETL Testing Laboratories, Inc., Cortland, NY (Accelerated Dust Clog Test, Self-Ignition Temperature Test), United States Testing Company, Inc. Fairfield, NJ (Air Permeability Test), Penwalt Laboratories, CA (UV Stability Test), Atochem, CT (Standard Tear and Tensile Test, Cold Crack Resistance Test).

Technical Data

Property	Test	Values
Air Permeability	ASTM D737	>>760 cu. ft. per minute
Tear and Tensile Strength	ASTM D1294-86	Tear: Machine 42 p.s.i. Counter 35.5 p.s.i.
	ASTM D2261-83	Tensile: Machine 55 p.s.i Counter 64 p.s.i
Self-Ignition Temperature	ASTM D1929	963° F.
Cold Crack Resistance	ASTM C115	-25° F.

BUILDING SECTION

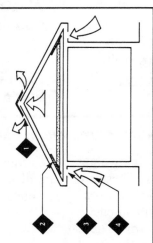

1. COBRA™ RIDGE VENT attic ventilation system under cap shingle.
2. COBRA™ SOFFIT VENT.
3. BERGER Vinyl Soffits for proper airflow. (Check local building codes for minimum ventilation requirements.)
4. Air flow.

RIDGE DETAIL

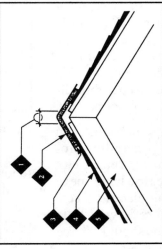

1. 1 1/2" opening in roof sheathing (3 1/2" opening in roofs with ridge board).
2. COBRA™ RIDGE VENT under cap shingles.
3. 5/8" nominal space between cap shingle and roof shingle.
4. Roof shingle on sheathing.
5. Roof truss.

Capture the wind's power for electricity

Q. Because of President Clinton's proposed energy tax, I want to install a windmill to generate my own electricity for my house and help protect the environment. Are there any small residential-size windmills?

A. There are many sizes of electric-generating windmills available for homes. The smallest ones are portable and weigh only 20 pounds. You can mount one on a piece of 2-inch pipe. Most windmills are sold as entire do-it-yourself kits - poles, wiring, controls, etc..

Using wind energy is virtually non-polluting. It is also an excellent complement to solar cell (PV) panels on your house to produce even more electricity. In 1991 in California alone, the utility companies' wind generating farms reduced carbon dioxide emissions by 2.7 billion pounds.

Depending on your budget, you can install a small windmill to produce just a fraction of the electricity your family requires to a large one to supply most of your electric needs. Once installed, there is very little maintenance and you should get free electricity for many years.

At times when the windmill produces more electricity than you need, many utility companies will purchase the extra electricity from you. You should still remain connected to the utility company's line for times when the wind is calm and it isn't sunny (if you also have solar PV panels).

A typical whole-house residential-size windmill has a rotor blade diameter of 15 feet and a rated output of 4,000 watts of electricity. An automatic computerized "brain" controls the electricity output and frequency to match your utility company's output.

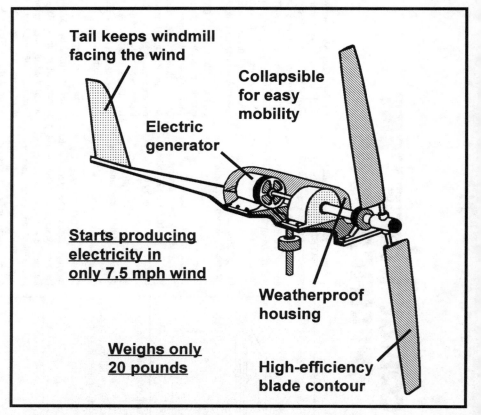

Tail keeps windmill facing the wind

Collapsible for easy mobility

Electric generator

Starts producing electricity in only 7.5 mph wind

Weatherproof housing

Weighs only 20 pounds

High-efficiency blade contour

Small windmill produces free clean electricity

There are portable lightweight (about 20 lb.) windmills. These are ideal for home use, backyard workshop, or camping. You can easily carry them under your arm. These begin to produce electricity in a wind as light as 7.5 miles per hour. For stormy conditions, there is an automatic high-wind protection feature.

You can use these small windmills to power refrigerators, lights, TV's, power tools, etc. The ideal system is to wire it to car-type batteries and include a small solar PV panel. The windmill charges the batteries when you are not using your appliances. If the wind dies down or it is too cloudy for enough solar power, the batteries supply the electricity.

Before you invest in a larger whole-house windmill, check the typical wind conditions in your area to determine its feasibility. Keep in mind that the actual wind speed varies considerably over short distances.

Q: I bought an old electric range that I am going to put in my son's apartment. Is there anything that we can do so it uses less electricity?

A: Electric ranges are very simple devices. Check to make sure that all of the burner (element) controls work properly and actually adjust the heat from low to high. Also clean the chrome reflector drip pans or buy new ones. They are inexpensive and can improve its efficiency.

Check the accuracy of the oven thermostat with a thermometer. If it gets hotter than the setting, this wastes electricity. Check the gasket around the oven door for deterioration.

One of the best methods to use alternative energy to produce electricity is windmills. The list below shows manufacturers of wind generating systems. Pages **b** and **c** show detailed information on several of the systems. Once you make the initial purchase, the electricity is basically free. The price of windmills ranges from about $600-$900 for the small 20-lbs. ones to more than $15,000 for the very large ones.

Sizes of windmills range from very small (only 20 lbs.) portable windmills to large whole-house windmills. The chart below lists the rated output wattages and the rotor blade diameter to give you an idea of the physical size. For example, a 1.5-kilowatt unit typically has a 10-foot rotor (blade) diameter and weighs about 170 lbs. A true whole-house 10-kilowatt unit often has a 23-foot diameter rotor, multiple blades, and weighs over 1,000 lbs.

You can buy appliances and tools designed to operate on 12-volt d.c. current or get an inverter to convert the electricity to a.c. current. Some typical current usages of 12-volt appliances are -- TV-1 amp, stereo - .7 amp, lights - 2 amp, absorption type refrigerator - 2 amps. If you want to use a windmill to replace some of the electricity that you now buy from the utility company, you will need special interface couplers so that the windmill will not backfeed electricity into the utility's line when workmen are working . You can also get equipment to measure how much electricity you provide to the utility company. Some utility companies will pay you for extra electricity you generate.

MANUFACTURERS OF WINDMILL GENERATING SYSTEMS

MANUFACTURER	ROTOR DIAMETER	VOLTAGE OUTPUTS	OUTPUT (WATTS/KW)
BERGEY WIND POWER 2001 Priestley Ave., Norman, OK 73069 (405) 364-4212	10 ft. 23 ft.	12-120 v d.c. 120 v d.c.	1.5 kw 10 kw
L.V.M. PRODUCTS for boat or land P.O. Box 1086, Severna Park, MD 21146 (410) 544-4352	61 in.	12 v d.c.	200 w
NORTHERN POWER SYSTEMS P.O. Box 659, Moretown, VT 05660 (802) 496-2955	10 ft. 16 ft.	24 v d.c. 48 v d.c.	1 kw 3 kw
WIND BARON 3920 E. Huntington Dr., Flagstaff, AZ 86004 (602) 526-0997	60 in. 60 in	12 v d.c. 24 v d.c.	500 w 600 w
WINDBUGGER for boat or land P.O. Box 259, Key Largo, FL 33037 (305) 451-4496	54 in.	12-16 v d.c.	250 w
WINDSTREAM POWER SYS. for boat or land P.O. Box 1604, Burlington, VT 05402 (802) 658-0075	42 in.	12 v d.c.	100 w
WIND TURBINE INDUSTRIES CORP. 16801 Industrial Cr., Prior Lake, MN 55372 (612) 447-6064	23 ft. 26 ft.	240v a.c. 240v a.c.	10-12.5kw 15-17.5kw
WORLD POWER TECHNOLOGIES 19 N. Lake Ave., Duluth, MN 55802 (218) 722-1492	7 ft. 9 ft. 15 ft.	12-48 v or 64-240 v	600 w 1 kw 3 kw

PERFORMANCE

PERFORMANCE The Real Secret... The NEO's direct drive alternator has been developed with Neodymium Iron Boron Magnets which are the latest state of the art magnets available in the World. This leads to the highest power output and reliability in the small turbine industry. The alternator is designed for high output and efficiency at low R.P.M. The NEO is designed to match the available power from the wind to the performance of the alternator and thus providing the most efficient and reliable wind generator on the market today.

- Aircraft quality rotor
- Cast aluminum frame
- Direct drive, high efficiency alternator
- "Smart" regulator
- Mil-spec. electronic components in aluminum oxide epoxy
- Wind force regulator
- Sealed slip rings
- Heavy duty yaw assembly
- All stainless hardware
- Standard 2" pipe tower (other towers available)

US PATENT PENDING

SPECIFICATIONS:

RATED POWER:
12 Volt 500 Watts (32 Amps)
24 Volt 600 Watts (25 Amps)

MAXIMUM POWER:
12 Volt 550 Watts (35 Amps)
24 Volt 650 Watts (28 Amps)

MINIMUM WIND SPEED:
12 Volt 8 MPH (3.82 MPS)
24 Volt 8 MPH (3.82 MPS)

OUTPUT VOLTAGE Adjustable
12 Volt preset at 14.8 Volts
24 Volt preset at 29.5 Volts

SURVIVAL WIND SPEED:
120 + MPH (57.2 MPS)

WEIGHT:
20 Lbs.(9Kg)

ROTOR DIAMETER:
60 inches (1.52 meters)

MOUNTING:
Standard 2" Schedule 40 steel pipe.

TIP TO WIND SPEED RATIO:
12:1

AVAILABLE VOLTAGES:
12 Volt
24 Volt
36 Volt
48 Volt
90 Volt
120 Volt
180 Volt

CONTACT YOUR LOCAL DEALER FOR ADDITIONAL INFORMATION.

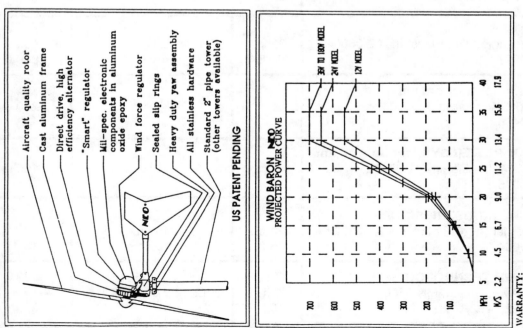

WIND BARON NEO
PROJECTED POWER CURVE

36V TO 180V MODEL
24V MODEL
12V MODEL

MPH	5	10	15	20	25	30	35	40
K/S	2.2	4.5	6.7	9.0	11.2	13.4	15.6	17.9

WIND BARON CORPORATION
3920 EAST HUNTINGTON DRIVE
FLAGSTAFF, ARIZONA 86004
Phone 602-526-6400 Fax 602-526-5498

WARRANTY:
One year parts and labor with prepaid freight to Wind Baron or your closet authorized service representative. Wind Baron will repair and return freight collect.

SYSTEM CONSIDERATIONS

SITING

Since the output of a wind turbine is a function of the cube of the wind velocity, the nature of the wind resource at the installation site is extremely important. For example, an increase in average wind speed from 11 mph to 14 mph can nearly double the output of a windpower generator. Anemometer data, tree flagging, weather station data, and the performance of nearby wind systems can help in evaluating the average local wind speed. Turbulence tends to reduce power output.

Wind speed increases and turbulence decreases with height above the ground. The tower height should place the machine at least 10m (33 ft) above obstructions within a radius of 100m (330 ft). Towers of 18m (60 ft) or higher are recommended, even in the most favorable conditions. Wire runs should be kept short on low voltage DC systems, but may be as long as 300m (1000 ft) for the BWC 1500-S and the BWC 1500-PD.

TOWERS

The AUTOFURL™ system greatly reduces the tower loading in high winds, allowing the use of a wide variety of towers, including wood poles, metal poles, and cable-braced truss towers.. BWC can furnish suitable towers or can advise on the appropriate clearance and strength requirements for customer-supplied towers.

INSTALLATION

Installing a BWC 1500 system is simple and can usually be accomplished in 8 to 15 hours, including tower erection. With the aid of our comprehensive installation manual, self-installation is a practical alternative. Only average mechanical skills are required, but experience with towers and electrical wiring will help.

PERFORMANCE

The performance specifications given below have been compiled in accordance with industry standards established by the American Wind Energy Association (AWEA). The Power Curve, shown in Figure 1, is based on measured performance under actual field conditions corrected to standard temperature and pressure. Figure 2 shows the estimated Annual Energy Output (AEO) for a BWC 1500 assuming the AWEA Standard (Rayleigh) Distribution of wind speed. High turbulence can cause a significant reduction in AEO and should be avoided. Multiple units may be used to increase the output at a given site.

APPLICATIONS

BATTERY CHARGING

The unique permanent magnet alternator of the BWC 1500 allows it to be used for charging batteries in remote areas. It is available in 12, 24, 36, 48, and 120 VDC versions. The batteries may be used to operate DC loads directly or, through a stand-alone inverter, can provide alternating current for AC appliances. The BWC 1500 may also be combined with photovoltaic cells or gas/diesel generators to satisfy specific needs in remote locations. Hybrid wind/photovoltaic systems are particularly attractive because of their complimentary daily and seasonal performance characteristics. The BWC 1500 is also well suited for harsh telecommunications sites, where it can typically support continuous loads in the range of 200-400 watts.

WATER PUMPING

The BWC 1500-PD can be used with single, multi-stage, surface-mounted or submersible pumps operating at flow rates up to 8.4 liters/second (125 gpm) and static heads up to 170 meters (557 ft). Standard off-the-shelf pumps can be selected for the specific site conditions. The BWC 1500-PD windpower generator can be located as much as 300 meters (1000 ft) from the well site to take advantage of improved wind conditions. A BWC 1500-PD installation is cost effective, providing higher delivery rates and twice the efficiency of a mechanical windmill at one-third the cost of comparable PV systems.

UTILITY INTERCONNECT

The BWC 1500-S operates through the POWERSYNC® inverter to feed electrical power directly into the home or building. Utility bills are reduced as the power from the BWC 1500 flows smoothly through the breaker box without flicker or distortion. In states and countries that allow "net billing", the BWC 1500-S can drive the utility company meter backwards when its output is greater than the power being used in the home or building.

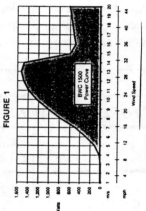

FIGURE 1

BWC 1500 Power Curve

m/s	2	4	6	8	10	12	14	16	18	20
mph	4	8	12	16	20	24	28	32	36	40	44

Wind Speed
Watts (0 to 1,600)

FIGURE 2

BWC 1500 Annual Energy Output
This curve is based upon a Rayleigh wind speed distribution. Your performance may vary.

| m/s | 2.5 | 3 | 4 | 4.5 | 5 | 5.5 | 6 | 6.5 | 7 | 7.5 | 8 | 8.5 | 9 | 9.5 | 10 |
| mph | 6 | | 10 | | 12 | 14 | | 16 | | 18 | 20 | | 22 |

Average Wind Speed
kWh's (0 to 7,000)

BWC 1500 SPECIFICATIONS

PERFORMANCE

START-UP WIND SPEED	3.6 m/s (8 mph)
CUT-IN WIND SPEED	3.6 m/s (8 mph)
RATED WIND SPEED	12.5 m/s (28 mph)
CUT-OUT WIND SPEED	None
FURLING WIND SPEED	13.4 m/s (30 mph)
MAXIMUM DESIGN WIND SPEED	54 m/s (121 mph)
RATED POWER	1,500 watts
ROTOR SPEED	100-500 RPM

MECHANICAL

TYPE	3 Blade Upwind
ROTOR DIAMETER	3.05 m (10 ft)
WEIGHT	76 kgs (168 lbs)
BLADE PITCH CONTROL	POWERFLEX®
OVERSPEED PROTECTION	AUTOFURL™
GEARBOX/BELTS	None, Direct Drive
TEMPERATURE RANGE	-40° to 60° C (-40° to 140° F)
SHIPPING DIMENSIONS	1 Carton, 150x50x60 cm, 98 kgs (59x20x24 in, 216 lbs)

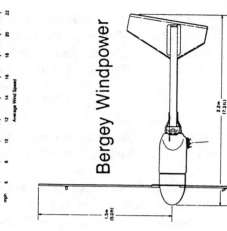

Bergey Windpower

2.2m (7.3ft)
1.5m (5.0ft)

HR3 Power Curve

HR3 Output/Month

Technical Data • North Wind HR3

Performance

Rated Power Output	3000 Watts @ 12.5 m/s (28 mph)
Peak Output	3200 Watts @ 14.5 m/s (32.5 mph)
Cut-in Windspeed	3.6 m/s (8 mph)
Design Life	25 years
Maintenance Interval	1 Year

Wind Turbine

Rotor Configuration	Horizontal axis, upwind, 3-bladed
Rotor Diameter	5 m (16.4 ft)
Blade Material	C-Lam® wood laminate
Transmission	None required(direct drive)
Yaw Control	Free yawing
Rotor Speed Control	VARCS™
Speed Control Initiation	9.4 m/s (21 mph)
Automatic Shutdown	47 m/s (105 mph)
Maintenance Shutdown	Winch-operated cable
Total Turbine Weight	315 kg (695 lb)
Overall Turbine Length	3.44 m (11.3 ft)

Electrical System

Voltage (nominal)	24, 48, or 110 VDC; options
Generator Type	3 Ø synchronous alternator
Field Configuration	Lundel type, shunt connected
Voltage Regulation	Solid state PWM field control
Rectification	Silicon diode full-wave bridge
Lightning Protection	Faraday shielding; MOV
Regulator Housing	20" x 20" x 8", NEMA 1, 22.7 kg (50 lb)

Tower

Types	Guyed; Self-Supporting
Standard Heights	12 m (40 ft) to 30 m (100 ft)
Foundation Options	Concrete piers or pads; Rock anchors
Structural Materials	High-strength steel, hot dip galvanized

Environmental Tolerances

Temperature	-60°C to +60°C (-76°F to +140°F)
Wind, Steady	54 m/s (120 mph)
Wind, Gusts	74 m/s (165 mph)
Rain, Dust, Marine	Sealed, corrosion-resistant construction

Shipping Dimensions

Turbine: 4 crates	
Total weight	399 kg (880 lbs)
Total volume	1.6 cu m (55 cu ft)
Tower (examples):	
12m (40 ft) guyed	
Weight	680 kg (1500 lbs)
Volume	3.9 cu m (137 cu ft)
18m (60 ft) self-supporting	
Weight	1,261 kg (2780 lbs)
Volume	2.8 cu m (100 cu ft)

North Wind HR3

High Reliability 3 kW Wind Energy System

The North Wind® HR series of high-reliability wind turbines supply power for telecommunications, radar, pipeline control, navigational aids, cathodic protection, and water pumping in 18 countries on all seven continents. They are engineered to operate unattended in harsh environments where system availability must exceed 99%.

As a sole power source, the HR3 provides primary power for high-reliability applications having loads of up to 1000 watts continuous where wind speeds average over 6 m/s (14-15 mph). In larger capacity MicroGrid™ systems it complements photovoltaics and fuel-fired generators.

ADVANTAGES

• **Reliability.** North Wind HR series turbines have logged more than 2.5 million hours of operation--many at sites near both the North and South Poles--with system availability exceeding 99%.

• **Maintainability.** Preventive maintenance is required only once each year. Design life is 25 years. Electronic components are mounted at ground level for easy accessibility.

• **Ruggedized, Simple Design.** Engineered for substantial safety factors. The HR3 has just three moving assemblies.

• **Survivability.** Installed HR series turbines have survived winds in excess of 71 m/s (160 mph). System design loading accommodates three inches of radial ice on all parts of the machine. Ice build-up within this range does not restrict turbine rotation and blade flexibility encourages shedding. Sealed construction and weather-tight fittings are field proven.

• **Ease of Installation.** An HR3 and tower can be installed in one day without a crane. Both are readily transportable to remote sites.

• **Cost Savings.** The HR3 can provide highly reliable power without any fuel costs at remote installations. HR3 systems require much less maintenance than comparable diesel-based power systems.

FEATURES

• **Passive Rotor Control.** The HR3's Variable Axis Rotor Control System (VARCS™) includes a torsion spring against which the rotor and generator tilt to control RPM and power in any wind speed. It provides both overspeed control and a maintenance shutdown mechanism while allowing the use of a fixed pitch rotor assembly and a fixed tail assembly. The VARCS eliminates the need for a mechanical brake.

• **Field Proven Electrical System.** A direct drive, slow speed Lundel alternator eliminates the need for a gearbox. Pulse-width modulation of the alternator field provides continuous voltage regulation. The charging voltage is field adjustable within 1% to allow for the precise matching of system output to load and battery requirements.

• **High Performance Materials.** High strength alloy steel resists embrittlement and will not fracture at any temperatures encountered in nature. Construction features full penetration, stress-relieved welds. The VARCS spring is cryogenically treated to tolerate extremes of cyclic loading. Corrosion resistant materials including copper-free aluminum alloys are used throughout the turbine and have been carefully selected to prevent galvanic reactions.

• **C-Lam® Wood Composite Blades.** Combining the superior flexibility and fatigue resistance of natural wood fibers with the durability of penetrating epoxy resins and two-part urethane coatings. Leading edge protection is state of the industry and helicopter proven.

Northern Power Systems

Solar cells generate good results

Q. I am interested in using solar cells to produce free and clean electricity for my home. I already use them on my camper. What types of solar cell systems are available for home use?

A. Electricity-generating solar cells (photovoltaics) naturally produce electricity when the sun shines on a panel of many interconnected solar cells. There is no sound, pollution, or waste produced. With no moving parts, a solar cell panel should last a very long time with proper care.

Although it is possible to utilize photovoltaics to provide all the electricity for a house, it is much less expensive to get your electricity from your electric utility company. However, for a remote home or cabin that is a long distance from existing power lines, it may be cheaper to install a photovoltaic system than to extend the electric power lines.

Another application for photovoltaics is to provide light or electricity for operating tools in a backyard work shed. The solar cell panels are connected to batteries that store the charge. The batteries can also be used as an emergency backup system for power outages.

You can buy special tools, refrigerators, lights, that operate on lower-voltage direct current (DC) coming from the batteries. By using an inverter and a more powerful solar cell system, you can also operate standard 110-volt alternating current (AC) power tools.

Small photovoltaic systems are very effective for campers and boats. These are usually used in the warmer weather when the days are longer

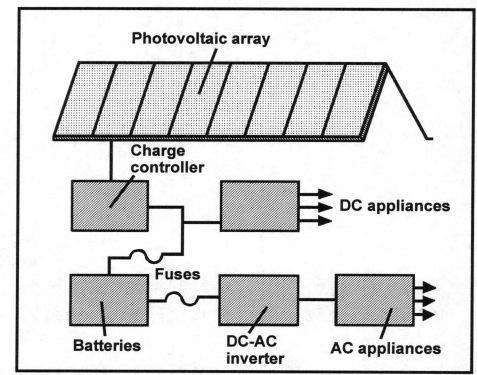

Photovoltaic array
Charge controller
DC appliances
Fuses
Batteries
DC-AC inverter
AC appliances

Typical photovoltaic (solar cell) AC-DC system

and the electricity output is greater. Very small solar cell panels can be used to keep the batteries at peak charge. Larger panels can produce enough electricity to power most of the appliances and lights in a camper.

One whole-house photovoltaic system provides 4 kilowatt-hours per day. This system could power four 60-watt and two 25-watt light bulbs for four hours per day, a 19-inch color TV and VCR for four hours a day, an automatic clothes washer and gas dryer five loads a week, a microwave oven used 15 minutes per day, a table saw one hour per week, or a water pressure booster pump.

You will still need natural gas or propane for space and hot water heating, and cooking. Electric heat-generating devices would consume too much power for the solar cells to provide. You can also get gas- or propane-powered refrigerators so you can operate more electrical appliances instead.

Q: I have many houseplants for decoration and to provide humidity in my home in the cooler weather. Will the higher humidity actually help to lower my utility bills?

A: The theory is that higher humidity levels improve your comfort and reduce cooling moisture evaporation from your skin. This allows you to lower your thermostat in the heating season without being uncomfortable.

Heat is absorbed when water evaporates, so unless you set your thermostat lower, it wastes energy. Also, houseplants may not be your best source of humidity. Many people are allergic to mold spores given off by houseplants. When you feel bad, you often set the thermostat higher.

UTILITY BILLS UPDATE

Solar cell photovoltaic systems for producing electricity from the sun are an effective, pollution-free method to generate electricity. Before you purchase any photovoltaic system, carefully analyze the payback from installing a system as compared to running electric lines from the standard utility-generated electric service. Environmentally, photovoltaic-generated electricity is almost perfectly clean and this may also figure into your decision of whether or not to install a system.

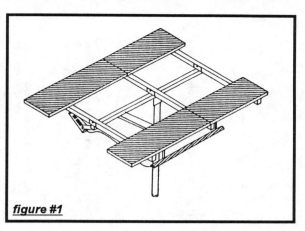

figure #1

Several suppliers of photovoltaic solar cell systems are listed below. There are additional local smaller retailers that purchase solar cell panels from these major manufacturers and assemble and market photovoltaic systems for home, trailer, and recreational use. Systems for recreational vehicles are very effective because of the large flat roofs.

Pages **b** and **c** show detailed specs. on several typical residential size systems (specs. for Kyocera America). Also listed below are special support racks used for mounting the solar cell panels (see figure #1). These are designed to automatically track the sun's position throughout the day to provide the maximum amount of electricity from a photovoltaic system. This also improves the payback.

SUPPLIERS OF PHOTOVOLTAIC (PV) SOLAR CELL SYSTEMS

KYOCERA AMERICA, 8611 Balboa Ave., San Diego, CA 92123 - (619) 576-2600

NORTHERN POWER SYSTEMS, 1 N. Wind Rd., Moretown, VT 05660 - (802) 496-2955

PHOTOCOMM, 7681 E. Gray Rd. Scottsdale, AZ 85260 - (800) 223-9580 (602) 948-8003

SIEMENS SOLAR, 4650 Adohr Ln., Camarillo, CA 93011 - (805) 482-6800

SOLAREX, 630 Solarex Ct., Frederick, MD 21701 - (301) 698-4200

SOLARMETRICS, 140 Bouchard, Manchester, NH 03103 - (800) 356-4751 (603) 668-3216

SUNNYSIDE SOLAR, RD4 Box 808, Green River Rd., Brattleboro, VT 05301 - (802) 257-1482

WINDSTREAM POWER SYSTEMS, P.O. Box 1604, Burlington, VT 05402 - (802) 658-0075

MANUFACTURERS OF SUN-TRACKING RACKS FOR SOLAR CELL PANELS

ARRAY TECHNOLOGIES, P.O. Box 751, Albuquerque, NM 87103 - (505) 242-8024

ROBBINS ENGINEERING, 1641 McCulloch, Lake Havasu City, AZ 86403 - (602) 855-3670

ZOMEWORKS CORP., P.O. Box 25805, Albuquerque, NM 87125 - (505) 242-5354

Standard Home Systems

System 1:
Remote Cabin, RV or Boat Mini System

Power Output: 100 Watt-hours per day - 8 amp-hours per day at 12 volts

System 1 is ideal for a cabin, boat or RV that is used on weekends. The battery charges all week and on the weekend you can run two 20 watt fluorescent lights for 10 hours, a portable stereo for 10 hours, a DC black and white TV for 8 hours and still have power left over to run a 12 volt blender or other small appliance. On Sunday night the battery will still be 50% charged and by the following Saturday it will be fully charged and ready to go again.

System 1 Components:
1 Kyocera 24 Watt Solar Module
  LD361C24
1 Mounting Bracket
1 100 Amp-Hour 12 Volt Deep Cycle
  Battery
1 6 Amp Charge Regulator
1 Wiring Harness

System 2:
Remote Cabin, RV or Boat Basic System

Power Output: 160 Watt-hours per day - 13 amp-hours per day at 12 volts

System 2 is ideal for heavier weekend use in cabins, boats, RVs or light continuous use. For weekend use you could use a DC color TV in place of the black and white, add one more light and still have power to spare.

For continuous use, with 13 amp-hours per day you can power a 20 watt fluorescent light for 4 hours, watch a black and white TV for 4 hours and listen to a portable stereo for 6 hours.

System 2 Components:
1 Kyocera 51 Watt Solar Module
  LD361K51
1 14 Amp Charge Regulator with
  Low Voltage Disconnect
1 Adjustable Mounting Bracket
2 100 Amp-Hour 12 Volt Deep Cycle
  Batteries
1 Wiring Harness
1 DC Fuse Box
Options:
Additional 51 Watt Solar Modules
100 Amp-Hour 12 Volt Deep Cycle
  Batteries

On a boat that's not in use, you can run a 7 amp bilge pump for almost 2 hours a day, enough to keep a leaky boat afloat without shore power. Best of all, the Kyocera 43 watt module is self regulating so you don't need a charge regulator.

System 2 Components:
1 Kyocera 45 Watt Solar Module
  LD361K45
1 Mounting Bracket
1 100 Amp-Hour 12 Volt Deep Cycle
  Battery
1 Wiring Harness

System 3:
Remote Home Starter System

Power Output: 400 Watt-hours per day - 32 amp-hours per day at 12 volts

With System 3 you can run two 20 watt fluorescent lights for five hours, listen to your portable stereo for 5 hours, watch a portable color TV for 3 hours every day of the week and still have power to spare. System 3 is expandable. Since the charge regulator can handle up to 4 modules you can add on as the need and budget allows. Just wire new modules in parallel to the existing ones and start using more power.

To protect your batteries, the charge regulator includes a low battery disconnect to prevent battery damage.

System 3 Components:
1 Kyocera 51 Watt Solar Module
  LD361K51
1 18 Amp Charge Regulator
1 Adjustable Mounting Bracket
4 100 Amp-Hour 12 Volt Deep Cycle
  Batteries
1 Wiring Harness
1 1500 Watt DC to AC Inverter
1 Pair of 2/0 Inverter Connection Cables
Options:
Additional 51 Watt Solar Modules
100 Amp-Hour 12 Volt Deep Cycle
  Batteries
Inverter
30 Amp Charge Regulator

System 4:
AC - DC Remote Home System

Power Output: 800 Watt-hours per day - 64 amp-hours per day at 12 volts

System 4 gives you everything in System 3 plus a 1500 watt inverter, that can supply 120 volt AC power to run kitchen appliances like a toaster or blender, a powerful vacuum cleaner or power tools as big as a worm drive skill saw.

The power generated by these 4 solar modules can run the DC loads described in System 3 and also run the toaster for 5 minutes a day, the blender 5 minutes a day and the vacuum cleaner 10 minutes a day.

Like System 3, this system is expandable, but in another dimension. Of course you can add solar modules and batteries to give you more power, but most inverters are cascadable, which means you can add a second inverter later on and have nearly 3000 watts of AC power available, enough to run an automatic washer or a pump in your hot tub.

To allow you to keep better track of your power, this system comes with a metered DC load center that tells you battery state of charge, charging amps and discharge amps.

System 4 Components:
1 Kyocera 51 Watt Solar Module
  LD361K51
1 50 Amp Charge Regulator
2 Adjustable Mounting Brackets
12 220 Amp-Hour 6 Volt Deep Cycle
  Batteries
1 Wiring Harness
2 1500 Watt DC to AC Inverters
2 Pairs of 2/0 Inverter Connection
  Cables
Options:
Additional 51 Watt Solar Modules
220 Amp-Hour 6 Volt Deep Cycle
  Batteries

System 5:
High Power AC - DC Remote Home System

Power Output: 2000 Watt-hours per day - 160 amp-hours per day at 12 volts

This Kyocera power system lets you run a family sized home in comfort. Five 20 watt fluorescent lights can light several rooms five hours a day, the inverter can power a 19 inch color TV and a VCR for 3 hours a day, you can run the vacuum cleaner for 30 minutes each week, you can do four loads of laundry each week and still have enough power to add a 16 cubic foot high efficiency refrigerator-freezer.

The two inverters can supply up to 3000 watts of 120 volt AC power at over 90% efficiency and the deep cycle 6-volt 220 amp hour batteries will let them surge to 8000 watts to start induction motors or run microwave ovens efficiently.

Expanding the system further is no problem either. The 50 amp charge regulator can handle up to 16 solar modules.

System 5 Components:
10 Kyocera 51 Watt Solar Module
  LD361K51
1 50 Amp Charge Regulator
2 Adjustable Mounting Brackets
12 220 Amp-Hour 6 Volt Deep Cycle
  Batteries
1 Wiring Harness
2 1500 Watt DC to AC Inverters
2 Pairs of 2/0 Inverter Connection
  Cables
Options:
Additional 51 Watt Solar Modules
220 Amp-Hour 6 Volt Deep Cycle
  Batteries

System 6:
High Power AC Remote Home System

Power Output: 2800 Watt-hours per day - AC POWER SYSTEM

This is an easily expandable AC power system. All house wiring is conventional, low-cost AC wiring. DC power stored in the batteries is converted to AC with over 90% efficiency to power readily available AC lights and appliances. The inverter used for this system can supply 2500 watts of 120/240 volt AC power. Up to two or more of these inverters can be cascaded together if more AC power is needed at one time.

The 30 amp charge regulator operates at 24 volts and can control up to 20 J48 modules, allowing for PV array expansion at a later date.

If attention is paid to buying energy efficient appliances, this power system could easily run four 60 watt and two 25 watt lights for 4 hours each, a 19 inch color TV and VCR for 3 hours a day, an automatic washer and gas dryer 4 times a week, a stereo component system 4 hours a day, a microwave oven used 15 minutes a day and a toaster and hair dryer for 5 minutes each, once a day.

System 6 Components:
14 Kyocera 51 Watt Solar Module LD361K51
1 30 Amp 24 Volt Charge Regulator
3 Adjustable Mounting Brackets
16 220 Amp-Hour 6 Volt Deep Cycle Batteries
1 Wiring Harness
1 Volt Meter
1 24 VDC to 120/240 VAC Inverter

Options:
Additional 51 Watt Solar Modules
220 Amp-Hour 6 Volt Deep Cycle Batteries
Additional 24 Volt-2500 Watt Inverter

System 7:
120/240 Volt AC Home Power System

Power Output: 4000 Watt-hours per day - AC POWER SYSTEM

This Kyocera power system gives you all of the convenience of a utility hook-up without utility bills. Standard AC house wiring can be used, since the DC system has been eliminated. A pair of 2500 watt inverters can supply 5000 watts of AC power, 120 and 240 VAC, at over 90% efficiency. With 20,000 watt surge capacity, this system can run pumps, large power tools and a microwave oven.

A typical system might have four 60 watt and two 25 watt light bulbs, run for 4 hours each day, a 19 inch color TV and VCR run for 4 hours a day, an automatic washer and gas dryer used 5 times a week, a microwave oven used 15 minutes per day, a 1 horsepower air compressor or table saw used 1 hour a week, a water system pressure booster pump, an electric lawn mower or weed whacker used 1 hour a week and an evaporative cooler used for 1 or 2 hours a day.

There will still be ample power for one possible addition, a 24 volt 16 cubic foot refrigerator-freezer. This refrigerator is so much more efficient than any available AC refrigerator it's worth running a 24 volt DC line to the kitchen. Of course, LP gas refrigeration is always an option in PV powered homes.

To help you keep track of the system operation, this power package comes with a digital metering and alarm system that can be mounted at a convenient place in the house. At the touch of a button, you can see battery voltage, charge and discharge current and be warned of high or low battery condition by an alarm.

Like all Kyocera PV systems, this one is easily expandable. Solar modules and batteries can be added when the need arises. If more AC power is needed, another 2500 watt inverter can be added, allowing the use of 7500 watts at once with 30,000 watts of surge capacity.

System 7 Components:
20 Kyocera 51 Watt Solar Module LD361K51
1 50 Amp 24 Volt Charge Regulator
5 4-Module Adjustable Mounting Brackets
28 220 Amp-Hour 6 Volt Deep Cycle Batteries
1 Wiring Harness
2 24 VDC to 120/240 VAC Inverters
1 Digital Meter and Alarm System

Options:
Additional 51 Watt Solar Modules
(Pairs required)
220 Amp-Hour 6 Volt Deep Cycle Batteries
Additional 2500 Watt Inverter

System 8:
120/240 Volt AC Advanced Home Power System

Power Output: 9600 Watt-hours per day - 2160 watt array - AC POWER SYSTEM

Though there is no limit on the size of a Kyocera power system, this one can do everything but heat your house and water. Instead of a utility hook-up, this is more like a utility company.

Three 2500 watt inverters can supply 7500 watts of AC power, 120 and 240 VAC, at over 90% efficiency. With 30,000 watt surge capacity, this system can run pumps, large power tools, even a welder. It can even run several big loads at once. Practically anything you find in a home, besides the electric furnace or electric water heater should fit into this energy budget. Keep cool in the summer with an evaporative cooler. In winter use electricity to run the blower of a gas fired central heating system. Try to use energy efficient house lighting and turn off lights in rooms you aren't using. Let a dishwasher clean your dishes and do one load of laundry in your automatic washer and gas dryer every day. Toast six slices of bread for the family and make coffee in the electric drip coffee maker every morning. Listen to the latest high tech stereo for a few hours a day and watch your color TV, VCR, satellite dish combination a few hours, too. Reheat the leftovers in the microwave oven or use the food processor to whip up something fancy. Even do a little work away from the office on your word processor.

A custom 100 amp 24 volt charge control can be programmed to feed array power directly or via the inverter to an electric heating element in a solar water heating storage tank, water pump or ventilation system when the battery becomes fully charged.

To help you keep track of the system operation, this power package comes with a digital metering and alarm system that can be mounted at a convenient place in the house. At the touch of a button, you can see battery voltage, charge and discharge current and be warned of high or low battery condition by an alarm.

As has been suggested before, the addition of a 24 volt 16 cubic foot refrigerator-freezer is appropriate if a propane refrigerator is not used.

System 8 Components:
48 Kyocera 51 Watt Solar Module LD361K51
1 100 Amp 24 Volt Charge Control
8 6-Module Adjustable Mounting Brackets
24 1470-Amp-Hour 2 Volt Deep Cycle Batteries
1 Wiring Harness
3 2500 Watt 24 VDC to 120/240 VAC Inverters
1 Digital Battery Voltage Monitor and Warning System

Solar fan is best to cool your attic

Q: My attic gets above 150 degrees in the sun and I plan to install a temperature-controlled attic vent fan to lower my air-conditioning costs. What type of vent fan is best and how large a vent fan should I get?

A: Installing an automatic attic vent fan can lower the air-conditioning load. By cooling the attic temperature as much as 50 degrees, you should also feel much more comfortable inside your house, especially in second floor bedrooms. High attic temperatures can also deteriorate the lumber.

There are several attic vent fans available. A solar-powered electric attic fan is the most efficient, easiest to install, and runs for free. Since it is powered by the sun, the brighter and hotter the sun is, the faster the fan runs. This makes it a perfect fit for attic cooling.

Some designs have the small solar cell panel (converts sunlight directly into electricity) built into the top of the vent fan. Others use a very small (less than one-foot square) solar cell panel on the roof next to the fan. You can use metal angles to face the small panel more directly toward the sun for more electricity output and better cooling.

You just remove a few shingles and saw a 12-inch hole in the roof. Nail the 12-volt fan in place and seal it. Replace the shingles. Run the wire from the solar cell panel to the fan and it starts. You can get solar-powered vent fans designed to mount vertically in gables.

An automatic temperature-controlled 120-volt electric attic vent fan is also very effective for cooling your attic. These can provide up to 1,600 cfm (cubic-feet-per-minute) of air flow to cool even large attics.

An adjustable thermostat is used to control the temperature at which the attic vent fan switches on. The thermostat keeps it from running too much and wasting electricity.

In the winter, you can install a humidistat to control the fan. This eliminates potential moisture prob-

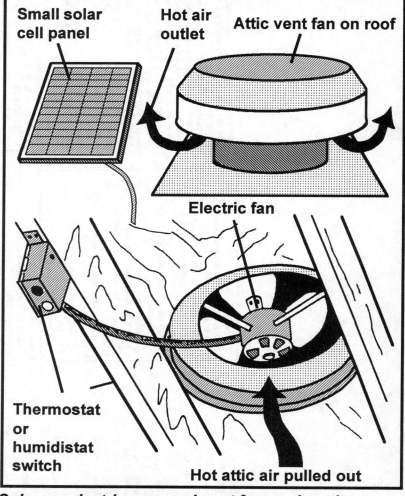

Small solar cell panel — **Hot air outlet** — **Attic vent fan on roof** — **Electric fan** — **Thermostat or humidistat switch** — **Hot attic air pulled out**

Solar- or electric-powered vent fan cools attic

lems during extremely cold spells. With adequate attic floor insulation, it will not increase your heating bills.

A rule of thumb for sizing an attic vent fan is that you have a minimum of 10 complete air changes per hour. With a typical pitched roof, a 900-square-foot attic would require a vent fan capacity of 630 cfm. A 1,500-square-foot attic would require 1,050 cfm vent fan. The best location for the inlet air vents is under the soffits (roof overhang).

Q: I have old permanent-type of window film on my windows and I want to remove it and install the self-cling film you wrote about. What is the easiest way to remove the old window film?

A: There are two methods. First, using a single edge razor blade or window scraper, scrape the film loose from the top edge. Spray the exposed area with a solution of half ammonia and half water. Slowly work your way diagonally across peeling it off from top to bottom.

If this doesn't work well, spray the film with the ammonia solution. Cover the window with plastic and let it stay wet for 10 to 12 hours. After sweating the film, the first removal method should be effective.

Using a fan to vent your attic helps lower your utility bills year-round. Keeping your attic cooler can lower your air conditioning costs and greatly improve your comfort. In the winter, you can operate it to keep the attic insulation from becoming damp. You can install an automatic humidistat to control it.

I have included a chart on the final page which shows the recommended size (air flow capacity - CFM - cubic feet per minute) vent fan. For a large home, you should consider installing two smaller fans to provide the total amount of air flow needed.

Be sure to install inlet air vents under the roof overhang (soffit) to get the most effective cooling. You can determine the amount of "net free" inlet vent area (square feet) needed by dividing the vent fan flow rate in CFM by 300. When you buy the soffit vent, the packaging should indicate the net free vent area. Installing ones with screening will block insects from getting into your attic. If you already have vents in the eave sides, block them off so the air is drawn in the soffit vents.

MANUFACTURERS OF 115-VOLT ELECTRIC ATTIC VENT FANS

Model No.	CFM	Model No.	CFM
AUBREY MANUFACTURING		**FASCO INDUSTRIES cont'd.**	
9000 louver	1000	RV16	1720
9000 shutter	1450	ASRV14	1000
9005 louver	900	GV16	1520
9090	900		
9105	1050	**KOOL-O-MATIC CORP.**	
9120	1200		
9130	1300	80	760
9150	1500	K-64	1230
9160	1600	A100	990
AC4011	1500	WA150	1110
AC4005	900	WA200	1830
4006	1100	LA100 louver	940
		LA150 louver	1040
BROAN MANUFACTURING CO.		LA200 louver	1450
350	1050	**NUTONE**	
353 louver	900		
353 shutter	1140	RF-49N	1020
355	1200	RF-59N	1250
356	1600	RF-68H	1530
358	1200	WF-57	2090
N350	1050		
N353 louver	900	GF-900	900
N353 shutter	1140	GF-1200	1200
N355	1200	RF-1000	1000
N356	1600		
		TPI CORPORATION	
FASCO INDUSTRIES		PDV405	1000
AGV14	1000	GV405	1075
APRV16	1200		

MANUFACTURERS OF SOLAR-POWERED ATTIC VENT FANS

ALTERNATIVE POWER & LIGHT, 701 S. Main, Estey, WI 54667 - (608) 625-4123
12-inch fan - up to 750 cfm

INTERNATIONAL ENERGY SYSTEMS, P.O. Box 588, Barrington, IL 60011 - (708) 381-0203
12-inch fan - up to 850 cfm

SOLAR ELECTRIC, 6930 McKinley, Sebastopol, CA 95472 - (707) 829-4554
12-inch fan - up to 500 cfm

SOLO POWER, 1011-B Sawmill Rd. N. W., Albuquerque, NM 87104 - (505) 242-8340
16-inch fan - up to 1,000 cfm

In the enclosed space of your attic, with the sun beating down on it day after day, the intense heat often builds up to 140°F. It's like living under a blanket all summer long, with this super-heated air up over your living area.

Hot attic air can be absorbed by ceilings in rooms underneath and spread throughout your home, adding to hot weather discomfort. And if you have air conditioning, it can cause your system to cycle on oftener using expensive high-wattage energy!

A NuTone Attic Fan can pull this hot air out of your attic automatically...at low wattage...saving you energy! Used in conjunction with a NuTone Whole-House Ventilator, an Attic Fan can exhaust super-heated attic air during the day, while you use your Whole-House Ventilator to pull in cooler air at night.

In addition, NuTone Attic Fans exhaust moisture and condensation that can cause premature deterioration of attic insulation, shingles, roof, rafters, wiring and outside paint.

NuTone Deluxe Attic Fans are all metal!
Choose from five NuTone Attic Fans...all durably designed of steel or aluminum for long life and service. All include automatic thermostats. The thermostats will turn the Fan on at whatever temperature setting you select...from 70°F to 130°F. You can also use a simple On/Off switch for manual control.

Aluminum Roof Fan—Model RF-68H

At 1530 CFM, this superb aluminum Fan is designed for larger attics. Extra quiet (¼ hp, 1530 RPM) ball-bearing motor has automatic reset thermal protection. Uses 120v AC 60 Hz.

14" aluminum axial flow blades (4 fins) with 32° pitch, 24" diameter heavy-gauge aluminum housing is 10⅞" high. Bird-guard is galvanized hardware cloth.

Large one-piece self-flashing flange and venturi design provide complete rain seal. Roof cutout: 14½" between rafters. Easy to install on flat* or pitched roofs. 🖐

**Three more roof fan choices—
Models RF-69N, RF-59N and RF-49N**

A trimmer silhouette with 22" diameter by 9" high housings, these Fans come in your choice of aluminum or baked enamel. Each features a sealed ball-bearing motor. 23" square, one-piece self-flashing flange and venturi design provide complete rain seal. All have expanded aluminum bird-guards. Roof cutout: 14½" between rafters. Easy to install on flat* or pitched roofs.

Aluminum Roof Fan—Model RF-69N

Designed for larger attics, delivers 1250 CFM. Quiet ⅛ hp sealed ball-bearing motor (1550 RPM). 14" aluminum axial flow blade has four fins, 28° pitch. 🖐

Enameled Roof Fan—Model RF-59N

Delivers 1250 CFM for larger attics. Quiet ⅛ hp sealed ball-bearing motor (1550 RPM). 14" aluminum axial flow blade has four fins, 28° pitch. Zinc-coated steel finished in baked enamel. 🖐

Enameled Roof Fan—Model RF-49N

For smaller and medium-sized attics, the RF-49N delivers 1020 CFM with a quiet ⅛ hp sealed ball-bearing motor (1550 RPM). 14" aluminum axial flow blade has three fins, 24° pitch. Zinc-coated steel finished in baked enamel.

Wall or Gable Fan—Model WF-57N

This powerful 2090 CFM automatic louvered Wall Fan is designed for the largest attics. The quiet ball-bearing motor (⅛ hp, 1050 RPM) has automatic reset thermal protection. Uses 120v AC 60Hz. 16" diameter aluminum fan blade (4 fins) with 40° pitch. Zinc-coated steel housing (16¾" diameter x 10½" deep) is finished in baked enamel. Louver

frame measures 18" wide x 19" high x 2". Aluminum louvers open when fan is on; close when fan is off. Comes assembled for quick installation in frame or brick construction.

**Attic Fan Accessories—
Humidity Control HU-100**

Sensitive to moisture build-up, the Humidity Control activates your NuTone Attic Fan at a pre-determined setting so it can effectively remove attic moisture which can cause mildew, damage sheathing and diminish the effectiveness of attic insulation. Especially helpful in fall, winter and early spring when attic temperatures may not be high enough to activate the fan. Wires in parallel with the automatic thermostats included with NuTone Fans. Can be adjusted from 0% to 90% relative humidity. Fits any standard single gang junction box. 120v, 6 amp. Comes complete with decorative cover plate.

Cannot be used with WF-57N Wall Fan.

Automatic Heat Sensor—AHS-200

Rated at 200°F, the AHS-200 Heat Sensor will automatically shut down NuTone Attic Fan when temperature in attic reaches this level for any reason, including fire. Mounted in 4" square junction box with nailing brackets, it installs 'in line' to 120v AC power supply. Rated 10 amps.

A guide to size for your attic
Multiply the square feet of your attic area by .7 CFM for *minimum* air delivery needed. Example: 1500 sq. ft. attic area x .7 CFM=1050 CFM. For dark roofs, add 15% to CFM. For exceptionally large attics or split level homes, use two or more attic fans.

If attic moisture is a special problem, choose a NuTone Attic Fan with a slightly larger CFM rating for added protection. See Humidity Control (HU-100) above.

*When used on flat roofs, fans should be mounted on built-up curbs, to raise them above standing water level.

NuTone

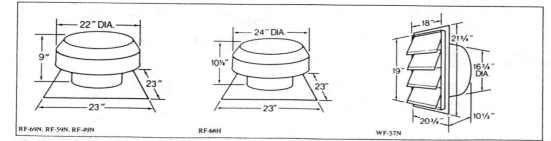

RF-69N, RF-59N, RF-49N   RF-68H   WF-57N

Size of Attic Vent Fan Required in cfm

Attic Width in feet

	20	22	24	26	28	30	32	34	36	38	40	42	44	46
20	280	308	336	364	392	420	448	476	504	532	560	588	616	644
22	308	339	370	400	431	462	493	524	554	585	616	647	678	708
24	336	370	403	437	470	504	538	571	605	638	672	706	739	773
26	364	400	437	473	510	546	582	619	655	692	728	764	801	837
28	392	431	470	510	549	588	627	666	706	745	784	823	862	902
30	420	462	504	546	588	630	672	714	756	798	840	882	924	966
32	448	493	538	582	627	672	717	761	806	851	896	941	986	1030
34	476	524	571	619	666	714	762	809	857	904	952	1000	1047	1095
36	504	554	604	655	706	756	806	857	907	958	1008	1058	1109	1159
38	532	585	638	692	745	798	851	904	958	1011	1064	1117	1170	1224
40	560	616	672	728	784	840	896	952	1008	1064	1120	1176	1232	1288
42	588	647	706	764	823	882	941	1000	1058	1117	1176	1234	1294	1352
44	616	678	739	801	862	924	986	1047	1109	1170	1232	1294	1355	1417
46	644	708	773	837	902	966	1030	1095	1159	1224	1288	1352	1417	1481
48	672	739	806	874	941	1008	1075	1142	1210	1277	1344	1411	1478	1546
50	700	770	840	910	980	1050	1120	1190	1260	1330	1400	1470	1540	1610
52	728	801	874	946	1019	1092	1165	1238	1310	1383	1456	1529	1602	1674
54	756	832	907	983	1058	1134	1210	1285	1361	1436	1512	1588	1663	1739
56	784	862	941	1019	1098	1176	1254	1333	1411	1490	1568	1646	1725	1803
58	812	893	974	1056	1137	1218	1299	1380	1462	1543	1624	1705	1786	1868
60	840	924	1008	1092	1176	1260	1344	1428	1512	1596	1680	1764	1848	1932
62	868	955	1042	1128	1215	1302	1389	1476	1562	1649	1736	1823	1910	1996
64	896	986	1075	1165	1254	1344	1434	1523	1613	1702	1792	1882	1971	2061
66	924	1016	1108	1201	1294	1386	1478	1571	1663	1756	1848	1940	2033	2125
68	952	1047	1142	1238	1333	1428	1523	1618	1714	1809	1904	1999	2094	2190
70	980	1078	1176	1274	1372	1470	1568	1666	1764	1862	1960	2058	2156	2254

Attic Length in feet (vertical axis label)

To determine what size attic vent fan you need to cool your attic effectively, find the length of your attic on the vertical column and the width of your attic on the horizontal column. Where the two columns intersect, you will find the required air flow capacity (in cubic feet per minute - cfm) of the attic vent fan needed.

MANUFACTURERS OF 115- VOLT ELECTRIC-POWERED ATTIC VENT FANS

AUBREY MANUFACTURING, 6709 S. Main St., Union, IL 60180 - (815) 923-2101

BROAN MANUFACTURING CO., P.O. Box 140, Hartford, WI 53027 - (414) 673-4340

FASCO INDUST., 810 Gillespie St., Fayetteville, NC 28302 - (800) 334-4126 (919) 483-0421

KOOL-O-MATIC CORP., P.O. Box 310, Niles, MI 49120 - (616) 683-2600

NUTONE, Madison & Red Bank Rds., Cincinnati, OH 45227 - (800) 543 - 8687 (513) 527-5100

TPI CORPORATION, P.O. Box T-CRS, Johnson City, TN 37602 - (615) 282-4131

Brighten your night with solar lights

Q: I want to add some outdoor accent and security lights, but it is difficult to get wiring to them. Are there new types of solar-powered lights available that work better than the old ones?

A: If you were dissatisfied with solar-powered outdoor lights several years ago, there are new designs and technologies that make them much more effective. With more efficient solar cells, lights, and batteries, they provide brighter and more hours of free light even after overcast days.

The new higher-efficiency solar cell panel is inconspicuously built into the top of the light. It is difficult to distinguish the new solar-powered accent lights from standard electric-powered lights. All the solar-powered lights have electric eyes to automatically switch them on at night.

For security and convenience, a motion-sensing solar floodlight is one of the most effective uses of solar power. I installed one (in only 10 minutes) on my house because it was difficult to run wiring to a standard light.

When motion is detected up to 75 feet away (the sensitivity distance can be shortened) the floodlight automatically comes on. You can adjust it to stay on for up to one minute after no more motion is detected. It also has an adjustable electric eye to control when it begins to operate at night.

With new high-capacity batteries and the brief on-time, these lights will operate 120 times on one full charge. Even if the sun does not shine for weeks, they will continue to operate. The replaceable rechargeable battery lasts for several years.

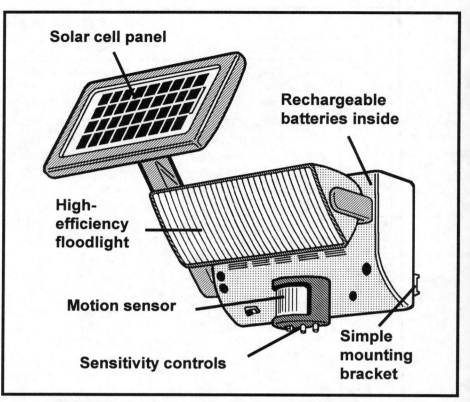

Solar cell panel

Rechargeable batteries inside

High-efficiency floodlight

Motion sensor

Sensitivity controls

Simple mounting bracket

New outdoor solar-powered lights are effective

Not all solar-powered lights are created equal. Accent, garden and walkway solar-powered lights with fluorescent bulbs provide the brightest and longest light at night. Single-crystal solar cell technology is the most efficient available.

Some models have two-level intensity switches. You can almost double the hours of light by switching to the low brightness setting. If you plan a party or have guests, you can switch it to the higher setting.

A high-temperature battery and vented battery improve efficiency and provide more hours of light at night. Double-protected solar cells and circuitry is best because it must withstand bad weather.

One convenience feature is an "easy mow" ground stake. You lift the light post out of a base that is flush with the ground so your mower passes over. Some models also have multiple lenses for even lighting. The upper prismatic lens directs light outward and the lower lens focuses it downward.

Q: The locks on our double-hung windows don't work well. Is it important to use the locks to make the weatherstripping seal properly?

A: On most newer windows, the locks hold the sashes together. This compresses the weatherstripping and provides a tighter seal.

On older warped windows, the locks can push the sashes slightly apart. You should check the air leakage with a stick of lighted incense on a windy day. You can buy new adjustable locks at most hardware stores. You may have to change the adjustment for summer and winter due to swelling.

Batteries in these lights are charged by the sun during the day. At night, when the electric eye senses no light, the solar light automatically comes on. On page **b**, I have listed the manufacturers of the best solar-powered lights and some information on their products. The type of solar cell used and several of the important design features are listed immediately after each manufacturer. After each model number, the suggested retail price and hours of light provided per charge is listed. These lights are often sold at discounted prices as are most products.

The style of each light is listed. On the bottom of this page, a sample illustration of each style is shown for your reference. After the style, the type of bulb and other features are listed for each model. A vented battery area keeps the batteries cooler. This allows them to operate most efficiently to store the greatest electricity charge during the day. A double protected and sealed solar cells compartment protects the cells against bad weather and humidity.

Single-crystal solar cells are the most efficient, but also the most expensive to produce. Greater efficiency means that they can generate more electricity for each square inch of cell area to charge the batteries. The next most efficient are semi-crystalline cells and the least efficient are amorphous cells. These amorphous (thin-film technology) are less expensive to make. You can get the same amount of electricity output, but the total area of the solar cells must be greater.

Fluorescent bulbs provide the brightest light - about four times brighter than incandescent bulbs for the same number of hours of light at night. They are also more expensive. If you want brighter light at times, for entertaining, and more hours of a dimmer light at other times, select a light with a high/low intensity switch.

At the low intensity setting, you also get twice as many hours of light from the batteries. The one "Pathmarker" light made by Siemens Solar is used just to mark a path. It uses a very efficient, yet dim, LED red light. It produces just a red glow for up to 12 hours per night. These are ideal for marking a driveway or walk entrance.

Motion-sensing security lights are an excellent fit with solar-powered light. Since these lights are on only for several minutes at a time when motion is detected, the light can operate for weeks without any sun. The motion sensitivity ranges up to 70 feet, but you will probably want to set it down from this. At 70 feet, you often pick up motion of neighbors or passing cars. You can also adjust the electric eye. This allows you to determine how dark it must be outdoors before the motion-sensing light begins to come on.

Page **c** shows some detail product information on several of these types of solar-powered lights. This will give you an idea of how they actually look and operate.

ILLUSTRATIONS OF STYLES OF LIGHTS

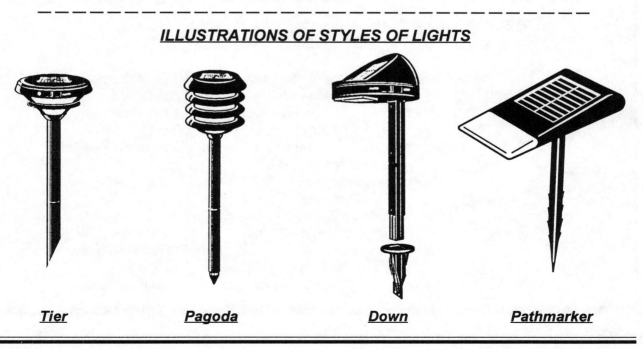

Tier   *Pagoda*   *Down*   *Pathmarker*

MANUFACTURERS OF SOLAR-POWERED OUTDOOR LIGHTS

BRINKMANN CORP., 4215 McEwen Rd., Dallas, TX 75244
(214) 387-4939

Semi-crystalline solar cells, vented battery area, double protected
SL-1 $34   light time - 5 hrs
          style - tier   bulb - incandescent
SL-4 $49   light time - 5 hrs/8 hrs (high/low)
          style - pagoda   bulb - incandescent   high/low switch
SL-5 $64   light time - 5 hrs
          style - down   bulb - fluorescent   easy-mow post
HOME GUARD $99   light time - 120 cycles
          style - motion   bulb - incandescent   70 ft. sensitivity

- -

HEATH ZENITH, P.O. Box 1288, Benton Harbor, MI 49023
(616) 925-6000

Amorphous solar cells, vented battery area, double sealed
SL-7001 $80   light time - 120 cycles
          style - motion   bulb - tungsten halogen   60 ft. sensitivity

- -

INTERMATIC, Intermatic Plaza, Spring Grove, IL 60081
(815) 675-2321

Amorphous solar cells, vented battery area, double sealed
LZ621 $55   light time - 3.5 hrs
          style - tier   bulb - incandescent
LZ682 $57   light time - 3.5 hrs
          style - down   bulb - incandescent

- -

SIEMENS SOLAR, P.O. Box 6032, Camarillo, CA 93011
(800) 325-9325 (805) 482-6800

Single-crystal solar cells, vented battery area, double protected
18431 $60   light time - 5 hrs/9 hrs (high/low)
          style - tier   bulb - fluorescent   high/low switch
17930 $60   light time - 5 hrs/9 hrs (high/low)
          style - pagoda   bulb - fluorsecent   high/low switch
18092 $60   light time - 6 hrs
          style - pagoda   bulb - fluorescent
16945 $50   light time - 6 hrs
          style - pagoda   bulb - incandescent
16953 $17   light time - 12 hrs
          style - pathmarker   bulb - red LED (soft red glow)
17935 $175   light time - 130 cycles
          style - motion   bulb - fluorescent   40 ft. sensitivity

Siemens Solar PRIME LIGHT™ FLUORESCENT

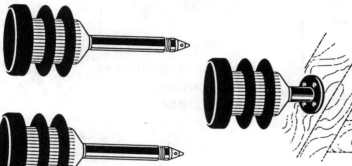

Our brightest, longest running solar light, thanks to Siemens Solar high technology design. Brightly illuminates driveways, patios, and walkways with 2 times the run time of ordinary fluorescent solar walkway lights.

- Up to 7 times brighter than competitive solar lights.
- Hi-low bulb offers choice of run times and brightness level:
  - 9-hour low-setting run time
  - 5-hour high-setting run time
- Full 2-year warranty.
- 2 times the run time of competitive fluorescent solar lights.
- Our highest capacity ALL WEATHER™ nickel cadmium batteries provide up to:
  - 50% longer run time
  - 4 times the life of other batteries
  - Easy to replace batteries; no soldering necessary.
- 3-year bulb life.
- 12-inch adjustable stake included.
- Accents driveways, garden, and walkways.

MODEL 17930

Technical Information

Solar Cell/Protection:	Single crystalline - potted silicone encapsulant; oven cured; covered with polycarbonate lens
Solar Panel Power:	1.4 watts
Battery:	2.0 Amp-hr. ALL WEATHER™ nickel cadmium; replaceable pack with wire lugs; 85% charge acceptance @ 50°C; 3-year life
Hours to Fully Charge:	6 hours
Run Time:	High setting = 5 hours; low setting = 9 hours
Bulb:	1-watt cold cathode fluorescent; plug-in connector; 3-year life; instant "ON" to -20°C; replaceable

Siemens Solar SENSOR LIGHT™

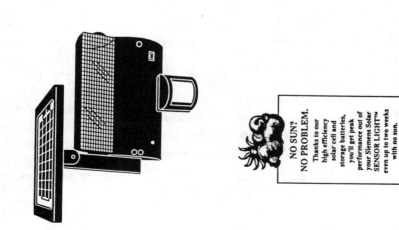

Built-in motion detector automatically turns on light when triggered. Automatically shuts off when you leave. Bright energy-efficient DULUX® fluorescent bulb lasts over 5 years. Unit mounts easily to wall, fascia, soffit or roof eave. No wiring or electrician required.

Solar powered convenience/security light with built-in motion sensor.

- Safety and security where you need it with no wiring.
- Up to 2 weeks of operation with no sun.
- Activated automatically by heat and motion (no timers or switches to set); welcomes you home and alerts you for safety.
- Bright energy efficient DULUX® bulb. Illuminates large areas evenly. Equivalent to a 75-watt flood light. 5-year bulb life.
- Installs in minutes with our universal mounting bracket. Hardware and bulbs included.
- SENSOR LIGHT™ mounts on eaves, soffits, walls, even posts. Place anywhere on or around your home or yard. For additional flexibility, solar module can be detached from unit. 14-foot cord included.
- Adjustable sensitivity control reduces false "triggers."
- No utility bills. Saves you money. Works even when the power is off.
- Full 2-year warranty.

MODEL 17935

NO SUN? NO PROBLEM.
Thanks to our high efficiency solar cell and storage batteries, you'll get peak performance out of your Siemens Solar SENSOR LIGHT™ even up to two weeks with no sun.

Technical Information

Solar Panel Cell Type/Protection:	Single crystalline; laminated EVA - Tedlar®
Solar Panel Output:	2.75 watts (± 5%)
Battery:	Sealed lead acid; 6.5 Amp-hr., up to 24-month shelf life; up to 5-year red LED light to tell when battery is low
Hours to Fully Charge:	12 hours
PIR:	Pulse count technology, eliminating false triggers; 40' range @ 110° view angle; full sensitivity and light level adjustments
Functions:	Dual operating switch modes; 3-position main operating switch: Auto -- Off -- Charge; 3-position run-time switch: Test -- 30 sec. -- 60 sec.
Run Time:	Maximum capacity = 130 60-second trips; up to 2 weeks without sun
Bulb:	9-watt DULUX® fluorescent SE; light output equivalent to 75-watt incandescent; quick start; replaceable; 5-year life

111-700093-01 REV. D

Electric car can shave driving costs

Q: Because of the gasoline tax, I want to convert my car to run on electricity or buy a new electric car. How much will it increase my monthly electric bills and can I easily convert a car myself?

A: Running a car on electricity can be less expensive than using gasoline. Electric cars require no tune-ups, no oil changes, no muffler replacements, etc., so the overall operating cost is low. From the outside and from the interior, you can not tell one from a standard gasoline-powered model.

Electric cars accelerate as fast as most cars. They have daily driving ranges of 60 miles or more and top speeds over 60 mph. One new electric sports car has "Porsche" acceleration and a top speed near 100 mph.

You dramatically reduce noise and air pollution by driving an electric car. It is more effective to control pollution at the electric utility's generating plant than at the tailpipes of millions of gasoline-powered cars.

You can either convert your existing car to electricity or buy a new complete "turnkey" model. Many companies make do-it-yourself conversion kits. These include the motor, electronic controls, wiring, gauges, and transmission adapter plate. All you have to supply are the batteries.

A high torque motor is mounted to the existing transmission by an adapter plate. This plate is designed for each car's stock transmission bolt pattern. The transmission works the same as before. The kits even have vacuum pumps for the power brakes and other accessories.

Compact cars, like Escorts, Rabbits, Corollas, are ideal for con-

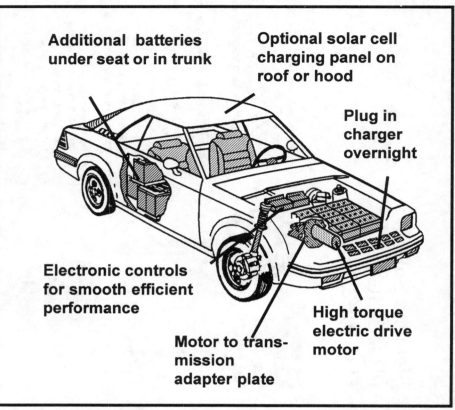

Additional batteries under seat or in trunk

Optional solar cell charging panel on roof or hood

Plug in charger overnight

Electronic controls for smooth efficient performance

Motor to transmission adapter plate

High torque electric drive motor

Kit makes electric car conversion a simple job

verting to electricity. You can mount the battery packs under the hood or in the trunk and solar cell panels on the roof for free solar battery charging.

For maintenance you can take your converted Escort, for example, to a Ford dealer for brakes, wipers, shocks, transmission repairs, etc. The electric motors and controls are the same as used in industrial lifts and trucks. Any industrial shop can repair those parts. The electronic controls and high-torque motors are reliable and require little maintenance.

Many turnkey electric cars are converted from standard new car models. They have warranties and all the options that the standard gasoline model has. You can also buy converted older models less expensively.

At 8 cents per kilowatt-hour, it costs about $1.50 to recharge a 96-

volt, 16-battery pack in the evening. If your utility company offers lower nighttime rates, the cost can be even lower. The batteries last about four years and cost about $50 each.

Q: I plan to replace my central air conditioner and furnace soon. Is there any rule of thumb to determine the size units that I need?

A: No. You should always have a contractor do a computerized analysis. Don't accept an "experienced guess". The energy needs of a house depend on too many variables for just an estimate. A furnace is rated by the heat content of the fuel it consumes. You can install a smaller high-efficiency furnace because it produces more usable heat from the same amount of fuel as a larger less efficient one.

Overall, an electric car can be cheaper to operate than a standard gasoline car. Figure 2 on this page shows the electric cost to recharge a 96-volt battery pack (sixteen 6-volt batteries). No tune-ups or oil changes needed. Many electric utility companies offer lower off-peak nighttime electric rates. This lowers your costs and it is also good for the utility company. By being able to utilize more of its generation capacity at night, when demand is typically low, the utility company can make more profit on its investment. This reduces the need for future rate increases.

Most electric cars use deep-cycle 6-volt batteries. 96 volts is adequate for small cars. For larger cars or ones with higher speeds and power, you can add more batteries. As figure 1 shows, the Chevy S-10 uses 20 batteries for 120 volts. More batteries are also heavier and bulkier, so you must consider overall weight and size for the car chassis you are converting. A single typical battery weighs about 50 pounds.

You can figure on spending about $50 per battery. If you take care of the batteries, they can last up to four years. It is important not to let batteries totally discharge. This shortens their life. Also charge them immediately when you return home. Maintain the proper water level.

Page **b** shows a list of manufacturers of conversion kits and components. Conversion kits usually contain all the major electrical components plus an adapter plate to mount the electric motor to the bell housing (transmission). You must specify what model car you are converting so the kit supplier can include the proper adapter plate. If you are handy with an end mill and welder, you can easily make your own adapter plate. Page **c** lists components of a conversion kit and prices.

Many of these suppliers are very small businesses (some do not even have a business telephone - you must write to them). Do not let this deter you from buying from them. Other than the adapter plate, all of the electrical components are similar to ones used by industrial lift trucks or golf carts. Replacement or accessory parts are available in most cities and other standard parts for the car are available at the car dealer for the type of car you are converting.

Complete electric car conversions, from brand new car models, are called turnkey cars.

New Conversions

Style:	Ford Escort sedan or wagon
Passengers:	five
Range:	30 to 60 miles
Top speed:	65 mph
Batteries:	108 volts
Price:	$22,485
Style:	Chevy S-10 pickup
Passengers:	three
Range:	30 to 60 miles
Top speed:	65 mph
Batteries:	120 volts
Price:	$22,985

figure 1

Suppliers of these are shown on Page **c**. Figure #1 on this page shows the cost of several models offered by Earth Options. They also plan to sell a futuristic mini-van for about $40,000 and a high performance sports car (90 mph top speed) for $75,000.

Power brakes are available for electric conversion cars. Since there is no gasoline engine to create the vacuum needed for the power brakes, you install a small electric vacuum motor. The standard power brakes on the car that you are converting work exactly the same as on the original car.

You can easily add a solar cell panel to let the sun help charge the battery for free while you drive or park the car. A panel will not provide enough extra electric power to greatly extend the driving range, but it will keep a trickle charge flowing to the battery pack. This improves its life.

Recharging Costs

Electric rate cents/kwh	Cost to recharge $
5.0	0.95
5.5	1.05
6.0	1.14
6.5	1.24
7.0	1.33
7.5	1.43
8.0	1.52
8.5	1.62
9.0	1.71
9.5	1.81
10.0	1.90
10.5	2.00
11.0	2.09
11.5	2.19
12.0	2.28
12.5	2.38
13.0	2.47
13.5	2.56

figure 2

SUPPLIERS OF ELECTRIC CAR CONVERSION KITS AND COMPONENTS

12 VOLT PRODUCTS, P.O. Box 664, Holland, PA 18966 - (215) 355-0525
  components, batteries, accessories

ALTERNATIVE AUTOS, P.O. Box 1249, Parker, CO 80134 - (303) 690-5031
  conversions, components

BREWER ASSOCIATES, 21511 Deerpath Ln., Malibu, CA 90265 - (213) 456-6236
  components

CALIFORNIA ELECTRIC CARS, 1669 Del Monte, Seaside, CA 93955 - (408) 899-2012
  kit car based on VW, conversions

DAVE PARES, 720 Laramie Dr., Lewisville, TX 75067 - (214) 221-4840
  conversions, components

E-MOTION, 515 W. 25th St., McMinnville, OR 97128 - (503) 434-4332
  conversions

ELECTRIC MOTOR CAR, 4301 Kingfisher, Houston, TX 77035 - (713) 729-8668
  conversions, components

ELECTRIC CAR CRAFTERS, 2S 643 Nelson Lake, Batavia, IL 60510 - (708) 879-0207
  conversions, components

EV CUSTOM CONVERSIONS, 1712 Nausika Ave., Rowland, CA 91748 - (818) 913-8579
  conversions

ELECTRIC VEHICLES INC., 2736 Windfield Dr., Mt. View, CA 94040 - (415) 964-3974
  conversions, components

ELECTRIC VEHILCES OF AMER., P.O. Box 59, Maynard, MA 01754 - (508) 897-9393
  conversions, components

ELECTRO AUTOMOTIVE, P.O. Box 1113, Felton, CA 95018 - (408) 429-1989
  conversions, components

EV MOTORSPORTS, 4073 County Rd., #187, W. Liberty, OH 43357 - (513) 599-1233
  components, kit bodies

EYEBALL ENGINEERING, 16738 Foothill, Fontana, CA 92335 - (714) 829-2011]
  conversions

HOWARD LETOVSKY, 116 Bellevue Rd., Watertown, MA 02172 - (617) 924-1663
  conversions

KAYLOR-KIT, 20000 Big Basin, Boulder Creek, CA 95006 - (408) 338-2200
  conversions

KTA SERVICES, 12531 Breezy Way, Orange, CA 92669 - (714) 639-9799
  conversions, components

MERCURY PRODUCTS, 1201 Camdon Ave., S.W. Canton, OH 44706 - (216) 456-3453
  components

NU-KAR ELECTRIC VEHICLES, 710 Hwy. 57, Collierville, TN 38017 - (901) 853-8021
  conversions, components

PERFORMANCE SPEEDWAY, 2810 Algonquin, Jackosnville, FL 32210 - (904) 387-9858
  components

SEBRING AUTO CYCLE, 3317 Maryland Ave., Sebring, FL 33872 - (813) 655-2131
  components

SEVCON, 40 North Ave., Burlington, MA 18003 - (617) 272-2000
  components

SOLAR CAR CORP., 1300 Lake Washington Rd., Melbourne, FL 32935 - (407) 254-2997
  conversions, components

EARTH OPTIONS, 6930 McKinley St., Sebastopol, CA 95472 - (800) 832-1986
  conversions, components

SOLECTRIA, 27 Jason St., Arlington, MA 02174 - (508) 658-2231
  components

SURPLUS CENTER, P.O. Box 822209, Lincoln, NE 68501 - (800) 488-3407
  components

WARD LEONARD ELECTRIC, 31 South St., Mt. Vernon, NY 10550 - (914) 664-1000
  components

SUPPLIERS OF COMPLETED TURN-KEY ELECTRIC CAR CONVERSIONS

CAL-START, 3601 Empire Blvd., Burbank, CA 91505 - (818) 565-5600

CALIFORNIA ELECTRIC CAR, 669 Del Monte Ave., Seaside, CA - (408) 899-2012

EARTH OPTIONS, 6930 McKinley St., Sebastopol, CA 95472 - (800) 832-1986

ELECTRIC MOTOR CAR SALES, 4301 Kingfisher St., Houston, TX 77035 - (713) 729-8668

ELECTRIC VEHICLE INDUSTRIES, 21 West St., Lawrence, MA 01841 - (617) 683-3675

ELECTRIC VEHICLES, 1776 "I" St., NW #850, Washington, DC 20006 - (202) 659-3950

LYMAN ELECTRIC PRODUCTS, 15 Meadow, S. Norwalk, CT 06856 - (203) 838-8491

PERFORMANCE SPEEDWAY, 2810 Algonquin, Jackosnville, FL 32210 - (904) 387-9858

SEBRING AUTO-CYCLE, P.O. Box 1479, Sebrin, FL 33871 - (813) 655-2131

SOLAR CAR CORP., 1300 Lake Washington Rd., Melbourne, FL 32935 - (407) 254-2997

SOLECTRIA CORP., 27 Jason St., Arlington, MA 02174 - (617) 894-6670

VEHMA INTERNATIONAL, 1200 Chicago Rd., Troy, MI 48083 - (313) 585-4800

ELECTRIC CAR NEWSLETTERS AND PUBLICATIONS

ALTERNATIVE ENERGY MAGAZINE, P.O. Box 19409, San Diego, CA 92119

BACKWOODS SOLAR, 8530 Rapid Lightning Creek Rd., Sandpoint, ID 83864

ELECTRIC VEHICLE NEWS, 1991 N. Ft. Myer Dr., Arlington, VA 22209

WORLD ELECTRIC TRANS. & SOLAR, P.O. Box 111, Yachats, OR 97498 - (503) 547-3506
(The owner/consultant asked to have you include $2.00 for complete info packet

---

RETROFIT KIT   K11 - $2,675.00

ORDER NO.:   K11

This kit is designed for upgrading existing EVs.

INCLUDES:
* Medium Advanced DC Motor
* Adaptor
* PMC 1221 Controller
* PB-6 Pot Box

BASIC CONVERSION KIT   K12 - $3,700.00

This is a generic kit for the conversion of a small manual transmission gasoline or diesel car to electric power. The adaptor plate will be custom-machined to suit the transmission. All other model-specific parts—motor mounts, brackets, battery racks, etc.—must be designed and fabricated by the builder. The included manual, Convert It, gives directions for designing and building these items. IN CALIFORNIA, THIS KIT IS EXEMPT FROM SALES TAX, AND CERTIFIED FOR UP TO $1,000 IN STATE PERSONAL INCOME TAX CREDITS.

INCLUDES:
* Medium Advanced DC Motor
* Adaptor
* PMC-1221 Controller
* PB-6 Potbox
* 110 Volt Charger
* Albright Main Contactor
* Heinemann Circuit Breaker
* Buss Fusible Link
* Empro Shunt
* Westach Gauge: 6 - 16 Volts
* Westach Gauge: 0 - 400 Amps
  Choice Of:
* Westach Gauge: 0 - 150 Volts OR
* Westach Gauge: 96 Volt Fuel Gauge
* Convert It Manual
ORDER NO.:   K12

DELUXE CONVERSION KIT   K13 - $4,100.00

This kit is identical to the Basic Kit listed above, with battery tools, and battery wiring supplies and tools added for your convenience. IN CALIFORNIA, THIS KIT IS EXEMPT FROM SALES TAX, AND CERTIFIED FOR UP TO $1,000 IN STATE PERSONAL INCOME TAX CREDITS.

INCLUDES:
* Medium Advanced DC Motor
* Adaptor
* PMC-1221 Controller
* PB-6 Potbox
* 110 Volt Charger
* Albright Main Contactor
* Heinemann Circuit Breaker
* Buss Fusible Link
* Empro Shunt
* Westach Gauge: 6 - 16 Volts
* Westach Gauge: 0 - 400 Amps
  Choice Of:
* Westach Gauge: 0 - 150 Volts OR
* Westach Gauge: 96 Volt Fuel Gauge
* Cable: Fifty Feet
* Belleville Washers: Thirty Five
* Shrink Tube: Four Feet of 1"
* Crimper
* Cable Shears
* Lugs: Forty 5/16" & Six 3/8"
* Noalox
* Battery Filler
* Termp. Correcting Hydrometer
* Convert It Manual
ORDER NO.:   K13

VOLTSRABBIT™ KIT   K14 - $6,975.00

This is the first ever truly bolt-in conversion kit—no design, fabrication, or welding necessary. Fits all manual transmission Rabbits. Features powder-painted battery rack and welded polypropylene battery box for acid resistance and electrical insulation. Seats 4 with cargo space. Can be installed in four days. IN CALIFORNIA, THIS KIT IS EXEMPT FROM SALES TAX. AND CERTIFIED FOR UP TO $1,000 IN STATE PERSONAL INCOME TAX CREDITS.

INCLUDES:
* Medium Advanced DC Motor
* Adaptor
* PMC 1221 Controller
* PB-6 Potbox
* 110 Volt Onboard Charger
* Sevcon DC/DC Convertor
* Albright Main Contactor
* Heinemann Circuit Breaker
* Buss Fusible Link
* Empro Shunt
* Westach Gauge: 0 - 400 Amps
* Westach Fuel Gauge: 96 Volts
* Power Brake Vacuum System
* Battery Racks & Holddowns
* Battery Box & Vent Fan
* Cable & Battery Interconnects
* Special Tools & Supplies
* Heavy-Duty Springs & Shocks
* Wiring Loom
* All Mounts & Brackets
* All Nuts, Bolts, & Hardware
* Grill & Starter Blockoffs
* Body Graphics
* Installation Instructions &
  Convert It Manual
ORDER NO.:   K14

ELECTRO AUTOMOTIVE, P. O. BOX 1113, FELTON, CA 95018-1113   (408) 429-1989

Heating with wood furnaces

Q: My heating bills are too high. Are there new types of high-efficiency central whole-house wood-burning furnaces or fireplace insert available? How can I determine if I will save much money using one?

A: The best and most-efficient method to use wood to heat an entire house is with a new high-efficiency central wood-burning furnace. It is located adjacent to your current furnace and is connected to the same duct system. It is about the same size as a typical forced-air furnace.

You can't tell whether the hot air is coming from your regular furnace or the wood-burning furnace. If the fire burns down, the regular furnace kicks on. You can also get furnaces that are located outdoors near your house. Then you don't have to carry the firewood indoors.

A wood-burning furnace can supply enough heat for most homes. It burns all night, about 8 to 12 hours, on one load of wood. A small combustion air blower is controlled by a wall thermostat, just like your regular furnace. When your house needs more heat, the blower comes on and makes the fire burn hotter.

There are also many high-efficiency wood-burning fireplaces available. These slide into your existing fireplace opening or can be added to an existing wall. Zero-clearance fireplaces are designed and insulated to rest against standard building materials without becoming a fire hazard. It is an easy do-it-yourself job to add one to your house.

Although the heat output from a fireplace is lower than from a wood-burning furnace, it is still adequate for most houses. The convection type, with a hot air blower, helps

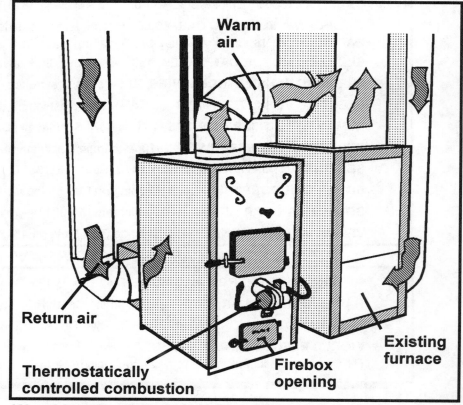

Warm air

Return air

Thermostatically controlled combustion

Firebox opening

Existing furnace

Wood-burning furnace is efficient and easy to use

circulate the heated air throughout your house.

It is a somewhat involved process to calculate whether or not heating with wood is less expensive than using your existing furnace. Since your furnace is not totally efficient, much of the energy you currently buy from the utility company is being lost up the flue.

For example, you can expect an older gas furnace to be in the 60 percent range. Knowing the efficiency and cost of gas, oil, or electricity, you can determine the cost of the heat that actually ends up heating your home.

When you compare wood-burning furnaces or fireplaces, the dealer should give you an estimate of their efficiencies. Based upon the price and type of the firewood that you buy, you can determine the cost of the same amount of heat from firewood

and compare it to your current heating costs.

Q: There are small holes drilled in the very bottom of my storm windows. It seems like they would leak cold air. Should I seal them?

A: Those holes are called weep holes and they are necessary. You can't totally stop water vapor from getting in between the storm and your primary window. It passes through tiny cracks and straight through the interior wall surface materials.

When it's cold outside, water vapor condenses in the windows and these holes let it escape. Since the holes are small, little air leaks in them. Also, cold air naturally settles to the bottom. With no entrance holes at the top, the energy loss is minimal.

Wood-burning furnaces are convenient to use. Some operate with thermostats, just like your regular gas or oil furnace. If you have a cheap source of firewood, a central wood-burning furnace is more effective than most fireplaces. Product information on wood burning furnaces is shown on page **c**.

You can use the Worksheet below to determine the savings from burning wood instead of using your conventional gas, oil, or electric central heating system. It basically calculates how much total heat your house used last year and compares the cost of using wood heat instead. You should not plan on using wood for 100% of your heat because there will be times when the furnace is down for cleaning or you run out of firewood. A target of 70% of your heat from firewood is reasonable. If you have an inexpensive and readily available source of firewood, you may increase this percentage to about 85%.

MANUFACTURERS OF HIGH-EFFICIENCY WOOD-BURNING FURNACES

CHARMASTER, 2307 E. Hwy. 2 W., Grand Rapids, MN 55744 - (800) 542-6360 (218) 326-6786
CENTRAL BOILER, Box 80, Greenbush, MN 56726 - (218) 782-2575
IRWIN ENTERPRISES, 346 Muddy Springs Rd., Lexington, SC 29072 - (803) 359-6737
HARDY MANUFACTURING CO., Rt. 4, Box 156, Philadephia, MS 39350 - (601) 656-5866
HORSTMAN INDUSTRIES, PO Box 66, Elroy, WI 53929 - (608) 462-8431
LONG MANUFACTURING, 111 Fairview St., Tarboro, NC 27886 - (919) 823-4151
TAYLOR MANUFACTURING, PO Box 518, Elizabethtown, NC 28337 - (919) 862-2576
YUKON ENERGY CORP., 3531 Nevada Ave. N., New Hope, MN 55427 - (612) 780-1720

WOOD HEAT EVALUATION WORKSHEET

1) Heating fuel you now use _____
2) Fuel unit (gal, cu. ft., etc.) _____
3) Number of Btu's per fuel unit - Chart A _____
4) Number of fuel units you used last year _____
5) Money that you spent for this fuel _____
6) Potential Btu's in the fuel you used (#3 x #4) _____
7) Efficiency of your heating system - Chart B _____
8) Btu's you actually received (#6 x #7) _____
9) Percentage of the heat load you want from wood _____
10) Convert to percentage (#9   100) _____
11) Type of wood you will burn _____
12) Cost of one cord of wood _____
13) Potential heat content in cord of wood - Chart A _____
14) Number of cords containing enough heat
       to heat your home (#8   #13) _____
15) Number of cords to supply the heat
       you need (#14 x #10) _____
16) Type of wood-burning device you install _____
17) Efficiency rating of device - Chart B _____
18) Number of cords you will need to buy (#15   #17) _____
19) Money you will spend on wood (#18 x #12) _____
20) Proportional cost of heat (#5 x #10) _____
21) Annual savings from burning wood (#20 - #19) _____

CHART A - HEAT CONTENT PER FUEL UNIT

Fuel	Unit	Btu/Unit
Oil	gallon	138,700
Kerosene	gallon	138,500
Natural Gas	therm	100,000
Natural Gas	cu. ft.	1,025
Electricity	kwh	3,414
Hardwood	cord	19,000,000
Mixed Woods	cord	17,000,000
Soft Woods	cord	15,000,000
Propane	cu. ft.	2,500
Propane	gallon	91,000
Propane	pound	21,500
Coal	ton	27,000,000

CHART B - HEATING SYSTEM EFFICIENCY RATINGS

Fuel	Heating Device	Efficiency
Oil or Kerosene	New high efficiency	.85
	Recently tuned with flue damper	.70
	Without flue damper	.60
	Average untuned	.50
Electricity	Resistance type	.95
	Heat pump	1.75
Natural gas or Propane	New high efficiency	.92
	Good condition with stack damper	.80
	Average condition	.70
	Untuned	.60
Coal	New high efficiency	.70
	Good with flue damper	.60
	Without flue damper	.55
Wood	High efficiency wood stove or furnace	.74
	Standard wood stove	.50

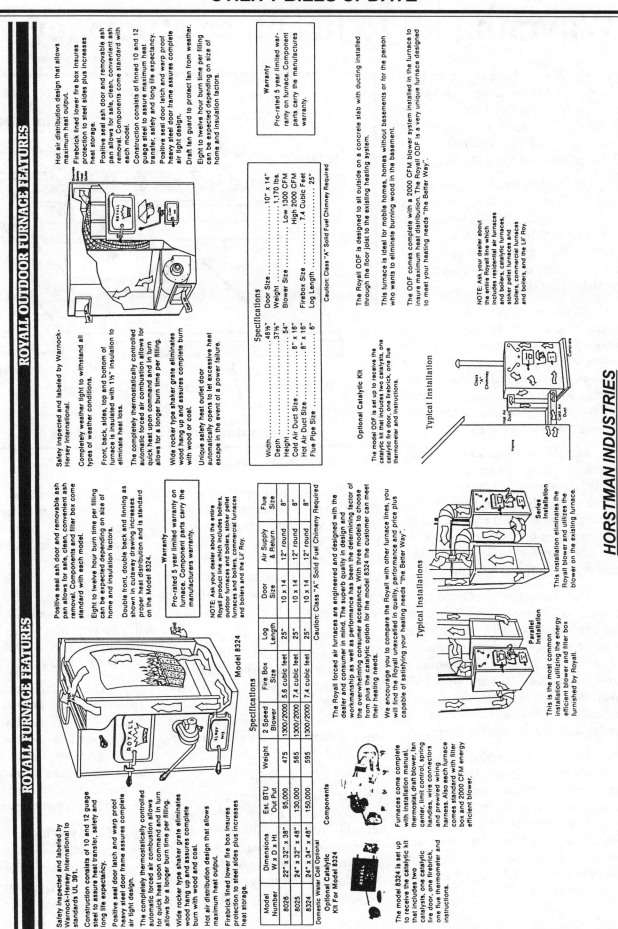

ROYALL FURNACE FEATURES

Safely inspected and labeled by Warnock-Hersey International to standards UL 391.

Construction consists of 10 and 12 guage steel to assure heat transfer, safety and long life expectancy.

Positive seal door latch and warp proof heavy steel door frame assures complete air tight design.

The completely thermostatically controlled automatic forced air combustion allows for quick heat upon command and in turn allows for a longer burn time per filling.

Hot air distribution design that allows maximum heat output.

Firebrick lined lower fire box insures protection to steel sides plus increases heat storage.

Positive seal ash door and removable ash pan allows for safe, clean, convenient ash removal. Components and filter box come standard with each model.

Eight to twelve hour burn time per filling can be expected depending on size of home and insulation factors.

Double front, double back and finning as shown in cutaway drawing increases proper heat distribution and is standard on the Model 8324.

Warranty
Pro-rated 5 year limited warranty on furnace. Component parts carry the manufacturers warranty.

NOTE: Ask your dealer about the entire Royall product line which includes boilers, outdoor furnaces and boilers, stoker pellet furnaces and boilers, commercial furnaces and boilers and the Lil' Roy.

Model 8324

Specifications

Model Number	Dimensions W x D x Ht	Est. BTU Out Put	Weight	2 Speed Blower	Log Length	Fire Box Size	Door Size	Air Supply & Return	Flue Size
8026	22" x 32" x 38"	95,000	475	1300/2000	25"	5.6 cubic feet	10 x 14	12" round	8"
8025	24" x 32" x 48"	130,000	565	1300/2000	25"	7.4 cubic feet	10 x 14	12" round	8"
8324	24" x 34" x 48"	150,000	595	1300/2000	25"	7.4 cubic feet	10 x 14	12" round	8"

Caution: Class "A" Solid Fuel Chimney Required

Components

Furnaces come complete with installation manual, thermostat, draft blower, fan center, limit control, spring handles, wire connectors and prewired wiring harness. Also each furnace comes standard with filter box and 2000 CFM energy efficient blower.

Domestic Water Coil Optional

Optional Catalytic Kit For Model 8324

The model 8324 is set up to receive the catalytic kit that includes two catalysts, one catalytic fire door, one firebrick, one flue thermometer and instructions.

ROYALL OUTDOOR FURNACE FEATURES

Safely inspected and labeled by Warnock-Hersey International.

Completely weather tight to withstand all types of weather conditions.

Front, back, sides, top and bottom of furnace is insulated with 1½" insulation to eliminate heat loss.

The completely thermostatically controlled automatic forced air combustion allows for quick heat upon command and in turn allows for a longer burn time per filling.

Wide rocker type shaker grate eliminates wood hang up and assures complete burn with wood or coal.

Unique safety heat outlet door automatically opens to let excessive heat escape in the event of a power failure.

Hot air distribution design that allows maximum heat output.

Firebrick lined lower fire box insures protection to steel sides plus increases heat storage.

Positive seal ash door and removable ash pan allows for safe, clean, convenient ash removal. Components come standard with each model.

Construction consists of finned 10 and 12 guage steel to assure maximum heat transfer, safety and long life expectancy.

Positive seal door latch and warp proof heavy steel door frame assures complete air tight design.

Draft fan guard to protect fan from weather.

Eight to twelve hour burn time per filling can be expected depending on size of home and insulation factors.

Warranty
Pro-rated 5 year limited warranty on furnace. Component parts carry the manufactures warranty.

Specifications

Width............48½"
Depth............37¾"
Height............54"
Cold Air Duct Size............8" x 16"
Hot Air Duct Size............8" x 16"
Flue Pipe Size............6"
Door Size............10" x 14"
Weight............1,170 lbs.
Blower Size............Low 1300 CFM / High 2000 CFM
Firebox Size............7.4 Cubic Feet
Log Length............25"

Caution: Class "A" Solid Fuel Chimney Required

Optional Catalytic Kit

The model ODF is set up to receive the catalytic kit that includes two catalysts, one catalytic fire door, one firebrick, one flue thermometer and instructions.

Typical Installation

The Royall ODF is designed to sit outside on a concrete slab with ducting installed through the floor joist to the existing heating system.

This furnace is ideal for mobile homes, homes without basements or for the person who wants to eliminate burning wood in the basement.

The ODF comes complete with a 2000 CFM blower system installed in the furnace to insure maximum heat distribution. The Royall ODF is a very unique furnace designed to meet your heating needs "the Better Way".

NOTE: Ask your dealer about the entire Royall line which includes residential air furnaces and boilers, catalytic furnaces, stoker pellet furnaces and boilers, commercial furnaces and boilers, and the Lil' Roy.

The Royall forced air furnaces are engineered and designed with the dealer and consumer in mind. The superb quality in design and workmanship as well as performance has been the determining factor of the overwhelming consumer acceptance. With three models to choose from plus the catalytic option for the model 8324 the customer can meet their heating needs.

We encourage you to compare the Royall with other furnace lines, you will find the Royall unexcelled in quality, performance and price plus capable of satisfying your heating needs "the Better Way".

Typical Installations

Parallel Installation
This is the most common installation utilizing the energy efficient blower and filter box furnished by Royall.

Series Installation
This installation eliminates the Royall blower and utilizes the blower on the existing furnace.

HORSTMAN INDUSTRIES

Warming up to fireplace efficiency

Q: When I burn my open fireplace, the house, including that room, seems to get colder. What can I do inexpensively to make it produce more heat yet still let me enjoy watching the fire?

A: Burning a typical open hearth fireplace actually increases your utility bills rather than cuts them. What's worse, it continues to waste energy (heated or cooled room air goes up the flue) when you are not using it.

There are several simple fireplace improvements that you can make yourself without spoiling the allure of the fire. These can easily convert your fireplace from a net energy waster to an energy producer (up to 40,000 Btuh from one design of heat circulating grate).

Installing glass doors is a must. These not only reduce the loss of heated room air when the fireplace is burning, but also when it isn't being used. Most have screens inside so you can open the glass doors sometimes if you want to hear the crackling while the fire is burning.

Don't buy the least expensive glass doors. They all look good, but the best glass doors have a tight fit with small gaps between the doors. Some have adjustable slot openings so you can control the amount of air to the fire. The back of the door frame should be stuffed with insulation to seal against the front of the fireplace.

For more heat, you can install a heat circulating grate. The grate itself is made of hollow tubing. Room air is circulated through the hot grate by a small blower. The blower is controlled by a thermostat so it continues to blow out warm air even after the fire burns down, for as long as the ashes are still hot.

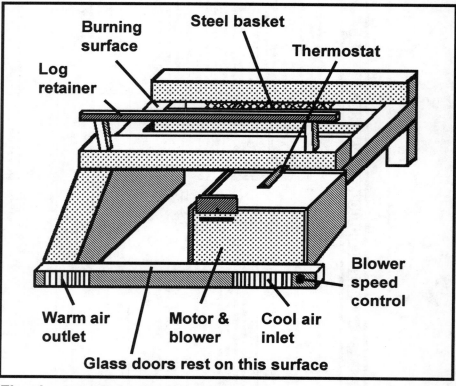

Fireplace grate heater warms room air

The most efficient models are designed to fit underneath the glass doors. Cool room air is drawn in one side and warm air is blown out the other. It raises the doors a little more than an inch. These models also are designed with the blower behind the glass doors so it is not visible.

An antique style "fire back" can also help. It is a decorative heavy metal plate which you put in the back of your fireplace. When the fire back gets hot, it radiates heat out into your room. The cast iron ones have the most decorative and interesting designs and shapes.

When you are not using your fireplace, which is most of the time, you can insert a very inexpensive reusable inflatable pillow seal in the flue opening. This totally blocks air leakage and provides insulation value. You simply put it up by the damper in the chimney and blow it up.

Using the proper type of firewood is important. High heat content wood produces more heat and reduces flammable creosote buildup in the chimney.

Q: I had wall insulation blown in years ago and it may have settled. The top of the walls feel cooler. How can I tell if it has settled?

A: Just small insulation voids result in a large energy losses. The fact that some sections of the wall feel cooler is a good indication that settling has occurred. The best way to determine the location and extent of the settling is with infrared (heat sensitive) pictures of your walls.

Once you locate the insulation voids, a 2-inch hole is usually drilled in the top of the wall above them. More insulation is carefully blown in.

There are several methods to make your fireplace more energy efficient. Manufacturers of various products are listed below and representative product information in shown on the following pages. The manufacturer of the inflatable pillow for sealing the chimney damper area (as discussed in my column) is made by Enviro/Energy, 6601 E. Mill Plain Blvd., Vancouver, WA 98661 - (206) 737-0622.

ENERGY EFFICIENT HEAT-CIRCULATING GRATES

CUSTOM FIRESCREEN, 108 Jefferson, Des Moines, IA 50314 - (515) 243-3942
 Heat circulating grate with blower

DIAMOND W PRODUCTS, 30 Railroad Ave., Albany, NY 12205 - (518) 459-6775
 Heat circulating grate with blower

HEAT-N-GLO, 6665 W. Hwy. 13, Savage, MN 55378 - (800) 669-4328 (612) 890-8367
 Heat circulating grate with blower

H. L. RADER CO., P.O. Box 7186, Columbus, GA 31908 - (800) 234-0504 (706) 322-5059
 Heat reflecting grate - no blower

THERMO-RITE, P.O. Box 1108, Akron, OH 44309 - (216) 633-8701
 Heat circulating grate with blower

HEAT RADIATING FIREBACKS

ADAMS CO., P.O. Box 268, Dubuque, IA 52004 - (319) 583-3591

VIRGINIA METAL CRAFTERS, 1010 E. Main St., Waynesboro, VA 22980 - (703) 949-9403

HIGH-QUALITY TIGHT-FITTING GLASS FIREPLACE DOORS

BECKWOOD INDUSTRIES, 889 Horan Dr., Fenton, MO 63026 - (314) 343-4100

CUSTOM FIREPLACE DOORS, Box 625, Walled Lake, MI 48390 - (313) 360-1919
 Custom-made doors only - order through local dealers

DIAMOND W PRODUCTS, see above

FIREPLACE DECOR USA, 1129 E. Curry Rd. #13, Tempe, AZ 85281 - (602) 921-2942

GOLDEN BLOUNT, 4200 Westgrove, Dallas Tx 75248 - (214) 250-3113

HEARTH CRAFT INC., 116 S. Tenth St., Louisville, KY 40402 - (502) 589-6220

HEAT-N-GLO, see above

PORTLAND WILLAMETTE, P.O. Box 13097, Portland, OR 97213 - (503) 288-7511

WILKENING FIREPLACE CO., HCR 73, Box 625, Walker, MN 56484 - (218) 547-3393

"The *Hearth Heater*® is designed with all the best features built right in."

CONVENIENT...
- Simple, removable motor box means easy maintenance of the motor or thermostat without having to remove the entire heater from the firechamber.
- 3-legged wood cradle design makes it easy to clean the fireplace and remove ashes.
- Thermostat automatically turns the heater on at 110° and off at 90°.
- Variable motor speed control for your comfort.

EFFICIENT...
- One intake and one heater duct: all air passes through the entire length of tubing for maximum heating power up to 40,000 BTU's.
- Curved grate design exposes more surface area of the heat exchanger to hot coals for best heat absorption and transfer.
- All heaters are designed with a special removable grating for easy replacement.

VERSATILE...
- Custom *Hearth Heaters* can be made to fit all shapes and sizes of fireplaces including See-through and Corner models.
- Made to fit most manufacturer's models of fireplace glass doors.

DURABLE...
- the *Hearth Heater*® is made with heavy, 1/8" welded, steel pipe construction and carries a three-year warranty.
- All electrical components including the blower are UL approved and carry a one-year warranty.

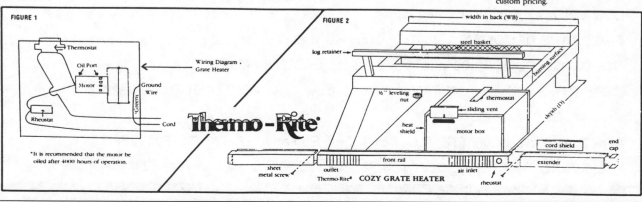

the Hearth Heater shown with Maxi-View II Trimline with top and bottom contemporary grille and fulbview bifold doors.

VISUALLY PLEASING LOG BASKET DESIGN

REMOVEABLE GRATE

EASY ACCESS FOR CLEANING

COOL ROOM AIR

WARM AIR

AIR TRAVELS THE ENTIRE LENGTH OF THE HEAT EXCHANGER TUBE

1-3/8" GRILLE

the Hearth Heater® is a great way to capture more of the heat produced by each fire in your fireplace.

SIZES:

Available in two sizes to fit all fireplaces:

21" W x 17"D   24"W x 21"D

OPTION:
- Air Tight® Doors for maximum efficiency - ask your dealer for more information.

Specially designed for placement inside your fireplace, Cozy Grate Heater generates up to 40,000 BTUs of heat per hour while hidden neatly behind your glass fireplace enclosure. And the variable speed blower (100 CFM) is equipped with a thermostat control that turns on automatically at 110 F. and off at 90 F.

HOW TO ORDER:
Measure fireplace width in back (WB) and the depth (D) to determine which model best suits your needs. Grate Heater dimensions need only be less than fireplace dimensions. All units come with a front grill 1-3/8" high and 51-1/4" wide.

Glass door will sit on top of front rail and will be elevated 1-3/8". If your door is an inside fit, you must have 1" extra depth to accomodate the depth of the grate heater.

For fireplaces with existing glass doors, simply cut heater grill to glass door width and elevate glass doors 1-3/8". Existing glass door hardware can be used to secure it to the heater grill.

MODEL	DEPTH	WIDTH	WEIGHT
TR-22	22''	24''	52#
TR-20	20''	22''	50#
TR-17	17''	20''	48#

- A unique air-flow design with one floor level outlet providing rapid heat circulation throughout the house.
- Manufactured of heavy 12 gauge steel for lasting durability.
- All electrical components UL approved.
- SAFETY—A proven 8 year safety and performance record.

The TR-36 & TR-42 Trim Bars will fit a Thermo-Rite® 36 and 42 wide series door exactly. No cutting required. The TR-54 is a 3 piece Trim Bar and must be used for Thermo-Rite® 30, 48 & 54 wide series doors. It can also be used with 36 & 42 wide series along with all competitive doors. Custom sizes and finishes are available.

CUSTOM COZY GRATE HEATERS
Custom Heaters can be ordered from the factory to fit virtually any fireplace—including see-through and corner fireplaces. Special finish grill is available.

for see-through fireplace

For two sided or see-through fireplaces you will need to know the exact depth from front to front, units will be made so that one front rail will be adjustable in case your measurement is slightly off. Specify your width.

For corner units we need a sketch showing floor dimensions of the fireplace along with the size grate heater you are ordering.

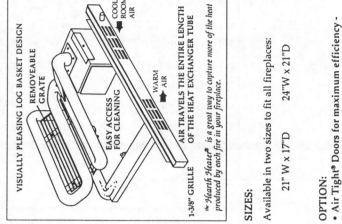

for corner fireplace

All stock and custom grate heaters come with the motor on the right. You may want the motor on the left if your electrical outlet is on the left. Refer to custom pricing.

FIGURE 1

Thermostat
Oil Port
Motor
Rheostat
Ground Wire
Green
Cord

Wiring Diagram . Grate Heater

Thermo-Rite®

*It is recommended that the motor be oiled after 4000 hours of operation.

FIGURE 2

width in back (WB)
steel basket
log retainer
burning surface
½" leveling nut
thermostat
sliding vent
heat shield
motor box
depth (D)
end cap
cord shield
extender
front rail
air inlet
rheostat
sheet metal screw
outlet

Thermo-Rite® COZY GRATE HEATER

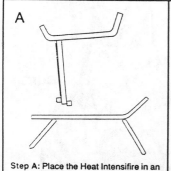

H. L. RADER COMPANY
P.O. Box 7186
1748 Northside Industrial Blvd.
Columbus, Georgia 31904
(706) 322-5059

With **HEAT INTENSIFIRE**,
20% more radiant heat is projected into
your living space.

A

Step A: Place the Heat Intensifire in an upright position at the rear of the standard grate. (see diagram A) Make sure that the Heat Intensifire balances on the lower level of the standard grate.

B

½" BOLT

STANDARD WASHER

MOUNTING BRACKET

LOCK WASHER

½" NUT

Step B: Put bolts, washers, and nuts together as shown in diagram. Tighten nuts and bolts with wrench. Make sure assembly is sturdy and bolts are fastened tightly.

C

Step C: The finished products. On grates 34" or wider, install two Heat Intensifires side by side.

Installation is usually easy, but it's much easier if you follow the instructions using this step-by-step guide.
There are many different fireplaces and your DraftStopper can be adapted to work in almost all of them. Even if you have an unusual construction, the following directions will help you make to a successful installation in less than 20 minutes. The time you spend installing the DraftStopper is one of the best investments you can make. It is the easiest and most inexpensive way to stop valuable warm air from leaving your home and minimizing drafts and odours from your fireplace.

DraftStopper™
A Patented Hi-Tech Product

Fig. 3

PERIMETER SEAL FLANGE

SEALING EDGES

DAMPER HANDLE SUITABLE AREAS

Fig. 2

DAMPER HANDLE LOCATIONS

TOP

BACK

BOTTOM SIDE

FRONT

PINCH CLASP

FIRE WARNING LABEL Fig. 1

FIRE BOX PREPARATION

To start, measure the firebox throat just below the damper level to ensure the DraftStopper will fit. (fig 4.)

In order to reach the full width you may need to use a foot pump or blow very hard to inflate fully (NOT more than 2 psi.).

The maximum firebox size for standard installations is 16 1/2" wide by 38" long.

If your opening is larger than this you have two choices. You are welcome to return the unit (unused) for full credit or you can spend some extra time installing the unit further up in the damper enclosure. You will find instructions for doing this on the other side of instruction sheet.

Next, get a flashlight and take a look at your firebox. (fig 5.) Check for anything that could puncture your DraftStopper. Puncture points could be metal spurs on the damper, damper hinge, damper retaining brackets or angle iron lintel. Any rough finished mortar should be chipped away and flattened with a hammer. If you have glass doors, bolt ends may need to be filed smooth or removed. This a good time to see, and measure where your damper handle is.

The walls of the firebrick or metal surfaces, where the unit will seal, should be brushed clean and wiped well with a damp cloth. (fig 6.) This will give you the best fit and tightest seal. You do not have to repeat this procedure with each installation, but check after every ten fires or so. You may want to brush & clean firebox again if necessary. This process also helps to reduce the transfer of soot to the unit and prevents dirt from getting into your house. Also clean DraftStopper if it is slippery from excess soot and dust.

Next, take a look at your damper handle, if you have one. If the handle is on either side of the firebox, DraftStopper will mold around it for a good seal. If the handle passes through the center of the firebox, remove it if you can.

If the handle cannot be removed easily, do not worry. As shown in fig 2. & fig 7, there are five places where you can cut a slit for your damper. Decide which slit you will use and with a sharp knife make an incision in the middle area that is slightly smaller than the damper handle. This is done to reduce air leakage. If the hole is too big you can fill it with a piece of foam rubber insulation or paper towel.

Note: If damper handle or crosspiece restricts installation for any reason, see if you can completely remove or dismantle damper handle and cross pieces. If you cannot, please see fig 21 and/or fig 19 or fig 22 on opposite side.

INSTALLATION PROCEDURE

Spread the DraftStopper out flat and inflate just enough to give it some shape. Seven or eight full breaths is usually enough to partially fill the DraftStopper.

Hold the DraftStopper in front of you as shown in fig 9. To begin installation the inflation tube must be on the bottom side and closest to you.

To install, wedge the DraftStopper into the upper-most back corner on a 15 degree angle (see fig 10) so that the bottom side creates the seal. The DraftStopper should be against the back wall of firebox immediately below the damper level.

When the backside is positioned, roll the front side of the DraftStopper up under the front lintel (fig 11) so that a good seal is formed along both front and back sides. Sometimes you must open the damper to allow unit to better fit into flue.

Note: the more the DraftStopper is inflated, the wider an area it fills. If air can pass by the unit then reposition until a tight seal is formed. You can use some paper towels to fill any air pockets that persist.

* If unit wants to slip out double check:
  1. Did I brush the bricks?
  2. Did I wipe the walls where unit touches?

If you have done the above and the unit is still not secure, check the instructions for specific kinds of fireplaces on other side of this sheet.

When the DraftStopper is installed and sealed, inflate it further until it is drum hard, no more than 2 psi. (fig 12.). Installation is very easy after you have done it a few times and your firebox has been properly prepared.

Fig. 4 Fig. 5 Fig. 6 Fig. 7 Fig. 8 Fig. 9 Fig. 10 Fig. 11 Fig. 12

Enviro/Energy Marketing Services

Store bought logs okay for quick fires

Q: On occasion, I use fireplace logs instead of wood for a fast-starting couple-of-hour-long fire. Do they burn as hot as real wood? How do I select the best types of real firewood to buy?

A: Fireplace logs, that you buy at your grocery store, are ideal for the quick evening fire. Depending on the brand, they produce more than twice as much heat per pound as real firewood and burn for more than three hours.

In addition to the ease of handling and lighting, fireplace logs are friendly to the environment. They burn much cleaner than real wood - 80% less carbon monoxide, 50% less smoke, 78% less creosote, 69% less particulate matter, and 50% less ash.

Fireplace logs are made of waste sawdust and a low-grade paraffin wax to bind it together. Before fireplace logs were developed, all of this sawdust ended up in landfills.

To get the maximum heat output from your fireplace, real wood is the best choice. It is important to buy the proper type of firewood for a long hot fire without building up chimney creosote or polluting the air.

When you select firewood, the most important factors to consider are its heat content and burning qualities. Also, the aroma given off as it burns is important. Many of the fruit, nut, and cedar woods give off pleasant scents.

The heat content of wood depends primarily on the weight of the wood. Most firewoods produce about 7,000 Btu of heat per pound. Resinous woods produce a little more heat, but they produce more chimney creosote too.

The weight of woods varies from about 25 to 70 pounds per cubic foot. Figure on about 90 cubic feet of usable wood per cord (depending on how tightly it is stacked).

Firewood is generally classified as hardwood or softwood. Deciduous trees are typically denser hardwoods and conifers are less-dense softwoods.

Don't just select all dense hardwoods to get the longest burning, cleanest fire. Resinous softwood is easier to light and is excellent for starting the fire. You can then add the denser hardwood heat content logs.

To make sure the wood is well-seasoned by looking for cracks and checks in the ends of the logs. Knock two logs together. Well-seasoned logs make a sharp ringing sound, not a dull thud.

Q: I plan to install ceramic tile on my foyer floor to capture solar heat. How rigid must the flooring be to keep the tiles from cracking?

A: The Tile Council of America specifies a deflection no greater than 1/360 of the span for the floors that will be covered with ceramic tile. This means a ten foot long floor should not deflect more than 1/3 of an inch. Remember, the tile and thin set are additional weight.

If your floor deflects too much, you should contact a structural engineer about the best method to support it for better rigidity. If you are tiling over two different surfaces, wood flooring and a concrete slab, lay down tar paper or plastic film. Float mortar reinforced with galvanized mesh under the tile.

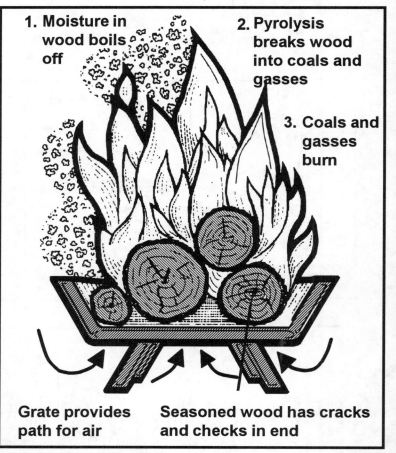

1. Moisture in wood boils off

2. Pyrolysis breaks wood into coals and gasses

3. Coals and gasses burn

Grate provides path for air

Seasoned wood has cracks and checks in end

How firewood burns in a fireplace

As the chart below shows, fireplace logs burn cleaner than real wood. They are safer because less carbon monoxide and chimney creosote are produced. (See manufacturers list and specifications. "*n/a*" means specs. are not available.) Also, fireplace logs are made from low-grade wax and sawdust that would otherwise end up as waste.

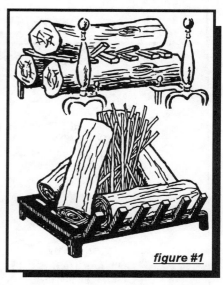

figure #1

The typical 5-lbs. fireplace log burns for about 3 hours and a 3-lbs. log burns for about 2 to 2-$\frac{1}{2}$ hours. It takes about 15 minutes for one to reach "full flame".

These logs are ideal for a short evening fire when you plan to go to bed in several hours. Even though they burn down quickly without hot coals like real wood, follow standard safety precautions as if you are burning real wood.

Pine Mountain logs are uniquely shaped like a quarter of a log with two flat sides. This reduces the possibility of their accidentally rolling out of the fireplace. Duraflame logs are the largest, at 6 lbs., so they burn longer and provide more heat per log. I sometimes use a fireplace log to start my wood fire when I run out of kindling. The 3-lbs. logs or several even smaller "starter logs" work well.

Pages **b** and **c** list many common types of firewood, the densities, and general burning characteristics. The heat content of wood is generally a function of the density of the wood. Hardwoods are usually the heaviest.

The densities are listed in lbs. per cubic foot for each type of wood. For seasoned firewood, there are approximately 7,000 Btu of heat per lb. of wood. Resinous wood has a slightly higher heat content than other wood of equivalent density. The resinous wood also lights easily, but it burns dirtier and can create more chimney creosote deposits.

Starting a fire with some soft resinous wood followed by denser hardwoods is a good fire building technique. Figure #1 shows several methods for laying a fire. The top method is commonly used in England.

The bottom method, teepee method, creates many narrow vertical paths to promote better draft between the logs. Place a layer of crumpled newspapers on top of the logs to warm the chimney and create a quick draft.

MANUFACTURERS OF FIREPLACE LOGS

CALIFORNIA CEDAR PROD., PO Box 1230, Stockton, CA 95201
"Duraflame" - 3.2 lbs. and 6 lbs. logs   (209) 461-6615

heat content - 15,000 Btu/lb.	*particulate* - 69% less
carbon monoxide - 88% less	*ash* - 90% less
creosote - 78% less	*smoke* - 50% less

FLAME GLO, 123 Industry St., Toronto, ONT, M6M 5B6
"Flame Glo" - 3 lbs. and 5 lbs. logs   (416) 763-5533

heat content - 14,105 Btu/lb.	*particulate* - 70% less
carbon monoxide - 90% less	*ash* - 92% less
creosote - 75% less	*smoke* - n/a

KROGER COMPANY, 1014 Vine St., Cincinnati, OH 45202
"Firelog or Northern" - 3 lbs. and 5 lbs. logs   (513) 762-4000

heat content - 15,000 Btu/lb.	*particulate* - n/a
carbon monoxide - n/a	*ash* - 92% less
creosote - 75% less	*smoke* - n/a

PINE MOUNTAIN, 1375 Grand Ave., Piedmont, CA 94610
"Pine Mountain" - 3 lbs. and 5 lbs. logs   (510) 654-7880

heat content - 15,000 Btu/lb.	*particulate* - 66% less
carbon monoxide - 78% less	*ash* - 50% less
creosote - 66% less	*smoke* - 57% less

Type of Tree	Density	General burning characterisitcs
Eastern Trees		
AMERICAN BEECH	52	Hard to split, slow burning
AMERICAN LINDEN	30	Very soft, poor flue
BLACK ASH	47	Easy to split, good fuel
BLACK CHERRY	42	Expensive, easy to split, good fuel
BLACK GUM	47	Can't split, fair fuel
BLACK HAW	62	Not need to split, good fuel
BLACK LOCUST	58	Easy to split, good fuel
BLACK OAK	51	Easy to split, good fuel
BLACK WALNUT	47	Easy to split, fair fuel
BOX ELDER	32	Easy to split, fair fuel
BROOM HICKORY	65	Hard to split, good fuel, slow burning
BUR OAK	55	Hard to split, good fuel
CANADA PLUM	51	Easy to split, good fuel
CHINKAPIN OAK	64	Difficult to split, excellent fuel
COMMON JUNIPER	31	Aromatic, resinous, fast burning
COTTONWOOD	32	Easy to split, fast burning, poor fuel
EASTERN HEMLOCK	30	Easy to split, resinous, fast burning
EASTERN IRONWOOD	60	Not need to split, slow burning
EASTERN RED CEDAR	36	Easy to split, resinous, fast burning
EASTERN WHITE OAK	57	Easy to split, slow burning, good fuel
FLOWERING DOGWOOD	60	Not need to split, excellent fuel
HACKBERRY	41	Easy to split, good fuel
HONEY LOCUST	52	Slow burning, excellent fuel
NORTHERN BALSAM	31	Easy to split, resinous, fast burning
NORTHERN RED OAK	50	Difficult to split, good fuel
OHIO BUCKEYE	33	Easy to split, fair fuel
PAPER BIRCH	47	Easy to split, bark is good starter
PECAN	54	Aromatic, difficult to split
PERSIMMON	62	Not need to split, excellent fuel
PIN OAK	51	Excellent fuel, slow burning
PIN CHERRY	37	Aromatic, fair fuel, easy to split
PITCH PINE	41	Easy to split, resinous, fast burning
RED ASH	47	Easy to split, good fuel
REDBUD	46	Easy to split, slow burning
RED MAPLE	45	Easy to split, good fuel
RED SPRUCE	32	Easy to split, resinous, fast burning
SASSAFRAS	38	Easy to split, fair fuel
SCARLET OAK	50	Easy to split, excellent fuel
SHADBUSH	60	Easy to split, excellent fuel
SHAGBARK HICKORY	63	Difficult to split, slow burning
SILVER MAPLE	39	Easy to split, fair fuel
SOURWOOD	55	Difficult to split, excellent fuel
SOUTHERN BALSAM	32	Easy to split, resinous, fast burning
SWAMP CEDAR	24	Easy to split, resinous, fast burning
STAGHORN SUMAC	32	Easy to split, poor fuel
SUGAR MAPLE	52	Easy to split, excellent firewood
SWAMP WHITE OAK	56	Easy to split, slow burning
SWEET BUCKEYE	30	Difficult to split, poor fuel
SWEET GUM	43	Easy to split, resinous, poor fuel
SYCAMORE	42	Slow burning, good fuel
TAMARACK	45	Easy to split, resinous, fast burning
TULIP TREE	33	Easy to split, fair fuel
WHITE ASH	48	Easy to split, good fuel
WHITE BASSWOOD	31	Poor fuel
WHITE PINE	30	Easy to split, resinous, fast burning
SWEET CRABAPPLE	52	Aromatic, easy to split
WITCH HAZEL	42	Aromatic, not need to split
YELLOW BIRCH	51	Difficult to split, good fuel

Type of Tree	Density	General burning characterisitcs
Western Trees		
ALPINE FIR	26	_Easy to split, resinous, poor fuel_
ARIZONA CYPRESS	36	_Aromatic, easy to split, resinous_
BALSAM POPLAR	26	_Easy to split, poor fuel_
BITTER CHERRY	33	_Easy to split, fair fuel_
BLACK COTTONWOOD	29	_Easy to split, fair fuel_
BLUEBERRY ELDER	37	_Easy to split, fair fuel_
BLUE SPRUCE	28	_Easy to split, resinous, poor fuel_
BROWN BIRCH	45	_Easy to split, good fuel_
BUR OAK	54	_Difficult to split, excellent fuel_
CALIFORNIA BUCKEYE	37	_Easy to split, fair fuel_
CANOE CEDAR	28	_Easy to split, resinous, fair fuel_
CASCARA BUCKTHORN	44	_Easy to split, good fuel_
COAST REDWOOD	30	_Easy to split, poor fuel_
DESERT CATALPA	44	_Good fuel_
DESERT SMOKETREE	41	_Not need to split, fair fuel_
DOUGLAS FIR	38	_Easy to split, resinous, fair fuel_
DWARF MAPLE	45	_Easy to split, good fuel_
ELEPHANT TREE	46	_Aromatic, resinous_
ENGELMANN SPRUCE	26	_Easy to split, poor fuel_
FIRE CHERRY	37	_Aromatic, easy to split, fair fuel_
GAMBEL OAK	63	_Excellent fuel_
GRAND FIR	26	_Easy to split, resinous, poor fuel_
INCENSE CEDAR	30	_Aromatic, easy to split, resinous_
MACNAB CYPRESS	41	_Aromatic, easy to split, resinous_
MOUNTAIN ALDER	36	_Not need to split, good fuel_
MOUNTAIN ASH	41	_Easy to split, fair fuel_
MOUNTAIN HEMLOCK	33	_Easy to split, resinous, poor fuel_
BLACK COTTONWOOD	29	_Easy to split, poor fuel_
NETLEAF HACKBERRY	27	_Not need to split, good fuel_
NEW MEXICAN LOCUST	60	_Not need to split, excellent fuel_
NOBLE FIR	34	_Easy to split, resinous, poor fuel_
OREGON ALDER	36	_Easy to split, good fuel_
OREGON ASH	42	_Easy to split, good fuel_
OREGON WHITE OAK	55	_Excellent fuel_
PACIFIC DOGWOOD	56	_Excellent fuel_
PACIFIC PLUM	48	_Aromatic, good fuel_
PORT OXFORD CEDAR	34	_Aromatic, easy to split, resinous_
SILVER FIR	32	_Easy to split, resinous, poor fuel_
SUGAR PINE	26	_Easy to split, poor fuel_
TAN OAK	51	_Easy to split, excellent fuel_
TRUE MESQUITE	57	_Aromatic, excellent fuel_
UTAH JUNIPER	41	_Aromatic, resinous_
VALLEY OAK	55	_Easy to split, excellent fuel_
VELVET ASH	50	_Easy to split, excellent fuel_
VINE MAPLE	50	_Easy to split, excellent fuel_
WESTERN CHINQUAPIN	41	_Easy to split, good fuel_
WESTERN HEMLOCK	38	_Easy to split, resinous, fair fuel_
WESTERN LARCH	55	_Easy to split, good fuel_
WESTERN MULBERRY	57	_Difficult to split, excellent fuel_
WESTERN SUGAR MAPLE	55	_Easy to split, excellent fuel_
WESTERN SYCAMORE	36	_Difficult to split, fair fuel_
WHITE FIR	27	_Easy to split, resinous, poor fuel_
WHITE PINE	33	_Easy to split, resinous, poor fuel_
WILD RED PLUM	47	_Aromatic, easy to split, good fuel_
WILLOWS	40	_Not need to split, fair fuel_
YELLOW OAK	64	_Easy to split, excellent fuel_
YELLOW PINE	35	_Easy to split, resinous, fair fuel_

Coolest fireplaces keep houses warm

Q. I want to add a wood-burning fireplace to my living room. I want it to provide some heat, but I don't want an ugly insert with tiny glass doors. What types of regular-looking fireplaces should I consider?

A. Adding a new attractive and energy-efficient fireplace, or replacing an old one, is an excellent investment. Not only will you enjoy it and reduce your utility bills, but you generally get more back in higher resale value than its initial cost. You should easily be able to install a prebuilt zero-clearance fireplace yourself.

An old open hearth fireplace loses more heat than it generates. Most of the heat loss is the result of already-heated room air being drawn up the chimney. This pulls cold outside air into your home. You feel toasty warm in front of the fireplace, but the rest of your house feels like an icebox.

There are many energy-efficient "regular-looking" fireplaces available. The most important features to look for are tight fitting doors, a tight damper, heat-circulating blower, and provisions for outdoor air. These features are all needed to reduce the indoor air loss up the chimney.

For the maximum heat output and energy efficiency, you should consider heat-circulating types of fireplaces. These look like regular fireplaces, but they have an extra shell around the back of the fireplace firebox.

A small blower circulates room air around the hot firebox and blows heated air out into your room. This increases the efficiency dramatically and reduces the load on your furnace to heat the rest of your house. The

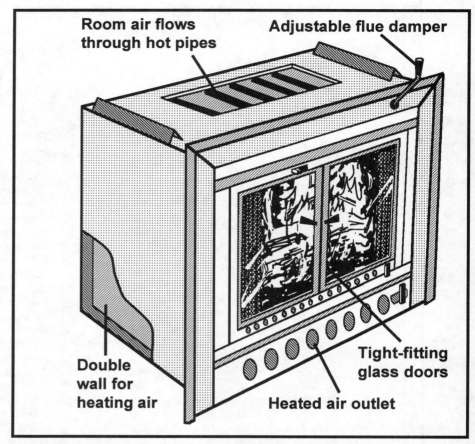

Room air flows through hot pipes

Adjustable flue damper

Double wall for heating air

Heated air outlet

Tight-fitting glass doors

Circulating fireplaces are efficient and attractive

more expensive models have thermostats and multi-speed quiet blowers.

When making your selection of a fireplace, inspect the quality of the fit and finish, especially around the doors. The hinges and latches should be heavy-duty. Shine a flashlight around the closed doors to find gaps. If there are gaps, you may see the light shine into the fireplace.

To realize the maximum heat output and enjoyment from your fireplace, you should only burn well-seasoned wood. With a lower moisture content, seasoned wood starts easier and burns hotter. Harder woods tend to burn cleaner and minimize creosote buildup in your chimney.

Q: When we take showers in the morning, there is only enough hot water for one shower. Our 50-gallon electric water heater is not leaking. Do I need a new one or can I fix this one?

A: When there is only a small supply of very hot water from an electric water heater, it is usually caused by a faulty lower heating element. You can easily install a new heating element yourself. Purchase one at your hardware store and follow the simple installation instructions.

Old water heaters are not well insulated. While you are at the hardware store, get a water heater tank insulation jacket or make one yourself using old wall insulation batts.

If you want a regular heat-circulating fireplace, select one with provisions for outdoor combustion air. This reduces the amount of already-heated room air that is sucked up the chimney. In the following manufacturers list, "outdoor combustion air" refers to air ducted into the firebox.

Where it is listed as "indirect", the outdoor air is mixed with the room air. This is slightly less efficient, but it brings some fresh air into your home. Many of the fireplace manufacturers publish maximum heat outputs in Btu/hour. The outputs are listed after the manufacturers. This heat output figure will vary considerably depending on the type of wood that you burn, so use it only as a general reference to compare fireplaces.

With an electric blower to circulate the room air through the fireplace heat exchangers, the heat output is usually greater. Natural convection uses no blower, but relies on the principal that hot air rises. Cool room air is drawn in the bottom as the heated room air naturally flows out the top. Some other options to consider are the types of controls. Some of the fireplaces have built-in internal thermostats to control the blower. Others can use a remote wall thermostat, like on a furnace, to control the blower and heat output.

MANUFACTURERS OF HEAT-CIRCULATING FIREPLACES

ASHLEY HEATER CO., P.O. Box 128, Florence, AL 35631 - (205) 767-0330
Natural convection or blower, outdoor combustion air

COUNTRY FLAME, 1200 Industrial Park, Mt. Vernon, MO 65803 - (417) 466-7161
Blower, outdoor combustion air, 175,000 Btu/hr.

DERCO INC., P.O. Box 9, Blissfield, MI 49228 - (517) 486-4337
Blower, no outdoor combustion air, 36,500 Btu/hr.

DOVRE, 401 Hankes Ave, Aurora, IL 60505 - (800) 468-7387   (708) 844-3353
Natural convection or blower, outdoor combustion air, 60,000 Btu/hr.

FIREPLACE MFG., 2701 S. Harbor, Santa Ana, CA 92704 - (800) 888-2050 (714) 549-7782
Natural convection or blower, outdoor combustion air

FOURTH BAY, 10500 Industrial Dr., Garrettsville, OH 44231 - (800) 321-9614   (216) 527-4343
Natural convection, indirect outdoor combustion air

FUEGO FLAME, P.O. Box 3551-2618, Quincy, IL 62305 - (800) 445-1867   (217) 223-3473
Natural convection, no outdoor combustion air, 50,000 Btu/hr.

HEATILATOR INC., 1915 W. Saunders, Mt. Pleasant, IA 52641 - (800) 247-6798
Natural convection or blower, outdoor combustion air

HEAT-N-GLO, 6665 W. Hwy. 13, Savage, MN 55378 - (800) 669-4328   (612) 890-8367
Natural convection or blower, outdoor combustion air, 60,000 Btu/hr.

KOZY HEAT, P.O. Box 577, Lakefield, MN 56150 - (800) 253-4904   (507) 662-6641
Natural convection or blower, outdoor combustion air, 65,000 Btu/hr.
Internal thermostat, gold plated doors

MAJESTIC, 1000 E. Market St., Huntington, IN 46750 - (800) 962-3123   (219) 356-8000
Natural convection or blower, outdoor combustion air, 55,000 Btu/hr.

MENDOTA FORGE, 1890 Wooddale, St. Paul, MN 55125 - (800) 825-2858 (612) 731-5367
Natural convection or blower, outdoor combustion air, 60,000 Btu/hr.

MANUFACTURERS OF HEAT-CIRCULATING FIREPLACES - cont'd.

RUEGG FIREPLACES, 216 Hwy. 206, Ste. 12, Somerville, NJ 08876 - (908) 281-9555
Blower, indirect outdoor combustion air, 55,000 Btu/hr.

SUPERIOR FIREPLACE CO., 4325 Artesia Ave., Fullerton, CA 92633 - (714) 521-7302
Natural convection or blower, outdoor combustion air

VERMONT CASTINGS INC., Prince St., Randolph, VT 05060 - (802) 728-3181
Blower, outdoor combustion air, 50,000 Btu/hr. Wall-mounted thermostat

WILKENING FIREPL., HCR 73, Box 625, Walker, MN 56484 - (800) 367-7976 (218) 547-1988
Natural convection or blower, outdoor combustion air, 130,000 Btu/hr.
24 ct. gold plated doors

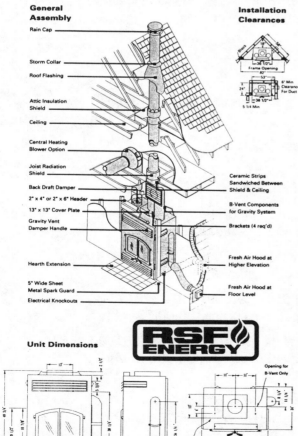

General Assembly

- Rain Cap
- Storm Collar
- Roof Flashing
- Attic Insulation Shield
- Ceiling
- Central Heating Blower Option
- Joist Radiation Shield
- Back Draft Damper
- 2" x 4" or 2" x 6" Header
- 13" x 13" Cover Plate
- Gravity Vent Damper Handle
- Hearth Extension
- 5" Wide Sheet Metal Spark Guard
- Electrical Knockouts

Installation Clearances

- Ceramic Strips Sandwiched Between Shield & Ceiling
- B-Vent Components for Gravity System
- Brackets (4 req'd)
- Fresh Air Hood at Higher Elevation
- Fresh Air Hood at Floor Level

Unit Dimensions

RSF ENERGY

The Opel 2000 Specifications

BTU/Hour EPA Test	10,680–49,735
BTU/Hour (actual)	5,000–70,000
Heating Capacity	1,500–3,000 sq ft*
Flue Size	7" or 8" diameter
USA; approved with the following chimneys:	Ameritec HS
	ICC EXEL HT
	GSW JSC
	ProJet 3103
	Metal-fab TG
	Ryder FP HT/Commander 5103
	Security ASHT
	Selkirk Metalbestos SSII
	Simpson Dura-vent SDP
Canada; approved with the following chimneys:	ULC-S629 chimney—all makes
	ICC EXEL/2100
	Security ASHT
	ProJet 3103
	GSW JSC
	Ryder FP HT/Commander 5103
	Selkirk Metalbestos SSII
Firebox (firewood length 18")	22"w x 16"h x15"d
Outside Dimensions	36 1/2"w x 49 3/4"h x 24"d
Weight	450 lbs
Clearance to Combustibles	Zero clearance sides, top and back to stand-offs
Outside Combustion Air	5" diameter intake, meets R2000 standards

*Dependent on: R factor, ceiling height, window surface area, weather zones etc.

Part #	Options	
FFHB5	Internal Blower	Thermally activated with remote mounted rheostat control
	Gold Door	Tarnish-free gold
FDL	Gold Louvre	Tarnish-free gold
FEHC4	Thermostat Control	Wall-mounted electrical thermostat
FDFS	Screen Door	Slip-in installation
FDK	Rock Retainer Kit	Facing installation kit
FDK-1	Rock Retainer Kit	Facing installation kit for use when blocking top louvre
FEHC6	Central Heating Control Kit	Thermostat & 8" backdraft damper
FFHB6	Central Heating Blower	Variable speed
FDV	Gravity Vent Kit	8" start & finishing collars, grill & shut off valve
FFHCZ-1	Zone Heat Control	Solid state junction board
FFHCZ-2	Zone Heat Damper	Thermostat & 8" motorized damper
Gas Log Option		See Instruction Manual

The SunBurst™ Fireplace *Everything your hearth desires.*

The SunBurst fireplace offers all the features you expect from a quality engineered model—plus some of the unexpected. Like porcelain enamel exterior accents, striking brass plated or matching color grille, reversible door for left or right handed operation, brass spring handle, decorative log retainer and ash pan.

The SunBurst fireplace has models available with either a 6″ or 8″ chimney system to fit your specific needs.

Efficiency

The innovative design of the SunBurst fireplace produces radiant and convected heat for maximum heating efficiency. Convection occurs when cool room air is drawn under the firebox from the floor, heated as it passes over the surface of the cast iron, and flows out of the convection chamber through the top grille.

The SunBurst meets the U.S. Environmental Protection Agency fireplace requirements. (method 28A).

Construction

Materials: Cast iron firebox, grate, log retainer and door; high temperature insulation enclosed in an aluminized steel housing; ceramic fire viewing glass.

Standard Features: Removable door, sparkscreen, ash pan, grate, log retainer, decorative double wall fireback.

Options: Outside air kit, 125 CFM fan kit, natural or liquid propane gas kits, surround trim kits in choices of matte black, Bright Brass, Antique Brass or Silver finish. Window trim in brass or silver tone finish. Air deflector (for reduced mantel clearance) in matte black, Bright Brass, Antique Brass or Silver finish. Four colors of porcelain enamel finish include:

Grey Aristocrat	Cameo Creme
Brown Magellica	Black Ebony

SunBurst style upper air grille in choices of black, Bright Brass, Antique Brass or four porcelain enamel colors.

Louvered style upper and lower air grilles in choices of brass or silver tone finishes. Black available in upper grille only.

Installation

The zero clearance design of the SunBurst fireplace can be enclosed in a wooden framework or wall, which can then be covered with paneling, dry wall or any kind of masonry. Special footings are not required unless you are planning to construct a large masonry surround. The SunBurst fits into a standard 24″ deep chimney chase. For copy of complete installation and operation manual, send $1.00 with your name and address to Dovre.

Contact local building or fire official about restrictions and installations inspection requirements.

Specifications

BTU/hour	60,000 Maximum
Overall Efficiency	Over 60%
Color	Midnight Black
Safety Listing	Underwriters Labs. Inc. —UL 127
Flue Size *Refer to SunBurst installation manual for details.*	6″ or 8″ Insulated Chimney
Height	39″ (41″ including 2″ standoff— Nominal Dimensions)
Width	33″ (Nominal Dimensions)
Depth	22″ (Nominal Dimensions)
Weight	410 lbs.
Exposed Glass Surface	25″ Diagonal
Log Length Capacity	22″ Maximum
Firebox Size	3 Cubic Feet

Important Use only completely dried wood. When burning wood with a high moisture content, a significant quantity of energy will be lost in drying the wood.

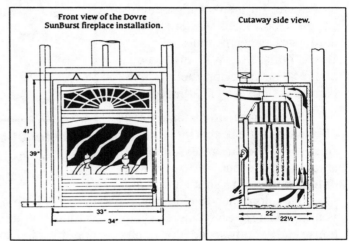

Front view of the Dovre SunBurst fireplace installation.

Cutaway side view.

The design of the Dovre SunBurst is a trademark of Dovre, Inc., 1987. All rights reserved.

10 Year Limited Warranty

Product design, specifications, color availability and hue are subject to change without notice. BTU rating is to be used as a guideline only, and does not imply a guarantee of the heating capacity of this unit. Factors affecting the heating capabilities of this unit include: climate, building construction and condition, amount of insulation, location of the unit, and air movement in the room. Heat output also depends on the condition and type of wood used as fuel, and on the draft and type of chimney system used in the installation.

Authorized Dovre Dealer

Dovre®

A New Generation in Fireplace Technology

401 Hankes Avenue
Aurora, Illinois 60505-1716
Toll Free 1-800-DOVRE US
Inside IL 708-844-3353

Member
WOOD HEATING ALLIANCE

Corn-burning stoves offer efficient heat

Q: I want to lower my heating bills and use "American-made", environmentally-safe fuel. Explain how super-efficient corn-burning stoves work and can they burn other renewable fuels?

A: New small corn-burning stoves are energy efficient and one can produce enough heat for an average home. Using kernels as a heat for homes means fewer American dollars spent on foreign fuel supplies and more jobs and profits for American farmers.

In addition to burning corn, with a simple modification, some of these stoves can burn small high-energy pellets made from waste sawdust, cardboard, paper, peanut shells, sunflower hulls, etc.. With efficiencies above 80%, these corn/pellet stoves can cut your overall heating costs.

Since these stoves operate so efficiently, little heat is lost with the flue gases. The flue gases (almost no smoke) are cool enough to be vented outdoors through a small horizontal pipe. You don't need a chimney, so you can locate one anywhere in your house and a multi-speed blower circulates the heated air. Some models have built-in air filters.

Corn/pellet stoves are very convenient to operate. You simply pour a bag of corn or pellets into a hopper on the back of the stove. One hopper full can provide more than a full day's heat. Once you light the fire in the stove, you just fill the hopper each day. It stays lit.

You can control the corn/pellet stove with a wall thermostat. When your house needs heat, a slow-moving auger inside the stove speeds up and feeds more corn or pellets to the small super-efficient fire chamber. When your house is warm enough,

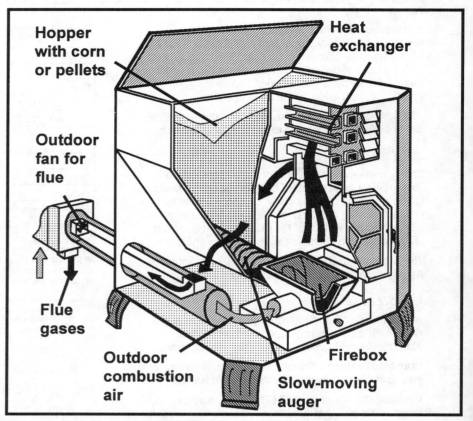

Corn/pellet stove is efficient and clean-burning

the auger slows down again to a "pilot light" rate.

For both safety and efficiency, combustion air is drawn in from outdoor by a fan and the flue gases are forced outdoors. This forced combustion air flow over the small pellets (about one inch long) or kernels of corn produces the very hot and extremely-clean burning fire.

These stoves, especially when burning low-ash pellets, produce less than 1.5 grams of emissions per hour with virtually no sulfur emissions which can cause acid rain. This is much lower than EPA regulations.

Corn/pellet stoves are available as freestanding units or fireplace inserts. A freestanding unit is the size of a small wood-burning stove. Some models have attractive and colorful metal cabinets with gold-plated trim.

Q: Over the past several years, I have made my house more energy efficient by caulking and insulating. Now, during extremely cold weather, there is window condensation, especially in the kitchen and bathroom. Why?

A: Condensation on windows and walls is caused by too much moisture in the air inside your home. When the temperature of the windows drops to the dew point, they begin to sweat.

Since your house is more airtight, moisture that used to leak outdoors is trapped inside. With a more airtight efficient house, you will have to run your kitchen and bathroom exhaust fans more often when using these rooms. Also, make sure there are no leaks in your clothes dryer vent duct.

Many of the freestanding models do not require chimneys. They vent outdoors through a small horizontal pipe through the wall. Several of the stoves listed below will require a major modification when switching from corn to wood pellets, so it may not be feasible to burn both types of these fuels in the stove. Some burn only corn or only pellets. There is a slight difference in the design of the fire pot for corn or pellets. Some of the pellet stoves can burn a mixture of 70% pellets and 30% corn without being modified. The types of fuels each uses is listed below with the manufacturer.

Corn is a little more difficult to burn than pellets. The corn first forms a liquid before it burns. This leaves a "clinker" in the firepot which must periodically be cleaned out. When burning wood or other types of pellets, there is very little maintenance required other than to empty the ash tray every several days. The motor bearings require a few drops of oil each year.

It is important to keep the heat exchanger surfaces clean for the best heat transfer. You should clean the soot off of the heat exchanger surfaces several time each year. This just requires using a stiff wire brush on the metal surfaces. Some models require you to remove small sheet metal panels. These are easily accessible through the large front door.

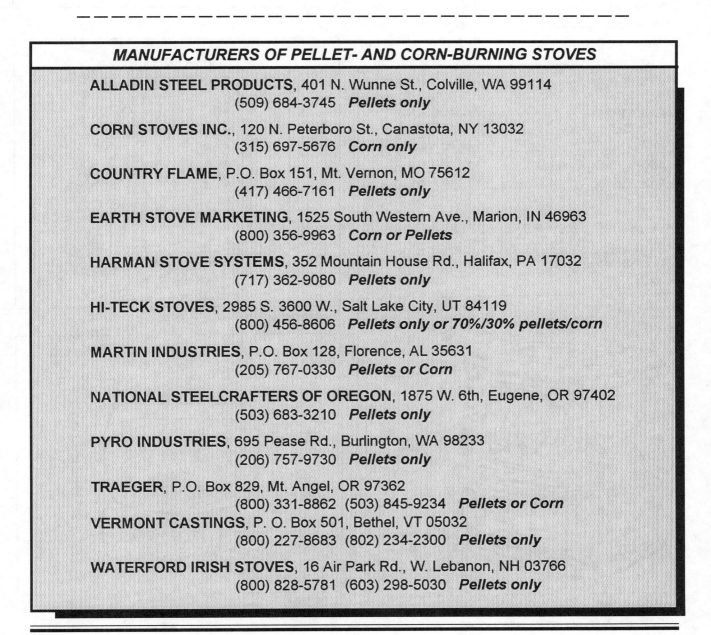

MANUFACTURERS OF PELLET- AND CORN-BURNING STOVES

ALLADIN STEEL PRODUCTS, 401 N. Wunne St., Colville, WA 99114
(509) 684-3745 *Pellets only*

CORN STOVES INC., 120 N. Peterboro St., Canastota, NY 13032
(315) 697-5676 *Corn only*

COUNTRY FLAME, P.O. Box 151, Mt. Vernon, MO 75612
(417) 466-7161 *Pellets only*

EARTH STOVE MARKETING, 1525 South Western Ave., Marion, IN 46963
(800) 356-9963 *Corn or Pellets*

HARMAN STOVE SYSTEMS, 352 Mountain House Rd., Halifax, PA 17032
(717) 362-9080 *Pellets only*

HI-TECK STOVES, 2985 S. 3600 W., Salt Lake City, UT 84119
(800) 456-8606 *Pellets only or 70%/30% pellets/corn*

MARTIN INDUSTRIES, P.O. Box 128, Florence, AL 35631
(205) 767-0330 *Pellets or Corn*

NATIONAL STEELCRAFTERS OF OREGON, 1875 W. 6th, Eugene, OR 97402
(503) 683-3210 *Pellets only*

PYRO INDUSTRIES, 695 Pease Rd., Burlington, WA 98233
(206) 757-9730 *Pellets only*

TRAEGER, P.O. Box 829, Mt. Angel, OR 97362
(800) 331-8862 (503) 845-9234 *Pellets or Corn*

VERMONT CASTINGS, P. O. Box 501, Bethel, VT 05032
(800) 227-8683 (802) 234-2300 *Pellets only*

WATERFORD IRISH STOVES, 16 Air Park Rd., W. Lebanon, NH 03766
(800) 828-5781 (603) 298-5030 *Pellets only*

Specifications

VERMONT CASTINGS, INC.

Fuel size/type .... Wood/cardboard pellets*
Maximum pellet capacity .... 48 lbs. (21.7 kg.)
Maximum burn time .... 30 hours
Range of heat output .... 8,000-40,000 Btu's/hr.
Maximum heat output .... 40,000 Btu's/hr.**
Area heated .... 1,600 ft² (148 m²)
EPA Emissions rate .... EPA Exempt***
Efficiency rating 80.0%
Loading .... Top
Exhaust vent .... 3" (75 mm)
Exhaust vent position .... Rear
Ash handling system .... Removable ash pan
Front glass panel .... High-temperature ceramic
Top glass panel .... Tempered glass
Weight .... 375 lbs. (171 kg.)
Width .... 24-3/4" (780 mm)
Depth .... 19-1/4" (488 mm)
Height .... 31-1/2" (800 mm)

*As s specified by the A.P.F.I. and F.F.I.

**Maximum heat output based on laboratory testing using full loads of wood pellets

***Method 28A

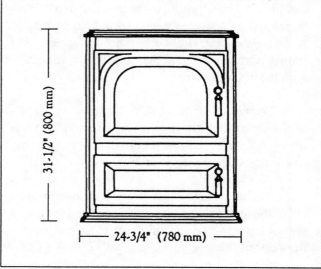

Front elevation

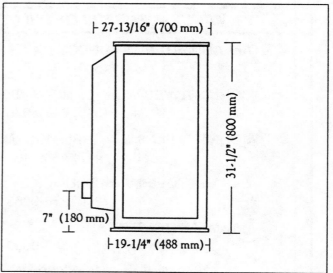

Side elevation

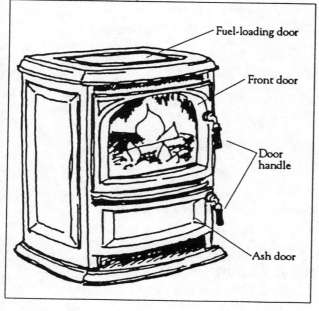

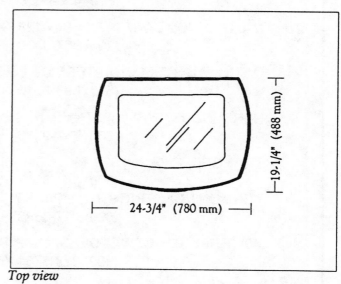

Top view

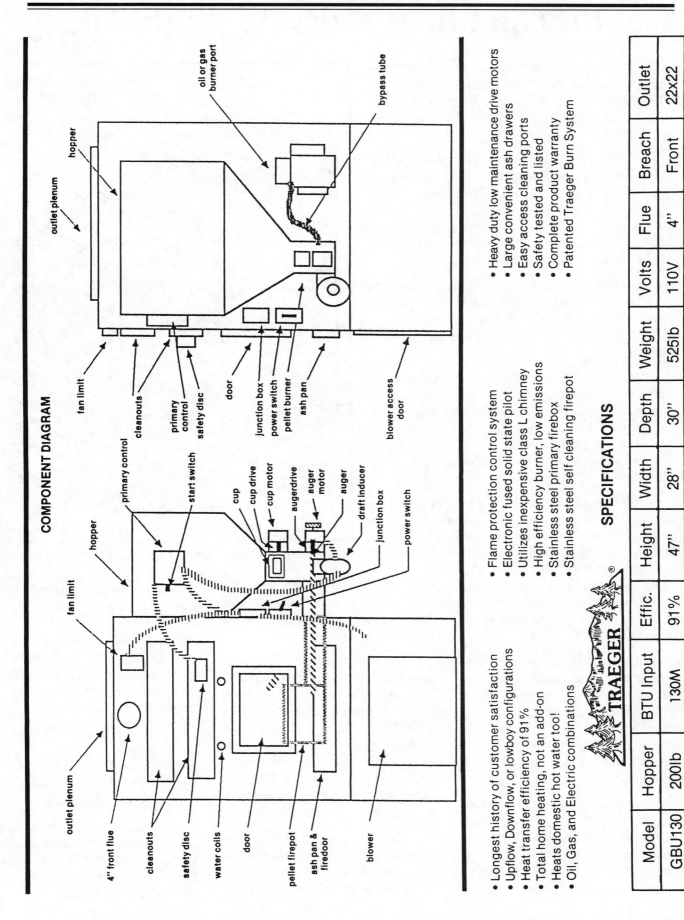

COMPONENT DIAGRAM

(component diagram labels)

outlet plenum — hopper — oil or gas burner port — bypass tube — fan limit — cleanouts — primary control — safety disc — door — junction box — power switch — pellet burner — ash pan — blower access door

hopper — primary control — start switch — cup — cup drive — cup motor — augerdrive — auger motor — auger — draft inducer — junction box — power switch — fan limit

outlet plenum — 4" front flue — cleanouts — safety disc — water coils — door — pellet firepot — ash pan & firedoor — blower

- Longest history of customer satisfaction
- Upflow, Downflow, or lowboy configurations
- Heat transfer efficiency of 91%
- Total home heating, not an add-on
- Heats domestic hot water too!
- Oil, Gas, and Electric combinations

- Flame protection control system
- Electronic fused solid state pilot
- Utilizes inexpensive class L chimney
- High efficiency burner, low emissions
- Stainless steel primary firebox
- Stainless steel self cleaning firepot

- Heavy duty low maintenance drive motors
- Large convenient ash drawers
- Easy access cleaning ports
- Safety tested and listed
- Complete product warranty
- Patented Traeger Burn System

SPECIFICATIONS

TRAEGER ®

Model	Hopper	BTU Input	Effic.	Height	Width	Depth	Weight	Volts	Flue	Breach	Outlet
GBU130	200lb	130M	91%	47"	28"	30"	525lb	110V	4"	Front	22x22

Geothermal heat units do double duty

Q. I need a new central air conditioner. I've heard of ground-source heat pumps that produce $4 of free heat for each $1 on my utility bills. Are they also super efficient for air-conditioning?

A. The correct name is "geothermal heat pump" and they are also super-efficient central air conditioners. Replacing a ten-year-old central air conditioner with a geothermal heat pump can cut your air-conditioning bills by up to 50%. The steady high cooling capacity insures comfort even on the hottest days.

Even if you have a gas furnace, it may be economical to add on a geothermal heat pump. With some of the new geothermal units, you pay only 20 cents on your electric bill for each $1 of heat you get in the winter.

Another advantage of geothermal heat pump is free hot water in the summer. The waste heat removed from your house runs through a special heat exchanger. This transfers the heat to your water heater, so you get free hot water all summer. It can heat water in the winter cheaper than an electric water heater.

A geothermal heat pump is very efficient for heating and cooling because it uses the earth as a source for heat in the winter and a sink to exhaust heat in the summer. Since a condenser fan is not needed, the entire system (in a sound-proof cabinet) is located inside your utility room or basement. It's indoors, so there's little maintenance and risk of damage.

In the summer, ground temperatures several feet deep can be 30 degrees cooler than the outdoor air. This makes it easier for the heat pump to exhaust heat from your house. In the winter, the ground can be 40 to 50 degrees warmer than the air, so it is easier to draw out the free heat.

A closed-loop geothermal heat pump system circulates a water/anti-freeze solution in a small plastic pipe buried in the ground. This long pipe can be laid horizontally in a very narrow, several-feet deep trench. An-

other closed-loop system uses a long vertical pipe in a hole in the ground. An open-loop system can use water from ponds or wells.

There are several design variations that effect efficiency. One manufacturer has a two-speed compressor. It runs in the super-efficient slow speed 80% of the time. It switches to high-speed only during very hot or cold weather. Many models now use new low-maintenance scroll or inertia compressors. Other models have multi-speed blowers for comfort.

Another design runs the refrigerant through the pipes in the ground. This eliminates one of the heat exchangers and therefore increases ef-

ficiency. A vertical "fence" of pipes is used in a narrow trench.

Q: My gasoline lawn mower quit yesterday and I am considering an electric one. Does an electric lawn mower use more energy?

A: An electric lawn mower is more energy-efficient than a gasoline mower. Small gasoline engines are inefficient, require tune-ups, are noisy, and severely pollute the air.

A typical electric lawn mower has a motor that draws about 11 amperes. At an electric rate of 9 cent per kilowatt-hour, for example, it costs about 12 cents per hour's use.

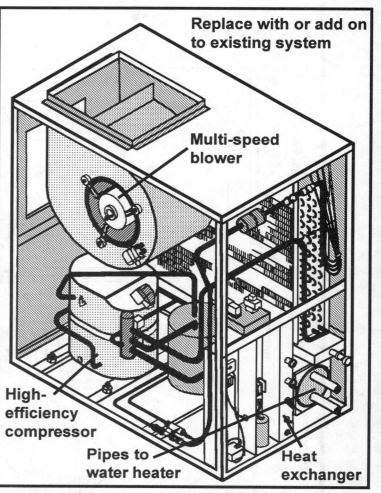

Replace with or add on to existing system

Multi-speed blower

High-efficiency compressor

Pipes to water heater

Heat exchanger

Geothermal heat pump is efficient year-round

Geothermal heat pumps are the most efficient electric heating method for your house. It is also the most efficient central air conditioner available. The following chart compares operating costs for various heating systems. The geothermal efficiency is shown at COP=3.3.

A geothermal heat pump is efficient because it uses the heat storage capacity of the earth for heating and cooling. In the heating mode, the earth acts as a giant solar collector. Although the air temperature can drop to below zero, the ground temperature stays warm.

In the winter, a geothermal heat pump draws its heat from this warm ground. In early fall, when the ground is warmest after a long summer, some geothermal heat pumps can provide 6 Btu of heat for each 1 Btu which shows on your utility bill (coefficient of performance - COP of 6). At the end of the winter, when the ground is colder, you may only get 3 Btu of heat for each 1 Btu you pay for (COP = 3). In cold weather, a standard air-type heat pump may have only COP = 1.2

In the summer, a geothermal heat pump exhausts your house heat to the cool ground, not to hot and humid 90° outdoor air. This cuts your cooling bills. You can install a water heater option which uses the waste heat from your house to heat the water in your water heater. This gives _free_ hot water whenever the heat pump is running in the cooling mode.

Page **b** and **c** lists the manufacturers of geothermal heat pumps and specifications on their products. One manufacturer, U.S. Power, circulates the refrigerant through copper pipes in the ground (called "DX" system).

The cooling and heating output specifications (per ARI 330 specifications for closed-loop systems) are listed after each manufacturer. If you have an open-loop system using water from wells or ponds, the efficiencies will probably be even higher.

Most efficient units (EER = 20+) use two-speed compressors. They only switch to high-speed during severely hot or cold weather. Scroll and inertia compressors are also very efficient, quiet, and reliable with fewer moving parts than a reciprocating compressor. The entire heat pump system is located inside your home in a soundproof cabinet, about the size of a standard furnace.

The prices for geothermal heat pumps vary significantly. Your contractor must size one for your specific house depending on the length of ground loop, local conditions, and your budget.

Several manufacturers gave me typical prices, but most would not because of the individuality of each home. An average single-speed 3-ton (36,000 Btuh cooling) unit costs in the range of $3,800 to $4,800. Add to this an average installed cost of $600 to $800 per each ton of cooling capacity for the ground pipe loop. Total installed "DX" system (U.S. Power) averages $7,500. A water heater option costs $500 to $1,000. If you now use an electric water heater, definitely get this option.

How Energy Costs Compare
(Space Heating)

100% Eff. Electric Resistance [Cents/kWhr]	330% Eff. Earth Energy Heat Pump [Cents/kWhr]	60% Eff. Fuel Oil Furnace [$/Gal.]	60% Eff. Propane Furnace [$/Gal.]	90% Eff. Propane Furnace [$/Gal.]	60% Eff. Natural Gas Furnace [$/MCF]	90% Eff. Natural Gas Furnace [$/MCF]
2.0	6.0	.49	.32	.48	3.51	5.27
3.0	9.0	.73	.48	.72	5.27	7.91
5.0	15.0	1.21	.80	1.21	8.79	13.18
7.0	21.0	1.70	1.13	1.69	12.30	18.45
9.0	27.0	2.18	1.45	2.17	15.82	23.73
11.0	33.0	2.67	1.77	2.65	19.33	29.00

READING THIS CHART: Each line represents typical energy costs for electric resistance heat and corresponding costs for the earth energy heat pump and alternative systems. For example, to equal the cost of a high efficiency earth energy heat pump system at 9¢ per kWhr, electric resistance heat must operate at 3¢ per KWhr, a 60 percent efficient propane furnace must operate at 48¢ per gallon, and a 60 percent efficient natural gas furnace must operate at $5.27 per MCF, etc.

Use these formulas to compare energy costs in your area:

ASSUMPTIONS

Fuel Source	BTU Heat Content	Annual Seasonal Operating Efficiency
Electricity	3.414 BTU/kWhr.	100%
#2 Fuel Oil	138,000 BTU/Gal.	60%
Propane	91,500 BTU/Gal.	60% or 90%
Natural Gas	1,000,000 BTU/MCF	60% or 90%

FORMULAS

ALTERNATE FUEL PRICE TO ELECTRIC RATE CONVERSION FORMULA:
(Fuel Price) ÷ (Efficiency) X (341,400) ÷ (BTU Heat Content) = (Electric Rate)
Example of $0.72/Gal Propane to Electricity with a Super Efficient Furnace
(0.72) ÷ (0.90) X (341,000) ÷ (91,500) = 3.0¢/kWhr.
ELECTRICITY RATE TO ALTERNATE FUEL PRICE CONVERSION FORMULA:
(Electric Rate) X (Efficiency) X (BTU Heat Content) ÷ (341,400) = (Fuel Price)
Example of 2.8¢/kWhr Electricity Rate to #2 Fuel Oil with a Regular Furnace
(2.8) x (0.60) x (138,000) ÷ (341,000) = $0.68/Gal.

ADDISON PRODUCTS, 7050 Overland Rd., Orlando, FL 32810 - (407) 292-4400
Compressor type -   single-speed rotary or scroll
Special features -   humidistat option to switch blower to a very low speed at desired temp.

Model #	Cooling	Heating
WPG024-1A	22,000 @ 14.7	16,000 @ 3.1
WPG030-1A	28,000 @ 15.0	19,800 @ 3.1
WPG036-1A	35,600 @ 15.0	24,800 @ 3.2
WPG042-1A	41,500 @ 14.8	30,000 @ 3.2
WPG048-1A	47,500 @ 14.4	34,000 @ 3.1

BARD MANUFACTURING CO., P.O. Box 607, Bryan, OH 43506 - (419) 636-1194
Compressor type -   single-speed scroll

Model #	Cooling	Heating
WQS30A	30,000 @ 12.5	22,600 @ 2.9
WQS36A	37,400 @ 12.0	26,800 @ 3.0
WQS42A	40,500 @ 11.9	31,000 @ 2.8

CLIMATE MASTER INC., P.O. Box 25788, Oklahoma City, OK 73179 - (405) 745-6000
Compressor type - single-speed reciprocating

Model #	Cooling	Heating
024	24,000 @ 11.5	19,000 @ 3.0
030	30,000 @ 11.0	22,000 @ 2.8
036	36,000 @ 11.2	28,000 @ 3.0
042	43,000 @ 11.3	31,400 @ 2.8
048	50,000 @ 10.9	37,400 @ 3.0

FLORIDA HEAT PUMP, 601 N.W. 65th Ct., Ft. Lauderdale, FL 33309 - (305) 776-5471
Compressor type -   two-speed reciprocating and single-speed scroll

Model #		Cooling	Heating
SX024		* 26,200 @ 16.6	* 16,000 @ 3.3
SX030		31,200 @ 16.0	21,200 @ 3.5
SX036		39,500 @ 15.4	25,400 @ 3.4
SX048	lo	28,400 @ 22.2	22,400 @ 4.7
	hi	49,000 @ 14.1	32,800 @ 3.3
SX060	lo	36,800 @ 19.7	29,600 @ 4.3
	hi	61,000 @ 12.2	43,500 @ 3.0
SX072	lo	45,000 @ 18.3	33,200 @ 3.8
	hi	74,000 @ 11.1	53,500 @ 2.7

> **Heating**
> **16,000 Btuh @ 3.3 COP**
> **Cooling**
> **26,200 Btuh @ 16.6 EER**
>
> * *This is what the figures to the right mean for each model*

HEAT CONTROLLER, P.O. Box 1089, Jackson, MI 49204 - (517) 787-2100
Compressor type -   single-speed scroll and reciprocating

Model #	Cooling	Heating
022-J	21,800 @ 10.8	16,100 @ 2.8
028-J	26,400 @ 10.8	20,100 @ 2.8
032-J	30,300 @ 10.8	22,000 @ 2.8
036-JA	34,000 @ 10.3	24,700 @ 2.8
044-J	41,700 @ 10.2	30,500 @ 2.9
054-JA	49,300 @ 9.6	39,400 @ 2.9
064-JA	59,300 @ 9.7	46,600 @ 2.9

MAMMOTH REFRIGERATION, P.O. Box 9333, Minneapolis, MN 55441 - (612) 559-2711
Compressor type -   single-speed scroll

Model #	Cooling	Heating
014	13,600 @ 13.3	10,800 @ 3.0
020	19,000 @ 12.3	15,600 @ 3.0

Models are available between these sizes, but current specs. were not available

070	72,000 @ 12.3	57,500 @ 3.1

MARVAIR, P.O. Box 400, Cordele, GA 31015 - (912) 273-3636
Compressor type - single-speed reciprocating

Model #	Cooling	Heating
WHP25HP	24,300 @ 11.2	20,200 @ 3.0
WHP31HP	31,900 @ 10.7	27,600 @ 3.2
WHP36HP	37,900 @ 12.0	29,700 @ 3.0
WHP43HP	40,400 @ 11.0	34,800 @ 3.3

TETCO, 1290 US 42 N., Delaware, OH 43015 - (800) 468-3826 (614) 363-5002
Compressor type - single-speed interia

Model #	Cooling	Heating
ES-20	22,200 @ 15.1	20,000 @ 3.6
ES-25	30,400 @ 15.0	26,600 @ 3.7
ES-30	36,400 @ 15.5	32,400 @ 3.8
ES-35	42,000 @ 14.4	37,400 @ 3.6
ES-40	48,000 @ 14.6	43,000 @ 3.6
ES-45	53,500 @ 15.0	47,500 @ 3.7
ES-50	57,000 @ 13.6	53,000 @ 3.4

TRANE, P.O. Box 7916, Waco, TX 76714 - (817) 840-3244
Compressor type - single-speed reciprocating

Model #	Cooling	Heating
GSUD028	30,600 @ 17.6	25,000 @ 4.3
GSUD035	39,900 @ 17.5	27,500 @ 3.5
GSUD041	45,000 @ 18.4	31,800 @ 3.6
GSUD051	54,500 @ 17.8	37,000 @ 3.5
GSUD061	66,400 @ 16.0	49,900 @ 3.6

U.S. POWER, 954 Marcon Blvd., Allentown, PA 18103 - (800) 669-1138 (215) 266-9500
Compressor type - single-speed interia
Special features - uses a DX system with refrigerant flowing through copper piping in the ground. The cooling EER's on all units average 14.7 (from 12 to 20) and the heating COP's average 4.7 (ranges 3 to 6 in the winter).

Model #	Cooling	Heating
C-2400	24,000	24,000
C-3000	30,000	30,000
C-3600	36,000	36,000
C-4200	42,000	42,000
C-4800	48,000	48,000
C-6000	60,000	60,000

WATER FURNACE INT'L., 9000 Conservation Way, Ft. Wayne, IN 46809 - (219) 432-5667
Compressor type - two-speed reciprocating
Special features - variable-speed blower for better comfort and efficiency

Model #		Cooling	Heating
AT045	lo	27,800 @ 20.1	22,400 @ 4.3
	hi	49,000 @ 14.0	33,000 @ 3.1
AT057	lo	36,000 @ 19.2	29,600 @ 4.3
	hi	61,000 @ 12.6	42,000 @ 3.0
AT070	lo	43,500 @ 17.1	36,800 @ 4.0
	hi	73,000 @ 10.6	53,000 @ 2.7

Compressor type - single-speed scroll or rotary

Model #	Cooling	Heating
ATV016	13,300 @ 15.6	9,900 @ 3.3
ATV022	23,400 @ 16.8	15,700 @ 3.4
ATV034	33,600 @ 14.4	25,000 @ 3.3
ATV046	48,000 @ 14.9	35,000 @ 3.4

Generators good backup power source

Q: We sometimes have electric power outages. To keep my furnace blower, sump pump, refrigerator, freezer, lights, etc. running, I plan to buy an emergency generator. What are available and are they efficient?

A: Electric utility power outages can be a problem. Even if you have a gas- or oil-fired furnace, without electricity for the blower, there is no heat. Extended power outages can allow frozen foods to thaw and spoil. Home security systems often stop functioning.

The most effective and convenient types of home emergency standby generators are 8 to 10 kilowatt (KW) output systems. These systems are located outside your house and look very similar to an outdoor central air conditioner unit. You can get systems as large as 20 KW output.

Inside your house, near your existing circuit breaker panel, you locate an automatic transfer switch. The electronic circuitry senses when the utility power goes off or the voltage is too low. Automatically, it starts the generator motor and switches your house power from the utility lines to your own generator.

Within less than a minute, you have electric power again during a utility power outage. It also starts (exercises) the generator motor once a week for a short period to make sure it is operating properly. Manual transfer switches are available which require you to physically throw the switch.

These small 8 KW to 10 KW systems utilized small air-cooled or water-cooled engines. These are similar to motorcycle or small automobile engines. They are designed to operate on natural gas, bottled gas, or gasoline. The home-sized generators are efficient. When powered on natural gas, the fuel cost alone is equivalent to about 12 cents per kilowatt-hour of electricity produced. The only additional operating cost is generally changing the engine oil once a year.

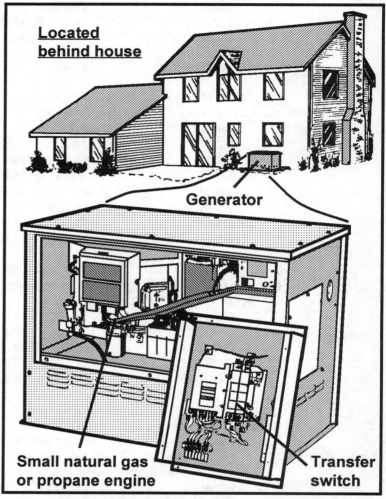

Located behind house

Generator

Small natural gas or propane engine

Transfer switch

Generator starts automatically at power outage

To determine the size of the emergency generator that you need, add up the watts used by the appliances and lights you want to keep running during a power outage. The wattage usage is usually shown somewhere on the products' nameplates.

For example, a furnace blower uses about 1000 watts of electricity, color TV - 300 watts, gas dryer - 400 watts, freezer - 500 watts, microwave oven - 800 watts.

Q: I always argue with my husband about the proper direction for a ceiling paddle fan to rotate in the winter. I think it should blow up, not down. Who is correct?

A: Chalk one up for you. The blades of a ceiling paddle fan should rotate to blow the room air upward. This slowly moves warm air near the ceiling upward and outward along the ceiling. The warm air then slowly flows down the walls without creating a chilly draft.

Most ceiling fans have a small reversing switch on the side of the motor housing. During the winter, operate the ceiling fan on the lowest speed to save electricity and not create a draft.

If you install a standby emergency generator for your house, it is most convenient to also install an automatic transfer switches. When there is a power outage, this will automatically switch on the generator and disconnect you from the utility company's lines. This gives you emergency power even when you are not home and it also protects the utility workers when they try to make repairs.

A typical generator output capacity for residential use is from 8 to 10 kilowatts. You can get generators as large as 20 kilowatts. The smaller ones have small air-cooled engines. For greater electrical output and longer life, particularly in areas where there are may power outages, you may consider a generator with a water-cooled engine.

These engines are very similar to a small motorcycle or automobile engine, except that they run on natural gas or propane. Engines run much cleaner on natural gas than they do on gasoline, so there is little regular maintenance. Propane burns as cleanly as natural gas. Some of the units have an automatic cycle to periodically switch on the generator and self-check its operation. Product information is shown on the following pages.

To determine the size of generator you need, refer to the chart below which shows the wattage used by various electric appliances in your home. These are typical wattages, so check the nameplate on your appliance for its exact wattage consumption. Then just sum up all the wattages. Unless you are on an unlimited budget, select a generator just large enough to power the essential electric appliances in your house - several lights, burglar alarm, furnace blower, radio or TV, etc.

MANUFACTURERS OF WHOLE-HOUSE STANDBY EMERGENCY GENERATORS

GENERAC CORP., P.O. Box 8, Waukesha, WI 53187 - (414) 544-4811

KOHLER POWER SYSTEMS, 444 Highland Dr., Kohler, WI 53044 - (414) 565-3381

ONAN CORP., 1400 73rd N.E., Minneapolis, MN 55432 - (800) 888-6626 (612) 574-5000

TYPICAL WATTAGES FOR VARIOUS HOUSEHOLD APPLIANCES

Appliance	Watts	Appliance	Watts
Air conditioner (room)	850	Humidifier	200
Clothes dryer (electric)	4,850	Jig saw	300
Clothes dryer (gas)	400	Lighting	1,000
Coffee maker	1,200	Microwave oven	800
Dehumidifier	300	Security system	250
Dishwasher	1,200	Sump pump	700
Electric skillet	1,250	Television (color)	300
Fan (attic)	350	Washing machine	500
Freezer	500	Water heater (electric)	2,700
Furnace blower	1,000	Well pump	1,000
Heater (portable)	1,350		

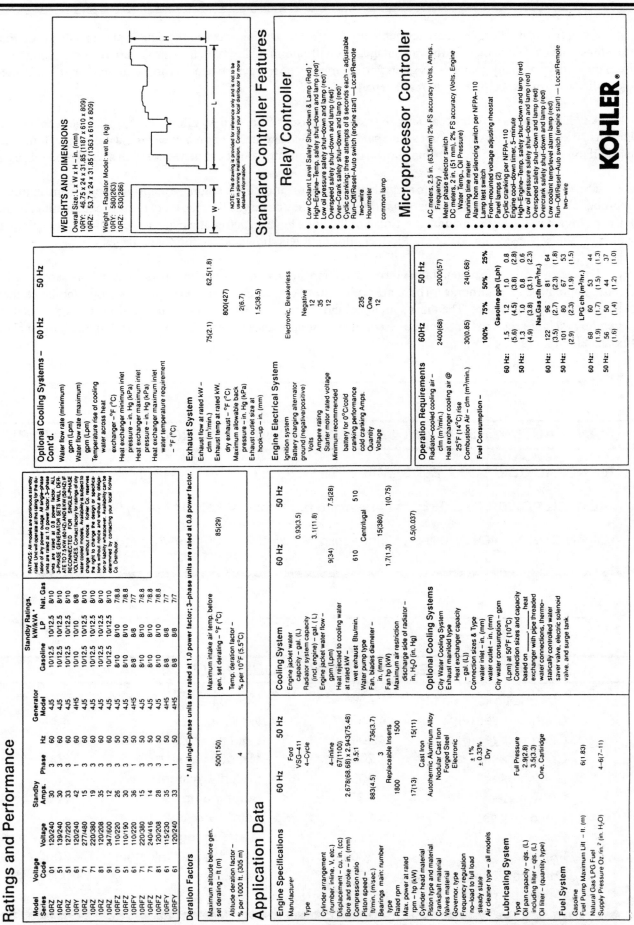

Ratings and Performance

Model Series	Voltage Code	Voltage	Standby Amps.	Phase	Hz	Generator Model	Standby Ratings, kW/kVA *		
							Gasoline	LP	Nat. Gas
10RZ	01	120/240	30	3	60	4J5	10/12.5	10/12.5	8/10
10RZ	51	139/240	30	3	60	4J5	10/12.5	10/12.5	8/10
10RZ	51	127/220	33	3	60	4J5	10/12.5	10/12.5	8/10
10RY	01	120/240	42	1	60	4H5	10/10	10/10	8/8
10RY	61	277/480	15	3	60	4J5	10/12.5	10/12.5	8/10
10RZ	71	220/380	19	3	60	4J5	10/12.5	10/12.5	8/10
10RZ	81	120/208	35	3	60	4J5	10/12.5	10/12.5	8/10
10RZ	91	347/600	12	3	60	4J5	10/12.5	10/12.5	8/10
10RFZ	01	110/220	26	3	50	4J5	8/10	8/10	7/8.8
10RFZ	51	110/190	30	3	50	4J5	8/10	8/10	7/7
10RFY	61	110/220	36	1	50	4H5	8/10	8/10	7/8.8
10RFZ	71	220/380	15	3	50	4J5	8/10	8/10	7/8.8
10RFZ	71	240/416	14	3	50	4J5	8/10	8/10	7/8.8
10RFZ	81	120/208	28	3	50	4J5	8/10	8/10	7/8.8
10RFY	61	115/230	35	1	50	4H5	8/8	8/8	7/7
10RFY	61	120/240	33	1	50	4H5	8/8	8/8	7/7

* All single-phase units are rated at 1.0 power factor; 3-phase units are rated at 0.8 power factor.

RATINGS: All models are continuous standby rated. Unit will operate at this rating for the duration of any power outage. All single-phase units are rated at 1.0 power factor. 3-phase units are rated at 0.8 power factor. ALL 3-PHASE GENERATOR SETS WILL DERATE TO 7.5 KW (60 HZ) AND 6 KW (50 HZ) IF RECONNECTED FOR SINGLE-PHASE VOLTAGES. Consult factory for ratings of any water cooled models. Availability is subject to change without notice. Kohler Co. reserves the right to change the design or specifications without notice and without any obligation or liability whatsoever. Availability can be determined by contacting your local Kohler Co. Distributor.

Deration Factors

	50 Hz
Maximum altitude before gen. set derating – ft (m)	500(150)
Altitude deration factor – % per 1000 ft. (305 m)	4
Maximum intake air temp. before gen. set derating – °F (°C)	85(29)
Temp. deration factor – % per 10° F (5.5°C)	7

Application Data

Engine Specifications

	60 Hz	50 Hz
Manufacturer	Ford	
Type	VSG-411	
	4-Cycle	
Cylinder arrangement (number, inline, V, etc.)	4-Inline	
Displacement – cu. in. (cc)	67(1100)	
Bore and stroke – in. (mm)	2.678(68.68) x 2.943(75.48)	
Compression ratio	9.5:1	
Piston speed – ft/min. (m/sec.)	883(4.5)	736(3.7)
Bearings main: number	3	
type	Replaceable Inserts	
Rated rpm	1800	1500
Max. power at rated rpm – hp (kW)	17(13)	15(11)
Cylinder head material	Cast Iron	
Piston type and material	Autothermic Aluminum Alloy	
Crankshaft material	Nodular Cast Iron	
Valves material	Forged Steel	
Governor, type	Electronic	
Frequency regulation no-load to full load	± 1%	
steady state	± 0.33%	
Air cleaner type – all models	Dry	

Lubricating System

Type	Full Pressure	
Oil pan capacity – qts. (L)	2.9(2.8)	
including filter – qts. (L)	3.5(3.3)	
Oil filter – (quantity, type)	One, Cartridge	

Fuel System

Gasoline Fuel Pump Maximum Lift – ft. (m)	6(1.83)	
Natural Gas LPG Fuel Supply Pressure Oz./in² (in. H₂O)	4–6(7–11)	

Cooling System

	60 Hz	50 Hz
Engine jacket water capacity – gal. (L)	0.93(3.5)	
Radiator system capacity (incl. engine) – gal. (L)	3.1(11.8)	
Engine jacket water flow – gpm (Lpm)	9(34)	7.5(28)
Heat rejected to cooling water at rated kW – wet exhaust Btu/min.	610	510
Water pump type	Centrifugal	
Fan, blades diameter – in. (mm)	15(380)	
Fan hp (kW)	1.7(1.3)	1(0.75)
Maximum air restriction discharge side of radiator – in. H₂O (in. Hg)	0.5(0.037)	

Optional Cooling Systems

City Water Cooling System
Exhaust manifold type: Heat exchanger capacity – gal. (L)
Connection sizes & Type: water inlet – in. (mm) / water outlet – in. (mm)
City water consumption – gpm (Lpm) at 50°F (10°C)

Connection sizes and capacity based on _____ heat exchanger with pipe threaded water connections, thermostatically controlled water saver valve, electric solenoid valve, and surge tank.

Optional Cooling Systems – Cont'd.

	60 Hz	50 Hz
Water flow rate (minimum) gpm (Lpm)		
Water flow rate (maximum) gpm (Lpm)		
Temperature rise of cooling water across heat exchanger – °F (°C)		
Heat exchanger minimum inlet pressure – in. Hg (kPa)		
Heat exchanger maximum inlet pressure – in. Hg (kPa)		
Heat exchanger maximum inlet water temperature requirement – °F (°C)		

Exhaust System

	60 Hz	50 Hz
Exhaust flow at rated kW – cfm (m³/min.)	75(2.1)	62.5(1.8)
Exhaust temp at rated kW, dry exhaust – °F (°C)		800(427)
Maximum allowable back pressure – in. Hg (kPa)		2(6.7)
Exhaust outlet size at hook-up – in. (mm)		1.5(38.5)

Engine Electrical System

Ignition system	Electronic, Breakerless	
Battery charging alternator ground (negative/positive)	Negative	
Volts	12	
Ampere rating	35	
Starter motor rated voltage	12	
Minimum recommended battery for 0°C/cold cranking performance cold cranking Amps.	235	
Quantity	One	
Voltage	12	

Weights and Dimensions

WEIGHTS AND DIMENSIONS

Overall Size: L x W x H – in. (mm)
10RY: 46.75 x 24 x 31.85 (1187 x 610 x 809)
10RZ: 53.7 x 24 x 31.85 (1363 x 610 x 809)

Weight – Radiator Model: wet lb. (kg)
10RY: 580(263)
10RZ: 630(286)

NOTE: This drawing is provided for reference only and is not to be used in planning installation. Contact your local distributor for more detailed information.

Standard Controller Features

Relay Controller

- Low Coolant Level Safety Shut-down & Lamp (Red) *
- High–Engine–Temp. safety shut-down and lamp (red) *
- Low oil pressure safety shut-down and lamp (red)
- Overspeed safety shut-down and lamp (red)
- Over–Crank safety shut-down and lamp (red)
- Cyclic cranking: three attempts of 8 seconds each – adjustable
- Run–Off/Reset–Auto switch (engine start) —Local/Remote two-wire
- Hourmeter

common lamp

Microprocessor Controller

- AC meters, 2.5 in. (63.5mm) 2% FS accuracy (Volts, Amps., Frequency)
- Meter phase selector switch
- DC meters, 2 in. (51 mm), 2% FS accuracy (Volts, Engine Water Temp., Oil Pressure)
- Running time meter
- Alarm horn and silencing switch per NFPA-110
- Lamp test switch
- Front-mounted voltage adjusting rheostat
- Panel lamps (2)
- Cyclic cranking per NFPA-110
- Engine cool–down timer, 5-minute
- High–Engine–Temp. safety shut-down and lamp (red)
- Low oil pressure safety shut-down and lamp (red)
- Overspeed safety shut-down and lamp (red)
- Overcrank safety shut-down and lamp (red)
- Low coolant temp/level alarm lamp (red)
- Run–Off/Reset–Auto switch (engine start) — Local/Remote two-wire

Operation Requirements

	60Hz	50 Hz
Radiator-cooled cooling air – cfm (m³/min.)	2400(68)	2000(57)
Heat exchanger cooling air @ 25°F (14°C) rise	30(0.85)	24(0.68)
Combustion Air – cfm (m³/min.)		

Fuel Consumption

		100%	75%	50%	25%
Gasoline gph (Lph)					
60 Hz:		1.5 (5.6)	1.2 (4.5)	1.0 (3.8)	0.8 (2.8)
50 Hz:		1.3 (4.9)	1.0 (3.8)	0.8 (3.1)	0.6 (2.3)
Nat.Gas cfh (m³/min.)					
60 Hz:		122 (3.5)	96 (2.7)	81 (2.3)	64 (1.8)
50 Hz:		101 (2.9)	80 (2.3)	67 (1.9)	53 (1.5)
LPG cfh (m³/min.)					
60 Hz:		68 (1.9)	60 (1.7)	53 (1.5)	44 (1.2)
50 Hz:		56 (1.6)	50 (1.4)	44 (1.2)	37 (1.0)

KOHLER®

Generac II Specifications

GENERATOR SET

Rated power (kW)*	8	8	12.5	16	20
60 Hz., Phase†	Single phase (all kW ratings) or three phase (16 - 20 kW)				
Voltage†	120/240V, single phase or 120/208V, three phase				
Amps @ 120/240V, 1 phase	66.6/33.3	66.6/33.3	104.2/52.1	133.3/66.6	166.6/83.3
Amps @ 120/208V, 3 phase	N.A.	N.A.	N.A.	96.3/55.6	120.4/69.5
Engine/alternator rpm	3600	1800	1800	3600	3600
Engine	480cc OHV V-twin	954cc 3 Cyl.	1.2L OHC 4 Cyl.	1.2L OHC 4 Cyl.	1.2L OHC 4 Cyl.
Fuel	Gas	Diesel	Gas	Gas	Gas
Engine cooling	Air	Liquid	Liquid	Liquid	Liquid
L x W x H (inches)	37.5 x 22.7 x 26.5	44 x 25 x 29	44 x 25 x 29	44 x 25 x 29	44 x 25 x 29
Shipping Wt. (lbs.)	447	592	582	623	645

*When gaseous fueled, kW rating is for gasoline. Natural gas and LPG ratings may decrease, depending on BTU content of local gas supply.

†Available in models with either 110/220 volts 1Ø, or 110/220 volts 3Ø. Voltage/phase must be specified when ordering.

CONTROLS

Start/stop control	Cyclic cranking: 7 sec. on, 7 rest. 90 sec. start and cooldown minimum.
Automatic low oil shutdown	Standard
Overspeed shutdown	Standard, 70 Hz.
High water temperature shutdown (liquid-cooled only)	Standard
Overcrank protection	Standard
Automatic voltage regulator w/ over-voltage protection	Standard
Engine warmup	15 seconds
Engine cooldown	1 minute
Safety fuse	Standard
Starter lockout	Starter cannot re-engage until 5 sec. after engine has stopped.
2 amp trickle battery charger	Standard
Mode switch	
Auto	Utility failure/ 7 day exercise
Off	Stops unit. Power is removed, control and charger still operate.
Manual/test (Start)	Start with starter control, unit stays on. If utility fails, transfer to load takes place.

TRANSFER SWITCH

Current rating (amps)	100
Voltage rating (VAC)	250
Dimensions (H x W x D, inches)	24 x 15 x 5
Utility voltage monitor (fixed)	80% pickup, 60% dropout
Return to utility	1 minute
Exerciser	15 minutes every 7 days.

Decks add style and value to your home

Q: I am planning to build a large deck on my house. I want it to be attractive and possibly help lower my air-conditioning and heating bills. Are there any special design characteristics to consider?

A: A well-designed deck can not only be an attractive and valuable addition to your house, but it can reduce your utility bills both summer and winter. Although a deck can be designed for any side of your house, building it on the west side is most effective for year-round savings.

In the summer, a deck can shade your house from the afternoon sun. It also can reduce the indirect heat that is reflected from sidewalks, patios, or driveways. In the winter, it becomes an effective windbreak to block the force of cold winds.

A good rule of thumb when sizing a deck is to plan on 20 square feet times the number of people that will typically be on the deck. Use pressure-treated, redwood, or cedar lumber for durability and weather resistance.

You should plan your deck so that the afternoon sun from the west is blocked. The summer sun is usually high enough in the sky near noon (when it's directly south) that it's blocked by the deck roof. When the sun is lower in the winter, you want it to shine through to warm your house.

A two-level west-facing deck is attractive and effective for shade. Cover the west side of the higher section with 1x6 louvers. It is most effective to cover the entire west side of both the upper and lower levels, but you may feel somewhat closed in.

Mount the side louvers so they slant outward from top to bottom.

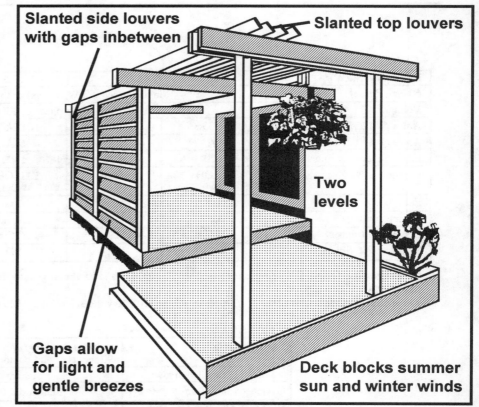

Well-designed deck saves energy year-round

Space the louvers to leave horizontal gaps between them. This lets you see through them for an open feel and lets gentle summer breezes pass through. In the winter, the louvers, even with gaps, slow the force of the cold winds.

With the winter sun lower in the sky, its rays shine through the gaps to help heat your house. In the summer, the sun is higher and it won't shine far enough through to reach your house.

Cover the top of the deck with louvers and slant them at the opposite angle (inward from top to bottom) from the side louvers. This also allows the winter sun to shine through, but blocks the higher summer sun.

For a south-facing deck, it is not necessary to cover the side with louvers. The summer sun is high in the sky and the top louvers should provide shade for your house. Just in-

stall a few top louvers near the house. Too many louvers will block the winter sun which is lower.

Q: I plan to caulk some inside angles around my windows. I hate to use my finger to smooth the bead and I'm not very good at it. Is there any sure-fire method to get a professional-looking job?

A: One method is to put masking tape along the sides of the joint I want to caulk. Lay a wide caulking bead so there is enough material to withstand thermal expansion.

Cut the corners off the end of a paint stirrer leaving the uncut flat edge the width of the bead you desire. After you lay the caulking, run the paint stirrer along the bead to smooth it. When dry, remove the tape.

The following designs of decks can be modified to meet your specific needs and house. Although it is slightly more difficult to build a deck with slanted louvers on the roof and sides, it allows more of the winter sun to shine through to your house.

A deck on the west side of your house provides the greatest potential for saving energy. The sun is lower in the sky in the afternoon, so it penetrates further into your house through unshaded windows. Also, the outdoor temperature is highest in late afternoon. Tilting the top louvers on the roof is most effective for a deck on the west side.

The position of the top louvers for a deck on the south side of your house is not as important. Since the sun is very high in the sky at noon in the summer, just a few standard vertical louvers on the roof of a deck on the south side will adequately block the sun. You can leave the sides totally uncovered to let the winter sun shine in and reach your house.

The design of a deck on the east side of your house will not significantly effect the energy efficiency of your house. However, proper positioning of the louvered sides will effect your comfort when you are on the deck by slowing cool breezes in early spring and late fall.

INSTRUCTIONS FOR MAKING DECK FOR WEST SIDE OF HOUSE

(design modifications for decks on east and south sides of house are described in sections M and N and diagrams are shown.)

A) Before you begin to build your deck, carefully plan your project. Check all local building codes and restrictions, zoning, and the location of any underground utilities. For a rough size estimate, plan on about 20 square feet times the maximum number of people that you will usually have on the deck.

Required Materials for Deck

- **4x4 pressure-treated wood posts**
- **2x4 lumber**
- **2x6 lumber**
- **1x6 lumber**
- **1x4 lumber**
- **2x10 lumber**
- **nails - stainless steel or plated**
- **joist hangers**
- **carriage bolts**
- **screws - stainless steel or plated**
- **polyethylene plastic film**
- **crushed rock**
- **concrete**

B) Lay out your deck position and stake the corner locations. Also stake the locations of the other vertical support posts. Dig the holes for the footers well below the frost line. Most builders can tell you how deep to dig in your area. You can either set the posts in concrete or crushed rock. Although concrete provides the best support, the posts can expand and sometimes cause the concrete to crack.

C) In order to retard the growth of weeds and grass under the deck, cover the area under the deck with polyethylene plastic film. A dark-colored film is usually used. You can use the same type of 4-mil plastic film that is used for vapor barriers for wall insulation. Make small slits in the plastic film to allow water to pass through it and not stand. Cover it lightly with gravel or bark to hold it in place.

D) Plan the size of the deck and height of the deck that you want. Try to balance its size with the size of your house and yard. Cut the 4x4 vertical supporting corner posts (*A*) to the proper length plus the amount that will set in the ground plus an extra several inches.

E) Put some gravel in the post holes to make sure the tops of the support posts are slightly higher than you want them to finally be. Place the posts in the holes and pour concrete around them. Use a plumb line to make sure they are vertical and stake them in position. Wait several days for the concrete to set up thoroughly. If you just set them in crushed rock, wait several days for it to settle. Saw the appropriate amount off of the tops to get the desired height.

F) Cut and attach the upper level floor joists (*B,C*) to the support posts. Use joist hangers to secure them in position. Attach the floor joists (*D,E,F*) for the lower level in the same manner. For the most secure and stable deck, screws are best to use for attaching the joist hangers.

G) Attach 2x6 nailer (**G-1**) to your house with screws. Recess it the thickness of the decking material. You can also attach piece (**G-2**) across the frame's side members for additional support.

H) Attach 2x4 supports (**H,I**) and 2x6 supports (**J**) to the framing. Using nails or joist hangers, attach 2x6 joists (**K,L**) to form the support for the flooring. Repeat the same flooring method for the lower level. Nail the 2x6 deck flooring to the joists.

I) Attach horizontal framing pieces (**Q,R**) to the tops of the support posts. Then bolt these framing piece/support posts to your house.

J) Attach short 2x4 pieces (**S**) to the corner support posts. Bolt horizontal framing (**T**) to pieces (**S**) and to the posts.

K) Although the diagram shows vertical top louvers which are easier to build and attach, slanted louvers are more effective for energy savings. They should slant toward your house from the top to the bottom of the louver. Loosely nail (leave the nail heads extended so your can pull them out easily) several in place to determine the best angle and spacing for summer sun control. Don't position them too closely together or they will also block the winter sun. For slanted roof louvers, cut spacer pieces (**W**) at the angle of slant that you desire. Toe nail the roof louvers (**U,V**) to the upper framing member.

L) Cut the 1x6 side louvers (**X**) and nail them between the vertical framing members (**Y**). Loosely nail several of them in place first with various gaps between them. Hold it up vertically and select the positioning which gives adequate sun control in the summer. The wider you leave the gaps, the more solar heat your house will get in the winter. Attach the side louver assembly to the front of the deck.

M) For the east side of your house, follow the same basic procedure. Add panels with louvers at either end of the deck to block winter winds and summer sun.

N) For the south side of your house, build the upper level of the deck only. Install only enough top louvers to block the midday sun. Since the sun is high in the sky when it is to the south, only a few top louvers will be needed. If you install too many, the lower winter sun will also be blocked. No side louvers are needed. Winter winds are seldom from the south.

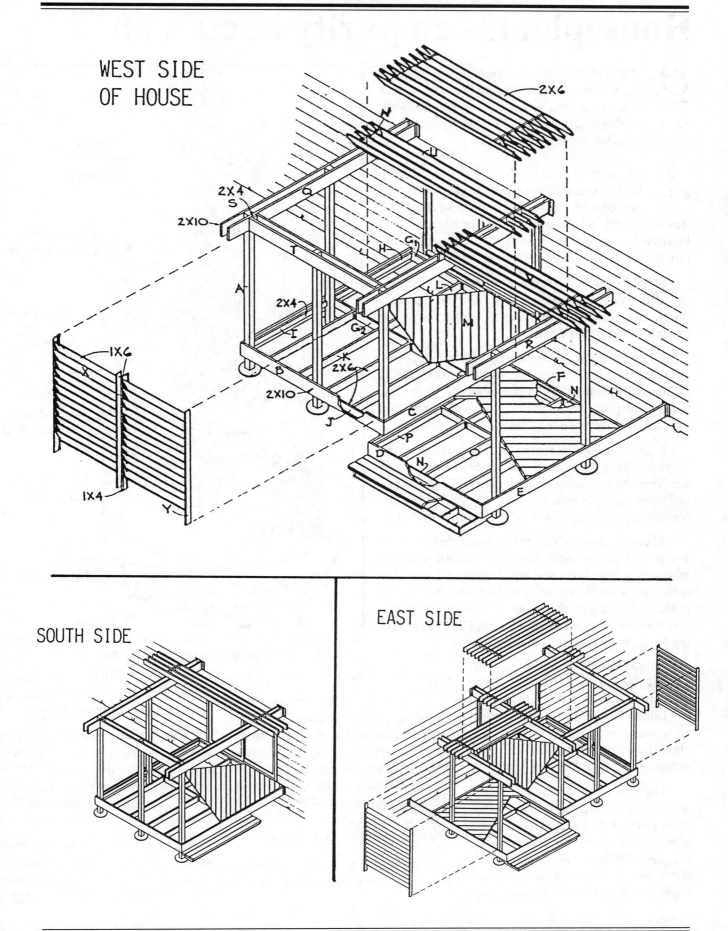

WEST SIDE
OF HOUSE

2X6

2X4
S
2X10

A

2X4
I

1X6
X

1X4

Y

B
2X10
J

2X6
K

P
D
E

SOUTH SIDE

EAST SIDE

Houseplants can purify home's air

Q: We made our house airtight to save energy, but we are concerned about the harmful and cancer-causing volatile chemicals indoors. Are houseplants very effective for purifying the air and how can we use them?

A: As more research is done, much of it by NASA, certain common houseplants are proving to be very effective natural air purifiers. Besides purifying the air inside your home, plants increase the oxygen level and provide natural moisture to the air.

Standard room and furnace-mounted air cleaners are effective for removing particles (dust, pollen, fungi, etc.) from the air. They do not remove the organic volatile chemicals.

These chemicals (formaldehyde, benzene, TCE, etc.) are emitted from carpeting, furniture, subflooring, cleaners, dry cleaned clothes, curtains, etc. Even your permanent-press shirts are treated with formaldehyde chemicals when they are made.

Some houseplants are more effective than others for removing particular volatile chemicals from the air. A combination of selected plants is best. Including some orchids and bromeliads is effective for nighttime purifying. Their leaf pores open at night.

There are special natural air purifying planters available. Current research indicates the roots and the microorganisms in the soil are also very effective for removing volatile chemicals from the air. These standard-looking planters take advantage of all three: leaf, root, and soil purifiers. There is a built-in watering gauge to avoid overwatering.

These planters are designed with a small electric fan in the base. This draws room air down through special soil filled with charcoal. As the room air passes through the charcoal and clay, the volatile chemicals are removed and trapped in the charcoal.

Trapped in the charcoal, these chemicals are broken down by the plant roots and "good" microorganisms in the soil into harmless food for the plant. In this way, the charcoal filter material is naturally bio-regenerated and does not have to be replaced. It is also good for the plant.

You should also consider using "low-toxic" natural cleaners and materials inside your home. Many companies manufacture special detergents, cleaners, paints, waxes, cloth, etc. from natural materials. Many of these environmentally-safe products are as effective as the typical mass-produced non-natural products.

Q: I am redecorating my living room and plan to hang some mirrors on the walls. Will hanging a mirror on an outside wall help to reflect the heat back indoors and save energy?

A: A typical mirror isn't effective for reflecting heat energy like it reflects visible light energy. If you really want to reflect heat, hang some type of artistic or sparsely-painted polished aluminum sheet on the wall.

If you do hang a large mirror, space it out slightly from the outside wall. This creates a dead air space behind it and saves a little energy.

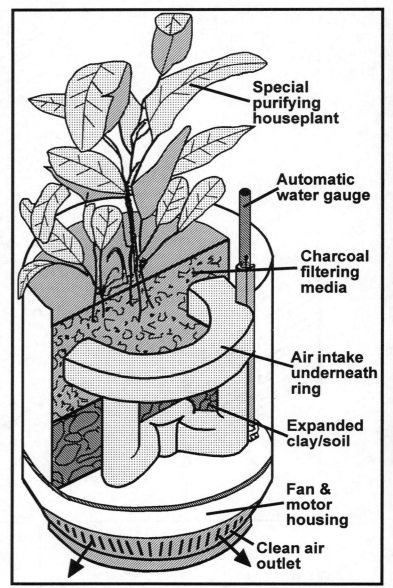

Special purifying houseplant

Automatic water gauge

Charcoal filtering media

Air intake underneath ring

Expanded clay/soil

Fan & motor housing

Clean air outlet

Houseplants and planter purify air

You can use plants to help purify the air inside your home. High-efficiency air cleaners, like electronic air cleaners in your furnace, are very effective for removing particles (dust, smoke, pollen, dander, etc.) from the air. On page **b,** I have included a list of manufacturers of purifying planters and a list of products that emit the most chemicals and the most effective houseplants to remove them. Below is information on a purifying planter.

On page **c,** I have also included a list of companies that sell "low-toxic" household cleaners and products. Although you cannot control the outgassing of chemicals from furniture, carpeting, cabinets, etc., you can reduce the problem by using these low-toxic household products wherever possible. Several "homemade" low-tox cleaning recipes are shown.

NATURE'S AIR FILTER, disguised as an attractive planter, is an effective and economical air-purifying machine. This unique filtering mechanism combines activated carbon and other filtering media with living plants and microorganisms to reduce and eliminate odors and pollutants in the air. This adsorptive filter material traps and holds the indoor pollutants. The plant roots and microorganisms living on and around the roots convert these harmful pollutants into harmless food for the plant. This concept was developed by a retired NASA scientist who performed research for the space program.

NATURE'S AIR FILTER uses a small fan built into the base of the filter to pull a room's contaminated air through the filter media, plant roots, and microorganisms. Smoke, odors, harmful chemicals, and other airborne pollutants are removed by the filter media and plant roots. The air, now clean, is returned to the room through slits in the bottom of the planter.

NATURE'S AIR FILTER does not require costly filter replacements like typical air cleaning systems. This is because the plant roots and microorganisms feed off the trapped air pollutants and continuously clean the filtering media. This cycle continues indefinitely as long as healthy plants are maintained. This process is a perfect example of how "nature's magic" can be used to clean our environment. The plant is grown hydroponically, (no dirt is used), in the filtering media that is supplied with NATURE'S AIR FILTER. The water gauge supplied with NATURE'S AIR FILTER indicates the minimum and maximum level of water for the planter. The water gauge should be on minimum for a few days before water is added. Plants require wet and dry cycles to grow properly. Liquid fertilizer should be added periodically to keep the plant healthy. When repotting the plants in the filter, small amounts of filter material may need to be added. This is available through your local distributor or by contacting Alliance Research & Manufacturing Corporation.

NATURE'S AIR FILTER filters the amount of air found in a typical 12' x 12' room in approximately 30 minutes. Under normal conditions, one filter per 12' x 12' room is recommended. For some home and office applications, additional units may be required. This will depend on the types of contaminants found in the air, the number of occupants, and the volume of the room. Electricity for each unit will cost approximately $1.00 per month when the filter is operated 8 to 12 hours per day.

Select a house plant based on your lighting conditions and personal preference. A partial list of suggested house plants that are attractive, and have been found to work well, are listed below. This does not mean that you must choose one of the plants listed. Most non-flowering house plants will work.

LOW LIGHT - Areas more than 6 feet from a window
Aglaonema
- CHINESE EVERGREEN
- GOLDEN EVERGREEN
- SILVER KING EVERGREEN

Sansevieria
- MOTHER-IN-LAW TONGUE

Scindapsus (Pothos)
- GOLDEN POTHOS
- SATIN POTHOS
- MARBLE QUEEN

Syngonium
- ARROWHEAD PLANT

Philodendron
- HEART LEAF
- RED PRINCESS

LOW TO MEDIUM LIGHT - Areas 4 to 6 feet from a window
Aspidistra
- CASTIRON PLANT

Peperomia
- EMERALD RIPPLE

Hedera Helix
- ENGLISH IVY

Spathiphyllum
- PEACE LILY

MEDIUM LIGHT - Areas 3 to 4 feet from a window
Chamaedorea
- BAMBOO PALM

Schefflera
- MINI SCHEFFLERA

MODEL NUMBER: AF-12   12" Diameter
AVAILABLE COLORS: White / Black / Dove Gray / Beige

SUPPLIERS OF SPECIAL PURIFYING PLANTERS WITH CIRCULATING FANS

ALLIANCE RESEARCH & MFG., P.O. Box 10, Taylorsville, MS 39168 - (601) 785-2282

ECOSOURCE, P.O. Box 1656, Sebastopol, CA 95473 - (707) 829-7562

SPACE BIOSPHERES VENTURES, P.O. Box 689, Oracle, AZ 85623 - (602) 825-6400

SOURCES AND PURIFYING PLANTS FOR COMMON CHEMICALS IN HOMES

Pollutant Chemicals	Sources	Effective Houseplants
Formaldehyde	foam insulation plywood particle board clothes carpeting furniture paper goods household cleaners water repellents	Aloe vera Boston fern Philodendron Chrysanthemum Golden pothos Dwarf date palm Bamboo palm Spider plant Janet Craig English ivy Weeping fig
Benzene	tobacco smoke gasoline synthetic fibers plastics inks oils detergents rubber	Gerbera daisy Corn plant Chrysanthemum Peace lily Warneckii Bamboo Palm Marginata Chinese evergreen Janet Craig
Trichloroethylene	dry cleaning inks paints varnishes lacquers adhesives	Gerbera Daisy Mother-in-law's tongue Marginata Peace lily Janet Craig Bamboo palm Warneckii

SUPPLIERS OF "LOW-TOXIC" HOUSEHOLD PRODUCTS

AFM ENTERPRISES, 1960 Chicago Ave. E7, Riverside, CA 92507 - (909) 781-6860

ECO DESIGN COMPANY, 1365 Rufina Cir., Santa Fe, NM 87501 - (505) 438-3448

ECOSOURCE, See preceeding page

GRANNY'S OLD FASHIONED PROD., P.O. Box 256, Arcadia, CA 91066 - (818) 577-1825

SEVENTH GENERATION, Colchester, VT 05446 - (802) 655-6777

HOMEMADE NATURAL "LOW-TOXIC" RECIPES

All-Purpose Household Cleaner
1 quart warm water
1 teaspoon liquid soap
1 teaspoon borax or tsp
squeeze of lemon or splash of vinegar
This solution can be used for cleaning jobs including countertops, floors, walls, rugs and upholstery.

Air Freshener
Leave open boxes of baking soda in refrigerators, closets, and bathrooms.
Open doors and windows for good ventilation.
Use stove fan when cooking.
Use flowers, herbs, and spices to add subtle fragrances to indoor air.

Chlorine Bleach
$1/2$ cup of borax per load of laundry to whiten and remove spots.

Degreaser (engine and tools)
Use a water-based cleaner such as Simple Green (well-diluted) in place of kerosene, turpentine, and commercial engine degreaser.

Degreaser (kitchen)
2 Tablespoons tsp in 1 gallon hot water or Nonchlorinated scouring powder (e.g., Bon Ami) with abrasive scouring pad or fine steel wool.

Disinfectant
Use $1/2$ cup borax in 1 gal. hot water. To inhibit mold and mildew, do not rinse off borax solution.

Fabric Softener
Use nonperfumed fabric softener sheets rather than liquid fabric softeners.

Floor Cleaner
Vinyl floors: $1/2$ cup vinegar or $1/4$ cup borax or tsp with 1 gallon water. Polish with club soda. Wood floors: damp mop with mild vegetable oil soap, such as Castile soap or Murphy Oil Soap.

Furniture Polish
1 pint mineral oil with a few drops of lemon juice.

Glass Cleaner
$1/4$ cup vinegar mixed in 1 quart warm water. (Do not use this as a windshield wiper solution because it may damage the pump; use plain water for this purpose.)

Laundry Detergents
Use soap flakes with $1/2$ cup added borax as a water softener. As a compromise, use a synthetic detergent that does not contain added fabric softeners (cationic surfactants) or bleach (sodium perborate or percarbonate).

Mildew Cleaner
Scrub with baking soda or borax; for extended mold inhibition, do not rinse off.

Oven Cleaner
Scrub with 2 Tablespoons or more of baking soda, tsp. or borax in 1 gallon of water, using very fine steel wool (0000). Wear gloves. For very baked-on spots, try scrubbing with pumice (available at hardware stores). As a last resort, use an aerosol oven cleaner with the words, "No caustic fumes", on the label.

Rug and Upholstery Cleaner
Use the All-purpose Cleaning Solution.

Scouring Powder
Use baking soda or a nonchlorinated commercial scouring powder.

Spot Removers
All-Purpose: $1/4$ cup borax in 2 cups cold water; soak the stain prior to washing as usual.
Blood: Pour 3% hydrogen peroxide solution directly on the stain, before rinsing with water. Then wash as usual.

Toilet Bowl Cleaner
Scrub with a solution or $1/2$ cup borax in 1 gallon water.

Tub/Tile Cleaners
Use scouring powder or baking soda.

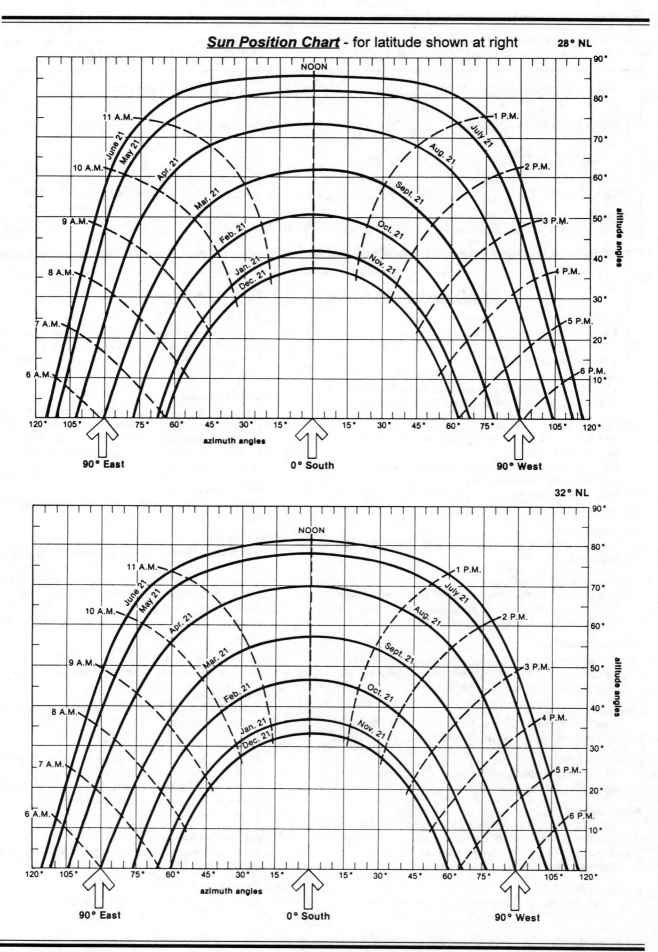

32° NL

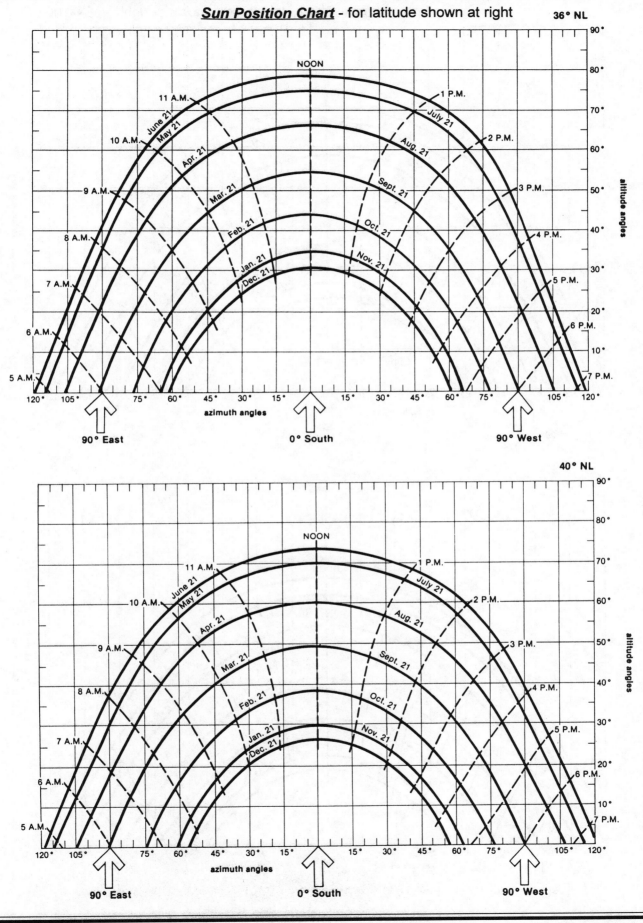

Sun Position Chart - for latitude shown at right

36° NL

40° NL

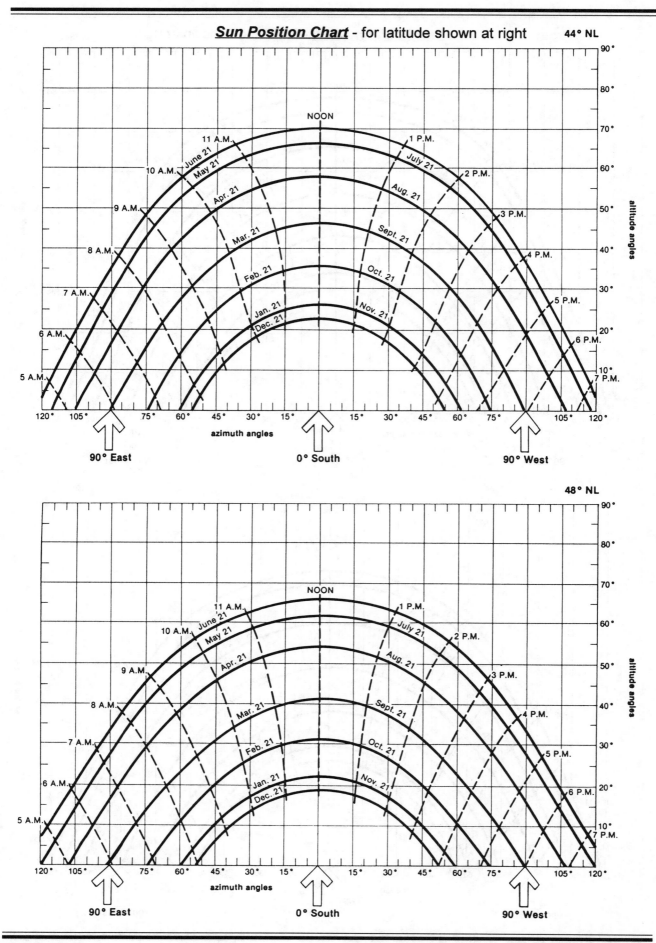

Sun Position Chart - for latitude shown at right

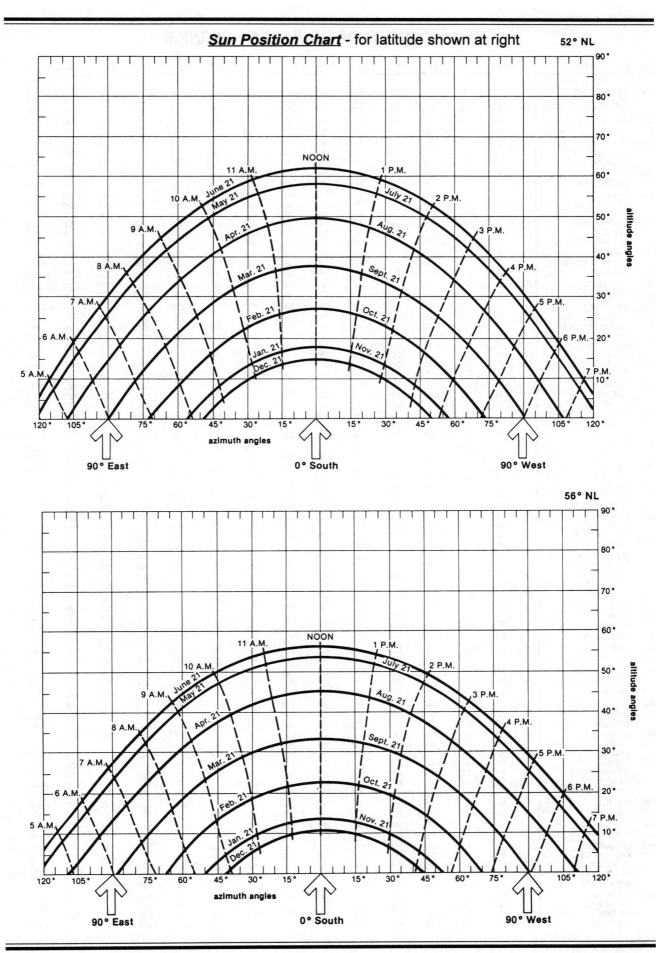

52° NL

NOON
11 A.M. · June 21 · 1 P.M.
10 A.M. · May 21 · July 21 · 2 P.M.
9 A.M. · Apr. 21 · Aug. 21 · 3 P.M.
8 A.M. · Mar. 21 · Sept. 21 · 4 P.M.
7 A.M. · Feb. 21 · Oct. 21 · 5 P.M.
6 A.M. · Jan. 21 · Nov. 21 · 6 P.M.
5 A.M. · Dec. 21 · 7 P.M.

altitude angles

90° · 80° · 70° · 60° · 50° · 40° · 30° · 20° · 10°

120° · 105° · 75° · 60° · 45° · 30° · 15° · 15° · 30° · 45° · 60° · 75° · 105° · 120°

azimuth angles

90° East · 0° South · 90° West

56° NL

NOON
11 A.M. · 1 P.M.
10 A.M. · June 21 · May 21 · July 21 · 2 P.M.
9 A.M. · Apr. 21 · Aug. 21 · 3 P.M.
8 A.M. · Mar. 21 · Sept. 21 · 4 P.M.
7 A.M. · Feb. 21 · Oct. 21 · 5 P.M.
6 A.M. · Jan. 21 · Nov. 21 · 6 P.M.
5 A.M. · Dec. 21 · 7 P.M.

altitude angles

90° · 80° · 70° · 60° · 50° · 40° · 30° · 20° · 10°

120° · 105° · 75° · 60° · 45° · 30° · 15° · 15° · 30° · 45° · 60° · 75° · 105° · 120°

azimuth angles

90° East · 0° South · 90° West

XIII - 1d

MEAN NUMBER OF HOURS OF SUNSHINE

STATE AND STATION		YEARS	JAN	FEB	MAR	APR	MAY	JUNE	JULY	AUG	SEPT	OCT	NOV	DEC	ANNUAL
AL	BIRMINGHAM	30	138	152	207	248	293	294	269	265	244	234	182	136	2662
	MOBILE	22	157	158	212	253	301	289	249	259	235	254	195	146	2708
	MONTGOMERY	30	160	168	227	267	317	311	288	290	260	250	200	156	2894
AK	ANCHORAGE	19	78	114	210	254	268	288	255	184	128	96	68	49	1992
	JUNEAU	29	71	102	171	200	230	251	193	161	123	67	60	51	1680
AZ	PHOENIX	30	248	244	314	346	404	404	377	351	334	307	267	236	3832
	PRESCOTT	14	222	230	293	323	378	392	323	305	315	286	254	228	3549
	TUCSON	13	255	266	317	350	399	394	329	329	335	317	280	258	3829
AR	FT. SMITH	30	146	156	202	234	268	303	321	305	261	230	174	147	2747
	LITTLE ROCK	30	143	158	213	243	291	316	321	316	265	251	181	142	2840
CA	FRESNO	29	153	192	283	330	389	418	435	406	355	306	221	144	3632
	LOS ANGELES	30	224	217	273	264	292	299	352	336	295	263	249	220	3284
	RED BLUFF	15	156	186	246	302	366	396	438	407	341	277	199	154	3468
	SACRAMENTO	30	134	169	255	300	367	405	437	406	347	283	197	122	3422
	SAN DIEGO	30	216	212	262	242	261	253	293	277	255	234	236	217	2958
	SAN FRANCISCO	30	165	182	251	281	314	330	300	272	267	243	198	156	2959
CO	DENVER	30	207	205	247	252	281	311	321	297	274	246	200	192	3033
	GRAND JUNCTION	30	169	182	243	265	314	350	349	311	291	255	198	168	3095
	PUEBLO	30	224	217	261	271	299	340	349	318	290	265	225	211	3270
CT	HARTFORD	30	141	166	206	223	267	285	299	268	220	193	137	136	2541
	NEW HAVEN	30	155	178	215	234	274	291	309	284	238	215	157	154	2704
DC	WASHINGTON	30	138	160	205	226	267	288	291	264	233	207	162	135	2576
FL	APALACHICOLA	26	193	195	233	274	328	296	273	259	236	263	216	175	2941
	JACKSONVILLE	30	192	189	241	267	296	260	255	248	199	205	191	170	2713
	KEY WEST	30	229	238	285	296	307	273	277	269	236	237	226	225	3098
	LAKELAND	7	204	186	222	251	285	268	252	242	203	209	212	198	2732
	MIAMI	30	222	227	266	275	280	251	267	263	216	215	212	209	2903
	PENSACOLA	30	175	180	232	270	311	302	278	284	249	265	206	166	2918
	TAMPA	30	223	220	260	283	320	275	257	252	232	243	227	209	3001
GA	ATLANTA	25	154	165	218	266	309	304	284	285	247	241	188	160	2821
	MACON	30	177	178	235	279	321	314	292	295	253	236	202	168	2950
	SAVANNAH	30	175	173	229	274	307	279	267	256	212	216	197	167	2752
HA	HILO	7	153	135	161	112	106	158	184	134	137	153	106	131	1670
	HONOLULU	30	227	202	250	255	276	280	293	290	279	257	221	211	3041
	LIHUE	10	171	162	176	176	211	246	246	236	246	210	170	161	2411
ID	BOISE	30	116	144	218	274	322	352	412	378	311	232	143	104	3006
	POCATELLO	30	111	143	211	255	300	338	380	347	296	230	145	108	2864
IL	CAIRO	15	124	160	218	254	298	324	345	336	279	254	181	145	2918
	CHICAGO	30	126	142	199	221	274	300	333	299	247	216	136	118	2611
	MOLINE	18	132	139	189	214	255	279	337	300	251	214	130	123	2563
	PEORIA	30	134	149	198	229	273	303	336	299	259	222	149	122	2673
	SPRINGFIELD	30	127	149	193	224	282	304	346	312	266	225	152	122	2702
IN	EVANSVILLE	30	123	145	199	237	294	322	342	318	274	236	156	120	2766
	FT. WAYNE	30	113	136	191	217	281	310	342	306	242	210	120	102	2570
	INDIANAPOLIS	30	118	140	193	227	278	313	342	313	265	222	139	118	2668
	TERRE HAUTE	24	125	148	189	231	274	302	341	305	253	235	150	122	2675
IA	BURLINGTON	19	148	165	217	241	284	315	353	327	270	243	175	147	2885
	CHARLES CITY	22	137	157	190	226	258	285	336	290	241	207	130	115	2572
	DES MOINES	30	155	170	203	236	276	303	346	299	263	227	156	136	2770
	SIOUX CITY	30	164	177	216	254	300	320	363	320	270	236	160	146	2926
KS	CONCORDIA	30	180	172	214	243	281	315	348	308	249	245	189	172	2916
	DODGE CITY	30	205	191	249	268	305	335	359	335	290	266	218	198	3219
	TOPEKA	18	159	160	193	215	260	287	310	304	263	229	173	149	2702
	WICHITA	30	187	186	233	254	291	321	350	325	277	245	206	182	3057
KY	LOUISVILLE	30	115	135	188	221	283	303	324	295	256	219	148	114	2601
LA	NEW ORLEANS	30	160	158	213	247	292	287	260	269	241	260	200	157	2744
	SHREVEPORT	19	151	172	214	240	298	332	339	322	289	273	208	177	3015
ME	EASTPORT	22	133	151	196	201	245	248	275	260	205	175	105	115	2309
	PORTLAND	30	155	174	213	226	268	286	312	294	229	202	146	148	2653
MD	BALTIMORE	30	148	170	211	229	270	295	299	272	238	212	164	145	2653
MA	BLUE HILL OBS.	10	125	136	165	182	233	248	266	241	211	181	134	135	2257
	BOSTON	30	148	168	212	222	263	283	300	280	232	207	152	148	2615
	NANTUCKET	22	128	156	214	227	278	284	291	279	242	208	149	129	2585
MI	ALPENA	24	86	124	198	228	261	303	339	285	204	159	70	67	2324
	DETROIT	30	90	128	180	212	263	295	321	284	226	189	98	89	2375
	LANSING	30	84	119	175	215	272	305	344	294	228	182	87	73	2378
	ESCANABA	30	112	148	204	226	266	283	316	267	198	162	90	94	2366
	GRAND RAPIDS	30	74	117	178	218	277	308	349	304	231	188	92	70	2406
	MARQUETTE	30	78	113	172	207	248	268	305	251	186	142	68	66	2104
	SAULT STE. MARIE	30	83	123	187	217	252	269	309	256	165	133	61	62	2117
MN	DULUTH	30	125	163	221	235	268	282	328	277	203	166	100	107	2475
	MINNEAPOLIS	30	140	166	200	231	272	302	343	296	257	193	115	112	2607
MS	JACKSON	12	130	147	199	244	280	287	279	287	235	223	185	150	2646
	VICKSBURG	30	136	141	199	232	284	304	291	297	254	244	183	140	2705
MO	COLUMBIA	30	147	164	207	232	281	296	341	298	262	225	166	138	2757
	KANSAS CITY	30	154	170	211	235	278	313	347	308	266	235	178	151	2846
	ST. JOSEPH	23	154	165	211	231	274	301	347	287	260	224	168	144	2766
	ST. LOUIS	30	137	152	202	235	283	301	325	289	256	223	166	125	2694
	SPRINGFIELD	30	145	164	213	238	278	305	342	310	269	233	183	140	2820
MT	BILLINGS	21	140	154	208	236	283	301	372	332	258	213	136	129	2762
	GREAT FALLS	19	154	176	245	261	299	299	381	342	256	206	132	133	2884
	HELENA	30	138	168	215	241	292	292	342	336	258	202	137	121	2742
	MISSOULA	25	85	109	167	209	261	260	378	328	246	178	90	66	2377

MEAN NUMBER OF HOURS OF SUNSHINE

STATE AND STATION		YEARS	JAN	FEB	MAR	APR	MAY	JUNE	JULY	AUG	SEPT	OCT	NOV	DEC	ANNUAL
NB	LINCOLN	30	173	172	213	244	287	316	356	309	266	237	174	160	2907
	NORTH PLATTE	30	181	179	221	246	282	310	343	304	264	242	184	169	2925
	OMAHA	30	172	188	222	259	305	332	379	311	270	248	166	145	2997
	VALENTINE	30	185	194	229	252	296	323	369	326	275	242	174	172	3037
NV	ELY	22	186	197	262	260	300	354	359	344	303	255	204	187	3211
	LAS VEGAS	8	239	251	314	336	386	411	383	364	345	301	258	250	3838
	RENO	30	185	199	267	306	354	376	414	391	336	273	212	170	3483
	WINNEMUCCA	30	142	155	207	255	312	346	395	375	316	242	177	139	3061
NH	CONCORD	23	136	153	192	196	229	261	286	260	214	179	122	126	2354
	MT. WASHINGTON OBS	18	94	98	133	141	162	145	150	143	139	159	89	87	1540
NJ	ATLANTIC CITY	30	151	173	210	233	273	287	298	271	239	218	177	153	2683
	TRENTON	30	145	168	203	235	277	294	309	273	239	206	160	142	2653
NM	ALBUQUERQUE	30	221	218	273	299	343	365	340	317	299	279	245	219	3418
	ROSWELL	21	218	223	286	306	330	333	341	313	266	266	242	216	3340
NY	ALBANY	30	125	151	194	213	266	301	317	286	224	192	115	112	2496
	BINGHAMTON	30	94	119	151	170	226	256	266	230	184	158	92	79	2025
	BUFFALO	30	110	125	180	212	274	319	338	297	239	183	97	84	2458
	NEW YORK	30	154	171	213	237	268	289	302	271	235	213	169	155	2677
	ROCHESTER	30	93	123	172	209	274	314	333	294	224	173	97	86	2392
	SYRACUSE	30	87	115	165	197	261	295	316	276	211	163	81	74	2241
NC	ASHEVILLE	30	146	161	211	247	289	292	268	250	235	222	179	146	2646
	CAPE HATTERAS	9	152	168	206	259	293	301	286	265	214	202	169	154	2669
	CHARLOTTE	30	165	177	230	267	313	316	291	277	247	243	198	167	2891
	GREENSBORO	30	157	171	217	231	298	302	287	272	243	236	190	163	2767
	RALEIGH	29	154	168	220	255	290	284	277	253	224	215	184	156	2680
	WILMINGTON	30	179	180	237	279	314	312	286	273	237	238	206	178	2919
ND	BISMARCK	30	141	170	205	236	279	294	358	307	243	198	130	125	2686
	DEVILS LAKE	30	150	177	220	250	291	297	352	302	230	198	123	124	2714
	FARGO	30	132	170	210	232	283	288	343	293	222	187	112	114	2586
	WILLISTON	29	141	168	215	260	305	312	377	328	247	206	131	129	2819
OH	CINCINNATI (ABBE)	30	115	137	186	222	273	309	323	295	253	205	138	118	2574
	CLEVELAND	30	79	111	167	209	274	301	325	288	235	187	99	77	2352
	COLUMBUS	30	112	132	177	215	270	296	323	291	250	210	131	101	2508
	DAYTON	10	114	136	195	222	281	313	323	307	268	229	152	124	2664
	TOLEDO	30	93	120	170	203	263	296	331	298	241	196	106	92	2409
OK	OKLAHOMA CITY	29	175	182	235	253	290	329	352	331	282	243	201	175	3048
	TULSA	18	152	164	200	213	244	287	314	308	281	241	207	172	2783
OR	BAKER	22	118	143	198	251	302	313	406	368	289	215	132	100	2835
	PORTLAND	30	77	97	142	203	246	249	329	275	218	134	87	65	2122
	ROSEBURG	30	69	96	148	205	257	278	369	329	255	146	81	50	2283
PA	HARRISBURG	30	132	160	203	230	277	297	319	282	233	200	140	131	2604
	PHILADELPHIA	30	142	166	203	231	270	281	288	253	225	205	158	142	2564
	PITTSBURGH	25	89	114	163	200	239	260	283	250	234	180	114	76	2202
	READING	30	133	151	195	220	259	275	293	259	219	198	144	127	2473
	SCRANTON	30	106	138	178	199	251	269	290	249	213	183	120	105	2303
RI	PROVIDENCE	30	145	168	211	221	271	285	292	267	226	207	153	143	2589
SC	CHARLESTON	30	188	189	243	284	323	308	297	281	244	239	210	187	2993
	COLUMBIA	30	173	183	233	274	312	312	291	283	243	242	202	166	2914
	GREENVILLE	26	166	176	227	274	307	300	278	274	239	232	192	157	2822
SD	HURON	30	153	177	213	250	295	321	367	320	260	212	142	134	2844
	RAPID CITY	30	164	182	222	245	278	300	348	317	266	228	164	144	2858
TN	CHATTANOOGA	30	126	146	187	239	290	295	278	266	247	220	169	128	2591
	KNOXVILLE	30	124	144	189	237	281	288	277	248	237	213	157	120	2515
	MEMPHIS	30	135	152	204	244	296	321	319	314	261	243	180	139	2808
	NASHVILLE	30	123	142	196	241	285	306	292	279	250	224	168	126	2634
TX	ABILENE	13	190	199	250	259	290	347	335	322	276	245	223	201	3137
	AMARILLO	30	207	199	258	276	305	338	328	288	260	229	205	205	3243
	AUSTIN	30	148	152	207	221	266	302	331	320	261	242	180	160	2790
	BROWNSVILLE	30	147	152	187	210	272	297	326	311	246	252	165	151	2716
	CORPUS CHRISTI	24	160	165	212	237	295	329	366	341	276	264	194	164	3003
	DALLAS	30	155	159	220	238	279	326	341	325	274	240	191	163	2911
	EL PASO	30	234	236	299	329	373	369	336	327	300	287	257	236	3583
	GALVESTON	30	151	149	203	230	288	322	305	292	257	264	194	164	3003
	HOUSTON	30	144	141	193	212	266	298	294	281	238	239	181	146	2633
	PORT ARTHUR	30	153	149	209	235	292	317	285	281	252	256	191	148	2768
	SAN ANTONIO	30	148	153	213	224	258	292	325	307	261	241	183	160	2765
UT	SALT LAKE CITY	30	137	155	227	269	329	358	377	346	306	249	171	135	3059
VT	BURLINGTON	30	103	127	184	185	244	270	291	266	199	152	77	80	2178
VA	LYNCHBURG	26	153	169	216	243	288	297	288	264	235	217	177	158	2705
	NORFOLK	30	156	174	223	257	304	311	296	282	237	220	182	161	2803
	RICHMOND	30	144	166	211	248	280	296	286	263	230	211	176	152	2663
WA	NORTH HEAD	22	76	97	135	182	221	214	226	186	170	123	87	66	1783
	SEATTLE	30	74	99	154	201	247	234	304	248	197	122	77	62	2019
	SPOKANE	30	78	120	197	262	308	309	397	350	264	177	86	57	2605
	TATOOSH ISLAND	30	70	100	135	182	229	217	235	190	175	129	71	60	1793
	WALLA WALLA	30	72	106	194	262	317	335	411	367	280	198	92	51	2685
W VA	ELKINS	24	110	119	158	198	227	256	225	236	211	186	131	103	2160
	PARKERSBURG	30	91	111	155	200	252	277	286	264	230	189	117	93	2265
WI	GREEN BAY	30	121	148	194	210	251	279	314	266	213	176	110	106	2388
	MADISON	30	126	147	196	214	258	285	336	288	230	198	116	108	2502
	MILWAUKEE	30	116	134	191	218	267	293	340	292	235	193	125	106	2510
WY	CHEYENNE	30	191	197	243	237	259	304	318	286	265	242	188	170	2900
	SHERIDAN	30	160	179	226	245	286	303	367	333	266	221	153	145	2884

State and Station	0-3 mph	4-7 mph	8-12 mph	13-18 mph	19-24 mph	25-31 mph	32-38 mph	39-46 mph	47 mph and over	Mean speed mph
ALABAMA										
Birmingham	27	22	30	17	3	1	•	•	•	7.9
Mobile	7	28	38	20	6	1	•	•	•	10.0
Montgomery	31	29	27	12	2	•	•	•	•	6.9
ALASKA										
Anchorage	28	35	25	11	2	•	•	•	•	6.8
Cold Bay	4	9	18	27	21	14	5	2	•	17.4
Fairbanks	40	35	19	5	1	•	•	•	•	5.2
King Salmon	11	20	30	24	10	4	1	•	•	11.4
ARIZONA										
Phoenix	38	36	20	5	1	•	•	•	•	5.4
Tucson	18	35	30	14	3	1	•	•	•	8.1
ARKANSAS										
Little Rock	12	30	39	16	2	•	•	•	•	8.7
CALIFORNIA										
Bakersfield	35	30	24	10	1	•	•	•	•	5.8
Burbank	52	26	18	4	1	•	•	•	•	4.5
Fresno	30	41	22	7	1	•	•	•	•	6.1
Los Angeles	28	33	27	11	1	•	•	•	•	6.8
Oakland	26	28	28	16	2	1	•	•	•	7.5
Sacramento	15	28	31	18	5	1	•	•	•	9.3
San Diego	28	38	28	6	•	•	•	•	•	6.3
San Francisco	16	21	26	22	11	3	1	•	•	10.6
COLORADO										
Colorado Springs	9	27	38	19	6	2	•	•	•	10.0
Denver	11	27	34	22	5	2	•	•	•	10.0
CONNECTICUT										
Hartford	13	26	32	24	6	1	•	•	•	9.8
DELAWARE										
Wilmington	15	31	30	19	4	1	•	•	•	8.8
FLORIDA										
Jacksonville	10	33	35	18	3	•	•	•	•	8.9
Miami	14	30	34	20	2	•	•	•	•	8.8
Orlando	18	28	32	17	4	•	•	•	•	8.6
Tallahassee	33	36	23	7	•	•	•	•	•	6.1
Tampa	9	31	40	16	2	•	•	•	•	8.8
West Palm Beach	9	22	36	27	6	1	•	•	•	10.5
GEORGIA										
Atlanta	13	24	36	21	6	1	•	•	•	9.7
Augusta	36	29	25	9	1	•	•	•	•	6.3
Macon	10	26	46	16	2	•	•	•	•	8.9
Savannah	12	34	37	14	3	•	•	•	•	8.4
HAWAII										
Hilo	7	34	43	15	1	•	•	•	•	8.7
Honolulu	9	17	27	32	12	2	•	•	•	12.1
IDAHO										
Boise	15	30	32	18	4	1	•	•	•	8.9

State and Station	0-3 mph	4-7 mph	8-12 mph	13-18 mph	19-24 mph	25-31 mph	32-38 mph	39-46 mph	47 mph and over	Mean speed mph
ILLINOIS										
Chicago (O'Hare)	8	22	33	27	8	2	•	•	•	11.2
Chicago (Midway)	7	26	36	25	5	1	•	•	•	10.2
Moline	14	23	32	24	7	2	•	•	•	10.0
Springfield	7	22	28	27	12	3	1	•	•	12.0
INDIANA										
Evansville	19	23	32	21	5	1	•	•	•	9.1
Fort Wayne	9	23	33	25	8	2	•	•	•	10.9
Indianapolis	9	22	34	26	7	2	•	•	•	10.8
South Bend	7	21	35	30	7	1	•	•	•	10.9
IOWA										
Des Moines	3	17	38	29	10	3	•	•	•	12.1
Sioux City	10	20	31	25	10	4	1	•	•	11.7
KANSAS										
Topeka	11	19	30	27	10	2	•	•	•	11.2
Wichita	4	12	30	31	16	5	1	•	•	13.7
KENTUCKY										
Lexington	8	25	39	22	6	1	•	•	•	10.1
Louisville	17	28	31	20	3	1	•	•	•	8.8
LOUISIANA										
Baton Rouge	17	29	34	17	3	•	•	•	•	8.3
Lake Charles	19	31	29	17	4	1	•	•	•	8.5
New Orleans	16	27	32	19	5	1	•	•	•	9.0
Shreveport	12	26	37	21	4	1	•	•	•	9.5
MAINE										
Portland	10	30	33	22	4	1	•	•	•	9.6
MARYLAND										
Baltimore	7	24	39	22	6	2	•	•	•	10.4
MASSACHUSETTS										
Boston	3	12	33	35	12	4	1	•	•	13.3
MICHIGAN										
Detroit (City AP)	8	23	37	26	5	1	•	•	•	10.3
Flint	9	24	34	26	7	1	•	•	•	9.0
Grand Rapids	14	23	32	23	5	1	•	•	•	9.8
MINNESOTA										
Duluth	6	15	33	31	11	4	•	•	•	12.6
Minneapolis	8	21	34	28	9	2	•	•	•	11.2
MISSISSIPPI										
Jackson	33	25	26	14	2	•	•	•	•	7.1
MISSOURI										
Kansas City	9	29	35	23	5	1	•	•	•	9.8
St. Louis	10	29	36	21	3	1	•	•	•	9.3
Springfield	4	13	34	32	13	3	1	•	•	12.9
MONTANA										
Great Falls	7	19	24	24	15	9	3	1	•	13.9
NEBRASKA										
Omaha	12	17	29	28	11	3	•	•	•	11.6

State and Station	0-3 mph	4-7 mph	8-12 mph	13-18 mph	19-24 mph	25-31 mph	32-38 mph	39-46 mph	47 mph and over	Mean speed mph
NEVADA										
Las Vegas	18	26	25	20	8	3	•	•	•	9.7
Reno	52	20	13	10	4	1	•	•	•	5.9
NEW JERSEY										
Newark	11	25	34	24	5	1	•	•	•	9.8
NEW MEXICO										
Albuquerque	17	36	26	13	5	2	•	•	•	8.6
NEW YORK										
Albany	23	24	27	21	4	1	•	•	•	8.6
Binghamton	11	23	35	25	5	1	•	•	•	10.0
Buffalo	5	17	34	27	13	3	1	•	•	12.4
New York (Kennedy)	7	21	35	30	7	1	•	•	•	12.0
New York (La Guardia)	6	17	35	28	10	4	1	•	•	12.9
Rochester	8	22	34	25	9	2	•	•	•	11.2
Syracuse	14	27	30	23	5	1	•	•	•	9.7
NORTH CAROLINA										
Charlotte	20	32	31	14	2	•	•	•	•	7.9
Greensboro	20	32	31	14	2	1	•	•	•	8.0
Raleigh	18	33	34	14	2	•	•	•	•	7.7
Winston-Salem	19	22	33	21	4	1	•	•	•	9.0
NORTH DAKOTA										
Bismarck	14	20	27	24	12	3	1	•	•	11.2
Fargo	4	13	28	31	15	7	2	•	•	14.4
OHIO										
Akron-Canton	7	25	35	26	5	•	•	•	•	10.4
Cincinnati	11	27	36	22	4	1	•	•	•	9.6
Cleveland	7	18	35	29	9	2	•	•	•	11.6
Columbus	26	23	26	18	6	2	•	•	•	8.2
Dayton	7	26	36	24	6	1	•	•	•	10.3
Youngstown	7	26	36	24	6	1	•	•	•	10.3
OKLAHOMA										
Oklahoma City	2	11	34	34	13	6	1	•	•	14.0
Tulsa	9	24	34	26	7	1	•	•	•	10.6
OREGON										
Medford	47	31	14	6	2	•	•	•	•	4.6
Portland	28	27	25	16	4	1	•	•	•	7.7
Salem	25	32	28	13	2	•	•	•	•	7.1
PENNSYLVANIA										
Harrisburg	28	31	25	13	3	1	•	•	•	7.3
Philadelphia	11	27	35	21	5	1	•	•	•	9.6
Pittsburgh	12	26	34	22	4	1	•	•	•	9.4
Scranton	11	33	35	18	2	•	•	•	•	8.8
RHODE ISLAND										
Providence	11	20	32	28	7	2	•	•	•	10.7
SOUTH CAROLINA										
Charleston	12	28	35	19	4	1	•	•	•	9.2
Columbia	15	35	35	12	2	•	•	•	•	7.0

State and Station	0-3 mph	4-7 mph	8-12 mph	13-18 mph	19-24 mph	25-31 mph	32-38 mph	39-46 mph	47 mph and over	Mean speed mph
SOUTH DAKOTA										
Huron	10	18	29	29	10	3	1	•	•	11.9
Rapid City	15	22	28	21	10	4	1	•	•	11.0
TENNESSEE										
Chattanooga	39	25	24	11	1	•	•	•	•	6.1
Knoxville	29	29	25	12	4	1	•	•	•	7.5
Memphis	14	26	34	20	5	1	•	•	•	9.4
Nashville	27	31	25	14	2	•	•	•	•	7.2
TEXAS										
Amarillo	5	15	32	32	12	4	1	•	•	12.9
Austin	13	25	34	23	5	1	•	•	•	9.7
Brownsville	10	17	25	30	14	3	•	•	•	12.3
Corpus Christi	11	16	26	33	12	1	•	•	•	11.9
Dallas	9	21	32	28	9	1	•	•	•	11.0
El Paso	10	22	32	22	9	4	1	•	•	11.3
Ft. Worth	4	14	34	34	10	2	•	•	•	12.5
Galveston	4	13	39	33	10	2	•	•	•	12.5
Houston	6	18	36	28	10	2	•	•	•	11.8
Laredo	6	15	32	34	12	1	•	•	•	12.3
Lubbock	4	11	33	34	13	5	1	•	•	13.6
Midland	9	22	38	26	4	1	•	•	•	10.1
San Antonio	18	23	32	22	4	1	•	•	•	9.3
Waco	3	14	36	35	10	2	•	•	•	12.5
Wichita Falls	5	22	41	27	5	•	•	•	•	10.5
UTAH										
Salt Lake City	12	33	36	14	4	2	•	•	•	8.7
VERMONT										
Burlington	24	24	28	22	2	•	•	•	•	8.3
VIRGINIA										
Norfolk	14	23	30	25	6	1	•	•	•	10.2
Richmond	14	37	36	11	1	•	•	•	•	7.8
Roanoke	31	22	23	17	5	2	•	•	•	8.3
WASHINGTON										
Seattle-Tacoma AP	13	16	35	26	8	2	•	•	•	10.7
Spokane	17	38	27	14	3	1	•	•	•	8.1
WASHINGTON, D.C.	11	26	35	22	5	1	•	•	•	9.7
WEST VIRGINIA										
Charleston	29	37	25	8	1	•	•	•	•	6.2
WISCONSIN										
Green Bay	8	22	32	26	10	2	•	•	•	11.2
Madison	15	22	30	23	7	2	•	•	•	10.1
Milwaukee	8	17	31	30	11	3	1	•	•	12.1
WYOMING										
Casper	8	16	27	27	13	7	2	•	•	13.3
PACIFIC										
Wake Island	1	6	27	48	17	2	•	•	•	14.6
PUERTO RICO										
San Juan	15	28	27	25	4	•	•	•	•	9.1

Source: Climatic Atlas of the United States.

FUEL COST COMPARISONS
Per Million BTUs

FUEL	PRICE	COST PER MILLION BTUs of USEABLE HEAT	FUEL	PRICE	COST PER MILLION BTUs of USEABLE HEAT
PELLETS	PER TON	PER MM BTUs	**ELECTRICITY**	PER KWH	PER MM BTUs
	$60.00	$4.41		$0.040	$11.83
8,500 BTUs per	$75.00	$5.51	3,415 BTUs per	$0.055	$16.27
Lb. (17 Million	$90.00	$6.62	Kilowatt Hour	$0.070	$20.70
BTUs per Ton	$115.00	$8.46		$0.085	$25.14
	$130.00	$9.56		$0.100	$29.58
Efficiency = 80%	$140.00	$10.29	Efficiency = 99%	$0.120	$35.49
ALDER FIREWOOD	PER CORD	PER MM BTUs	**ALDER FIREWOOD**	PER CORD	PER MM BTUs
Hardwood - Air	$60.00	$9.52	Hardwood - Air	$60.00	$6.67
Dried to 20%	$75.00	$11.90	Dried to 20%	$75.00	$8.33
Moisture Content	$90.00	$14.29	Moisture Content	$90.00	$10.00
18 Million BTUs	$115.00	$18.25	18 Million BTUs	$115.00	$12.78
per Cord	$130.00	$20.63	per Cord	$130.00	$14.44
Burned in Fire-	$145.00	$23.02	Burned in Typical	$145.00	$16.11
place w / Insert	$160.00	$25.40	Pre - 1986 Stove	$160.00	$17.78
Efficiency = 35%	$175.00	$27.78	Efficiency = 50%	$175.00	$19.44
PINE FIREWOOD	PER CORD	PER MM BTUs	**PINE FIREWOOD**	PER CORD	PER MM BTUs
Softwood - Air	$45.00	$4.62	Softwood - Air	$45.00	$4.00
Dried to 20%	$60.00	$6.15	Dried to 20%	$60.00	$5.33
Moisture Content	$75.00	$7.69	Moisture Content	$75.00	$6.67
15 Million BTUs	$90.00	$9.23	15 Million BTUs	$90.00	$8.00
Burned in Oregon	$115.00	$11.79	Burned in Oregon	$115.00	$10.22
DEQ Approved Non	$130.00	$13.33	DEQ Approved	$130.00	$11.56
Catalytic Stove	$145.00	$14.87	Catalytic Stove	$145.00	$12.89
Efficiency = 65%	$160.00	$16.41	Efficiency = 75%	$160.00	$14.22
PROPANE	PER GAL.	PER MM BTUs	**NATURAL GAS**	PER THERM	PER MM BTUs
	$0.50	$6.27	1 Therm =	$0.40	$5.71
	$0.60	$7.53	100,000 BTUs	$0.50	$7.14
93,800 BTUs	$0.70	$8.78		$0.60	$8.57
per Gallon	$0.80	$10.03	Conventional	$0.70	$10.00
	$0.90	$11.29	Prior to Pulse	$0.80	$11.43
	$1.00	$12.54	Type Furnace	$0.90	$12.86
	$1.10	$13.80		$1.00	$14.29
Efficiency = 85%	$1.20	$15.05	Efficiency = 70%	$1.10	$15.71
#2 OIL	PER GAL.	PER MM BTUs	**NATURAL GAS**	PER THERM	PER MM BTUs
138,00 BTUs	$0.80	$7.25	Therm = 100M BTU	$0.50	$5.56
per Gallon	$0.95	$8.61	(Pulse type)	$0.70	$7.78
Efficiency = 80%	$1.10	$9.96	Efficiency = 90%	$1.00	$11.11

FUEL	PRICE	COST PER MILLION BTUs of USEABLE HEAT
FIREWOOD (PINE)	PER CORD	PER MM BTUs
Softwood - Air	$45.00	$6.00
Dried to 20%	$60.00	$8.00
Moisture Content	$75.00	$10.00
15 Million BTUs	$90.00	$12.00
per Cord	$115.00	$15.33
Burned in Typical	$130.00	$17.33
Pre - 1986 Stove	$145.00	$19.33
Efficiency - 50%	$160.00	$21.33

INDEX

A

Absorptance, I-6
Air conditioner, III-3, VI-2, X-4
Algae, VIII-2
Appliance electricity usage, XII-2
Attic foil, III-3
Attic heat, VIII-1
Automobile, X-4

B

Batteries, X-4, IX-2
Biogas generator, VII-2
Blower, I-2
Blower, XI-2

C

Car conversion, X-4
Cardboard, VI-1
Caulking, XII-3
Ceiling paddle fan, XII-2
Ceramic tile, I-6, XI-3
CFC's, IX-1
Clothes dryer, I-3
Collector - air, I-1
Collector - concentrating, II-2
Collector - swimming pool, VIII-1
Collector - water, II-1
∗Cooling, III
Corn, XI-5
Creosote, XI-3

D

D.C. appliances, IX-2
Damper, XI-3
Deck, XII-3
Diffusivity, I-6
Direct gain windows, V-2
Direct vent, XI-5, XI-4
Distiller, II-2

E

Electric range, IX-2
Electricity, X-1, X-4, XII-2
Emittance, I-6

F

Fading rays, III-1, III-4, III-5
Fire back, XI-2
Fire logs, XI-3

F

Fireplace, XI-2, XI-4, I-5
Fireplace doors, XI-2
Fireplace grate, XI-2
Firewood, XI-3
Firewood selection, XI-3
Floors, I-6
Fluorescent lighting, X-3
Foam core panel, VII-2
Food cooking and preserving, VI
Fruits and vegetables, V-2
Fuel costs, XIII-4
Furnace, XI-1

G

Geothermal, XII-1
Greenhouses, IV

H

Heat circulating fireplace, XI-4
Heat pump, XII-1
Horsepower, II-2
Houseplants, X-1, XII-4
Humidistat, X-2

I, J, K

Indoor air quality, XII-4
Insulation, VII-2, I-3, XI-2

L

Lawn mower, XII-1
Lighting, VII-3, X-3
Lightwell, VII-3
Log house, V-1
Low emissivity, IV-3, VII-1, IV-2
Low-toxic cleaners, XII-4

M, N

Mirror, XII-4
Motion sensor, X-3

O

Outdoor combust. air, XI-5, XI-4
Outdoor furnace, XI-1

P

Passive solar, II-3, I-4, V-2
Passive solar houses, V
Pellets, XI-5
Percolator, II-2
Photovoltaics, X

R

Radiant heat, III-3
Refrigerator, VII-1, VIII-1
Ridge vent, III-3
Roof felt, III-1

S

Screening, III-1, IV-3
Security, III-5, X-3
Selective solar coating, I-5
Shutters, III-5, I-3,
Siding, I-1
Silver ions, VIII-2
Skylights, VII
Solar cells, X-1
Solar roof, V-2
Space heating, I
Storm windows, XI-1
Sun availability, XIII-2
Sun position, XIII-1
Sunlight tube, VII-3
Swimming pool, VIII

T

Television, I-6
Thermosiphoning, I-1
Thermostat, I-4, II-3
Toilets, II-1
Trombe wall, I-5, V-2
Turbine vent, IX-1, III-2

U

Urea formaldehyde, IV-1

V

Ventilation, IX-1, X-2, III-3
Vinyl film, III-1

W, X, Y, Z

Water heater, XI-4, XII-1
Water heating, II
Water tank, II-3
Wind energy, IX
Wind speed, XIII-3
Window condensation, XI-5
Window film, III-1, III-4
Wood energy, XI
Wood furnace, XI-1
Wood heat evaluation, XI-1

∗ bold faced heading indicates chapter topic